Love & Lies ①

LOVE and LIES by MUSAWO

CONTENTS

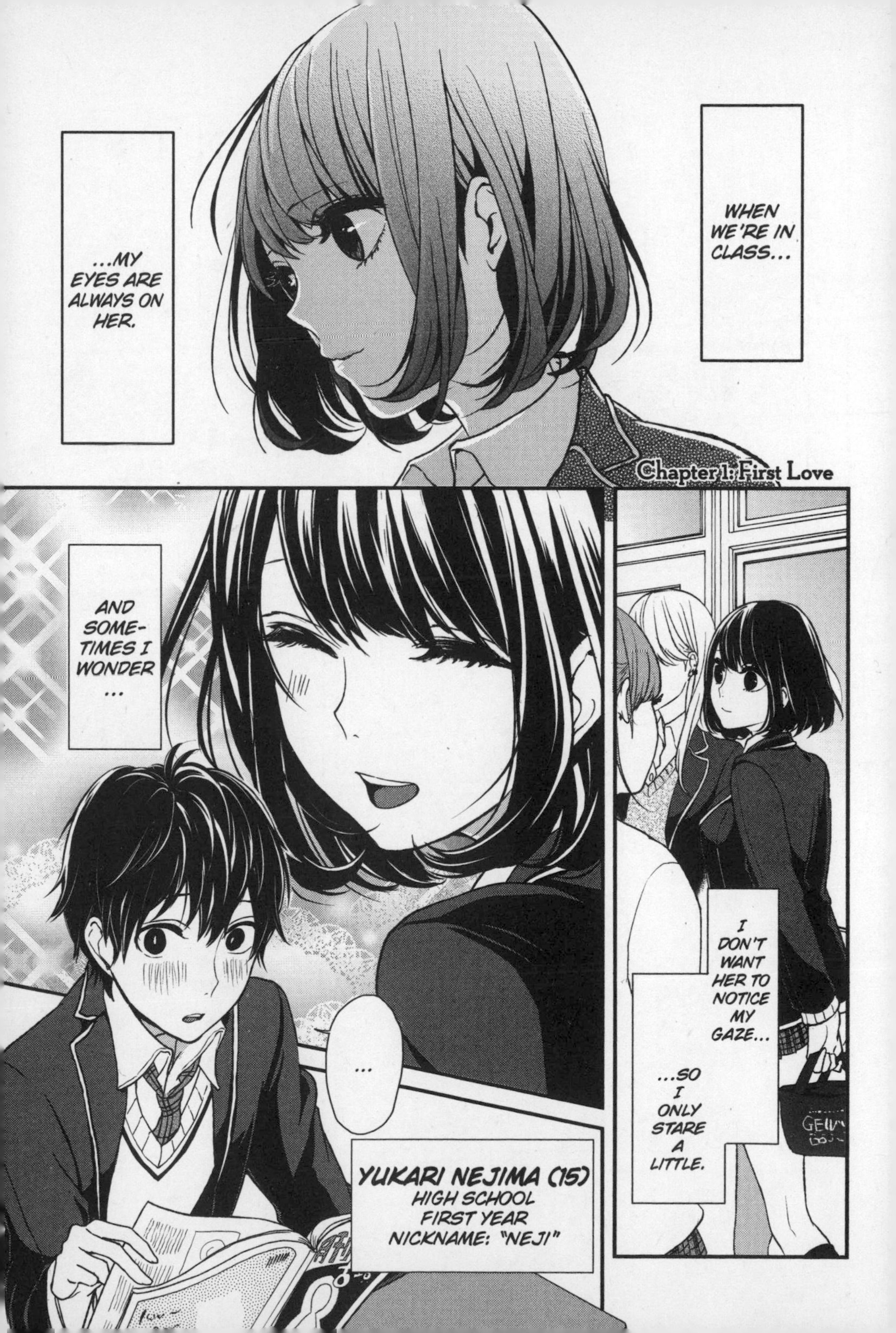
WHEN WE'RE IN CLASS...
...MY EYES ARE ALWAYS ON HER.
Chapter 1: First Love
I DON'T WANT HER TO NOTICE MY GAZE...
...SO I ONLY STARE A LITTLE.
AND SOME-TIMES I WONDER ...
...
YUKARI NEJIMA (15) HIGH SCHOOL FIRST YEAR NICKNAME: "NEJI"

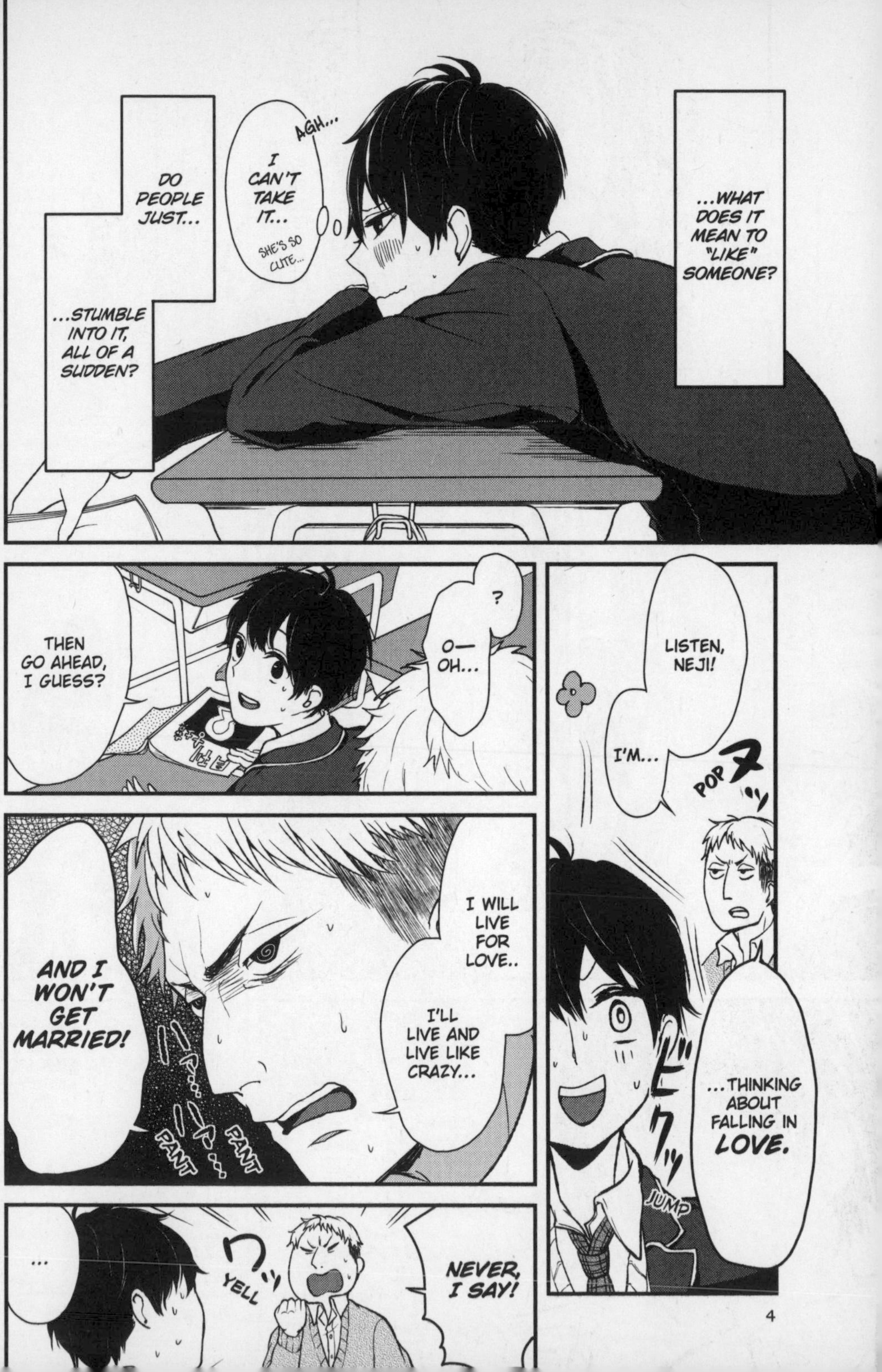
...WHAT DOES IT MEAN TO "LIKE" SOMEONE?
AGH...
I CAN'T TAKE IT...
SHE'S SO CUTE...
DO PEOPLE JUST...
...STUMBLE INTO IT, ALL OF A SUDDEN?
LISTEN, NEJI!
I'M...
POP
...THINKING ABOUT FALLING IN LOVE.
JUMP
?
O— OH...
THEN GO AHEAD, I GUESS?
I WILL LIVE FOR LOVE..
I'LL LIVE AND LIVE LIKE CRAZY...
AND I WON'T GET MARRIED!
PANT PANT
NEVER, I SAY!
YELL
...

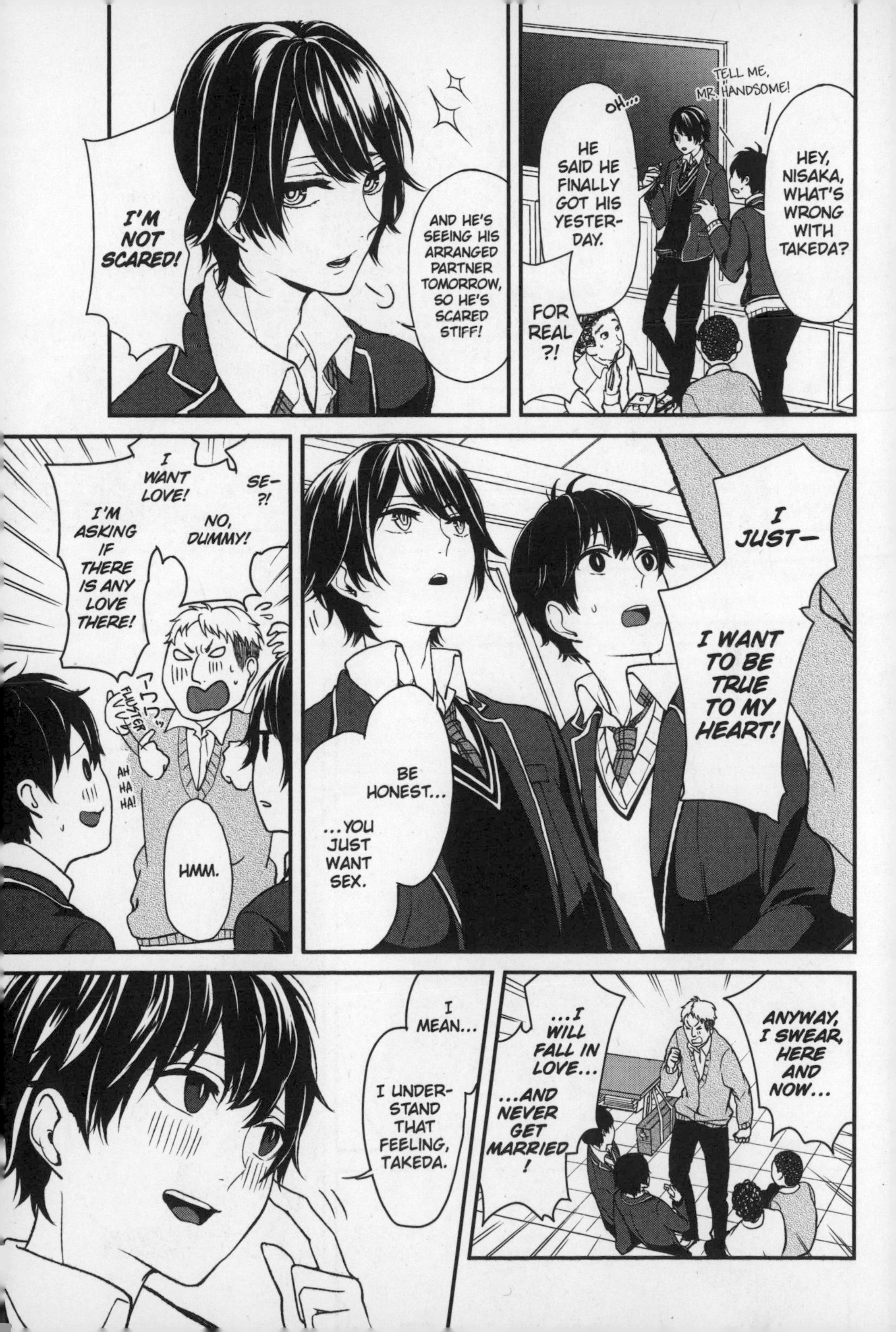
TELL ME, MR. HANDSOME!
HEY, NISAKA, WHAT'S WRONG WITH TAKEDA?
OH...
HE SAID HE FINALLY GOT HIS YESTER-DAY.
FOR REAL?!
AND HE'S SEEING HIS ARRANGED PARTNER TOMORROW, SO HE'S SCARED STIFF!
I'M NOT SCARED!
I JUST—
I WANT TO BE TRUE TO MY HEART!
BE HONEST...
...YOU JUST WANT SEX.
SE-?!
I WANT LOVE!
NO, DUMMY!
I'M ASKING IF THERE IS ANY LOVE THERE!
FLUSTER
AH HA HA!
HMM.
ANYWAY, I SWEAR, HERE AND NOW...
...I WILL FALL IN LOVE...
...AND NEVER GET MARRIED!
I MEAN...
I UNDER-STAND THAT FEELING, TAKEDA.

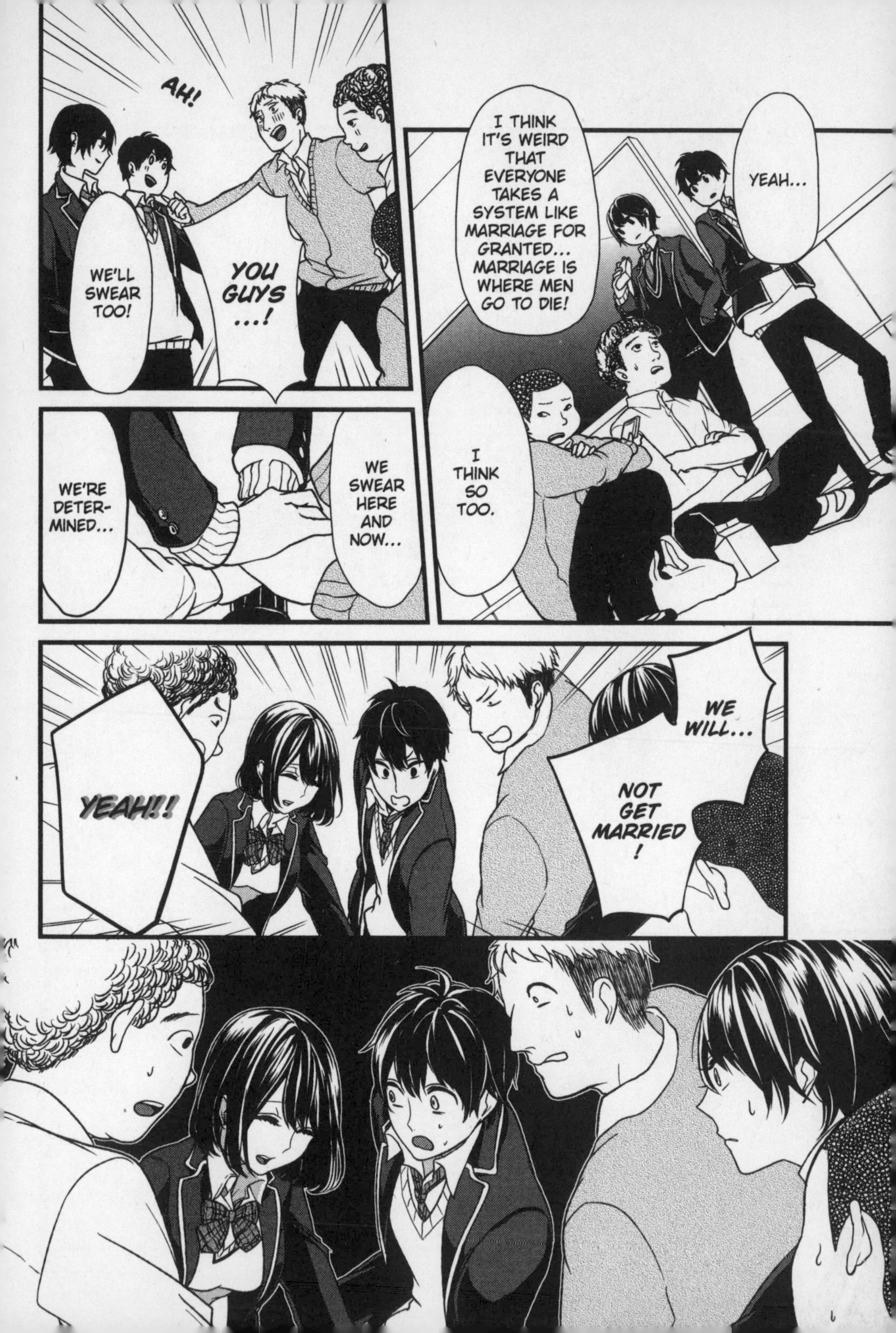
YEAH...
I THINK IT'S WEIRD THAT EVERYONE TAKES A SYSTEM LIKE MARRIAGE FOR GRANTED... MARRIAGE IS WHERE MEN GO TO DIE!
I THINK SO TOO.
AH!
YOU GUYS ...!
WE'LL SWEAR TOO!
WE SWEAR HERE AND NOW...
WE'RE DETERMINED...
WE WILL...
NOT GET MARRIED!
YEAH!!

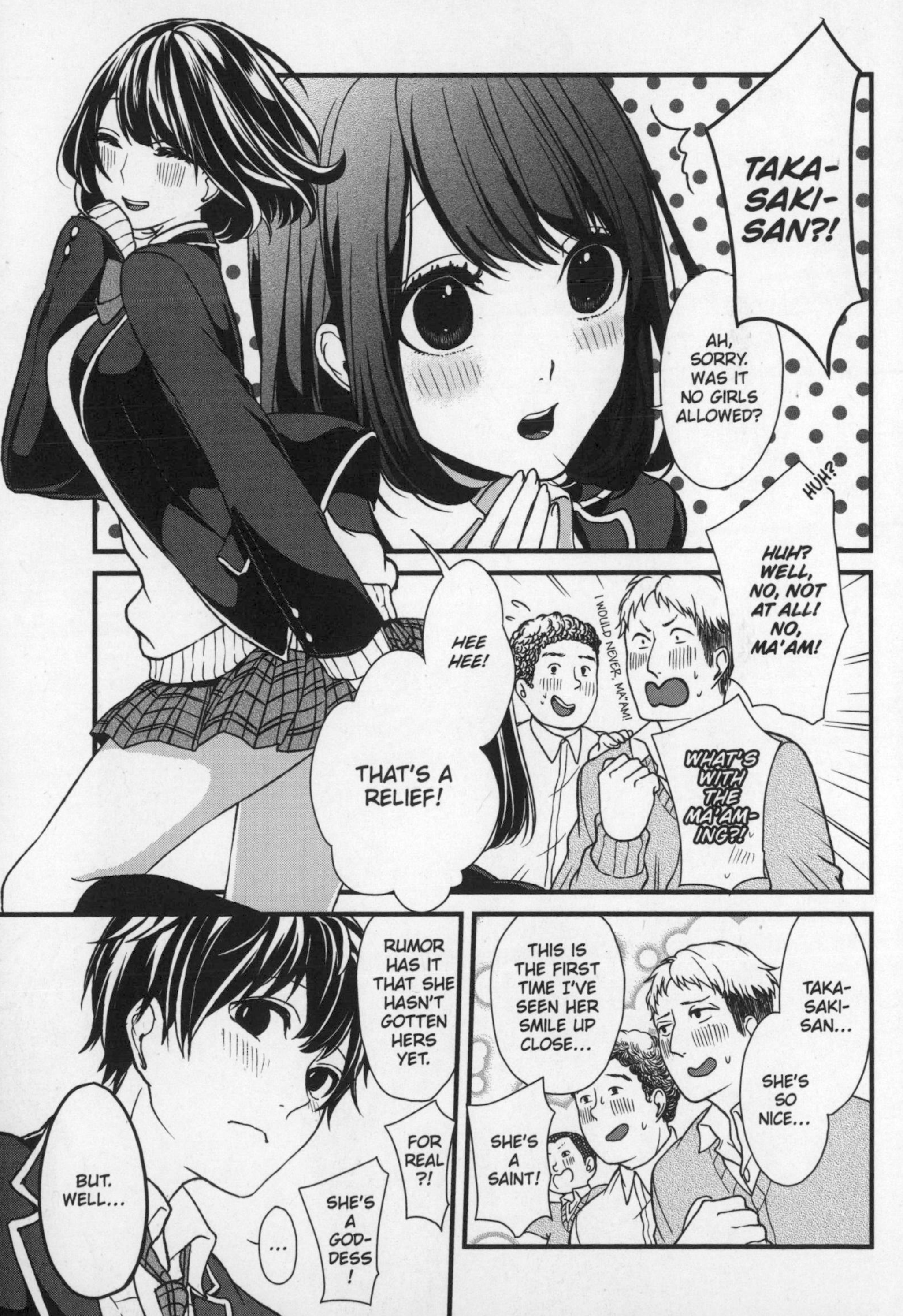
TAKA-SAKI-SAN?!
AH, SORRY. WAS IT NO GIRLS ALLOWED?
HUH?
HUH? WELL, NO, NOT AT ALL! NO, MA'AM!
I WOULD NEVER, MA'AM!
WHAT'S WITH THE MA'AMING?!
HEE HEE!
THAT'S A RELIEF!
TAKA-SAKI-SAN...
SHE'S SO NICE...
THIS IS THE FIRST TIME I'VE SEEN HER SMILE UP CLOSE...
SHE'S A SAINT!
RUMOR HAS IT THAT SHE HASN'T GOTTEN HERS YET.
FOR REAL?!
SHE'S A GOD-DESS!
...
BUT. WELL...

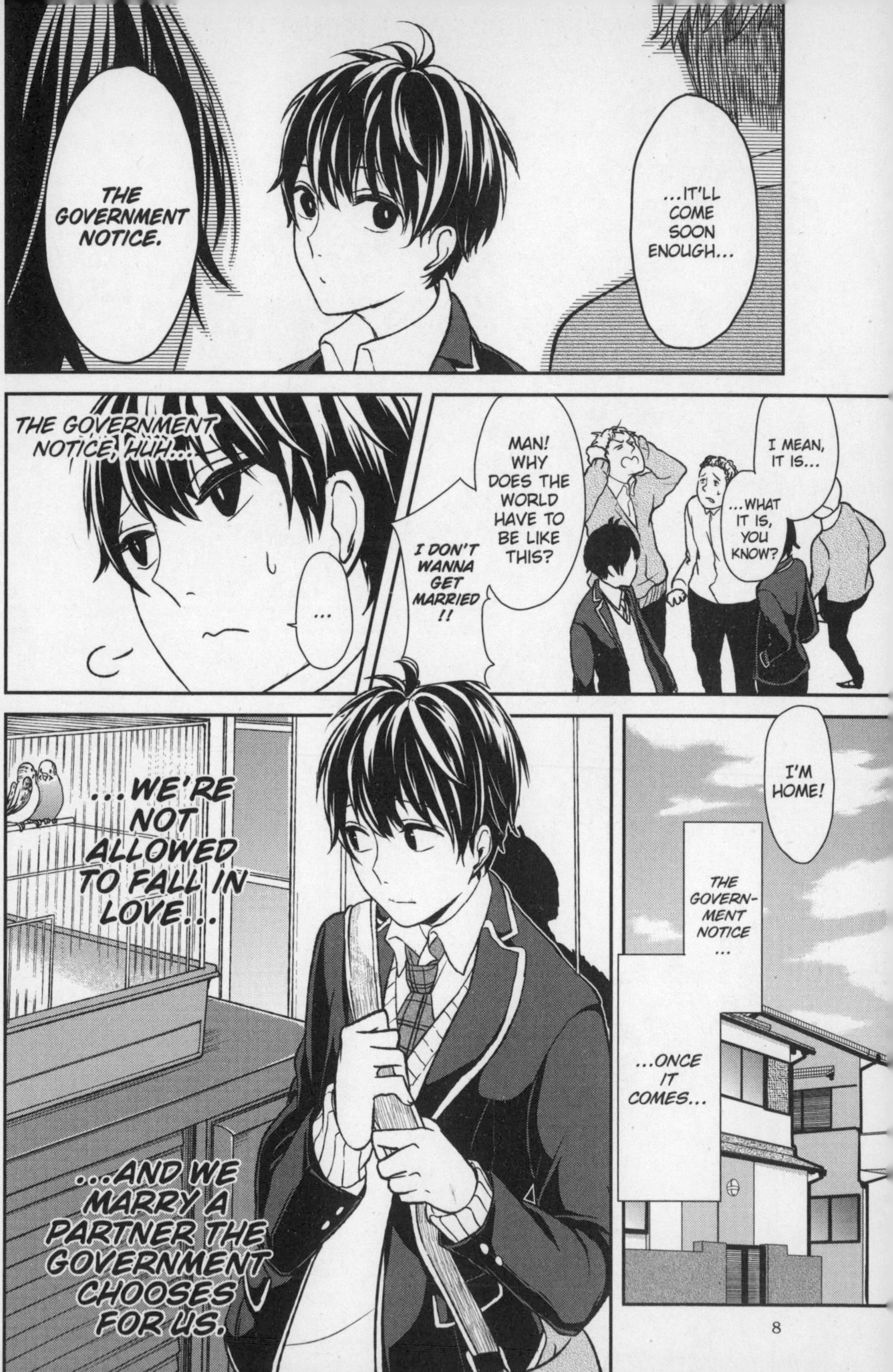
...IT'LL COME SOON ENOUGH...
THE GOVERNMENT NOTICE.
I MEAN, IT IS...
...WHAT IT IS, YOU KNOW?
MAN! WHY DOES THE WORLD HAVE TO BE LIKE THIS?
I DON'T WANNA GET MARRIED!!
THE GOVERNMENT NOTICE, HUH...
...
I'M HOME!
THE GOVERN-MENT NOTICE...
...ONCE IT COMES...
...WE'RE NOT ALLOWED TO FALL IN LOVE...
...AND WE MARRY A PARTNER THE GOVERNMENT CHOOSES FOR US.

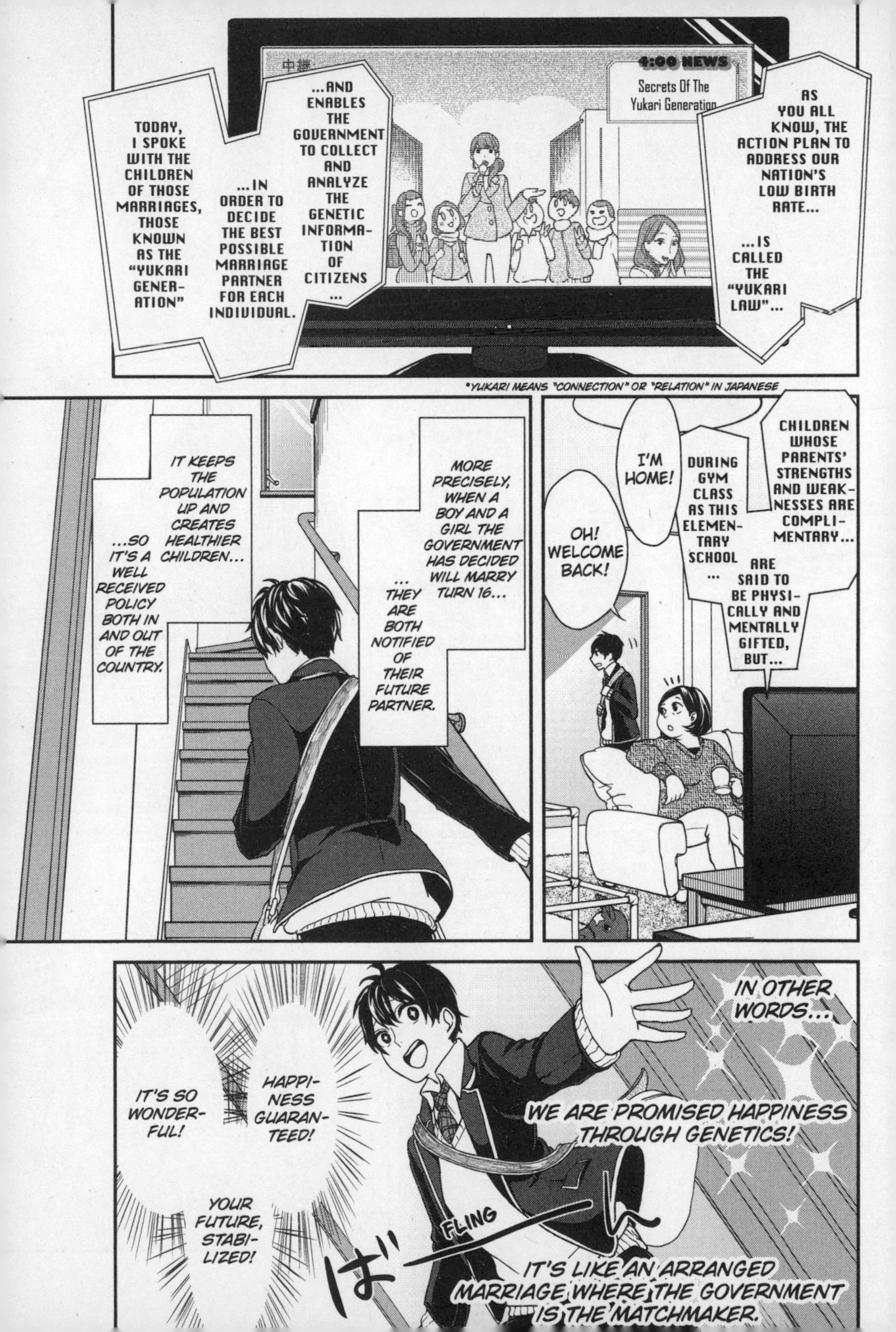
AS YOU ALL KNOW, THE ACTION PLAN TO ADDRESS OUR NATION'S LOW BIRTH RATE...
...IS CALLED THE "YUKARI LAW"...
4:00 NEWS
Secrets Of The Yukari Generation
...AND ENABLES THE GOVERNMENT TO COLLECT AND ANALYZE THE GENETIC INFORMATION OF CITIZENS...
...IN ORDER TO DECIDE THE BEST POSSIBLE MARRIAGE PARTNER FOR EACH INDIVIDUAL.
TODAY, I SPOKE WITH THE CHILDREN OF THOSE MARRIAGES, THOSE KNOWN AS THE "YUKARI GENERATION"
*YUKARI MEANS "CONNECTION" OR "RELATION" IN JAPANESE
CHILDREN WHOSE PARENTS' STRENGTHS AND WEAKNESSES ARE COMPLIMENTARY...
ARE SAID TO BE PHYSICALLY AND MENTALLY GIFTED, BUT...
DURING GYM CLASS AS THIS ELEMENTARY SCHOOL ...
I'M HOME!
OH! WELCOME BACK!
MORE PRECISELY, WHEN A BOY AND A GIRL THE GOVERNMENT HAS DECIDED WILL MARRY TURN 16...
...THEY ARE BOTH NOTIFIED OF THEIR FUTURE PARTNER.
IT KEEPS THE POPULATION UP AND CREATES HEALTHIER CHILDREN...
...SO IT'S A WELL RECEIVED POLICY BOTH IN AND OUT OF THE COUNTRY.
IN OTHER WORDS...
WE ARE PROMISED HAPPINESS THROUGH GENETICS!
HAPPINESS GUARANTEED!
IT'S SO WONDERFUL!
YOUR FUTURE, STABILIZED!
FLING
ば
IT'S LIKE AN ARRANGED MARRIAGE WHERE THE GOVERNMENT IS THE MATCHMAKER.

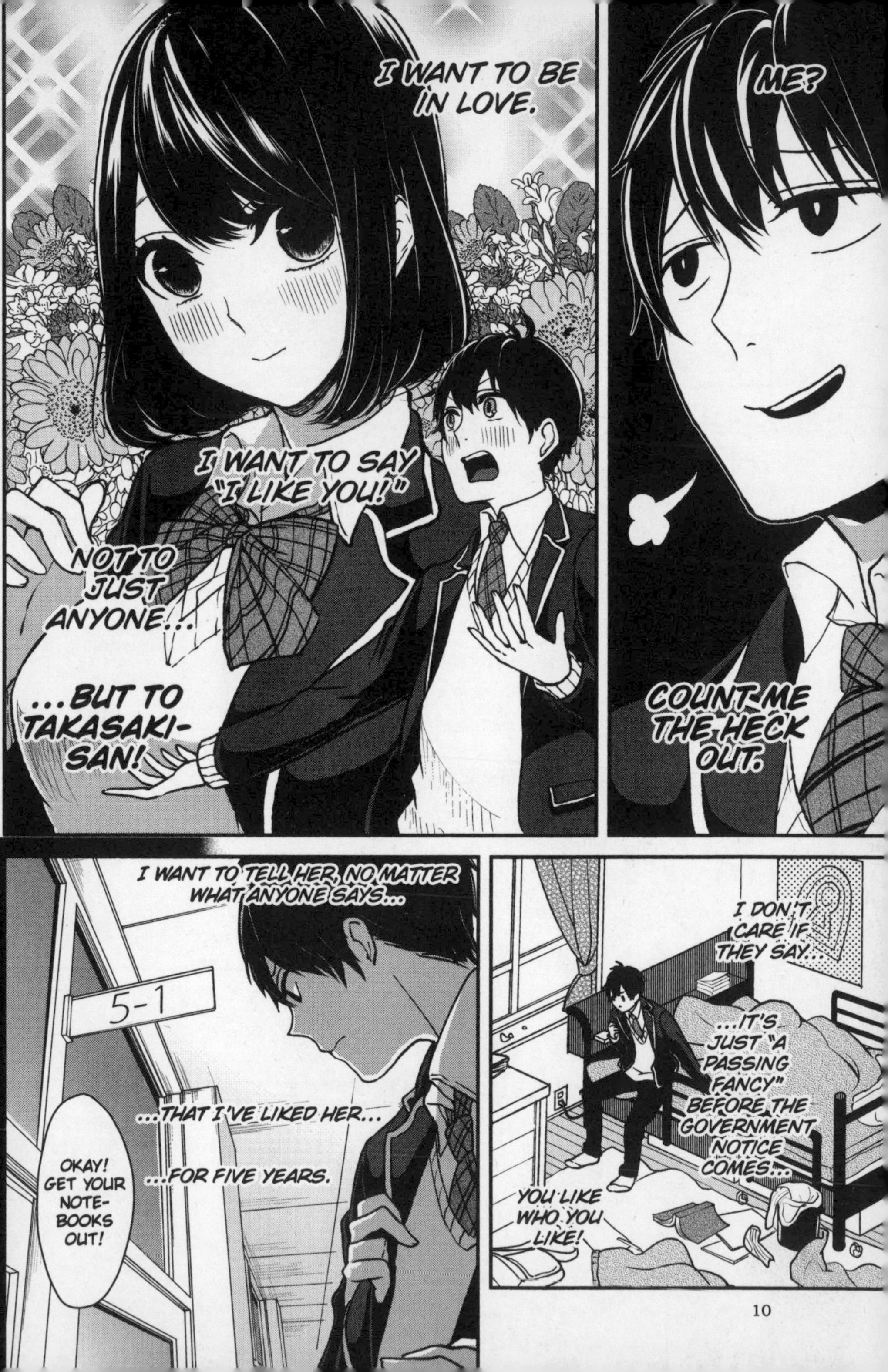
ME?
COUNT ME THE HECK OUT.
I WANT TO BE IN LOVE.
I WANT TO SAY "I LIKE YOU!"
NOT TO JUST ANYONE...
...BUT TO TAKASAKI-SAN!
I DON'T CARE IF THEY SAY...
...IT'S JUST "A PASSING FANCY" BEFORE THE GOVERNMENT NOTICE COMES...
YOU LIKE WHO YOU LIKE!
I WANT TO TELL HER, NO MATTER WHAT ANYONE SAYS...
5-1
...THAT I'VE LIKED HER...
...FOR FIVE YEARS.
OKAY! GET YOUR NOTE-BOOKS OUT!

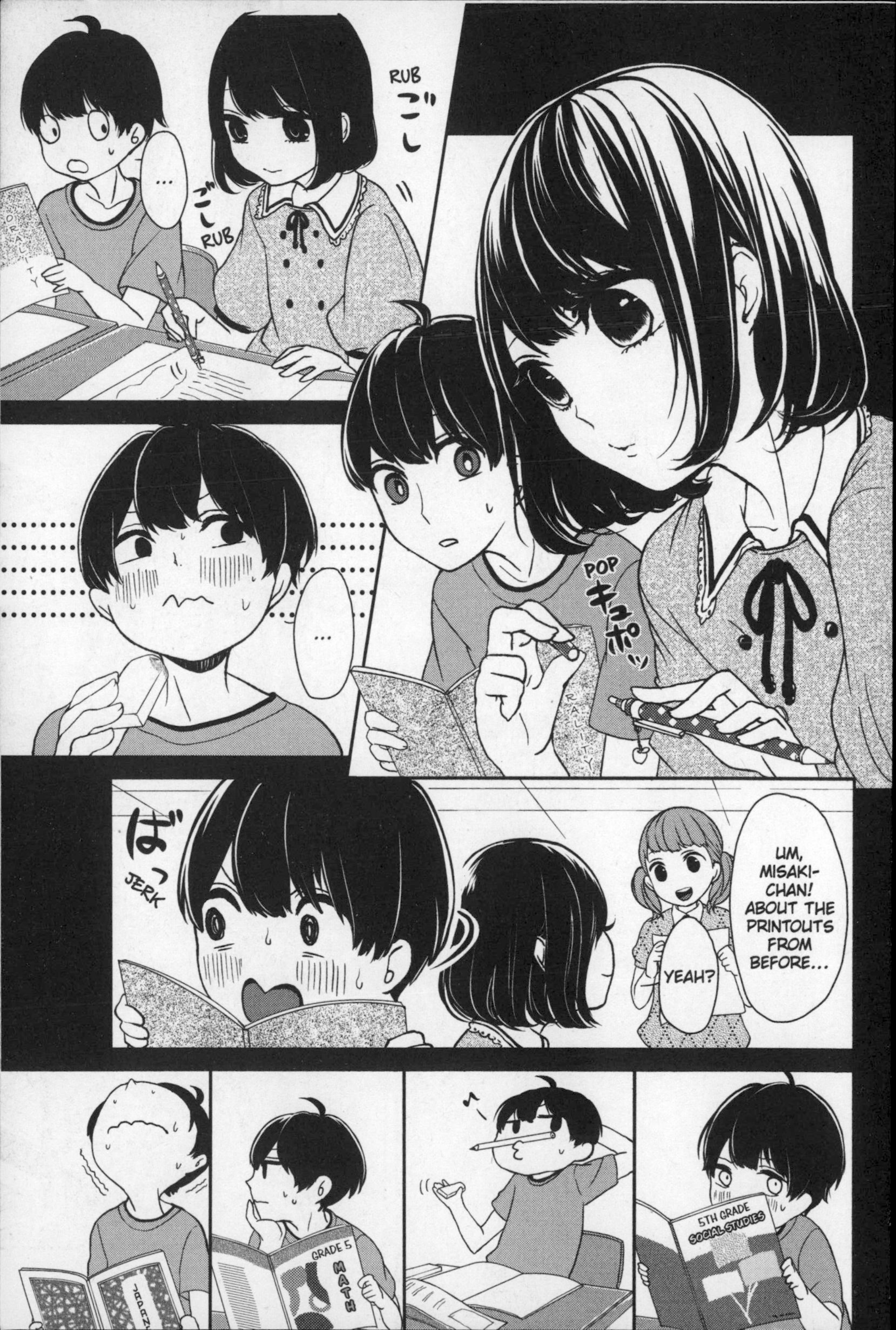
POP
キュポッ
RUB
ごし
...
ごし
RUB
...
UM, MISAKI-CHAN! ABOUT THE PRINTOUTS FROM BEFORE...
YEAH?
ばっ
JERK
5TH GRADE
SOCIAL STUDIES
GRADE 5
MATH

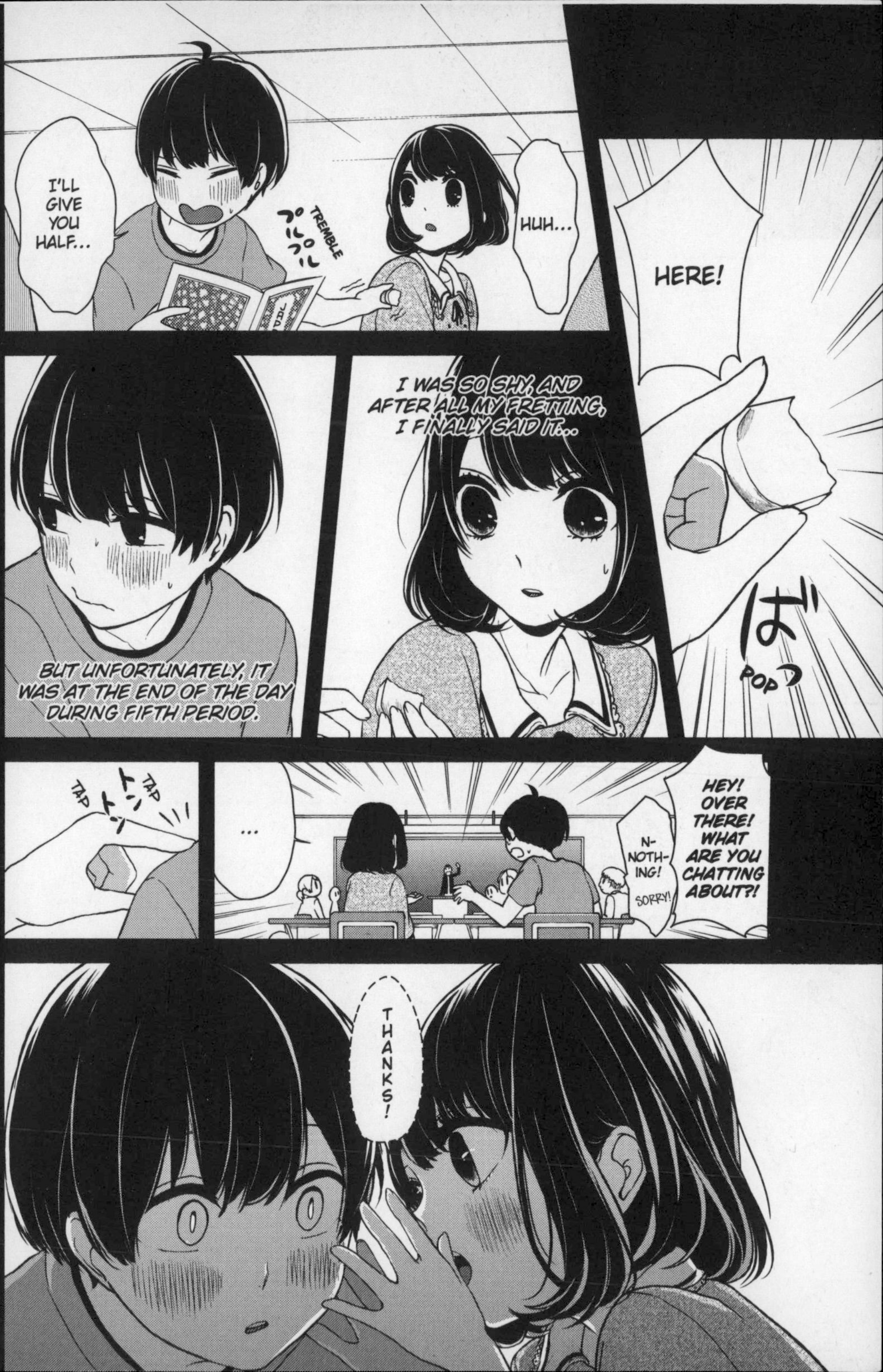
HERE!
ばっ
POP
HUH...
I'LL GIVE YOU HALF...
プルプル
TREMBLE
I WAS SO SHY, AND AFTER ALL MY FRETTING, I FINALLY SAID IT...
BUT UNFORTUNATELY, IT WAS AT THE END OF THE DAY DURING FIFTH PERIOD.
HEY! OVER THERE! WHAT ARE YOU CHATTING ABOUT?!
N-NOTHING!
SORRY!
...
トントン
TAP TAP
THANKS!

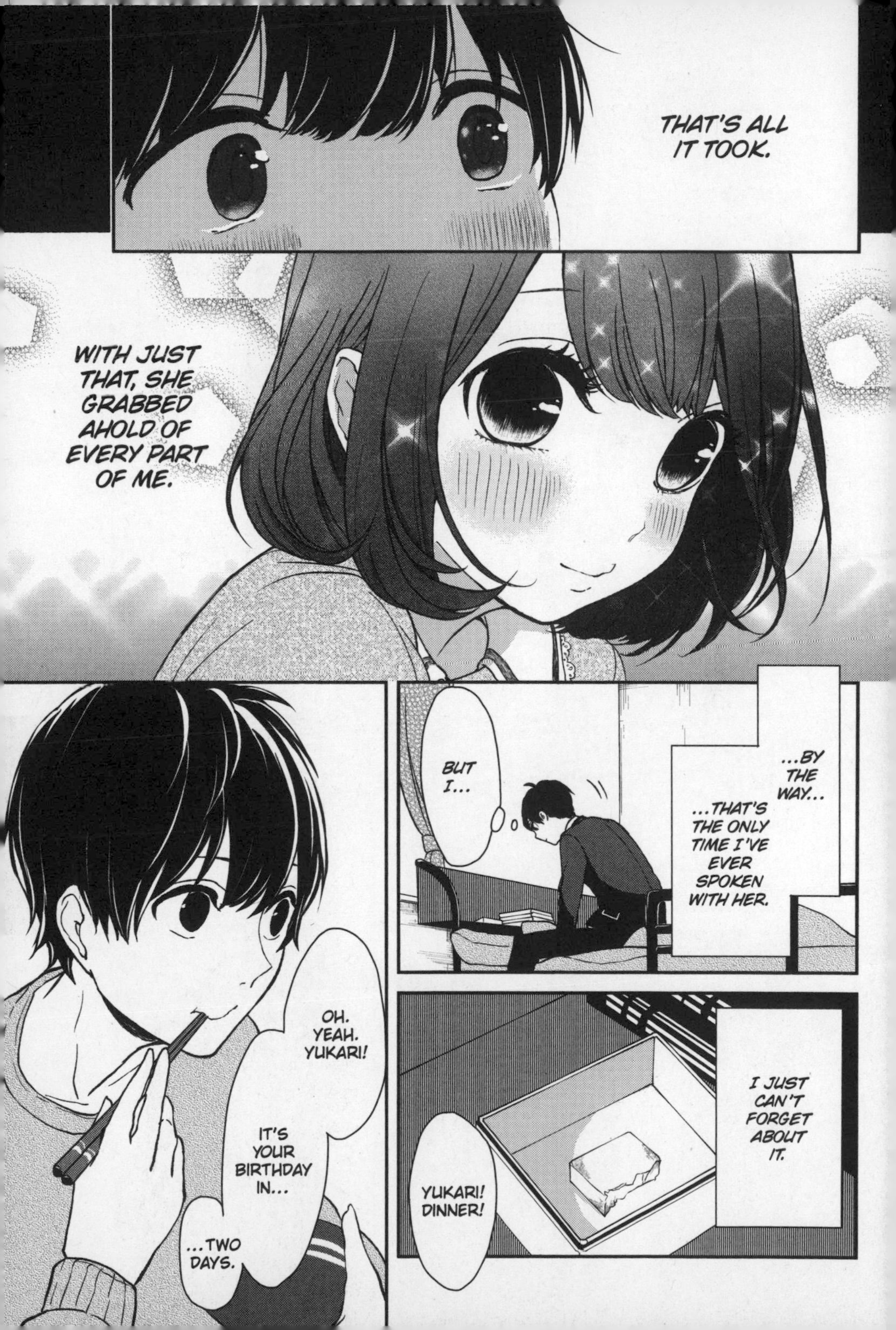
THAT'S ALL IT TOOK.
WITH JUST THAT, SHE GRABBED AHOLD OF EVERY PART OF ME.
...BY THE WAY...
...THAT'S THE ONLY TIME I'VE EVER SPOKEN WITH HER.
BUT I...
I JUST CAN'T FORGET ABOUT IT.
YUKARI! DINNER!
OH. YEAH. YUKARI!
IT'S YOUR BIRTHDAY IN...
...TWO DAYS.

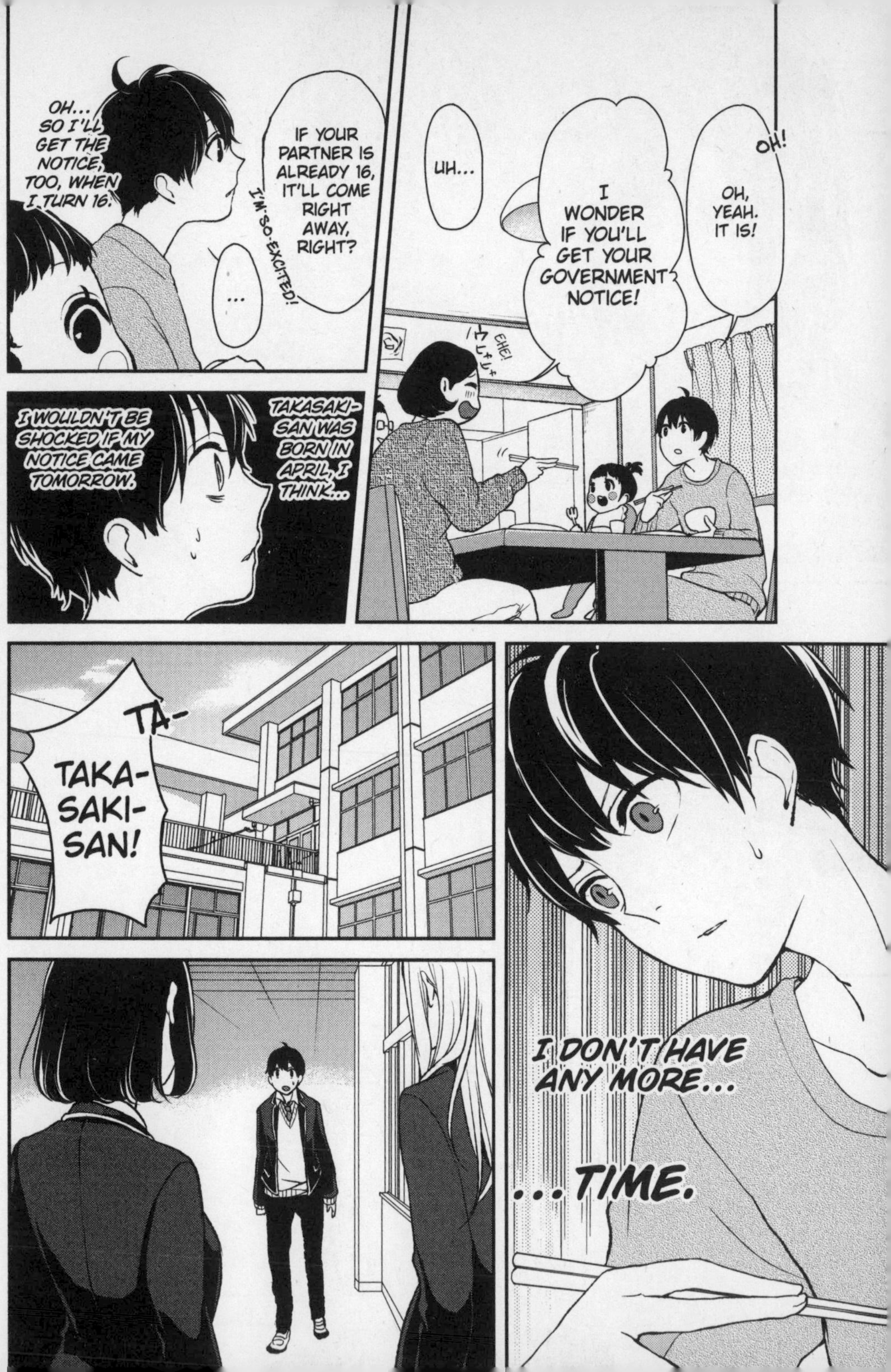

OH!
OH, YEAH. IT IS!
I WONDER IF YOU'LL GET YOUR GOVERNMENT NOTICE!
UH...
EHE!
IF YOUR PARTNER IS ALREADY 16, IT'LL COME RIGHT AWAY, RIGHT?
I'M SO EXCITED!
...
OH... SO I'LL GET THE NOTICE, TOO, WHEN I TURN 16.
TAKASAKI-SAN WAS BORN IN APRIL, I THINK...
I WOULDN'T BE SHOCKED IF MY NOTICE CAME TOMORROW.
I DON'T HAVE ANY MORE...
...TIME.
TA-
TAKA-SAKI-SAN!

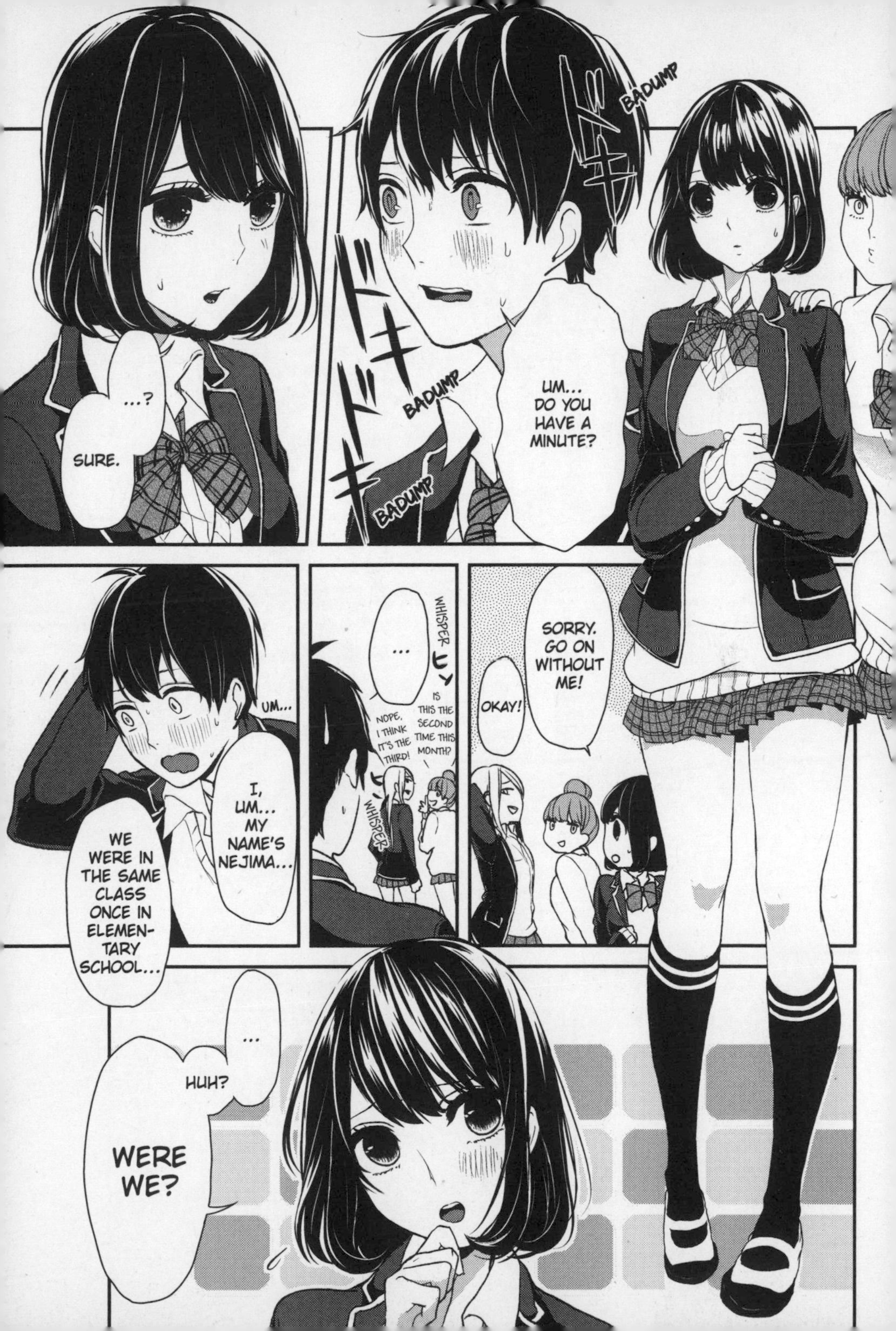
ドキ
BADUMP
ドキドキ
BADUMP
BADUMP
UM... DO YOU HAVE A MINUTE?
...?
SURE.
SORRY. GO ON WITHOUT ME!
OKAY!
...
ヒソ
WHISPER
IS THIS THE SECOND TIME THIS MONTH?
NOPE, I THINK IT'S THE THIRD!
WHISPER
UM...
I, UM... MY NAME'S NEJIMA...
WE WERE IN THE SAME CLASS ONCE IN ELEMENTARY SCHOOL...
...
HUH?
WERE WE?

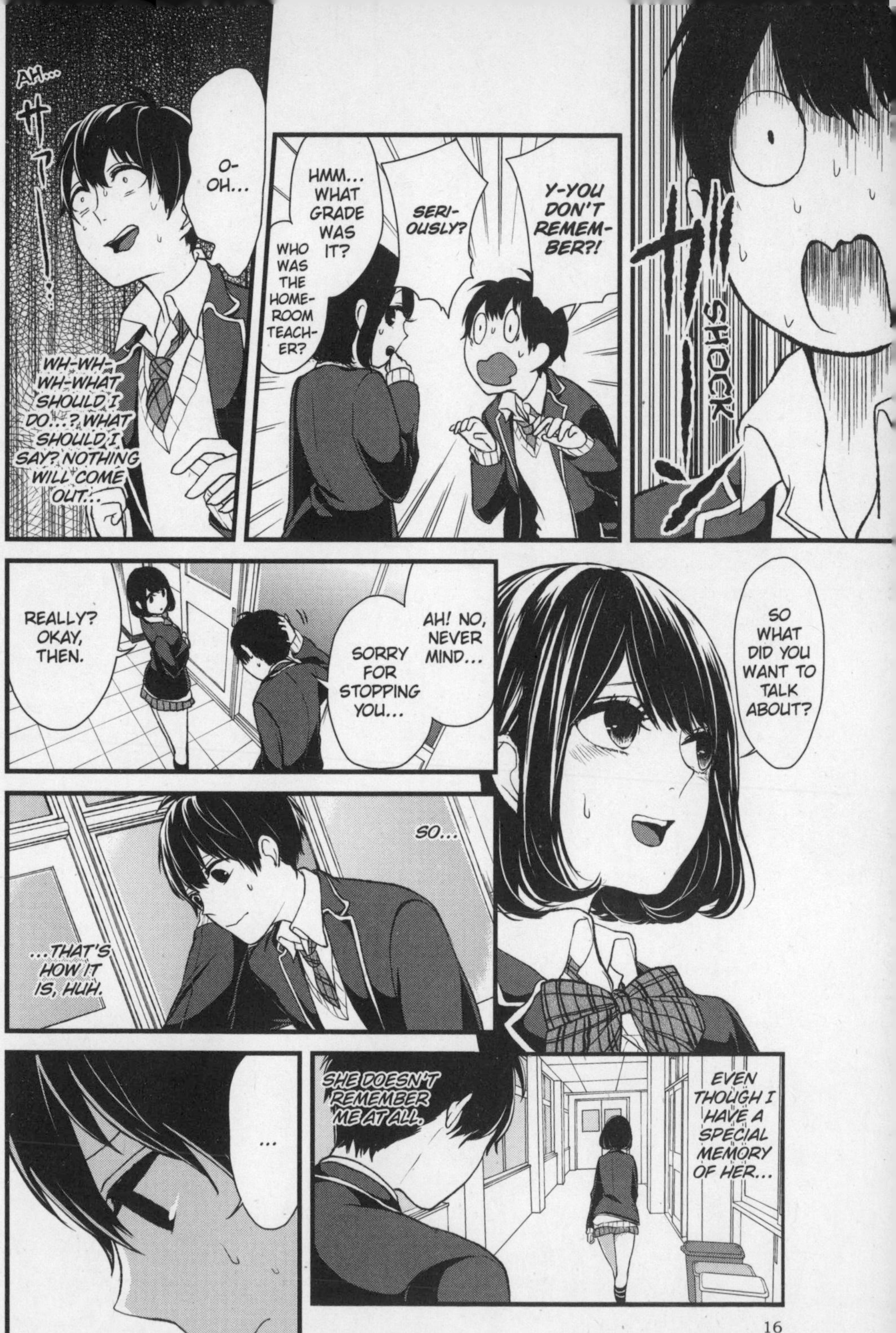
SHOCK
Y-YOU DON'T REMEMBER?!
SERI-OUSLY?
HMM... WHAT GRADE WAS IT?
WHO WAS THE HOME-ROOM TEACH-ER?
O-OH...
AH...
WH-WH-WH-WHAT SHOULD I DO...? WHAT SHOULD I SAY? NOTHING WILL COME OUT...
SO WHAT DID YOU WANT TO TALK ABOUT?
AH! NO, NEVER MIND...
SORRY FOR STOPPING YOU...
REALLY? OKAY, THEN.
SO...
...THAT'S HOW IT IS, HUH.
EVEN THOUGH I HAVE A SPECIAL MEMORY OF HER...
SHE DOESN'T REMEMBER ME AT ALL.
...

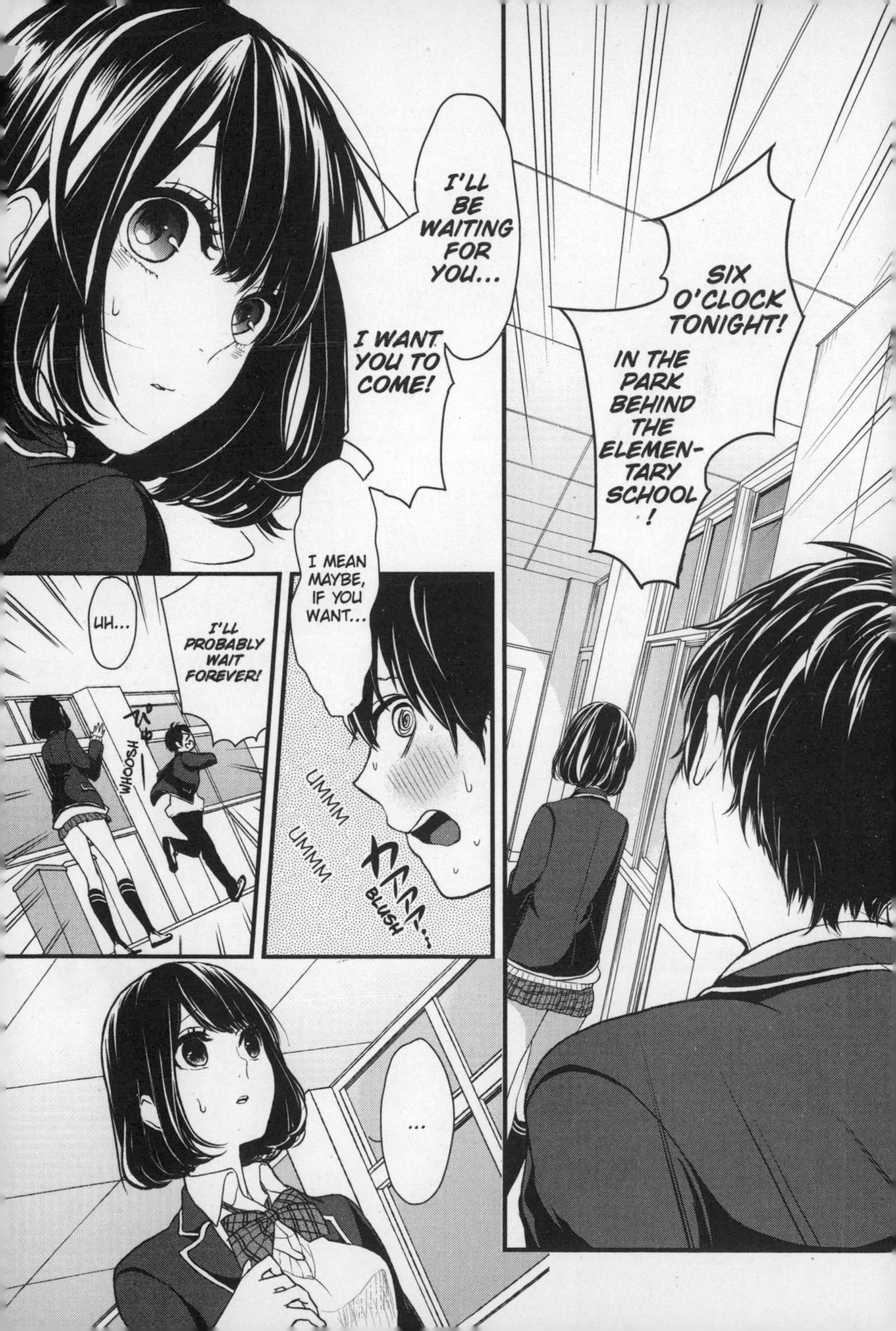
SIX O'CLOCK TONIGHT!
IN THE PARK BEHIND THE ELEMENTARY SCHOOL!
I'LL BE WAITING FOR YOU...
I WANT YOU TO COME!
I MEAN MAYBE, IF YOU WANT...
UMMM
UMMM
BLUSH
UH...
I'LL PROBABLY WAIT FOREVER!
WHOOSH
...

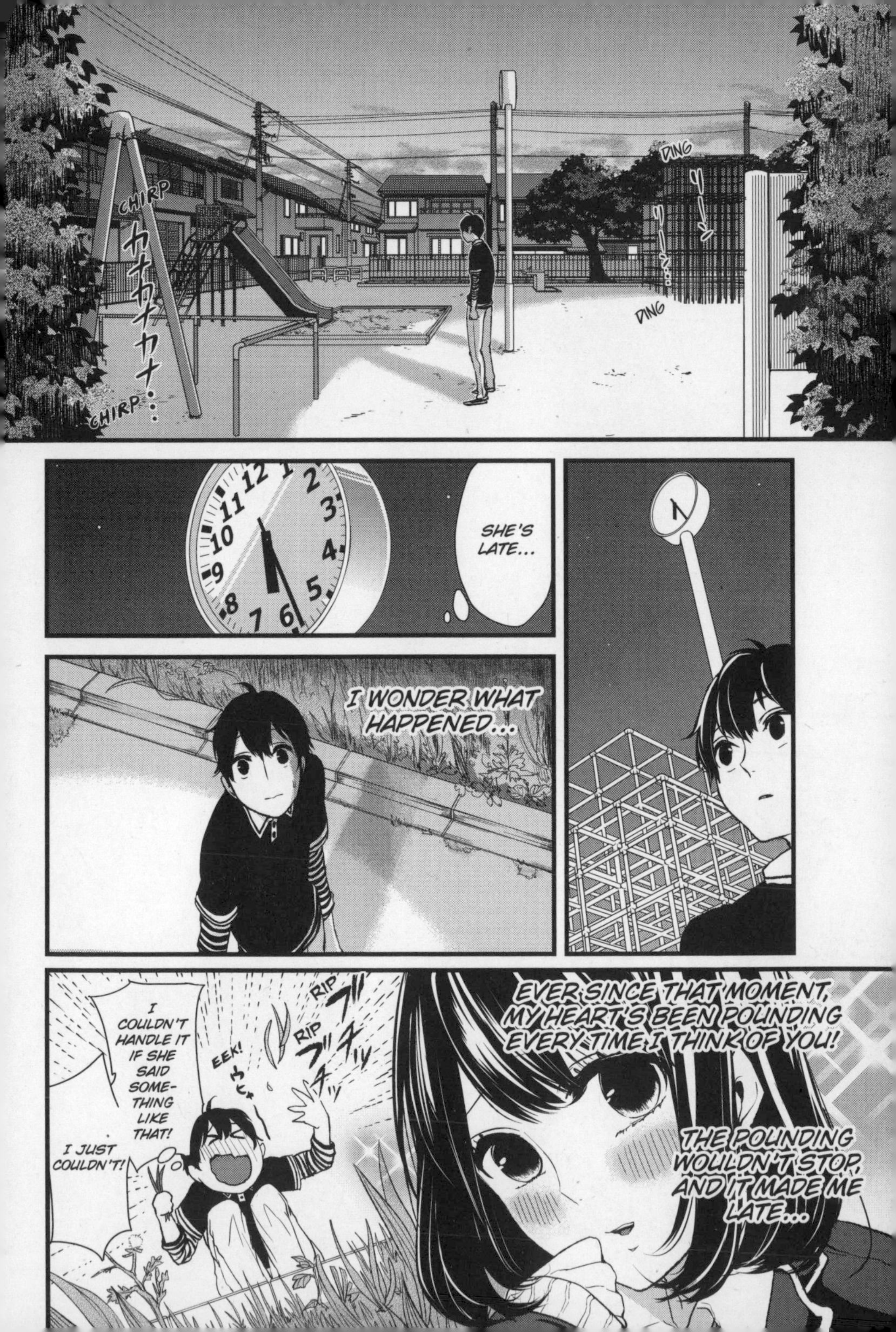
DING
DING
CHIRP
カナカナ…
CHIRP
SHE'S LATE…
I WONDER WHAT HAPPENED…
EVER SINCE THAT MOMENT, MY HEART'S BEEN POUNDING EVERY TIME I THINK OF YOU!
THE POUNDING WOULDN'T STOP, AND IT MADE ME LATE…
RIP
RIP
EEK!
I COULDN'T HANDLE IT IF SHE SAID SOME-THING LIKE THAT!
I JUST COULDN'T!

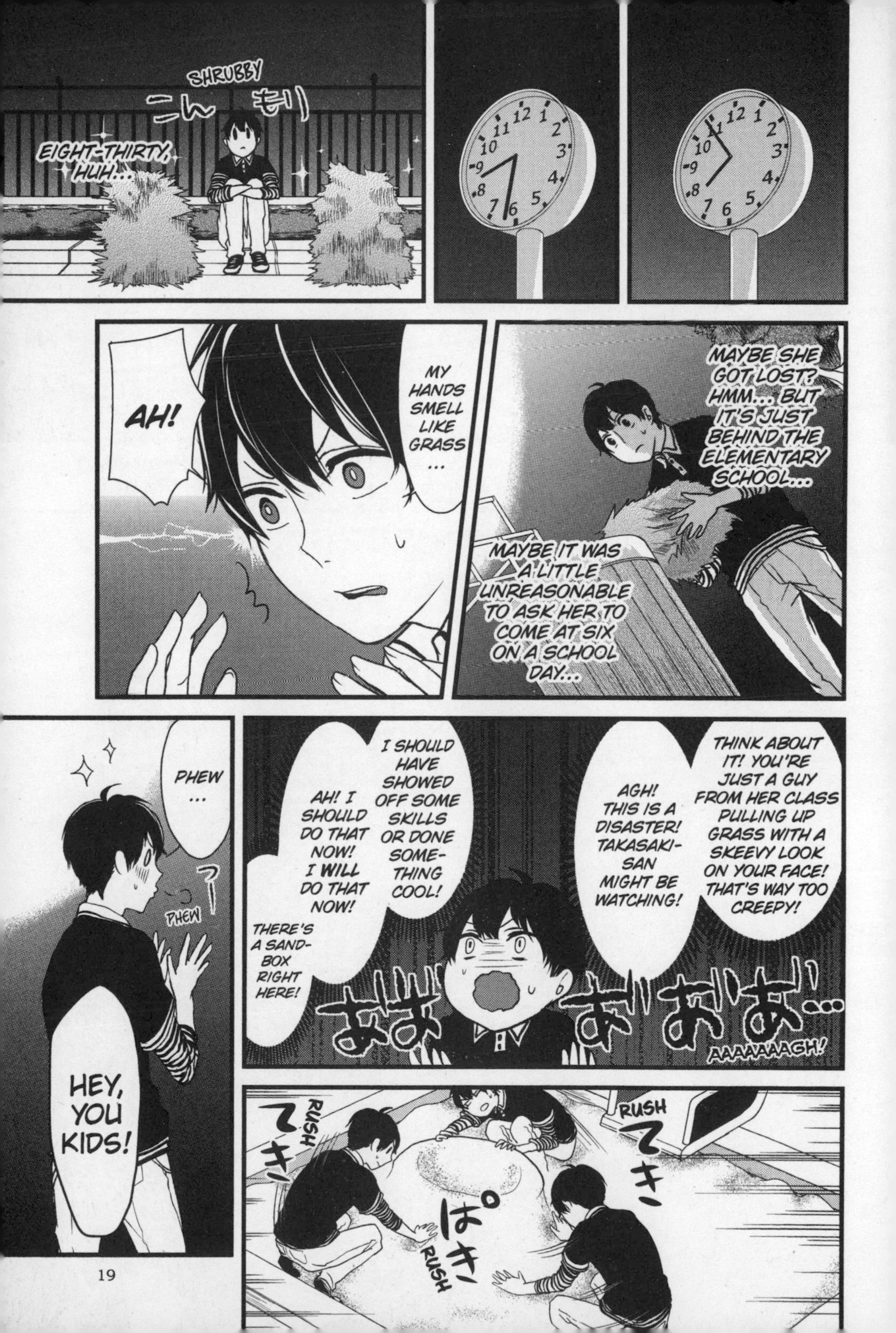

SHRUBBY
こんもり
EIGHT-THIRTY, HUH...
MAYBE SHE GOT LOST? HMM... BUT IT'S JUST BEHIND THE ELEMENTARY SCHOOL...
MAYBE IT WAS A LITTLE UNREASONABLE TO ASK HER TO COME AT SIX ON A SCHOOL DAY...
MY HANDS SMELL LIKE GRASS...
AH!
THINK ABOUT IT! YOU'RE JUST A GUY FROM HER CLASS PULLING UP GRASS WITH A SKEEVY LOOK ON YOUR FACE! THAT'S WAY TOO CREEPY!
AGH! THIS IS A DISASTER! TAKASAKI-SAN MIGHT BE WATCHING!
I SHOULD HAVE SHOWED OFF SOME SKILLS OR DONE SOME-THING COOL!
AH! I SHOULD DO THAT NOW! I WILL DO THAT NOW!
THERE'S A SAND-BOX RIGHT HERE!
あああああ…
AAAAAAAGH!
てき
RUSH
ぱき
RUSH
てき
RUSH
PHEW...
PHEW
HEY, YOU KIDS!

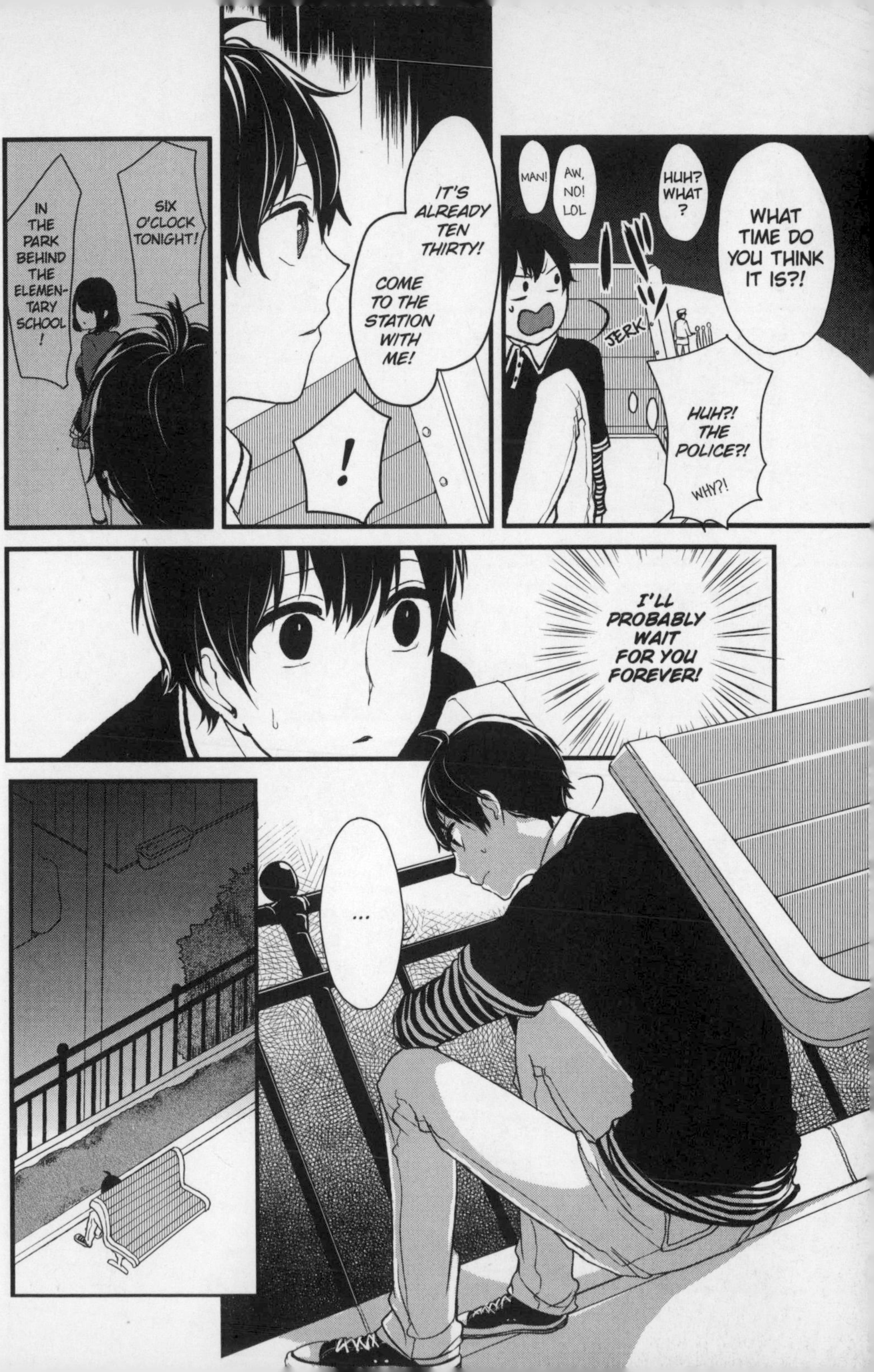
WHAT TIME DO YOU THINK IT IS?!
HUH? WHAT?
AW, NO! LOL
MAN!
JERK
HUH?! THE POLICE?!
WHY?!
IT'S ALREADY TEN THIRTY!
COME TO THE STATION WITH ME!
!
SIX O'CLOCK TONIGHT!
IN THE PARK BEHIND THE ELEMENTARY SCHOOL!
I'LL PROBABLY WAIT FOR YOU FOREVER!
...

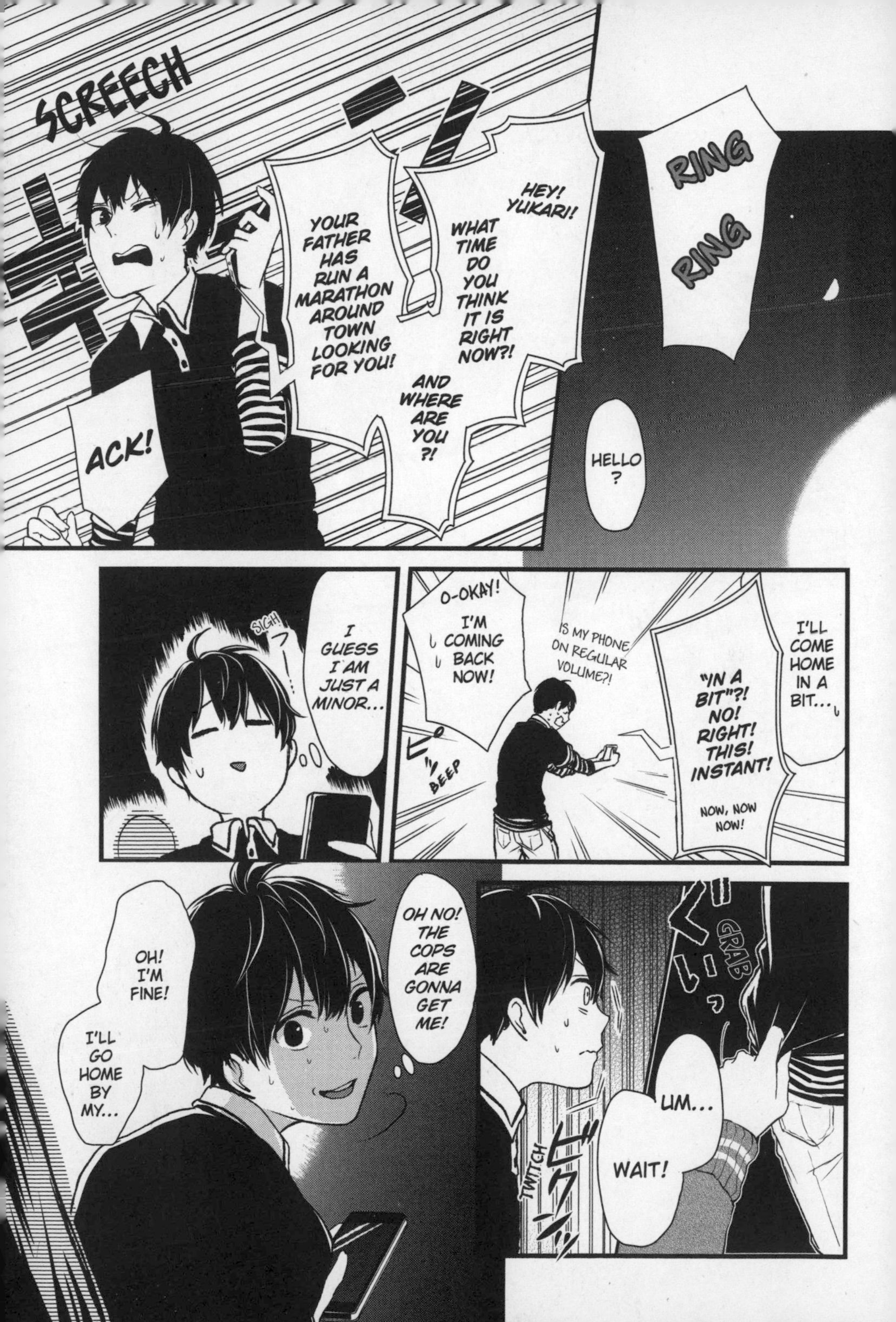
RING
RING
HELLO?
SCREECH
HEY! YUKARI!
WHAT TIME DO YOU THINK IT IS RIGHT NOW?!
AND WHERE ARE YOU?!
YOUR FATHER HAS RUN A MARATHON AROUND TOWN LOOKING FOR YOU!
ACK!
I'LL COME HOME IN A BIT...
"IN A BIT"?! NO! RIGHT! THIS! INSTANT!
NOW, NOW NOW!
IS MY PHONE ON REGULAR VOLUME?!
O-OKAY!
I'M COMING BACK NOW!
BEEP
SIGH
I GUESS I AM JUST A MINOR...
GRAB
UM...
WAIT!
TWITCH
OH NO! THE COPS ARE GONNA GET ME!
OH! I'M FINE!
I'LL GO HOME BY MY...

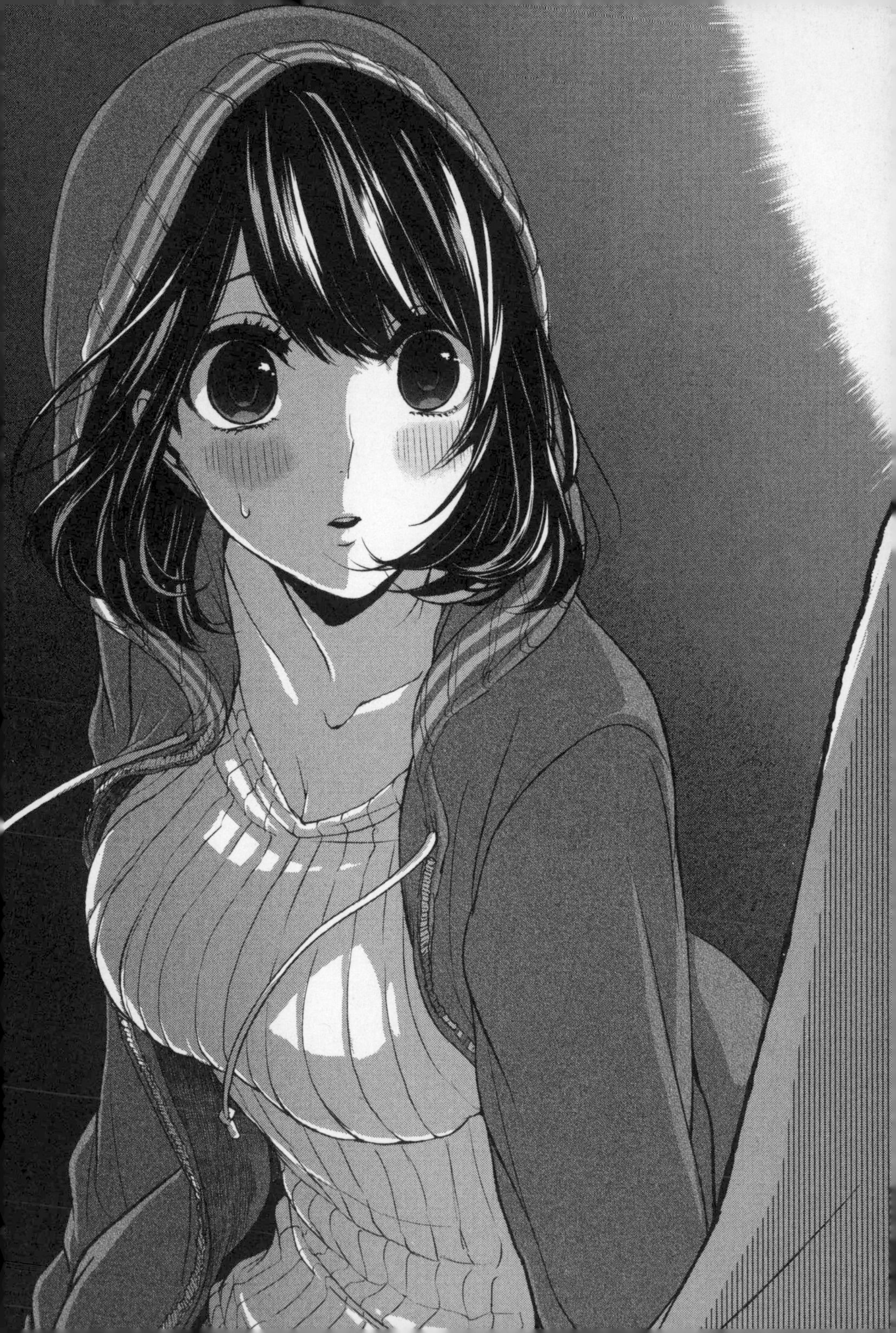

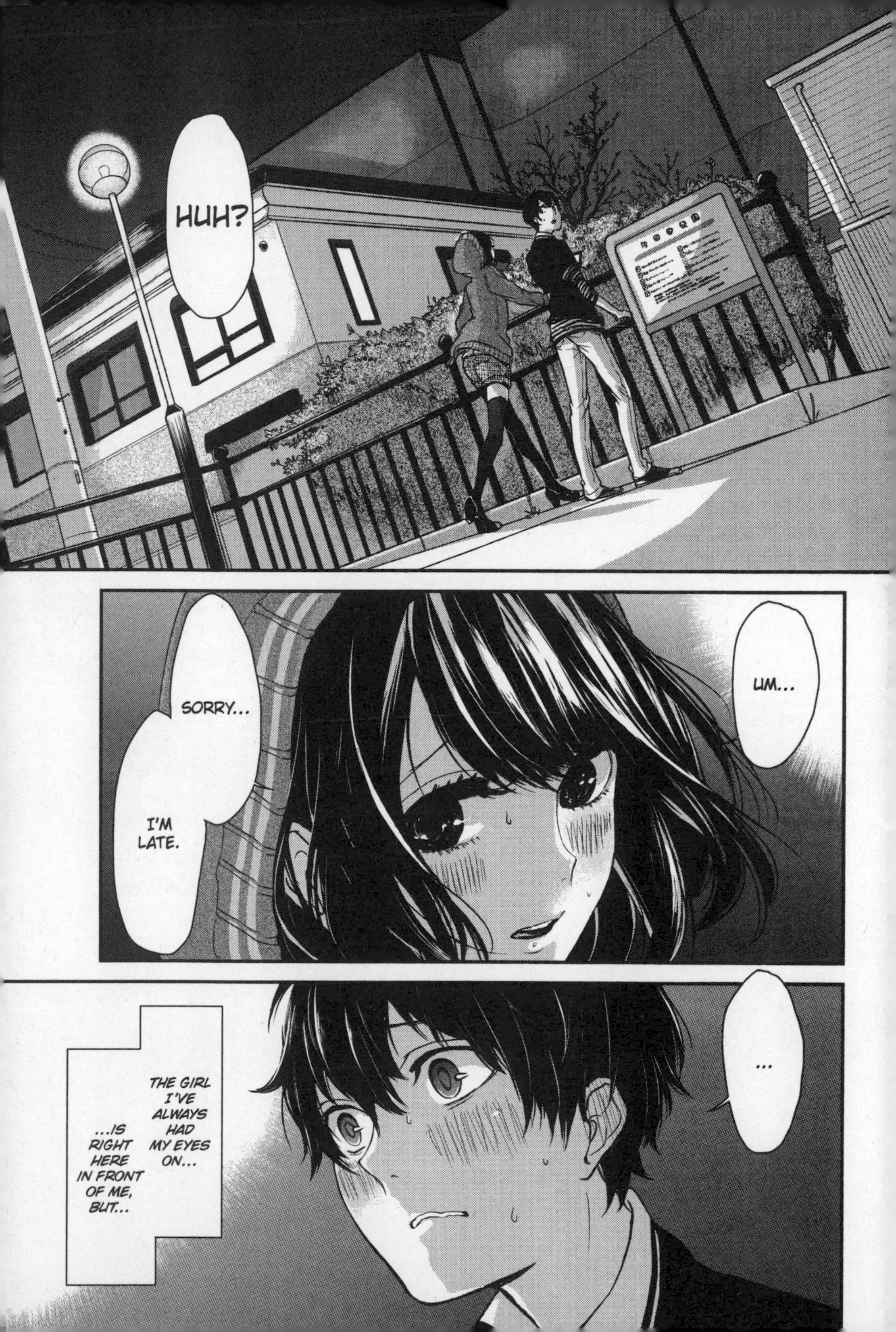
HUH?
UM...
SORRY...
I'M LATE.
...
THE GIRL I'VE ALWAYS HAD MY EYES ON...
...IS RIGHT HERE IN FRONT OF ME, BUT...

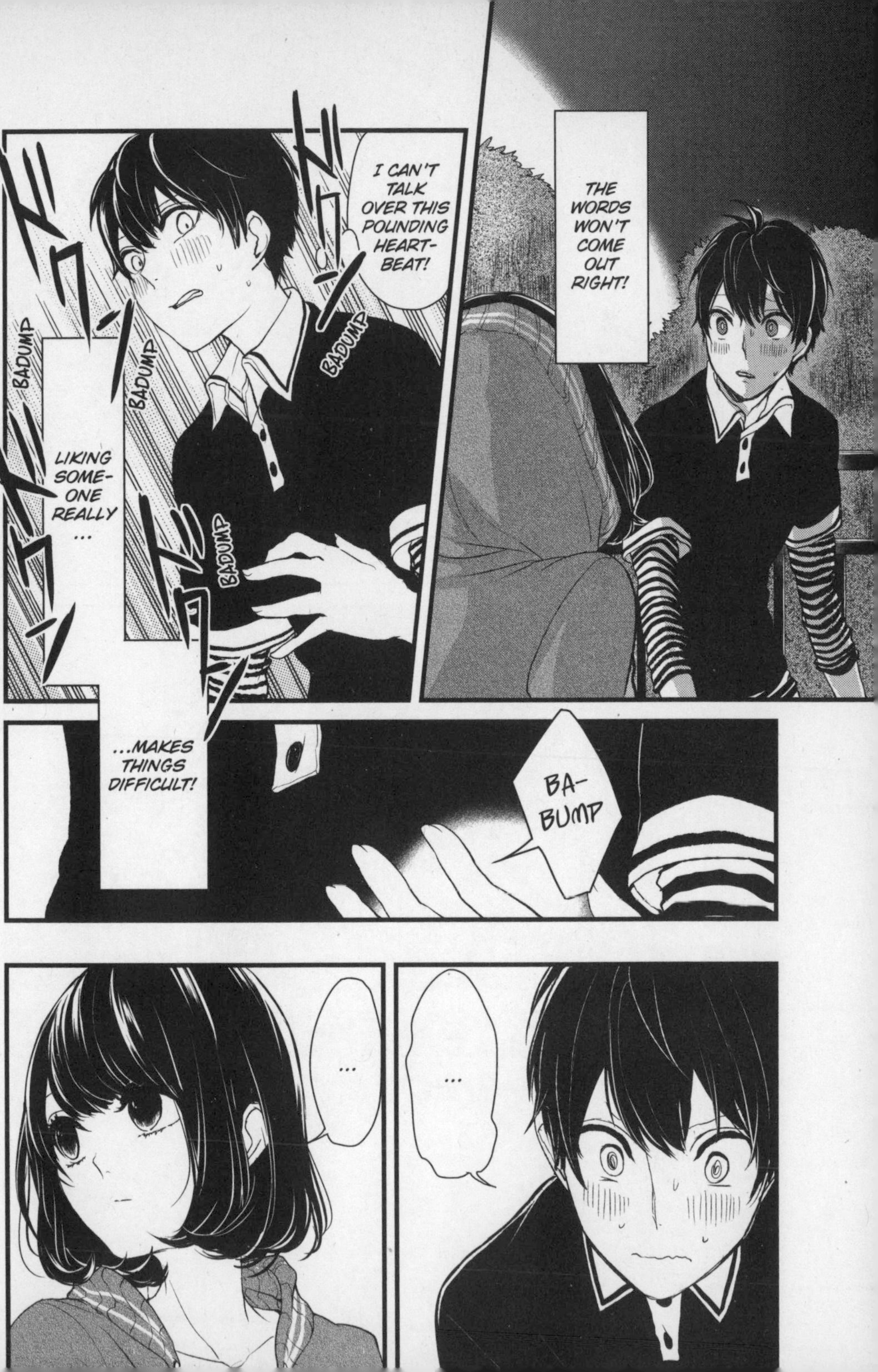
THE WORDS WON'T COME OUT RIGHT!
I CAN'T TALK OVER THIS POUNDING HEART-BEAT!
BADUMP
BADUMP
BADUMP
BADUMP
LIKING SOME-ONE REALLY ...
...MAKES THINGS DIFFICULT!
BA-BUMP
...
...

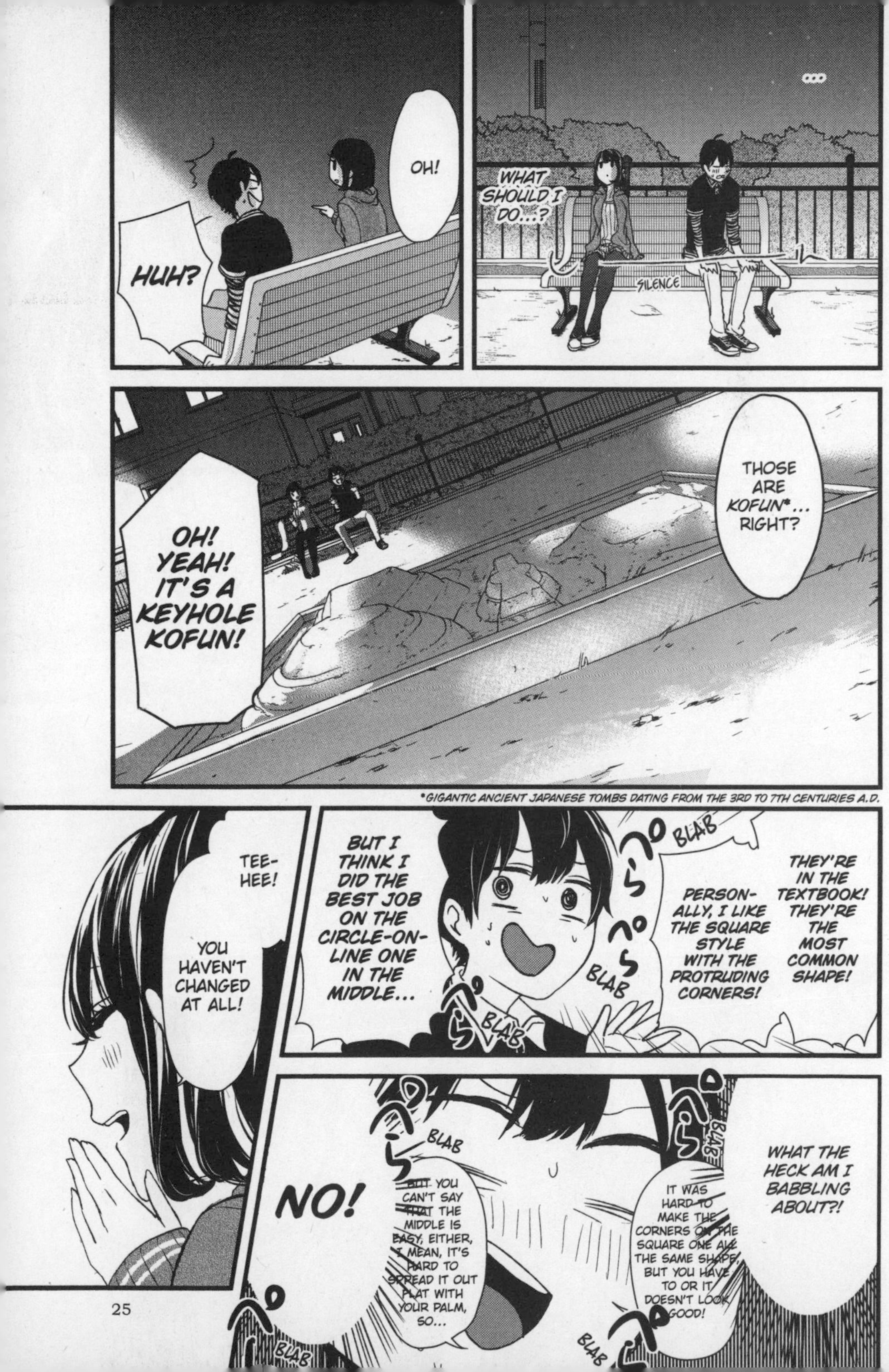
...
WHAT SHOULD I DO...?
SILENCE
OH!
HUH?
THOSE ARE KOFUN*... RIGHT?
OH! YEAH! IT'S A KEYHOLE KOFUN!
THEY'RE IN THE TEXTBOOK! THEY'RE THE MOST COMMON SHAPE!
PERSONALLY, I LIKE THE SQUARE STYLE WITH THE PROTRUDING CORNERS!
BUT I THINK I DID THE BEST JOB ON THE CIRCLE-ON-LINE ONE IN THE MIDDLE...
BLAB
BLAB
BLAB
WHAT THE HECK AM I BABBLING ABOUT?!
BLAB
IT WAS HARD TO MAKE THE CORNERS ON THE SQUARE ONE ALL THE SAME SHAPE, BUT YOU HAVE TO OR IT DOESN'T LOOK GOOD!
BUT YOU CAN'T SAY THAT THE MIDDLE IS EASY, EITHER, I MEAN, IT'S HARD TO SPREAD IT OUT FLAT WITH YOUR PALM, SO...
BLAB
NO!
BLAB
BLAB
TEE-HEE!
YOU HAVEN'T CHANGED AT ALL!

*GIGANTIC ANCIENT JAPANESE TOMBS DATING FROM THE 3RD TO 7TH CENTURIES A.D.

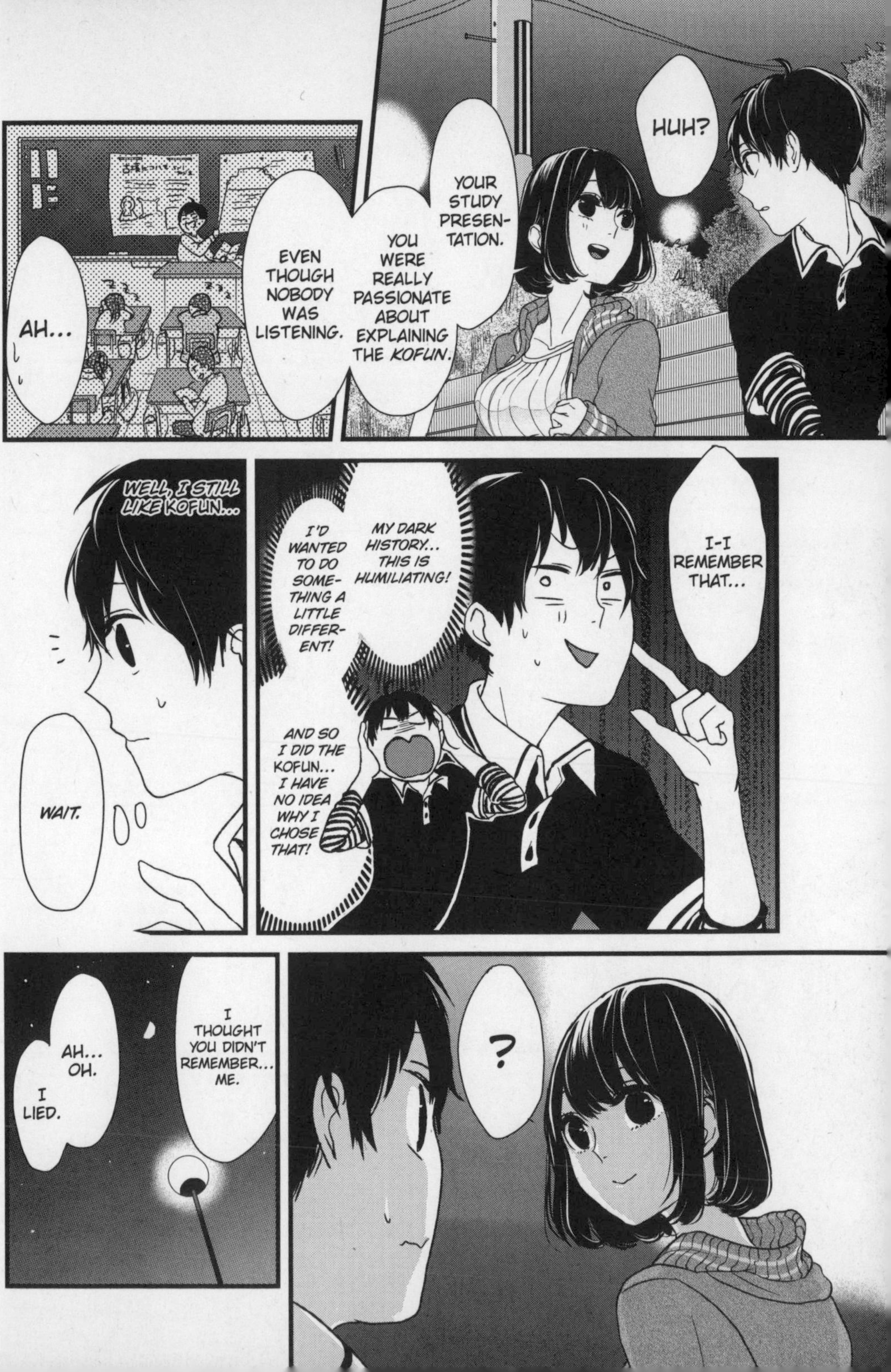
HUH?
YOUR STUDY PRESENTATION.
YOU WERE REALLY PASSIONATE ABOUT EXPLAINING THE *KOFUN*.
EVEN THOUGH NOBODY WAS LISTENING.
AH...
I-I REMEMBER THAT...
MY DARK HISTORY... THIS IS HUMILIATING!
I'D WANTED TO DO SOMETHING A LITTLE DIFFERENT!
AND SO I DID THE KOFUN... I HAVE NO IDEA WHY I CHOSE THAT!
WELL, I STILL LIKE KOFUN...
WAIT.
?
I THOUGHT YOU DIDN'T REMEMBER... ME.
AH... OH.
I LIED.

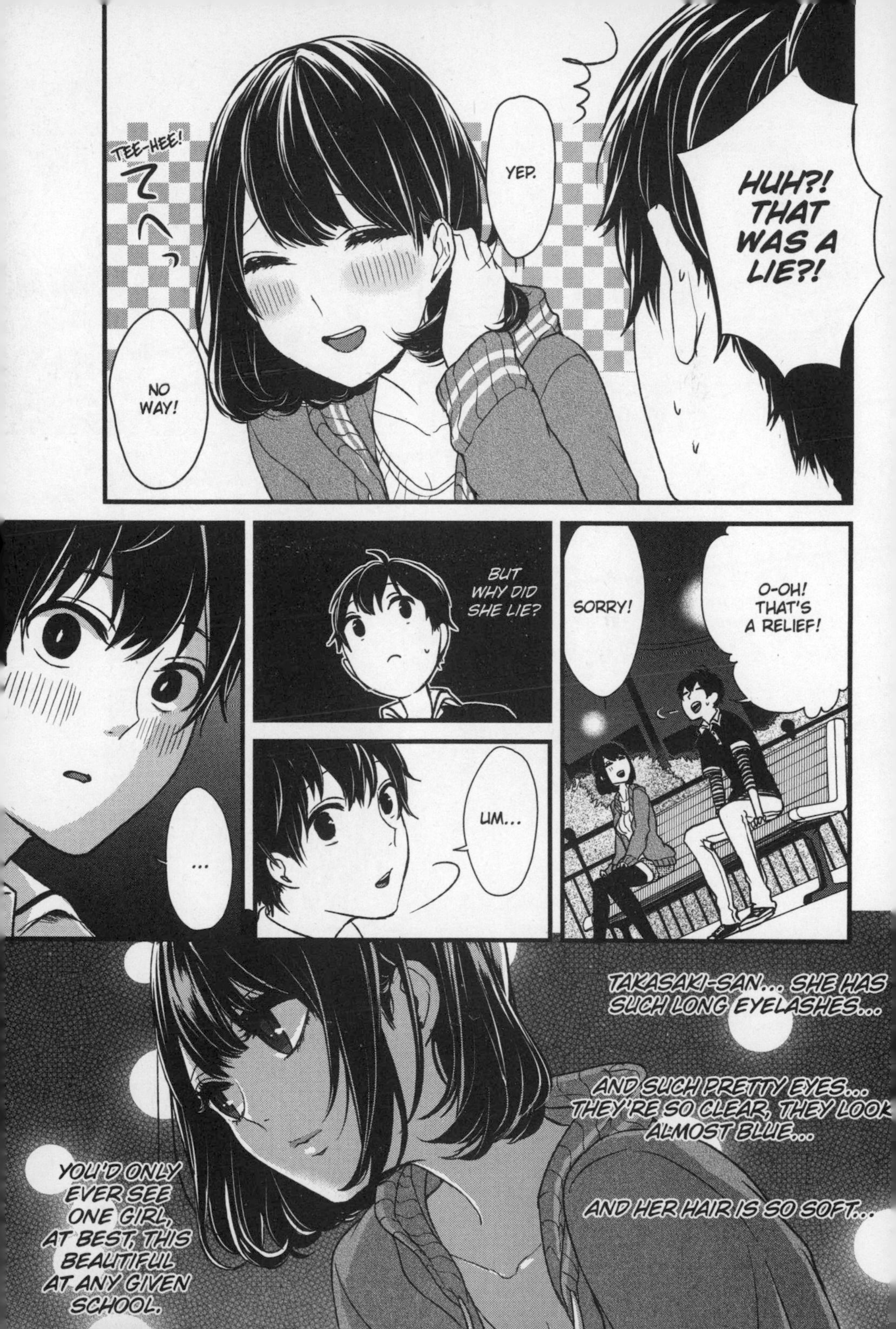
HUH?! THAT WAS A LIE?!
YEP.
TEE-HEE!
NO WAY!
O-OH! THAT'S A RELIEF!
SORRY!
BUT WHY DID SHE LIE?
UM...
...
TAKASAKI-SAN... SHE HAS SUCH LONG EYELASHES...
AND SUCH PRETTY EYES... THEY'RE SO CLEAR, THEY LOOK ALMOST BLUE...
AND HER HAIR IS SO SOFT...
YOU'D ONLY EVER SEE ONE GIRL, AT BEST, THIS BEAUTIFUL AT ANY GIVEN SCHOOL.

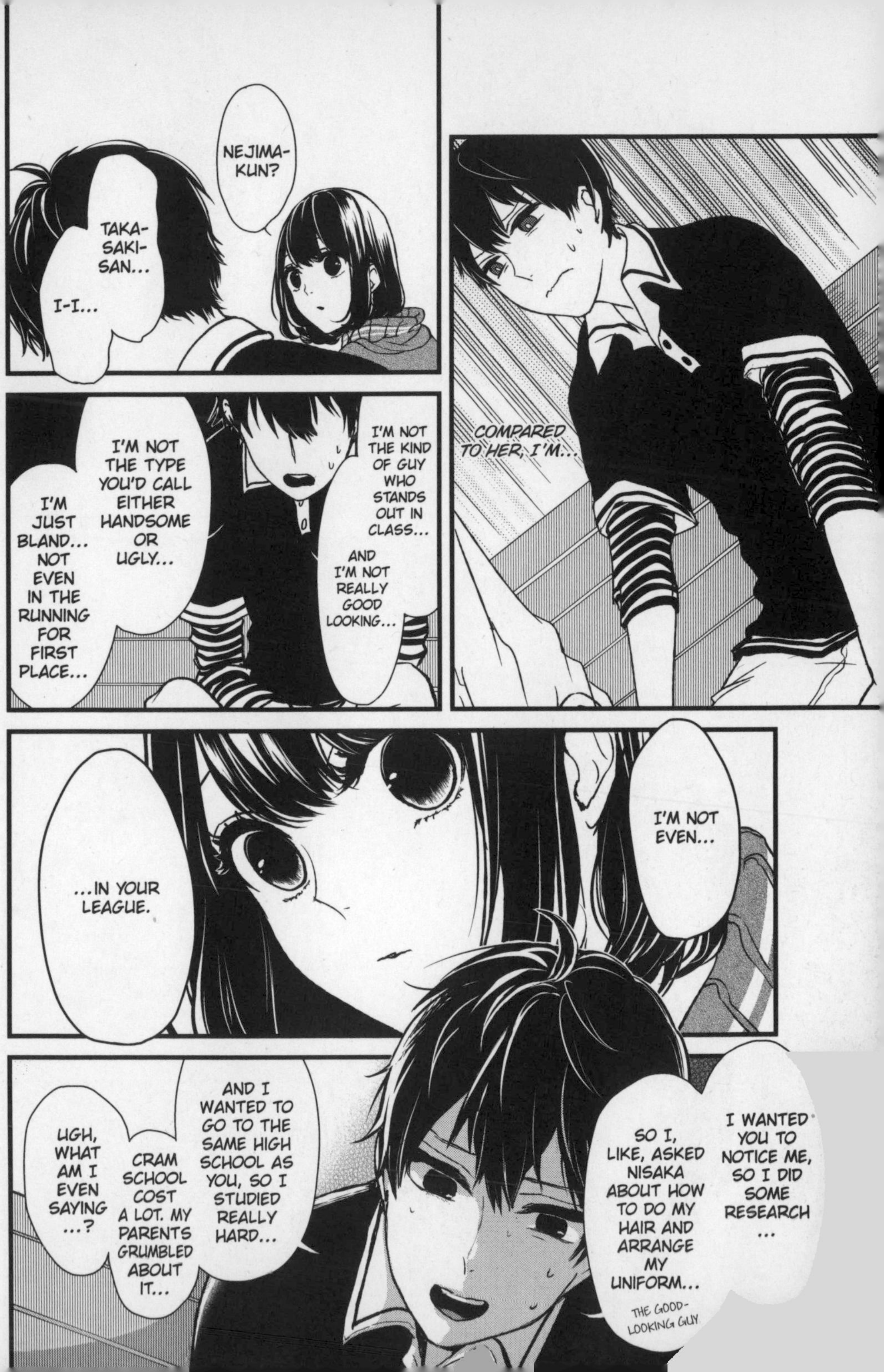
NEJIMA-KUN?
TAKA-SAKI-SAN...
I-I...
COMPARED TO HER, I'M...
I'M NOT THE KIND OF GUY WHO STANDS OUT IN CLASS...
AND I'M NOT REALLY GOOD LOOKING...
I'M NOT THE TYPE YOU'D CALL EITHER HANDSOME OR UGLY...
I'M JUST BLAND... NOT EVEN IN THE RUNNING FOR FIRST PLACE...
I'M NOT EVEN...
...IN YOUR LEAGUE.
I WANTED YOU TO NOTICE ME, SO I DID SOME RESEARCH...
SO I, LIKE, ASKED NISAKA ABOUT HOW TO DO MY HAIR AND ARRANGE MY UNIFORM...
THE GOOD-LOOKING GUY
AND I WANTED TO GO TO THE SAME HIGH SCHOOL AS YOU, SO I STUDIED REALLY HARD...
CRAM SCHOOL COST A LOT. MY PARENTS GRUMBLED ABOUT IT...
UGH, WHAT AM I EVEN SAYING ...?

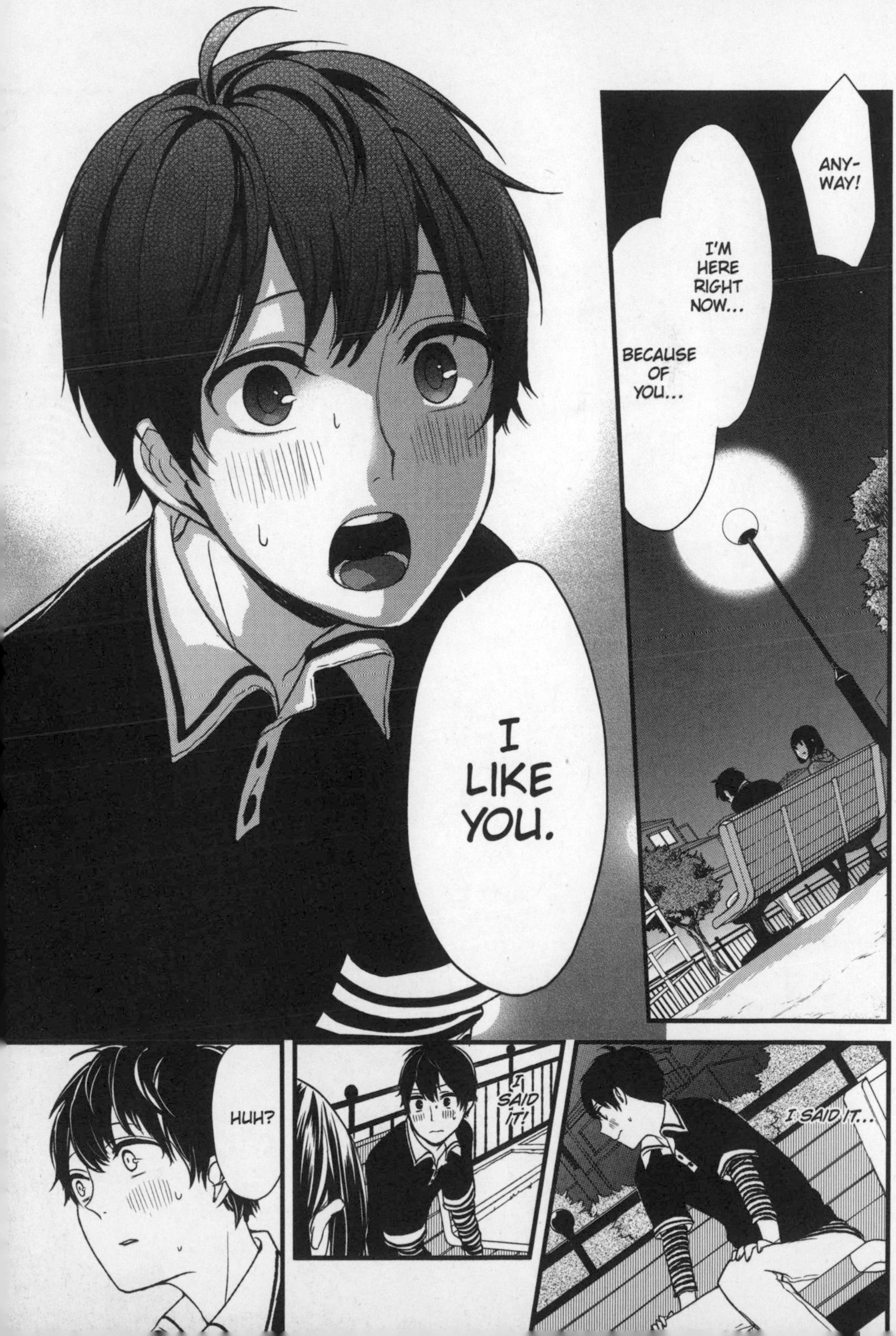
ANY-WAY!
I'M HERE RIGHT NOW...
BECAUSE OF YOU...
I LIKE YOU.
I SAID IT...
I SAID IT!
HUH?

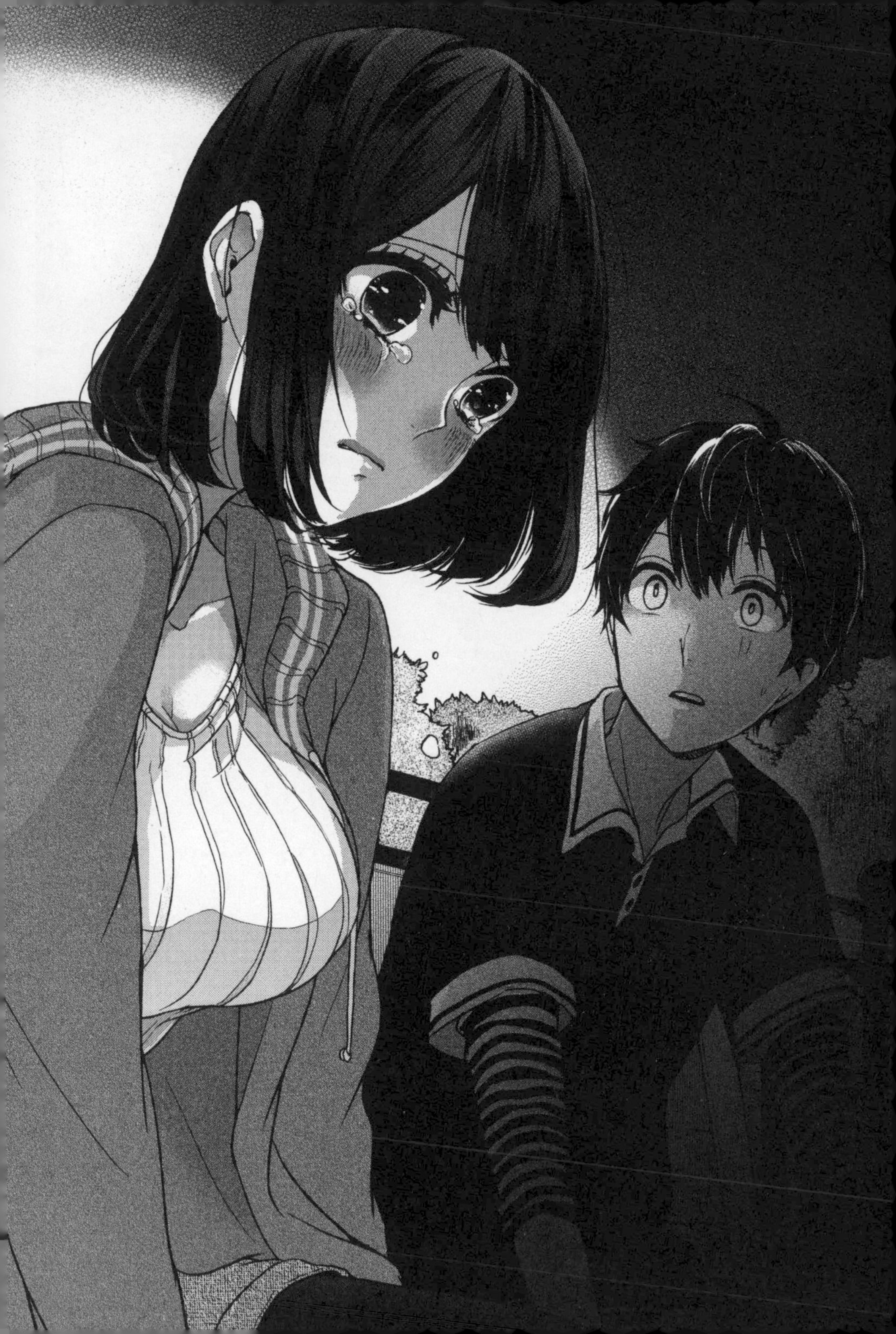

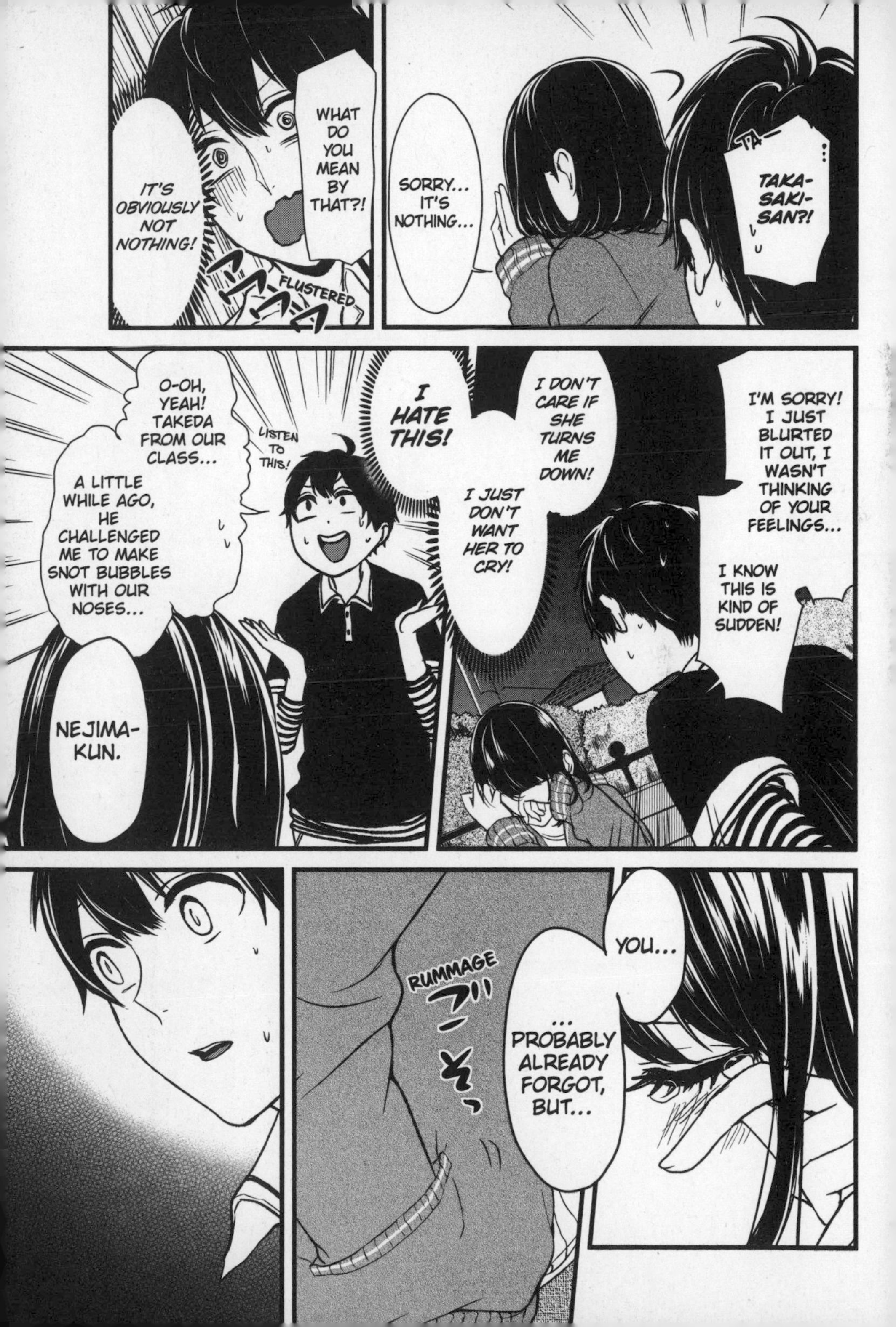
TA—
...
TAKA-SAKI-SAN?!
SORRY... IT'S NOTHING...
WHAT DO YOU MEAN BY THAT?!
IT'S OBVIOUSLY NOT NOTHING!
FLUSTERED
I'M SORRY! I JUST BLURTED IT OUT, I WASN'T THINKING OF YOUR FEELINGS...
I KNOW THIS IS KIND OF SUDDEN!
I DON'T CARE IF SHE TURNS ME DOWN!
I JUST DON'T WANT HER TO CRY!
I HATE THIS!
LISTEN TO THIS!
O-OH, YEAH! TAKEDA FROM OUR CLASS...
A LITTLE WHILE AGO, HE CHALLENGED ME TO MAKE SNOT BUBBLES WITH OUR NOSES...
NEJIMA-KUN.
YOU...
...PROBABLY ALREADY FORGOT, BUT...
RUMMAGE

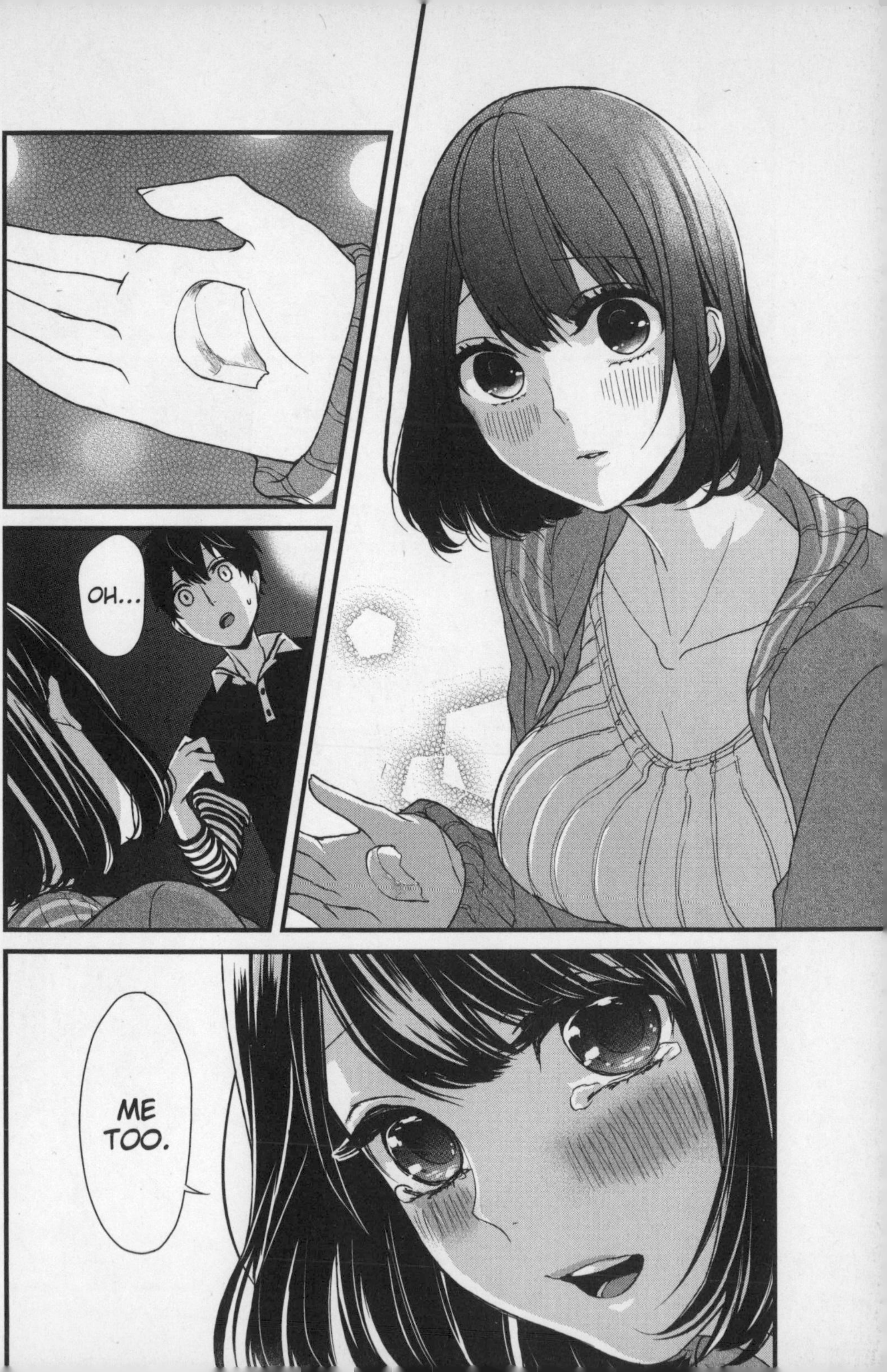
OH...
ME TOO.

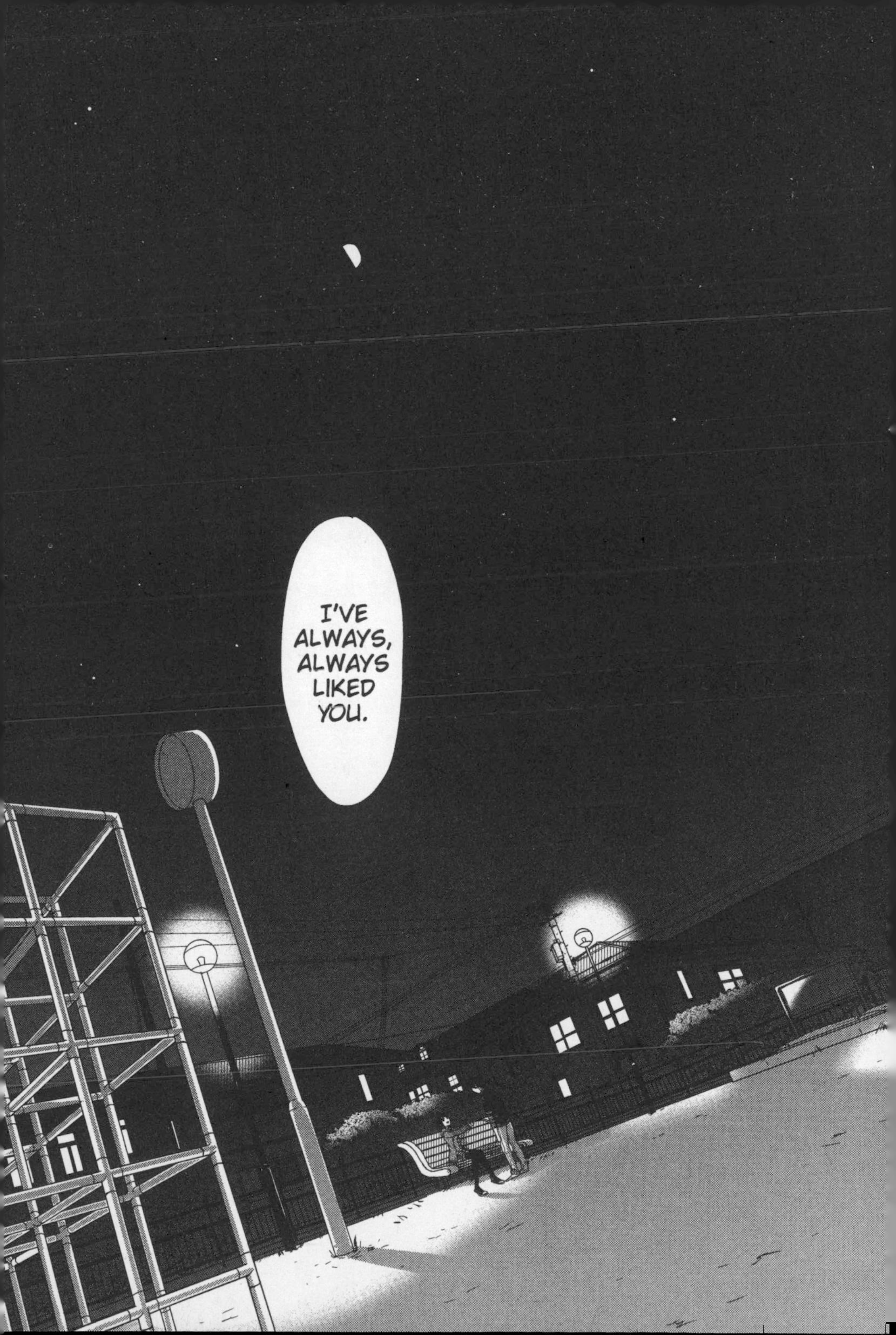
I'VE ALWAYS, ALWAYS LIKED YOU.

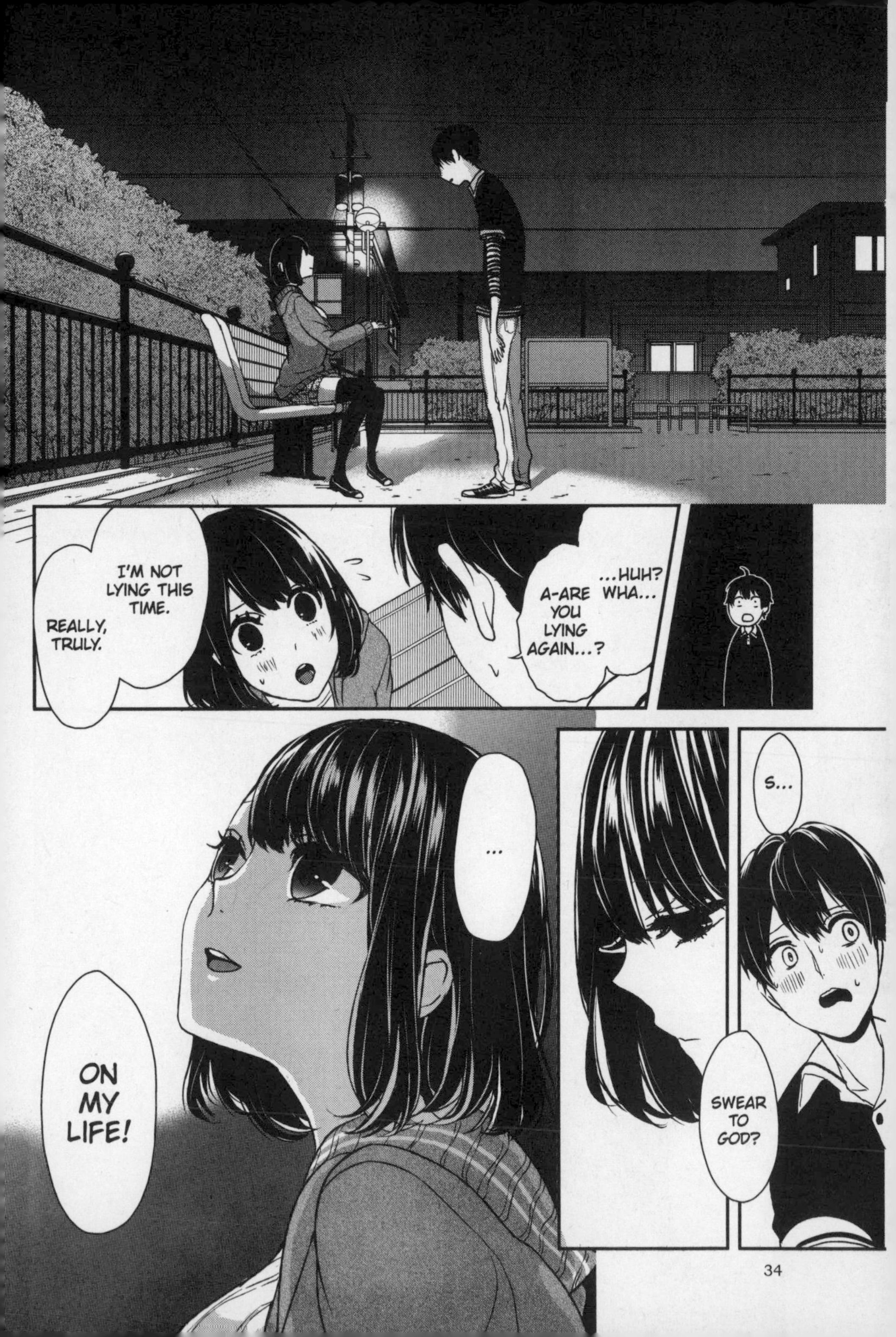
...HUH? WHA...
A-ARE YOU LYING AGAIN...?
I'M NOT LYING THIS TIME.
REALLY, TRULY.
S...
SWEAR TO GOD?
...
ON MY LIFE!

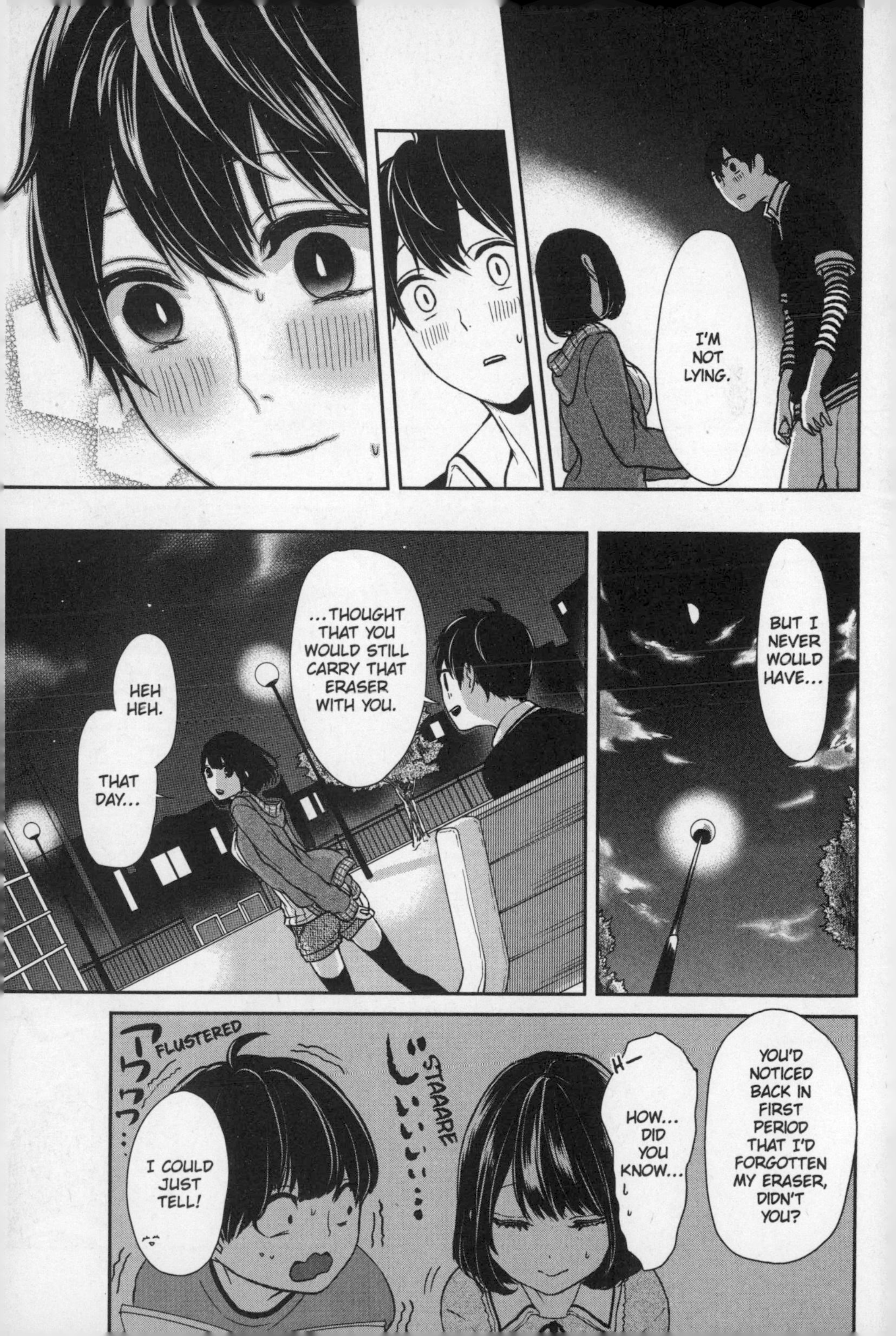
I'M NOT LYING.
BUT I NEVER WOULD HAVE...
...THOUGHT THAT YOU WOULD STILL CARRY THAT ERASER WITH YOU.
HEH HEH.
THAT DAY...
YOU'D NOTICED BACK IN FIRST PERIOD THAT I'D FORGOTTEN MY ERASER, DIDN'T YOU?
H—
HOW... DID YOU KNOW...
STAAARE
I COULD JUST TELL!
FLUSTERED

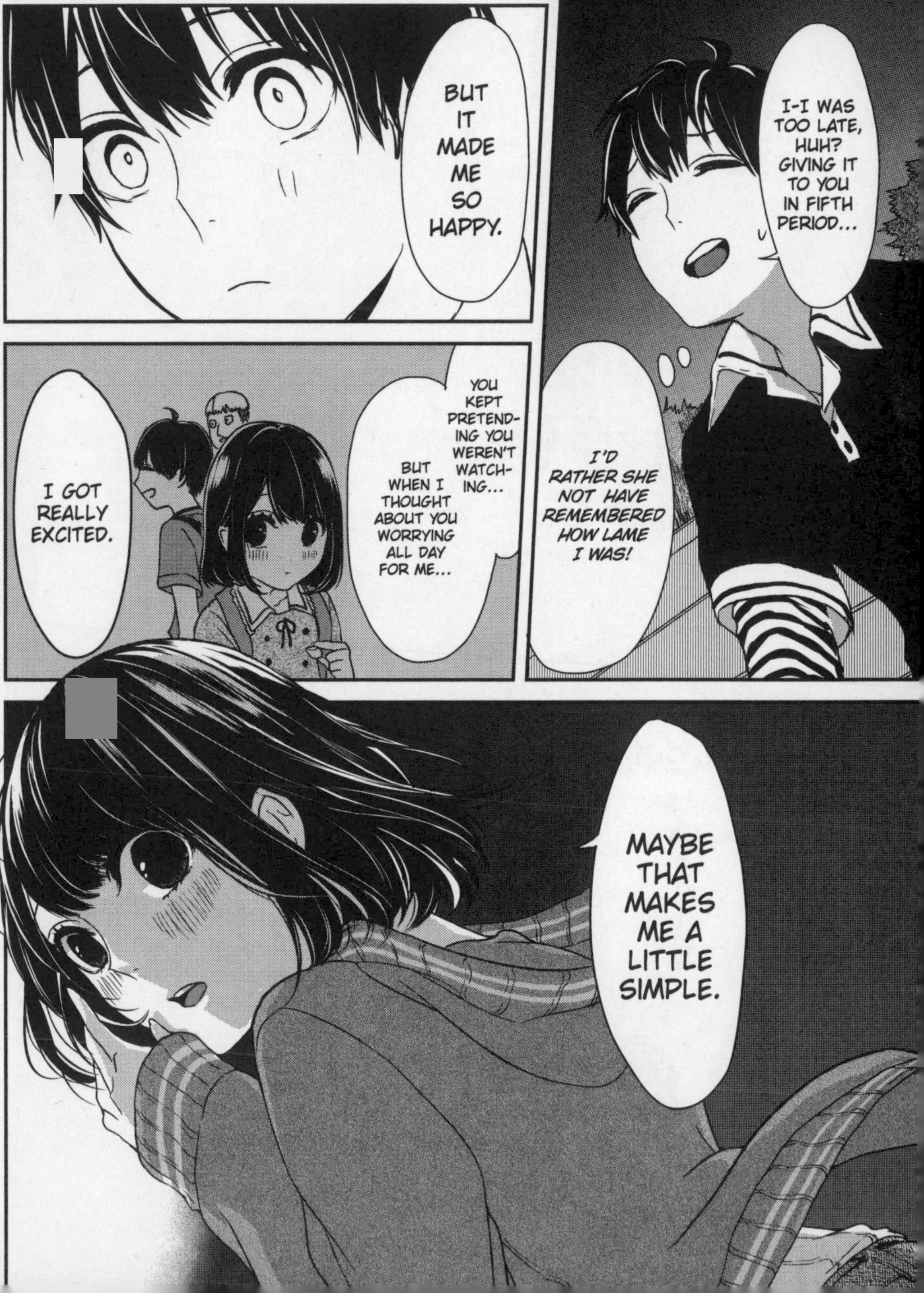
I-I WAS TOO LATE, HUH? GIVING IT TO YOU IN FIFTH PERIOD...
I'D RATHER SHE NOT HAVE REMEMBERED HOW LAME I WAS!
BUT IT MADE ME SO HAPPY.
YOU KEPT PRETEND-ING YOU WEREN'T WATCH-ING...
BUT WHEN I THOUGHT ABOUT YOU WORRYING ALL DAY FOR ME...
I GOT REALLY EXCITED.
MAYBE THAT MAKES ME A LITTLE SIMPLE.

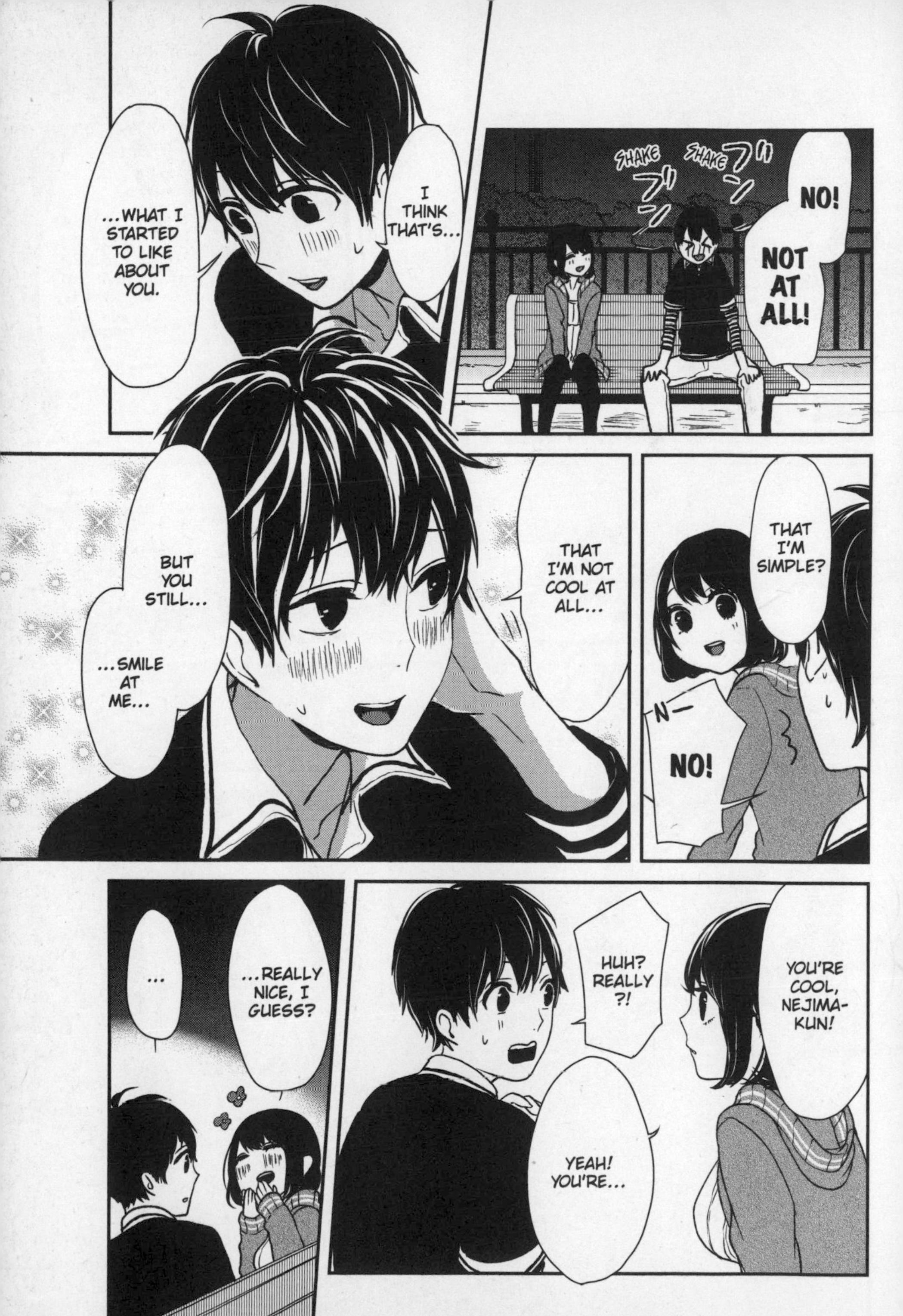
SHAKE SHAKE
NO!
NOT AT ALL!
I THINK THAT'S...
...WHAT I STARTED TO LIKE ABOUT YOU.
THAT I'M SIMPLE?
N— NO!
THAT I'M NOT COOL AT ALL...
BUT YOU STILL...
...SMILE AT ME...
YOU'RE COOL, NEJIMA-KUN!
HUH? REALLY?!
YEAH! YOU'RE...
...REALLY NICE, I GUESS?
...

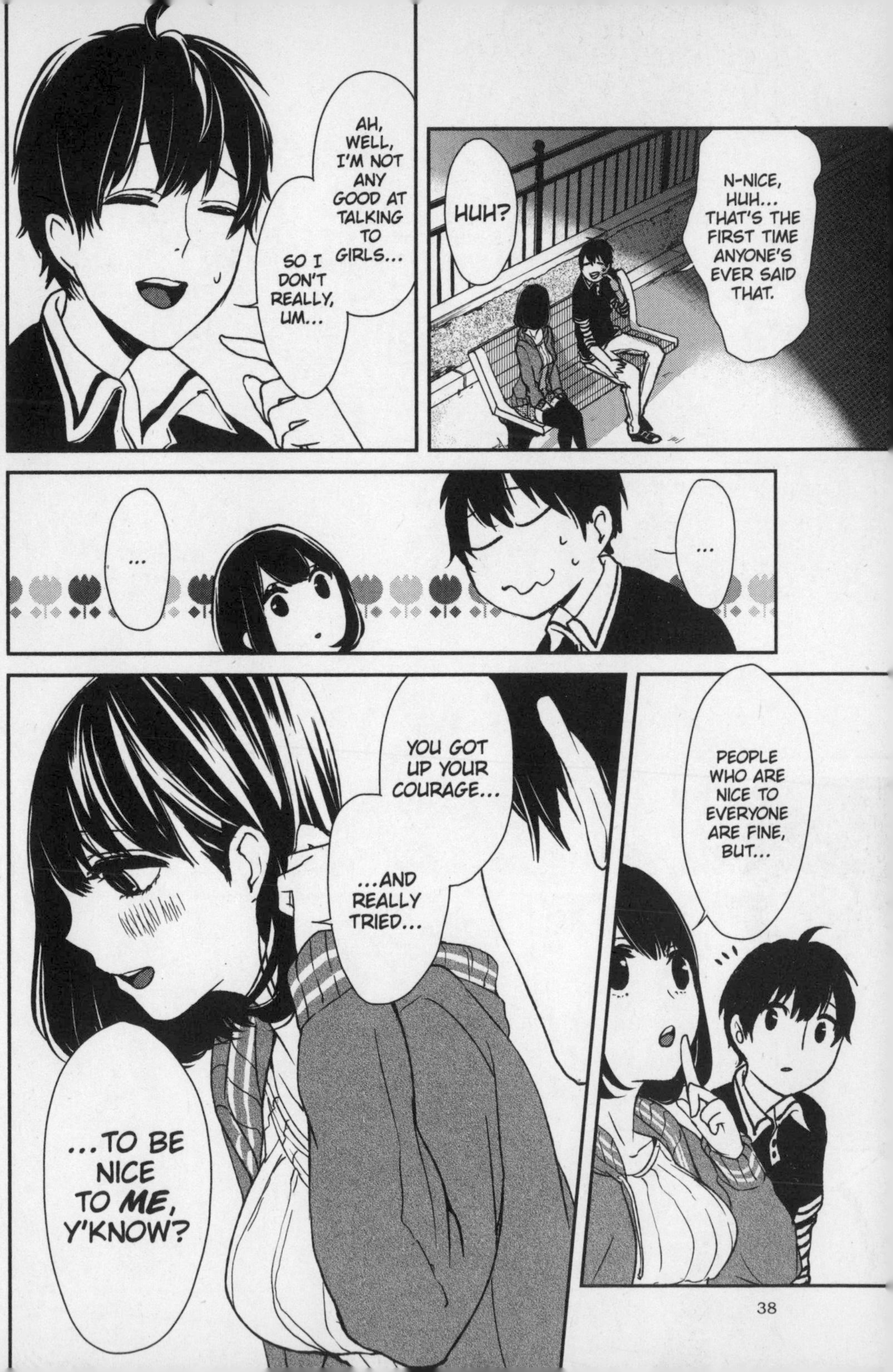
N-NICE, HUH... THAT'S THE FIRST TIME ANYONE'S EVER SAID THAT.
HUH?
AH, WELL, I'M NOT ANY GOOD AT TALKING TO GIRLS...
SO I DON'T REALLY, UM...
...
...
PEOPLE WHO ARE NICE TO EVERYONE ARE FINE, BUT...
YOU GOT UP YOUR COURAGE...
...AND REALLY TRIED...
...TO BE NICE TO *ME*, Y'KNOW?

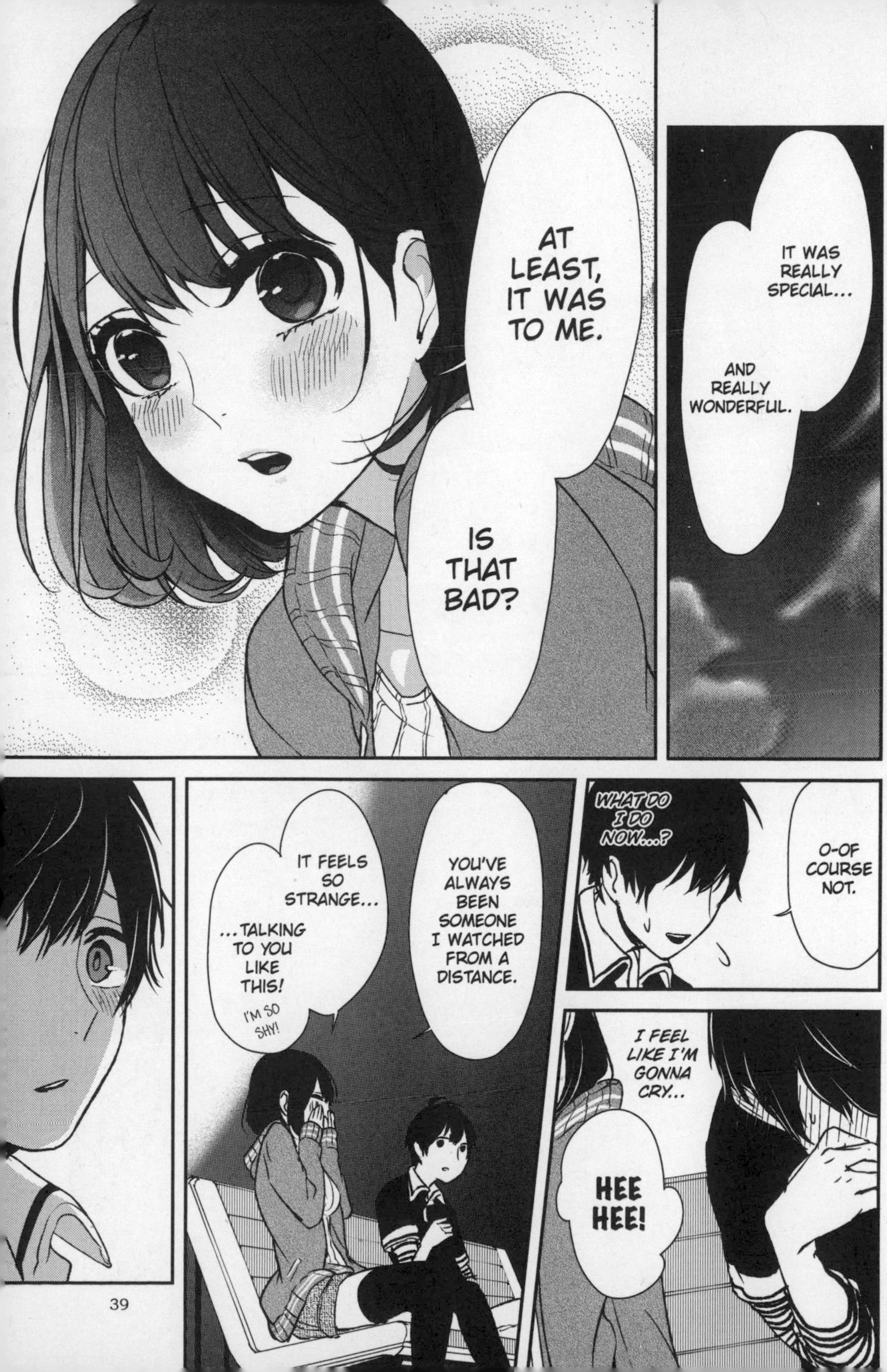
IT WAS REALLY SPECIAL...
AND REALLY WONDERFUL.
AT LEAST, IT WAS TO ME.
IS THAT BAD?
O-OF COURSE NOT.
WHAT DO I DO NOW...?
I FEEL LIKE I'M GONNA CRY...
HEE HEE!
YOU'VE ALWAYS BEEN SOMEONE I WATCHED FROM A DISTANCE.
IT FEELS SO STRANGE...
...TALKING TO YOU LIKE THIS!
I'M SO SHY!

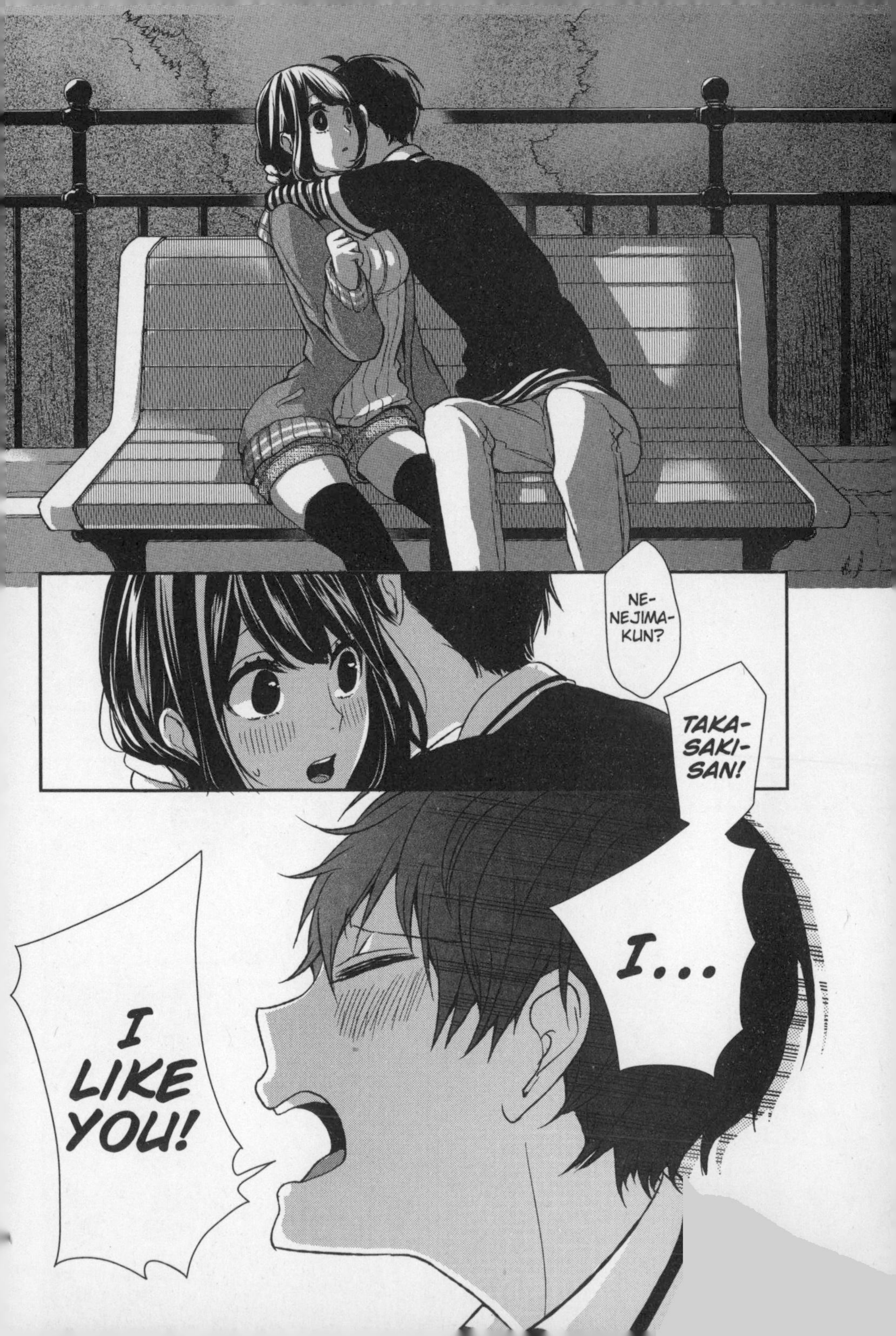
NE-NEJIMA-KUN?
TAKA-SAKI-SAN!
I...
I LIKE YOU!

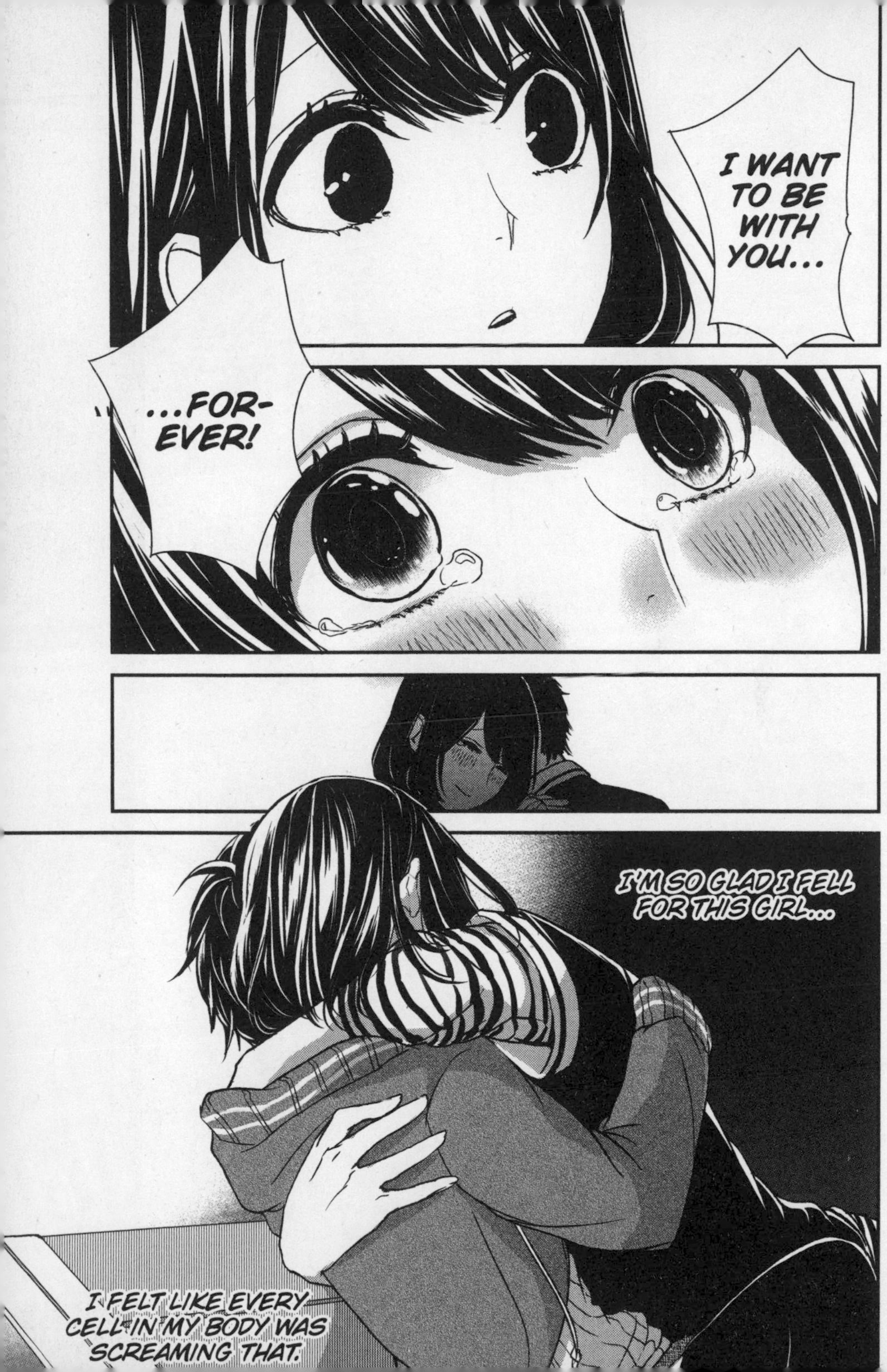
I WANT TO BE WITH YOU...
...FOR-EVER!
I'M SO GLAD I FELL FOR THIS GIRL...
I FELT LIKE EVERY CELL IN MY BODY WAS SCREAMING THAT.

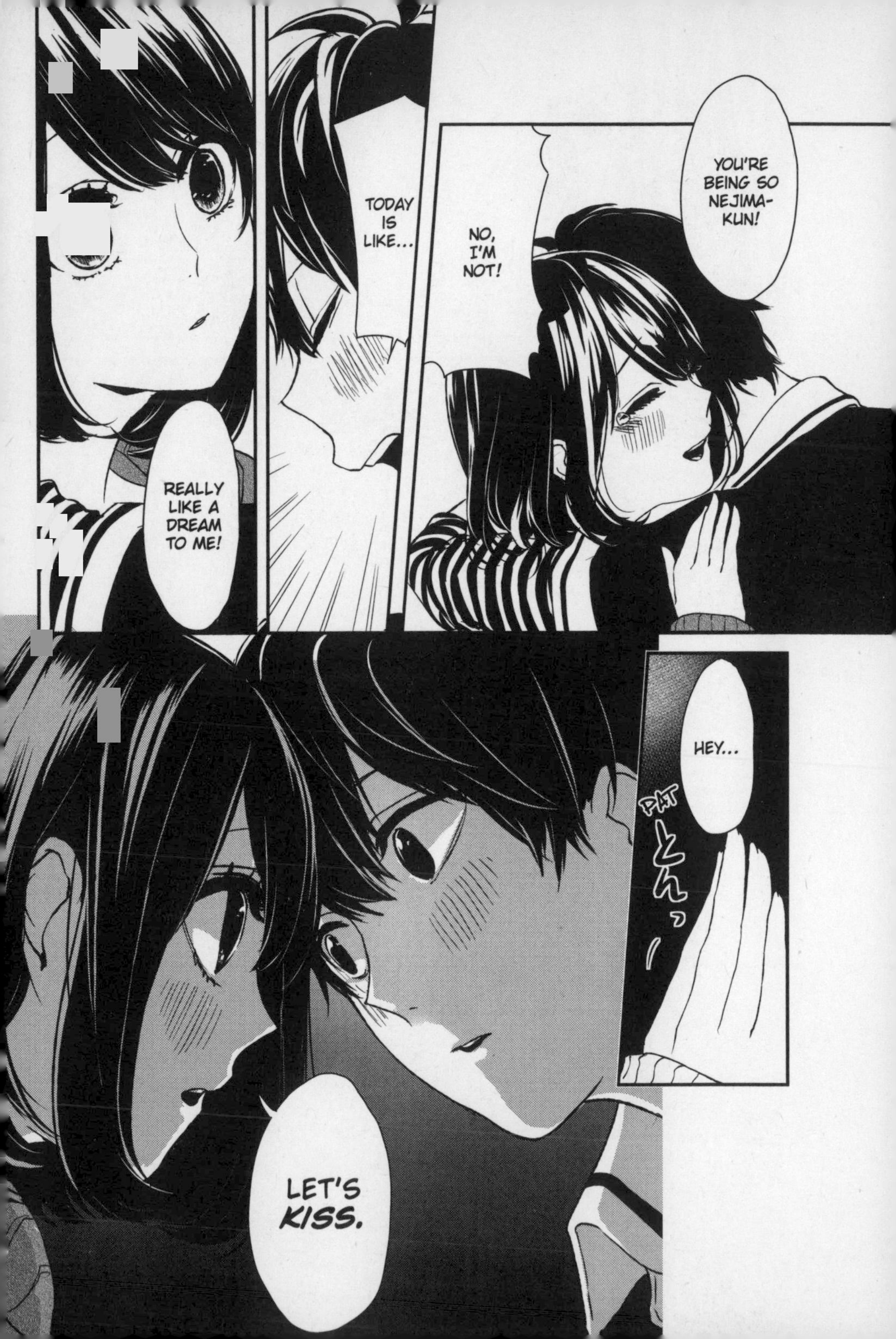
YOU'RE BEING SO NEJIMA-KUN!
NO, I'M NOT!
TODAY IS LIKE...
REALLY LIKE A DREAM TO ME!
HEY...
PAT
とんっ
LET'S KISS.

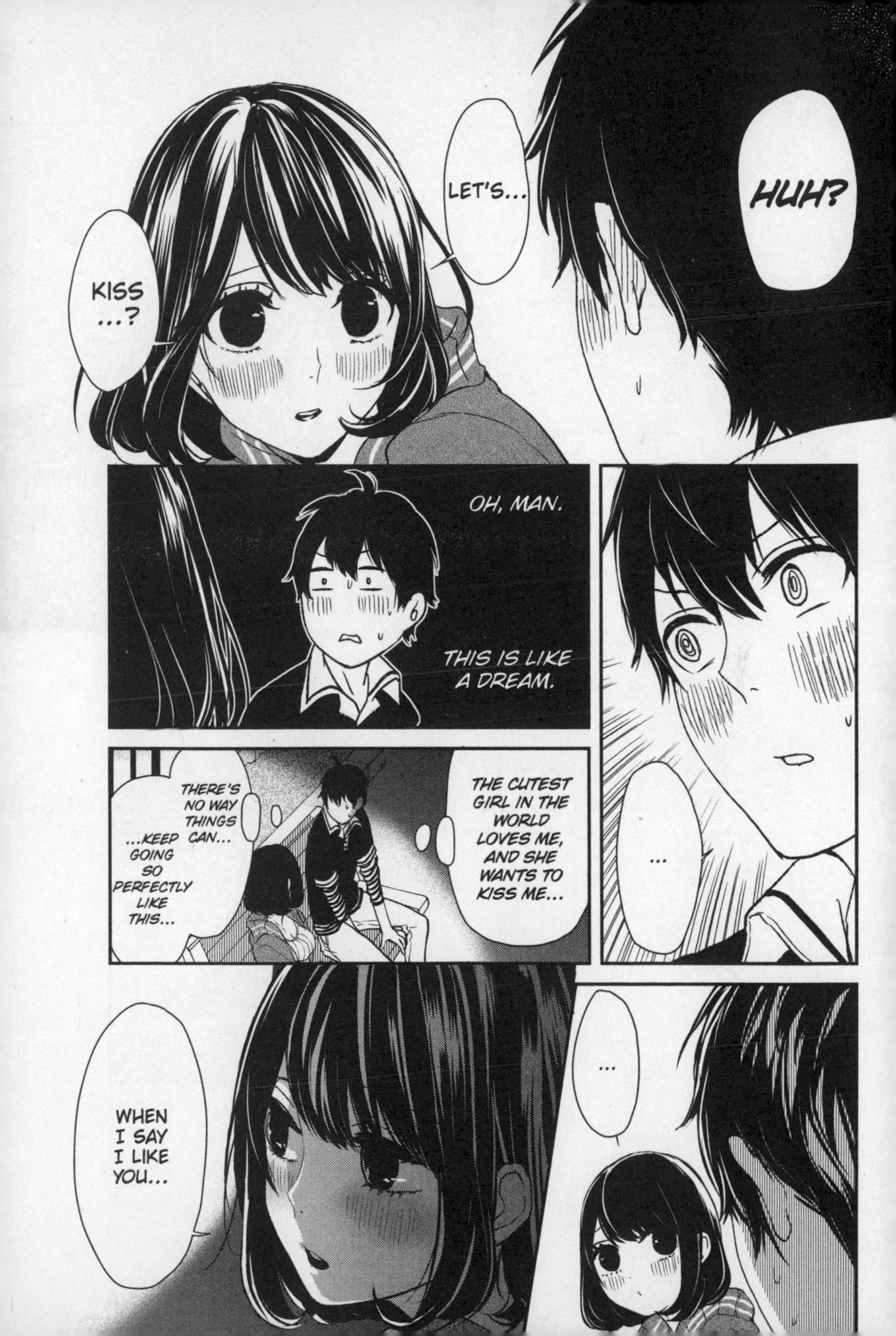
HUH?
LET'S...
KISS ...?
...
OH, MAN.
THIS IS LIKE A DREAM.
THE CUTEST GIRL IN THE WORLD LOVES ME, AND SHE WANTS TO KISS ME...
THERE'S NO WAY THINGS CAN...
...KEEP GOING SO PERFECTLY LIKE THIS...
...
WHEN I SAY I LIKE YOU...

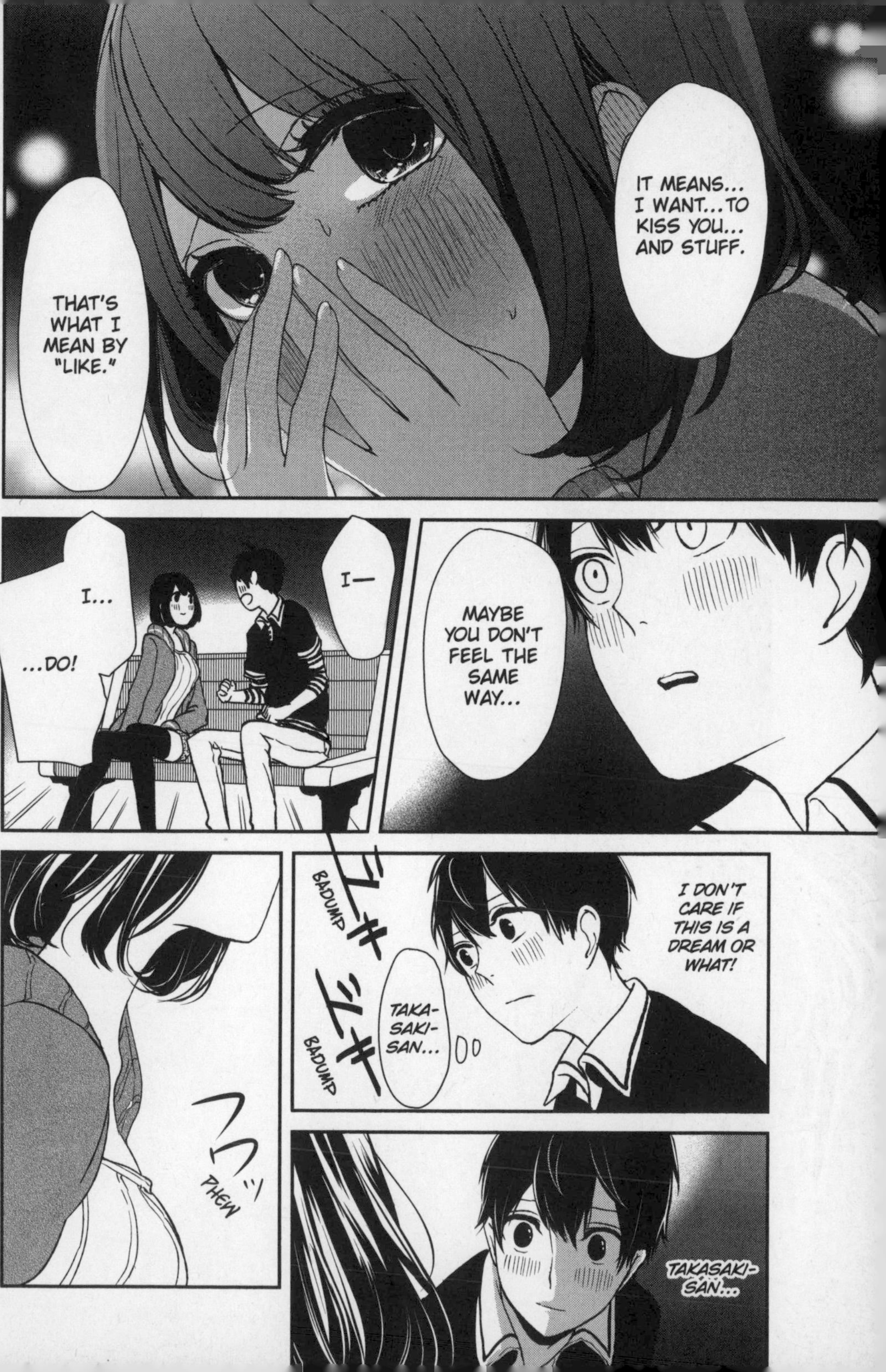
IT MEANS... I WANT...TO KISS YOU... AND STUFF.
THAT'S WHAT I MEAN BY "LIKE."
MAYBE YOU DON'T FEEL THE SAME WAY...
I—
I...
...DO!
I DON'T CARE IF THIS IS A DREAM OR WHAT!
BADUMP
BADUMP
TAKA-SAKI-SAN...
TAKASAKI-SAN...
PHEW

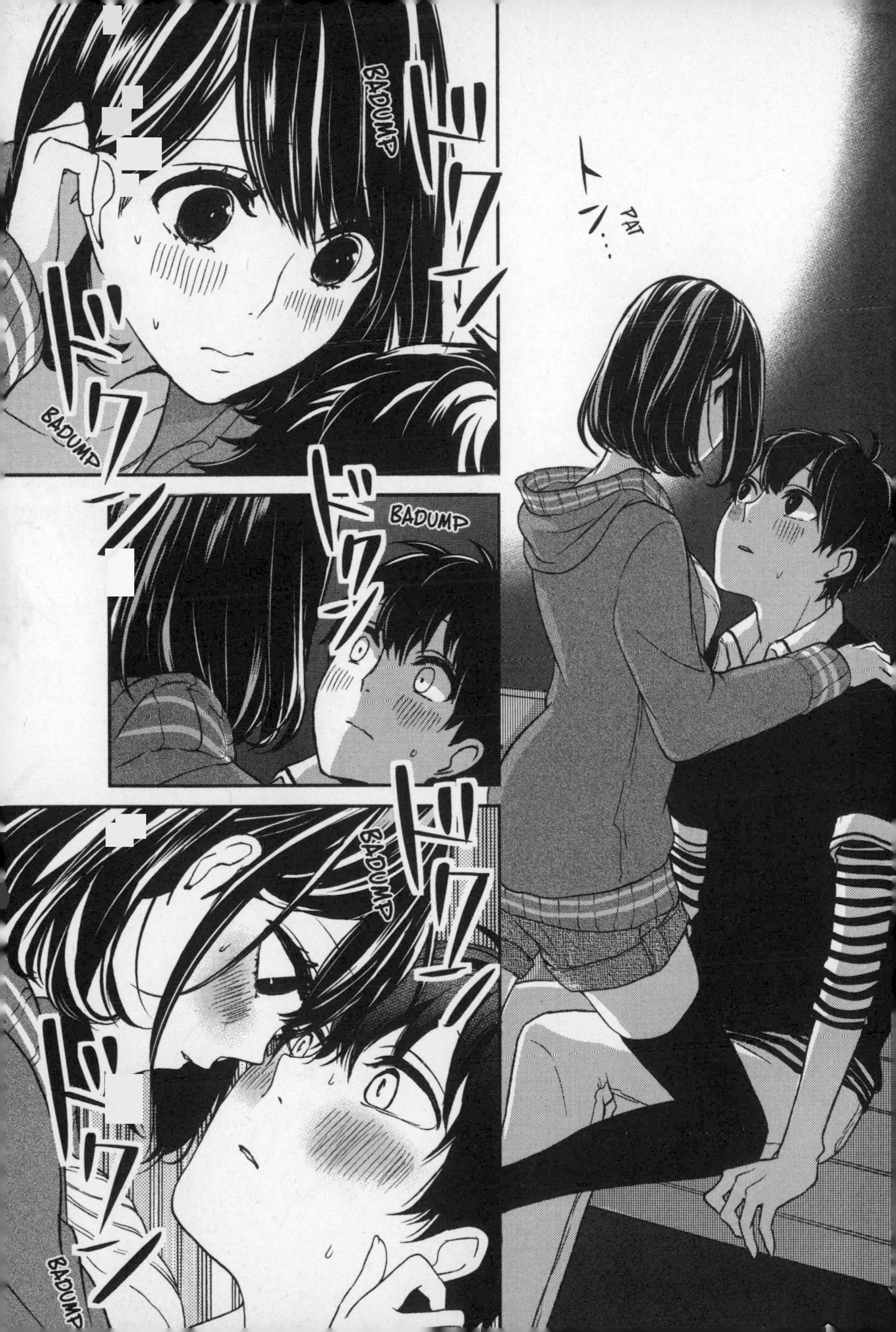
PAT
BADUMP
BADUMP
BADUMP
BADUMP
BADUMP

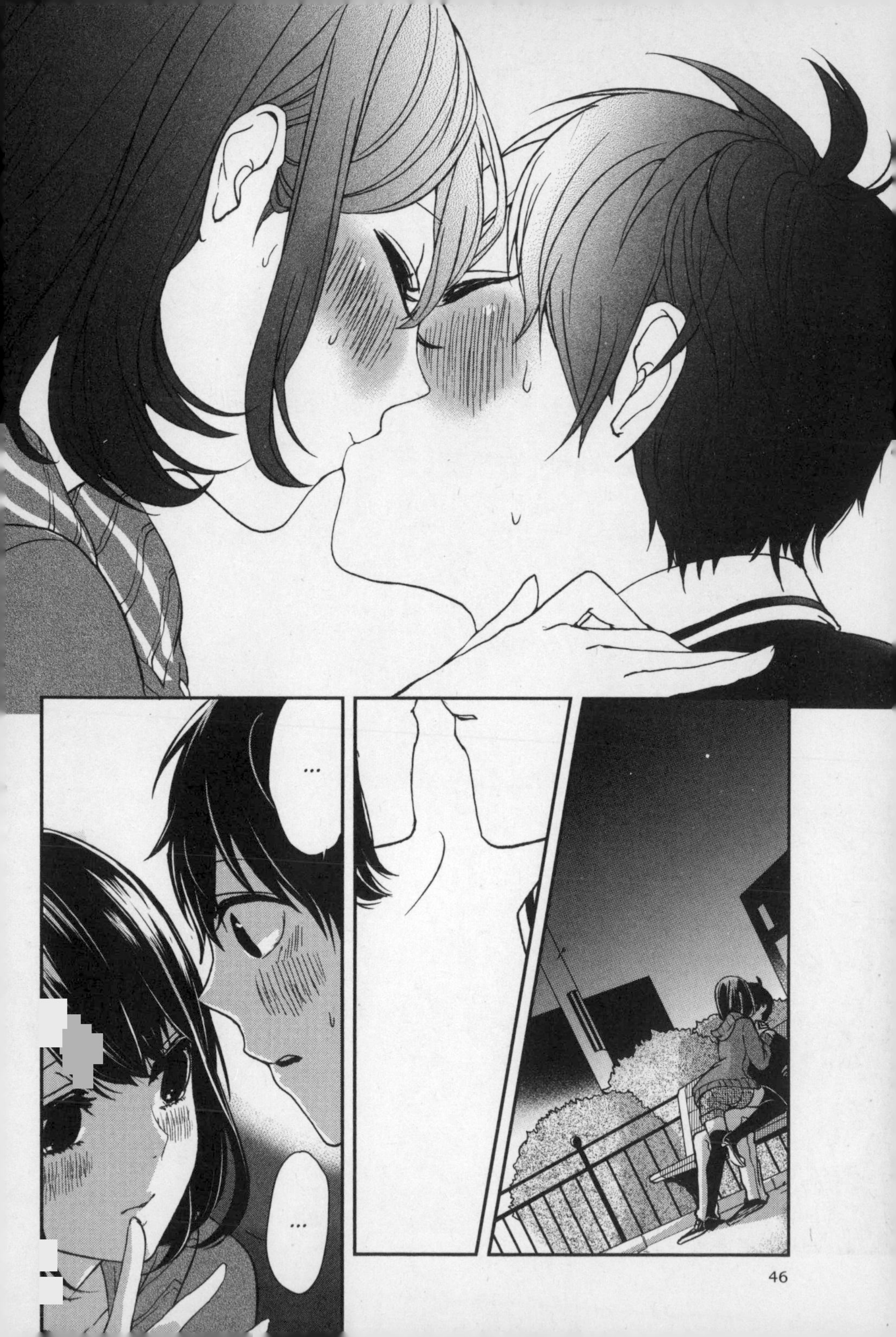
...
...

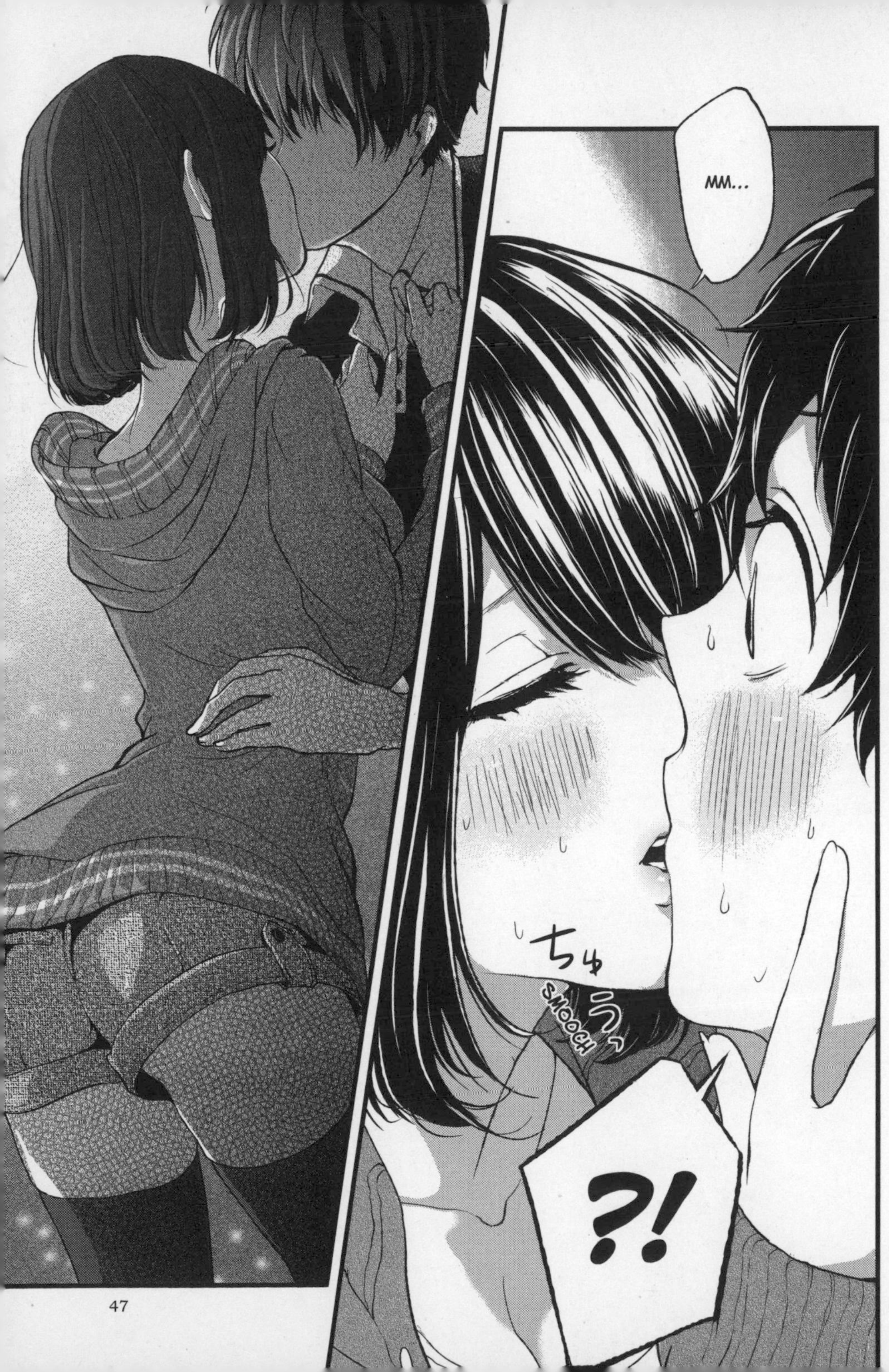
MM...
ちゅうぅ
SMOOCH
?!

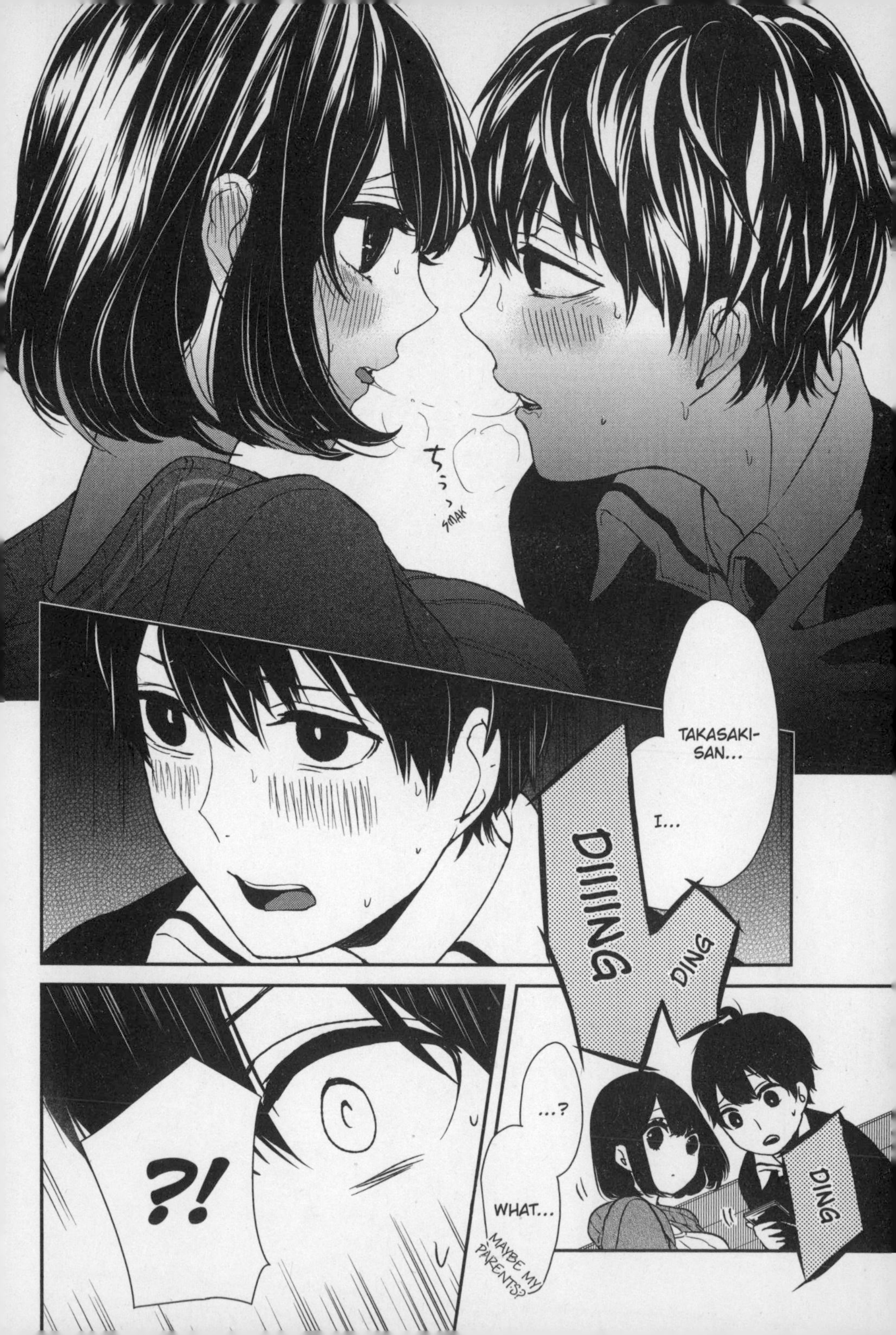
SMAK
TAKASAKI-SAN...
I...
DIIIING
DING
DING
...?
WHAT...
MAYBE MY PARENTS?
?!

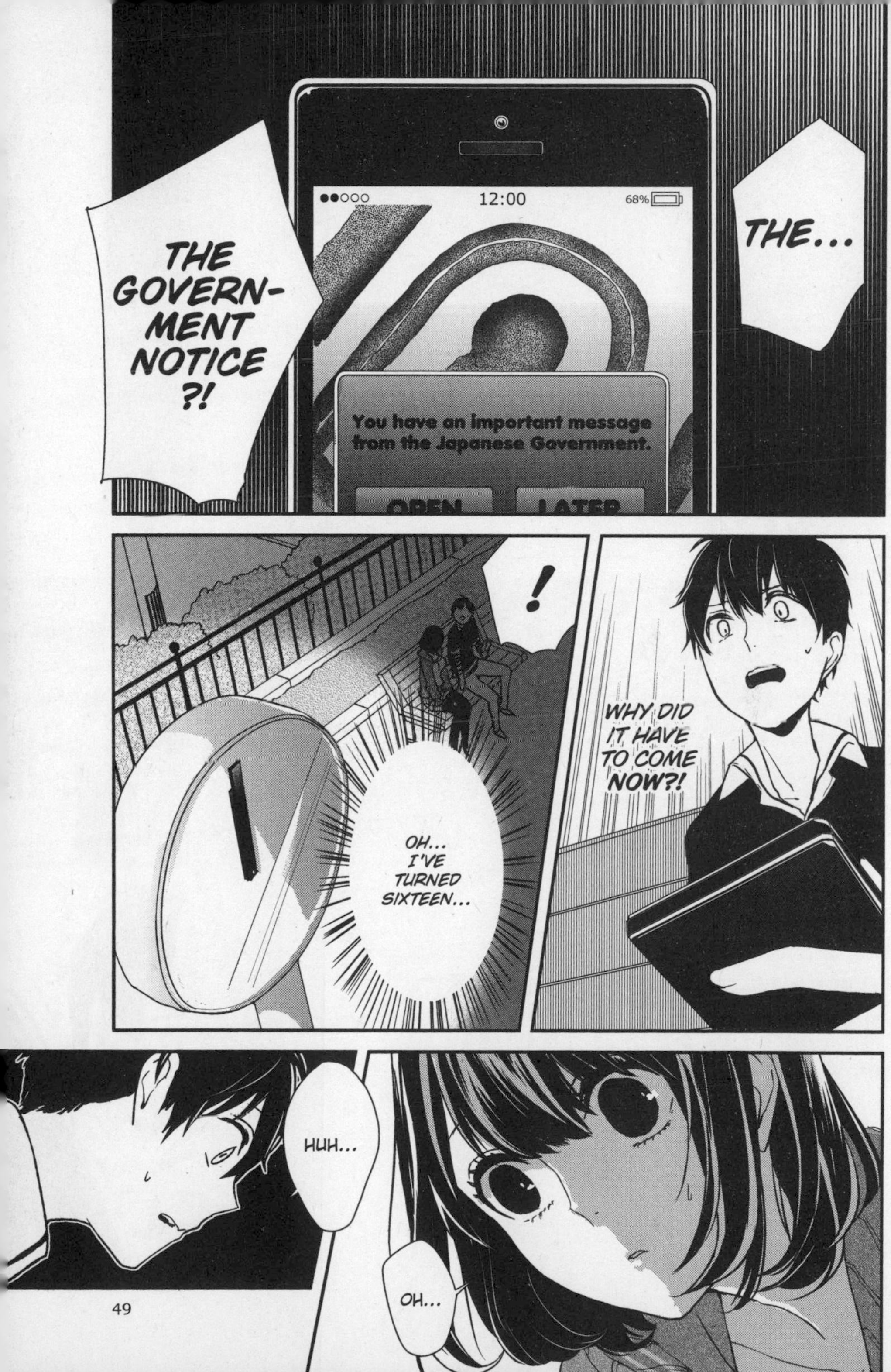
THE...
THE GOVERN-MENT NOTICE ?!
12:00
68%
You have an important message from the Japanese Government.
WHY DID IT HAVE TO COME NOW?!
!
OH... I'VE TURNED SIXTEEN...
OH...
HUH...

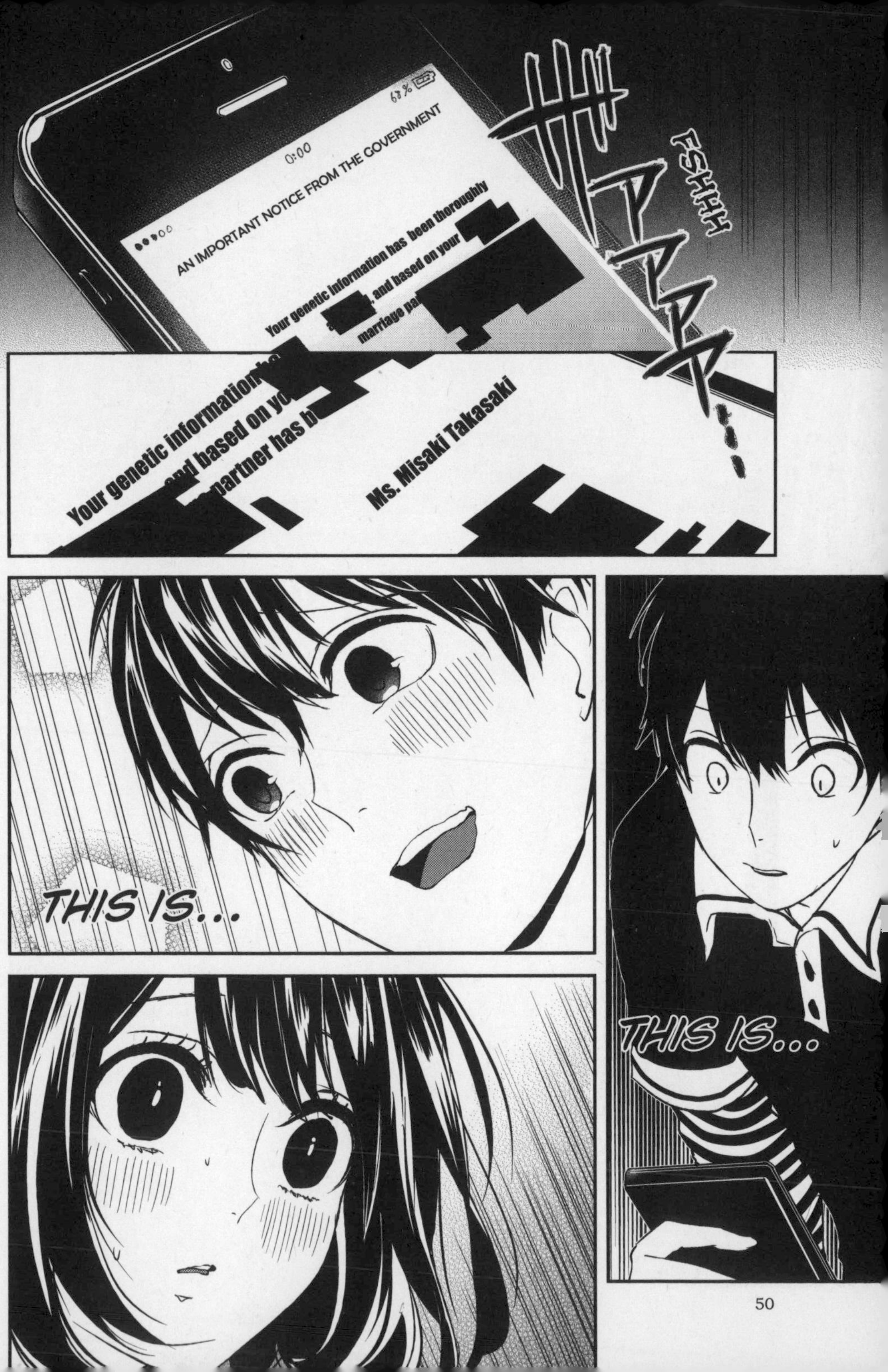

0:00
68%
AN IMPORTANT NOTICE FROM THE GOVERNMENT
Your genetic information has been thoroughly [redacted], and based on your [redacted]
marriage pa[redacted]
ザァァァ…
FSHHH
Your genetic information h[redacted] and based on yo[redacted] partner has b[redacted]
Ms. Misaki Takasaki
THIS IS...
THIS IS...

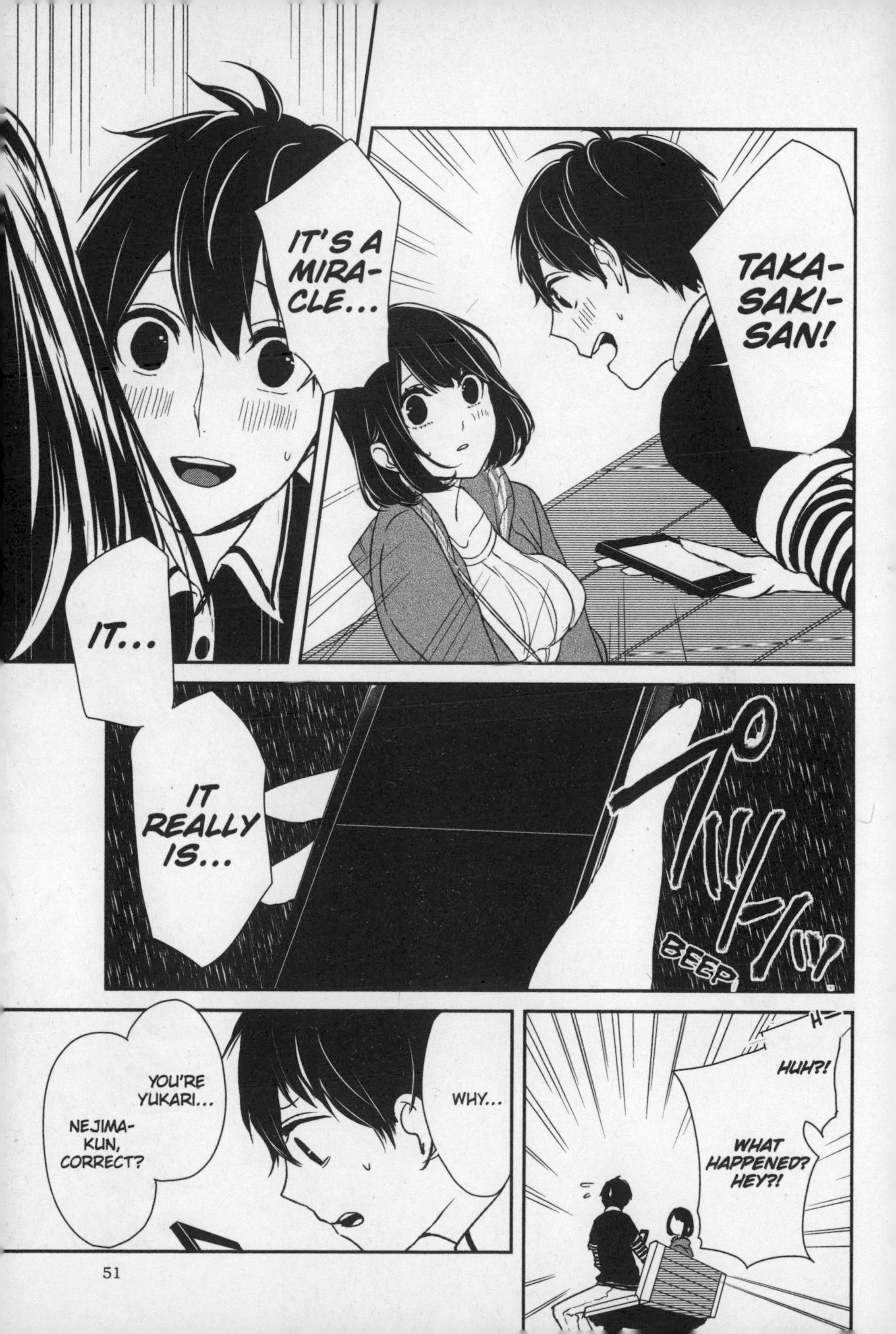
TAKA-SAKI-SAN!
IT'S A MIRA-CLE...
IT...
IT REALLY IS...
BEEP
H—
HUH?!
WHAT HAPPENED? HEY?!
WHY...
YOU'RE YUKARI...
NEJIMA-KUN, CORRECT?

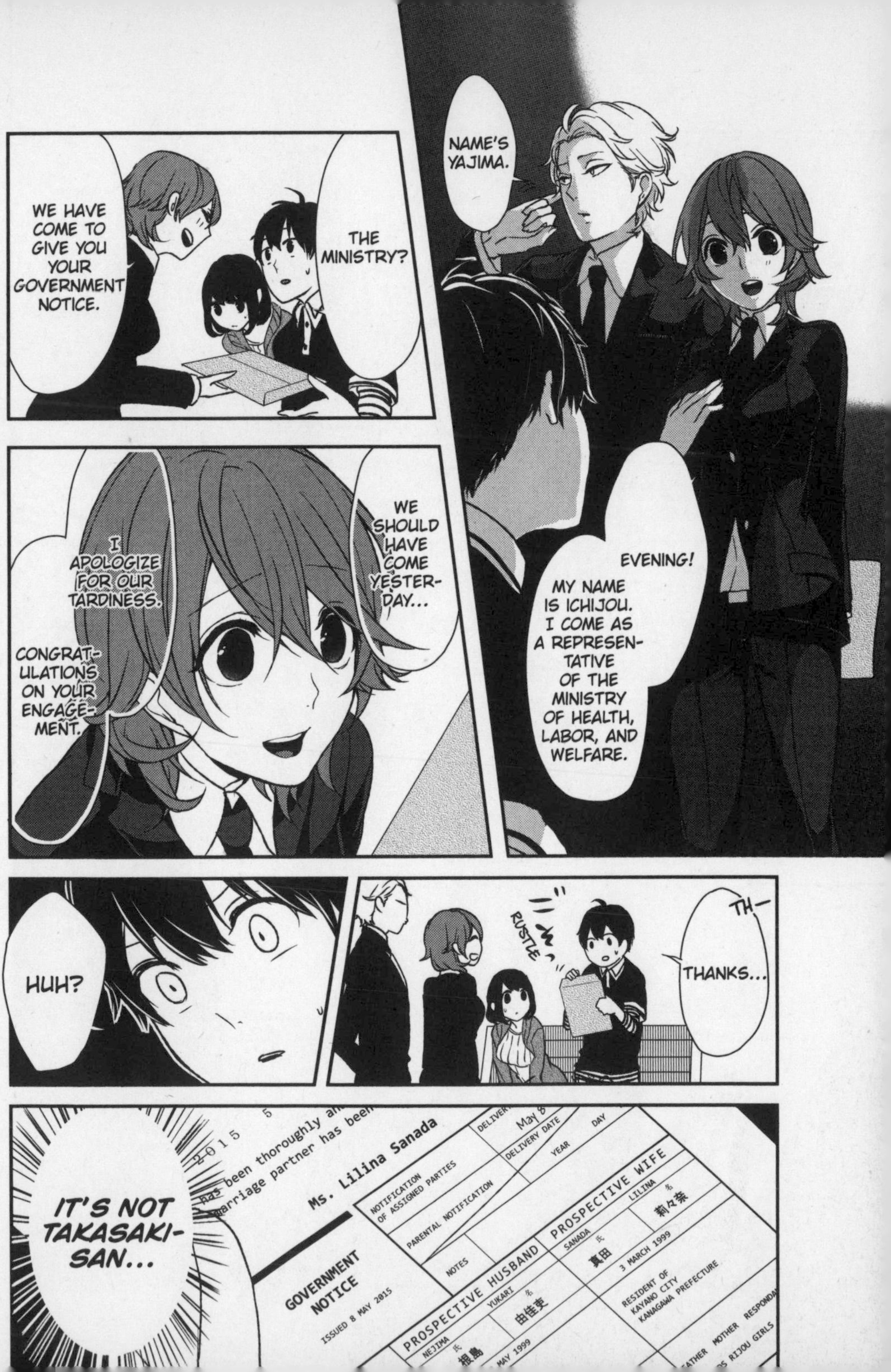
NAME'S YAJIMA.
EVENING!
MY NAME IS ICHIJOU. I COME AS A REPRESEN-TATIVE OF THE MINISTRY OF HEALTH, LABOR, AND WELFARE.
THE MINISTRY?
WE HAVE COME TO GIVE YOU YOUR GOVERNMENT NOTICE.
WE SHOULD HAVE COME YESTER-DAY...
I APOLOGIZE FOR OUR TARDINESS.
CONGRAT-ULATIONS ON YOUR ENGAGE-MENT.
TH-
THANKS...
RUSTLE
HUH?
IT'S NOT TAKASAKI-SAN...
GOVERNMENT NOTICE
ISSUED 8 MAY 2015
Ms. Lilina Sanada
has been thoroughly an
marriage partner has been
NOTIFICATION OF ASSIGNED PARTIES
PARENTAL NOTIFICATION
NOTES
DELIVERY DATE
YEAR
DAY
May 8
PROSPECTIVE WIFE
SANADA
真田
LILINA
莉々奈
3 MARCH 1999
RESIDENT OF KAYANO CITY KANAGAWA PREFECTURE
PROSPECTIVE HUSBAND
NEJIMA
根島
YUKARI
由佳吏
MAY 1999

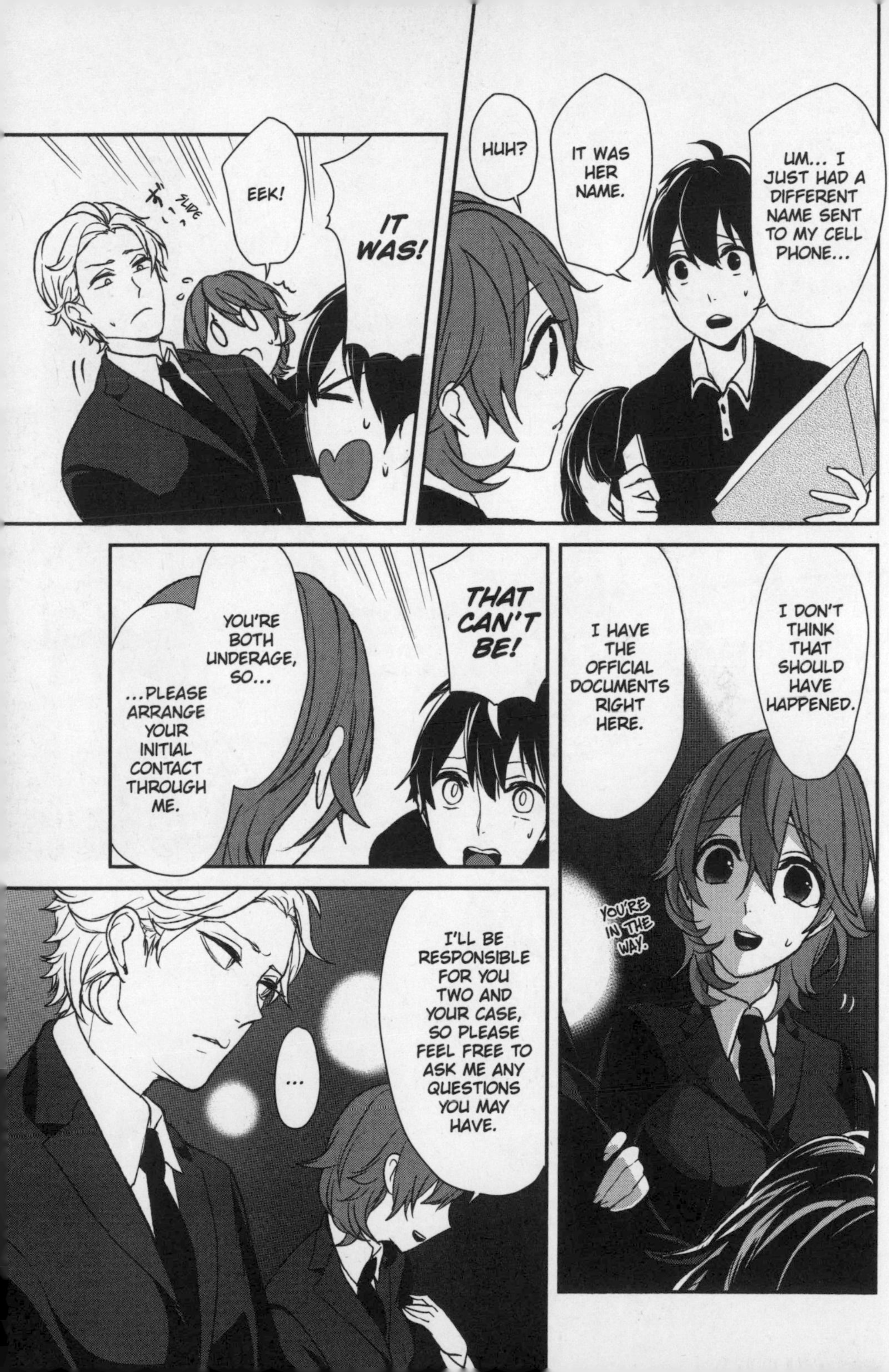
UM... I JUST HAD A DIFFERENT NAME SENT TO MY CELL PHONE...
IT WAS HER NAME.
HUH?
IT WAS!
EEK!
SLIDE
I DON'T THINK THAT SHOULD HAVE HAPPENED.
I HAVE THE OFFICIAL DOCUMENTS RIGHT HERE.
YOU'RE IN THE WAY.
THAT CAN'T BE!
YOU'RE BOTH UNDERAGE, SO...
...PLEASE ARRANGE YOUR INITIAL CONTACT THROUGH ME.
I'LL BE RESPONSIBLE FOR YOU TWO AND YOUR CASE, SO PLEASE FEEL FREE TO ASK ME ANY QUESTIONS YOU MAY HAVE.
...

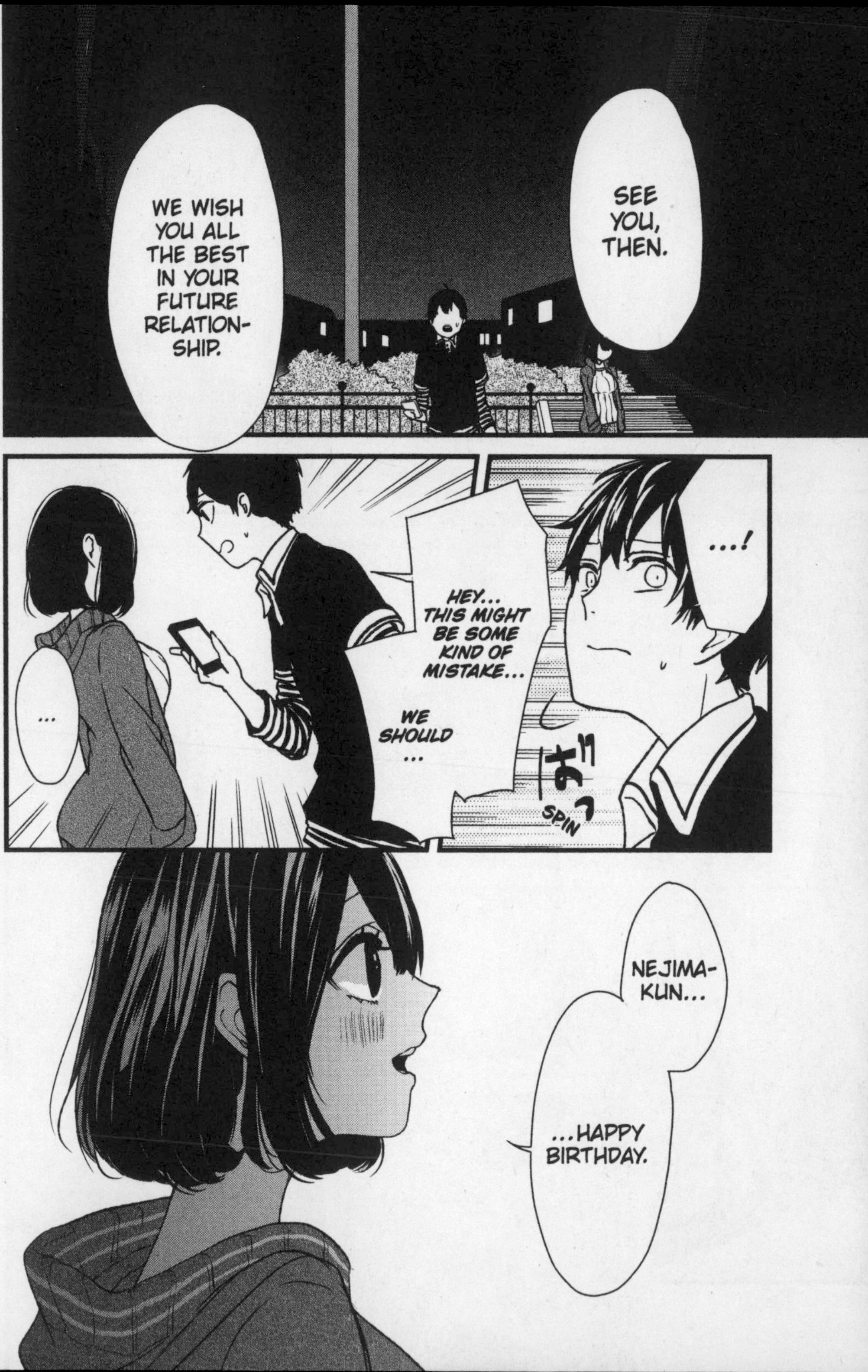
SEE YOU, THEN.
WE WISH YOU ALL THE BEST IN YOUR FUTURE RELATIONSHIP.
...!
HEY... THIS MIGHT BE SOME KIND OF MISTAKE...
WE SHOULD ...
SPIN
...
NEJIMA-KUN...
...HAPPY BIRTHDAY.

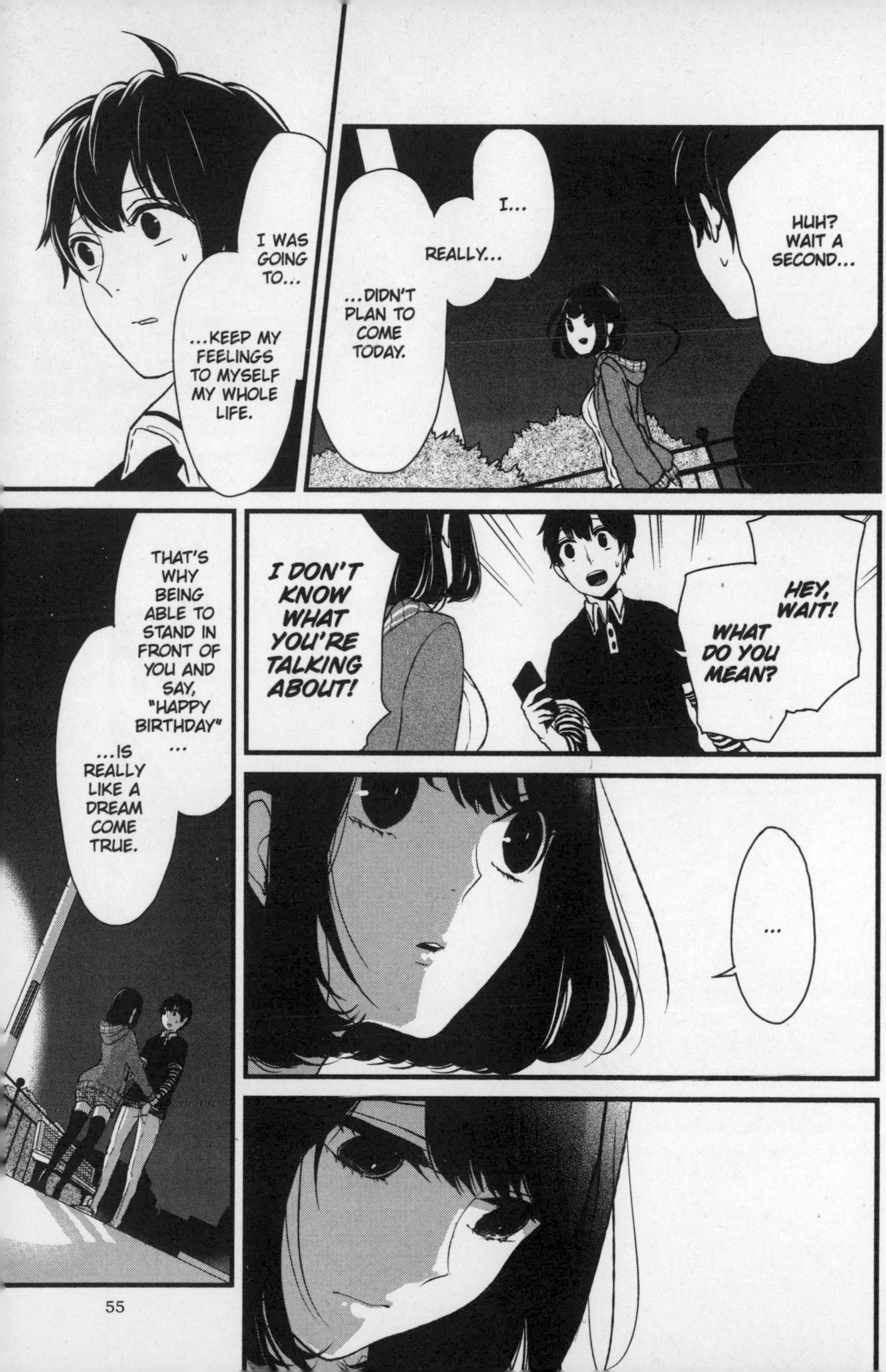
HUH? WAIT A SECOND...
I...
REALLY...
...DIDN'T PLAN TO COME TODAY.
I WAS GOING TO...
...KEEP MY FEELINGS TO MYSELF MY WHOLE LIFE.
HEY, WAIT!
WHAT DO YOU MEAN?
I DON'T KNOW WHAT YOU'RE TALKING ABOUT!
...
THAT'S WHY BEING ABLE TO STAND IN FRONT OF YOU AND SAY, "HAPPY BIRTHDAY"...
...IS REALLY LIKE A DREAM COME TRUE.

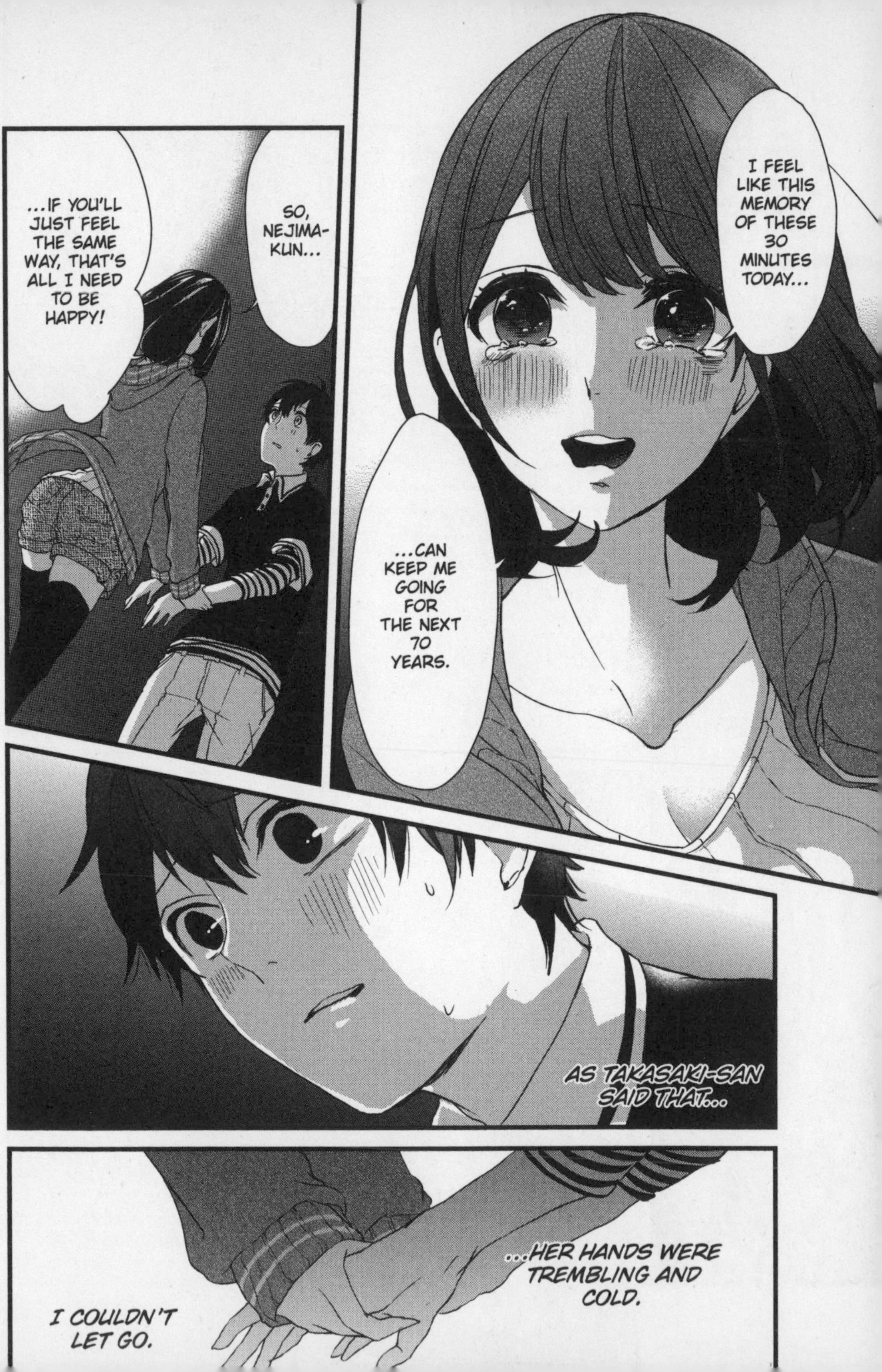
I FEEL LIKE THIS MEMORY OF THESE 30 MINUTES TODAY...
...CAN KEEP ME GOING FOR THE NEXT 70 YEARS.
SO, NEJIMA-KUN...
...IF YOU'LL JUST FEEL THE SAME WAY, THAT'S ALL I NEED TO BE HAPPY!
AS TAKASAKI-SAN SAID THAT...
...HER HANDS WERE TREMBLING AND COLD.
I COULDN'T LET GO.

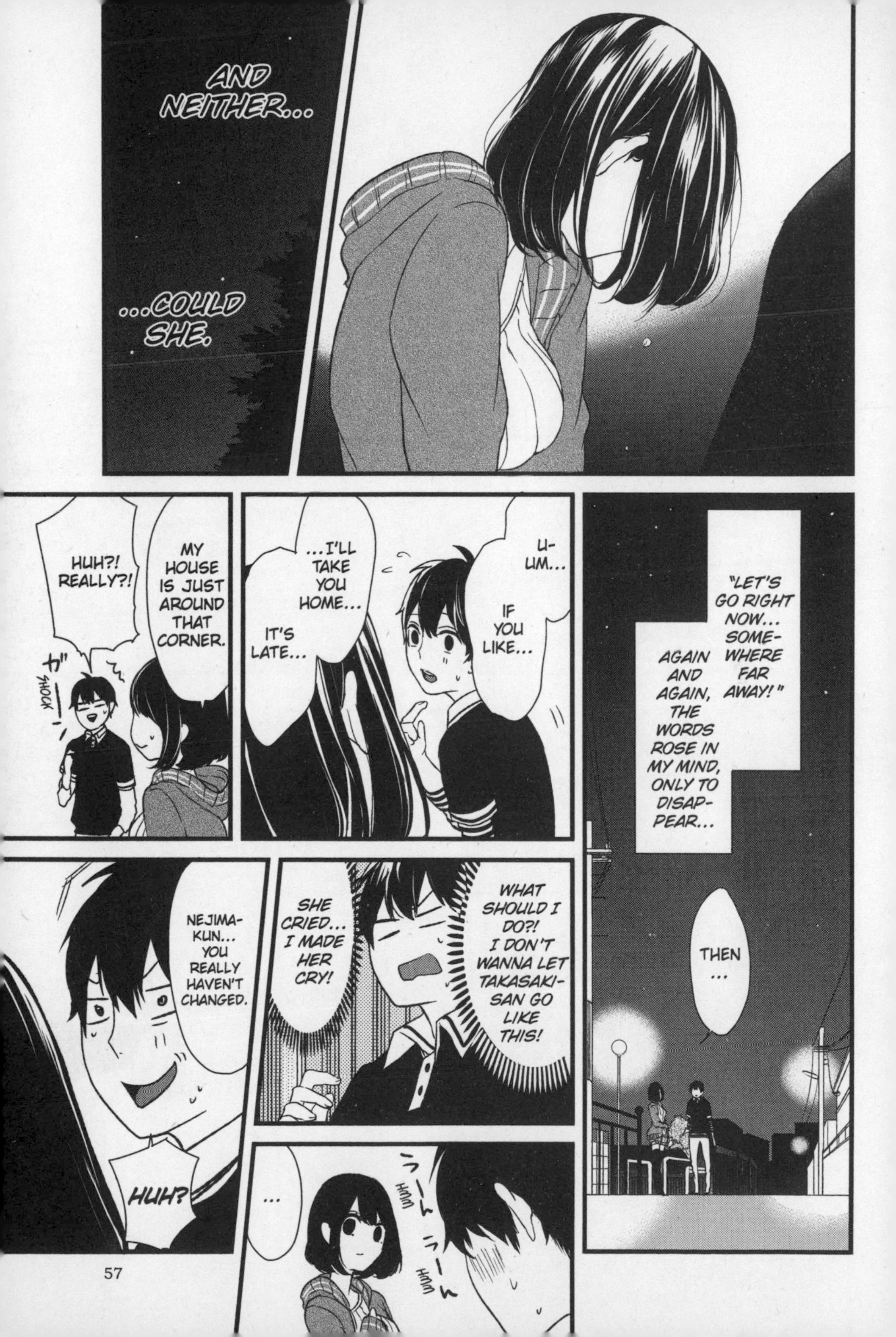
AND NEITHER...
...COULD SHE.
"LET'S GO RIGHT NOW... SOMEWHERE FAR AWAY!"
AGAIN AND AGAIN, THE WORDS ROSE IN MY MIND, ONLY TO DISAPPEAR...
THEN...
U-UM... IF YOU LIKE...
...I'LL TAKE YOU HOME... IT'S LATE...
MY HOUSE IS JUST AROUND THAT CORNER.
HUH?! REALLY?!
SHOCK
WHAT SHOULD I DO?! I DON'T WANNA LET TAKASAKI-SAN GO LIKE THIS!
SHE CRIED... I MADE HER CRY!
NEJIMA-KUN... YOU REALLY HAVEN'T CHANGED.
HUH?
HMM
HMM
...

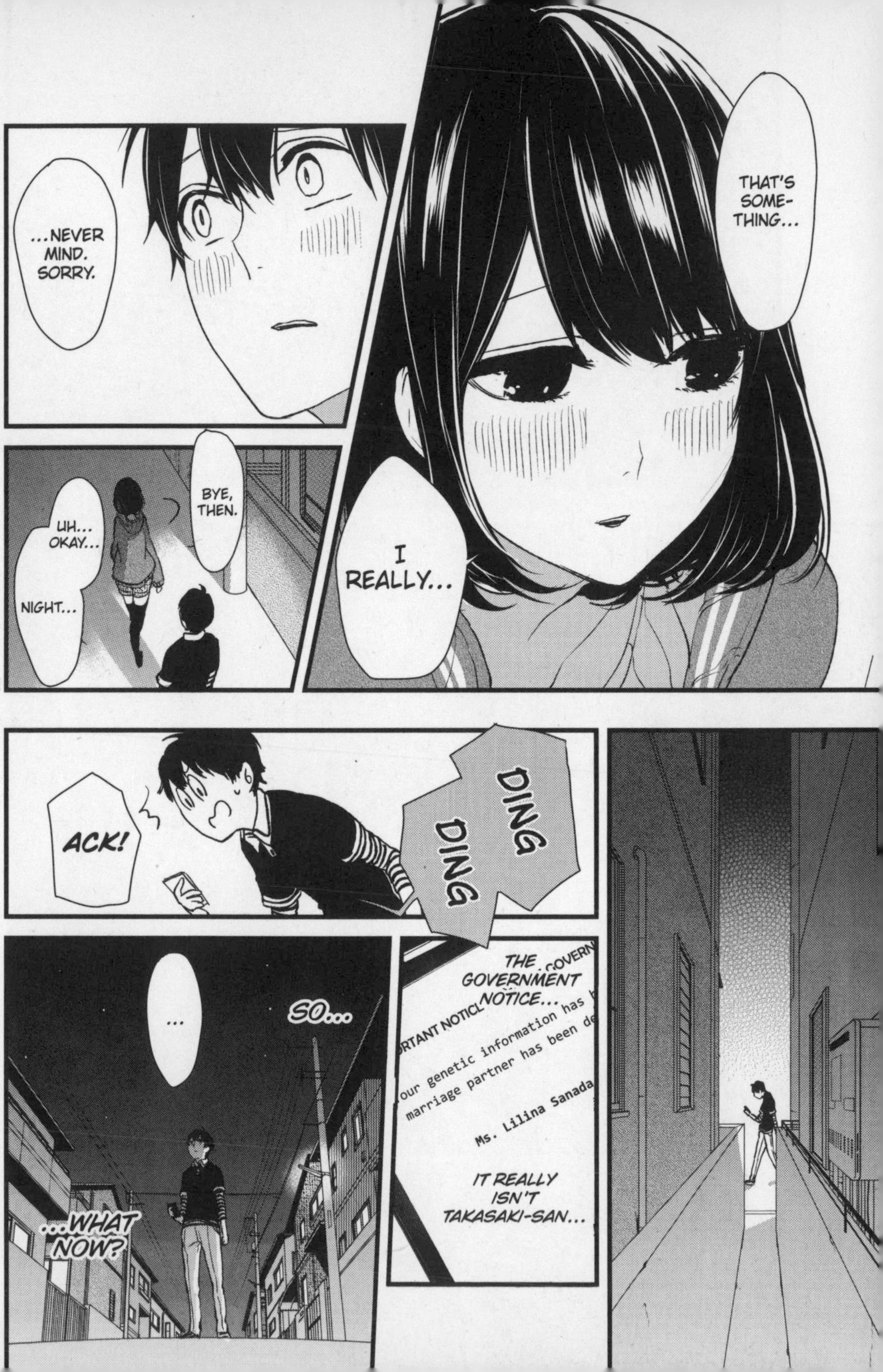
THAT'S SOME-THING...
I REALLY...
...NEVER MIND. SORRY.
BYE, THEN.
UH... OKAY...
NIGHT...
DING DING
ACK!
THE GOVERNMENT NOTICE...
RTANT NOTIC
our genetic information has b
marriage partner has been de
Ms. Lilina Sanada
IT REALLY ISN'T TAKASAKI-SAN...
...
SO...
...WHAT NOW?

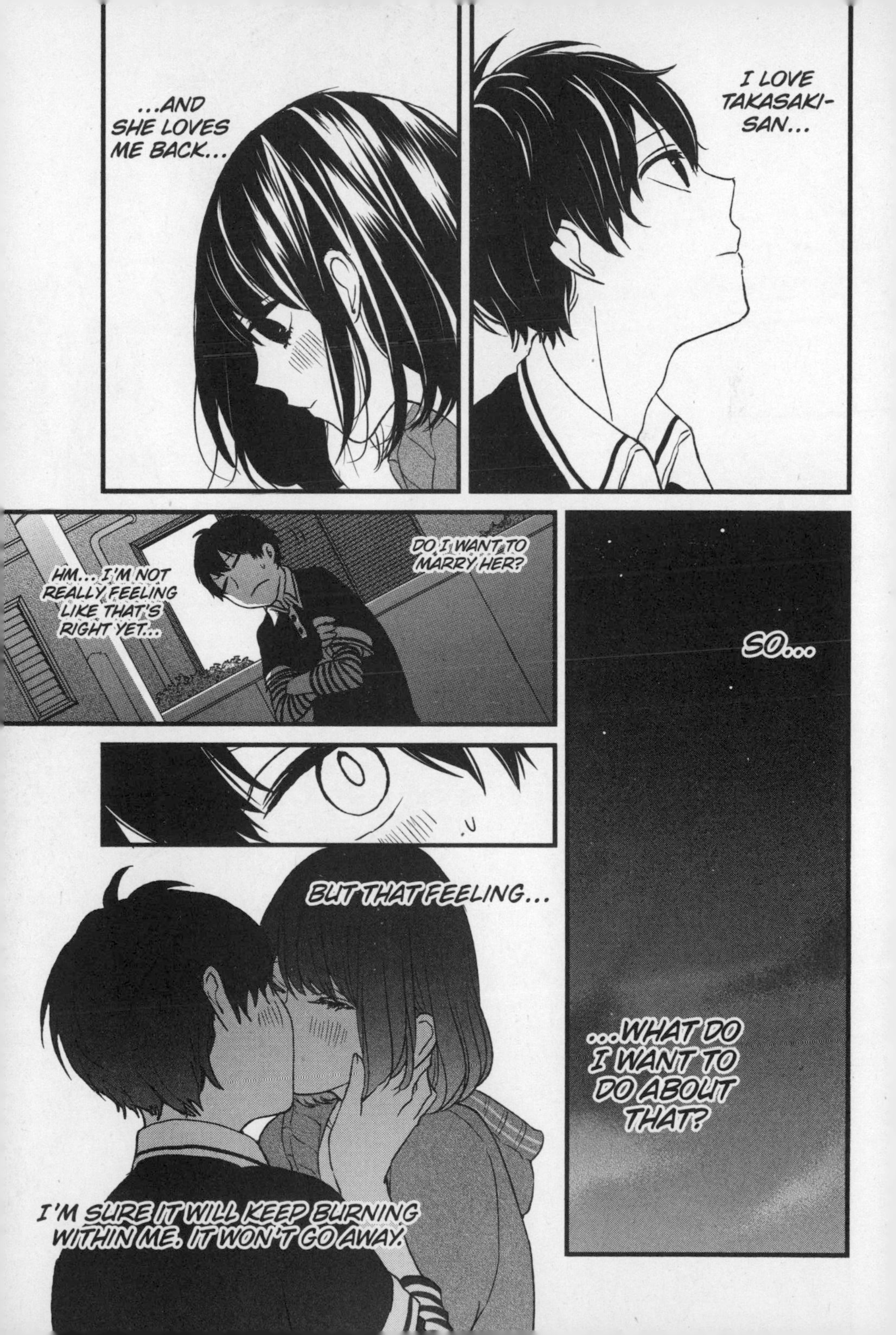
I LOVE TAKASAKI-SAN...
...AND SHE LOVES ME BACK...
SO...
...WHAT DO I WANT TO DO ABOUT THAT?
DO I WANT TO MARRY HER?
HM... I'M NOT REALLY FEELING LIKE THAT'S RIGHT YET...
BUT THAT FEELING...
I'M SURE IT WILL KEEP BURNING WITHIN ME. IT WON'T GO AWAY.

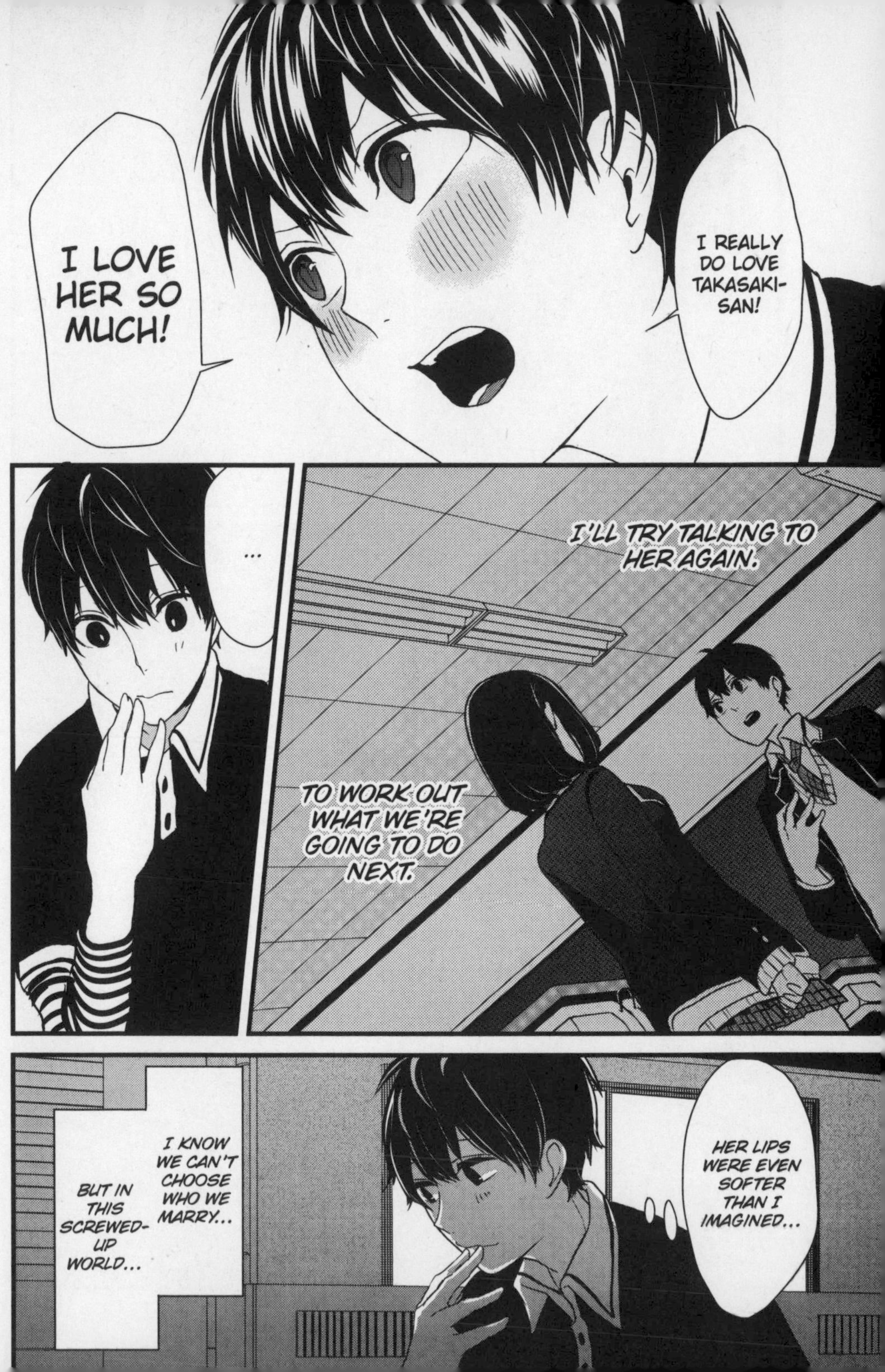
I REALLY DO LOVE TAKASAKI-SAN!
I LOVE HER SO MUCH!
I'LL TRY TALKING TO HER AGAIN.
TO WORK OUT WHAT WE'RE GOING TO DO NEXT.
...
HER LIPS WERE EVEN SOFTER THAN I IMAGINED...
I KNOW WE CAN'T CHOOSE WHO WE MARRY...
BUT IN THIS SCREWED-UP WORLD...

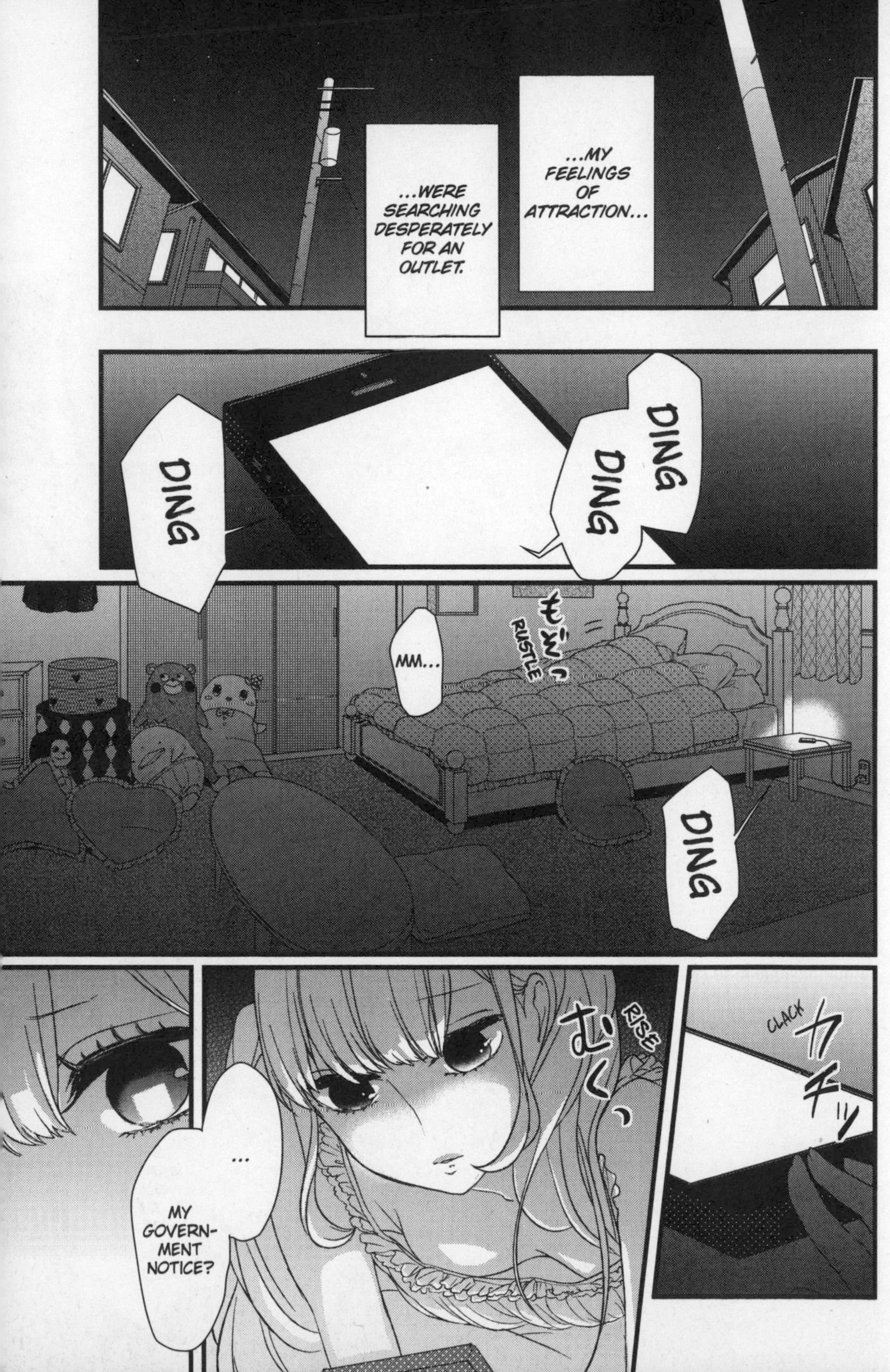
...MY FEELINGS OF ATTRACTION...
...WERE SEARCHING DESPERATELY FOR AN OUTLET.
DING DING
DING
もぞっ RUSTLE
MM...
DING
カチッ CLACK
むくっ RISE
... MY GOVERN-MENT NOTICE?

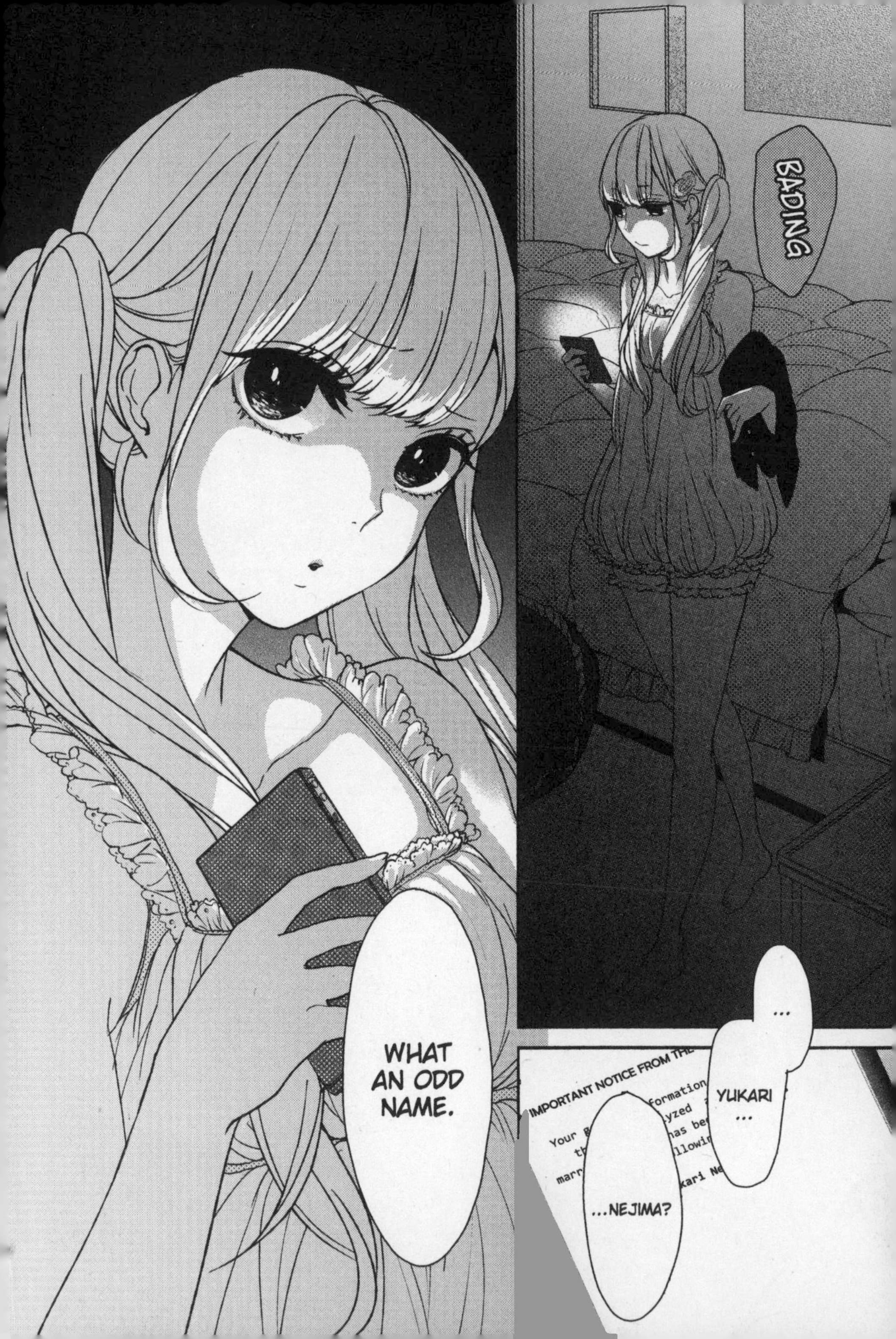
BADING
...
YUKARI ...
...NEJIMA?
IMPORTANT NOTICE FROM THE
WHAT AN ODD NAME.

Chapter 2: A Little Lie

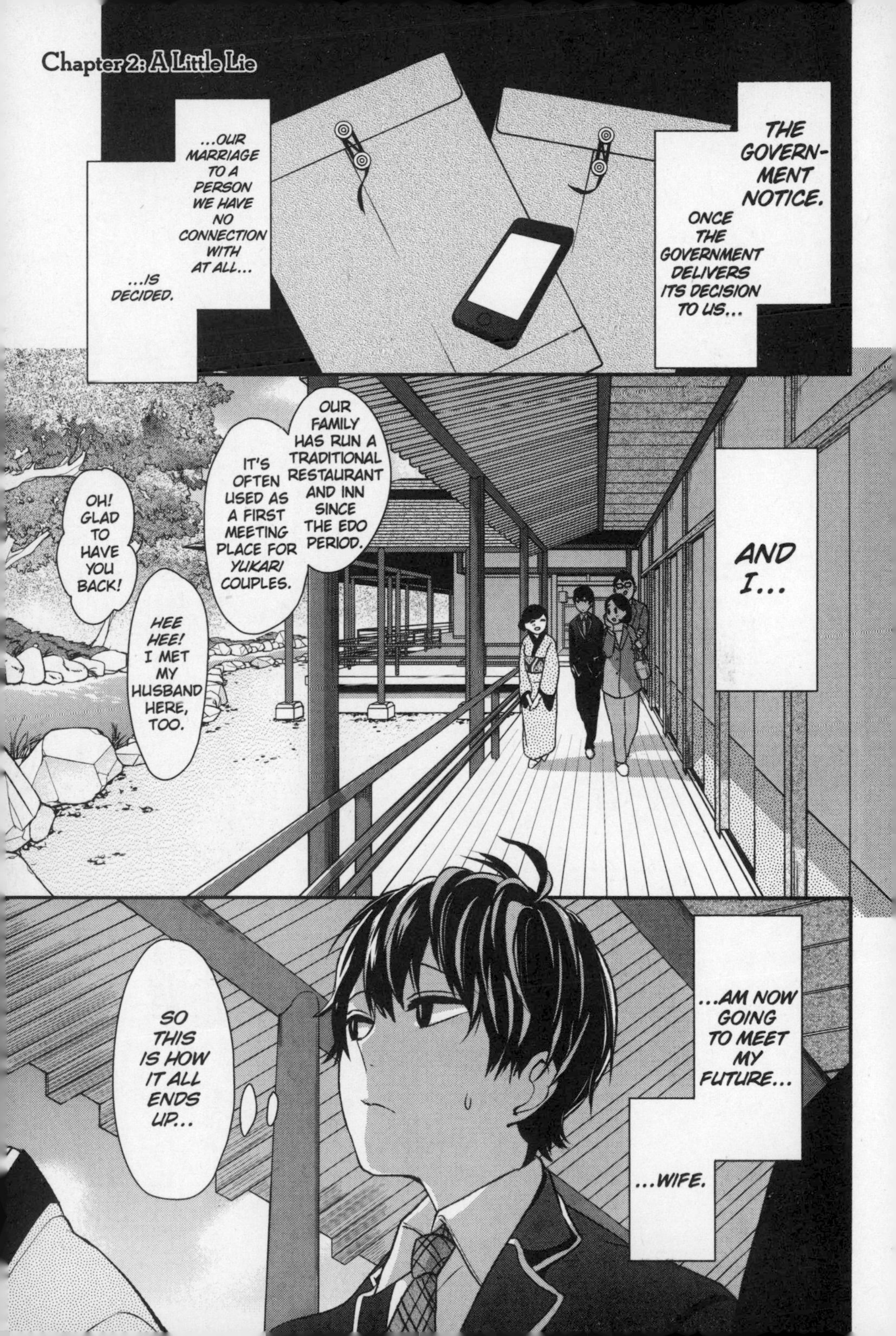
THE GOVERNMENT NOTICE.
ONCE THE GOVERNMENT DELIVERS ITS DECISION TO US...
...OUR MARRIAGE TO A PERSON WE HAVE NO CONNECTION WITH AT ALL...
...IS DECIDED.
AND I...
OUR FAMILY HAS RUN A TRADITIONAL RESTAURANT AND INN SINCE THE EDO PERIOD.
IT'S OFTEN USED AS A FIRST MEETING PLACE FOR YUKARI COUPLES.
OH! GLAD TO HAVE YOU BACK!
HEE HEE! I MET MY HUSBAND HERE, TOO.
...AM NOW GOING TO MEET MY FUTURE...
...WIFE.
SO THIS IS HOW IT ALL ENDS UP...

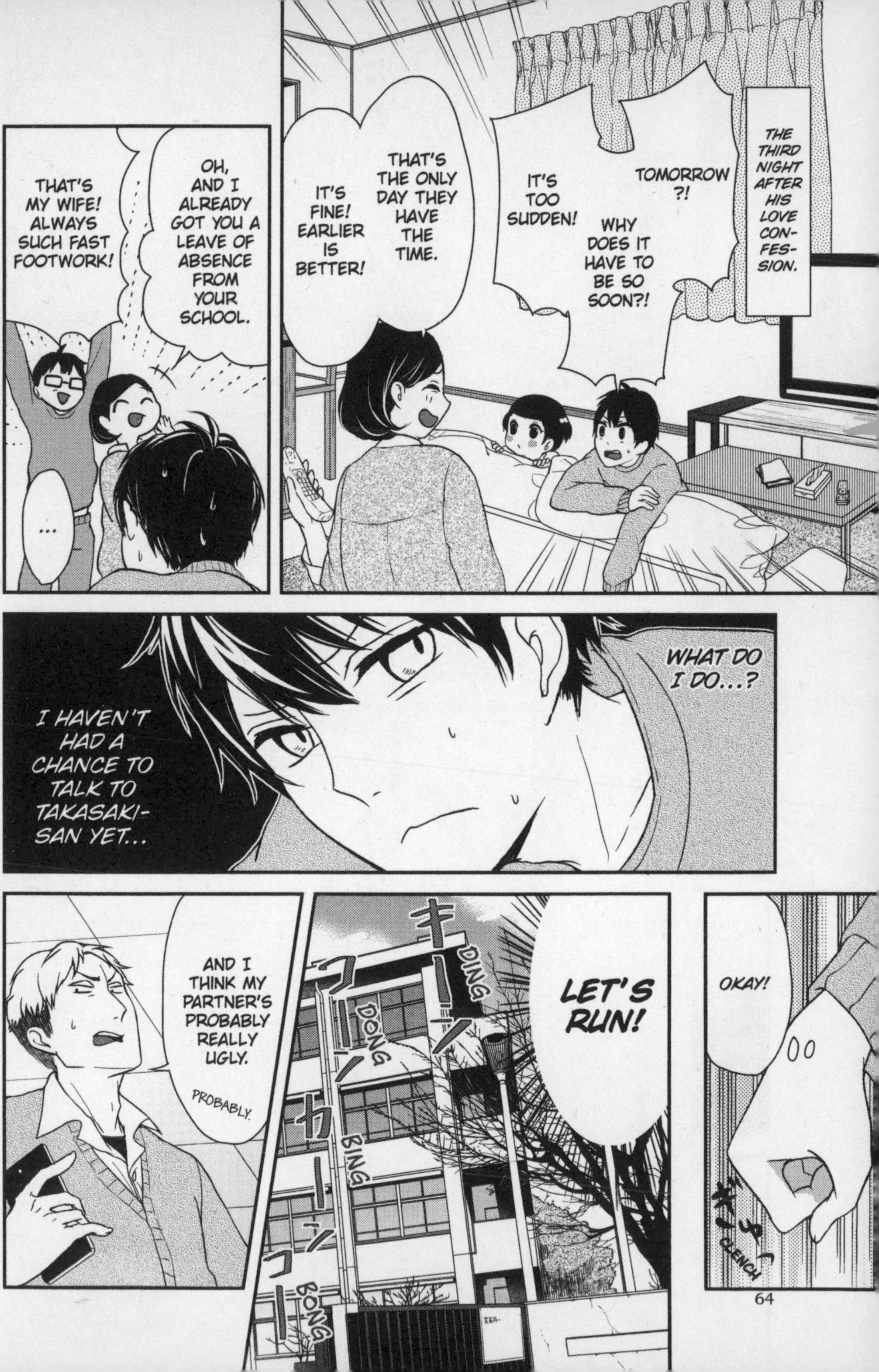
THE THIRD NIGHT AFTER HIS LOVE CON-FES-SION.
TOMORROW ?!
WHY DOES IT HAVE TO BE SO SOON?!
IT'S TOO SUDDEN!
THAT'S THE ONLY DAY THEY HAVE THE TIME.
IT'S FINE! EARLIER IS BETTER!
OH, AND I ALREADY GOT YOU A LEAVE OF ABSENCE FROM YOUR SCHOOL.
THAT'S MY WIFE! ALWAYS SUCH FAST FOOTWORK!
...
WHAT DO I DO...?
I HAVEN'T HAD A CHANCE TO TALK TO TAKASAKI-SAN YET...
OKAY!
CLENCH
LET'S RUN!
DING DONG BING BONG
AND I THINK MY PARTNER'S PROBABLY REALLY UGLY.
PROBABLY.

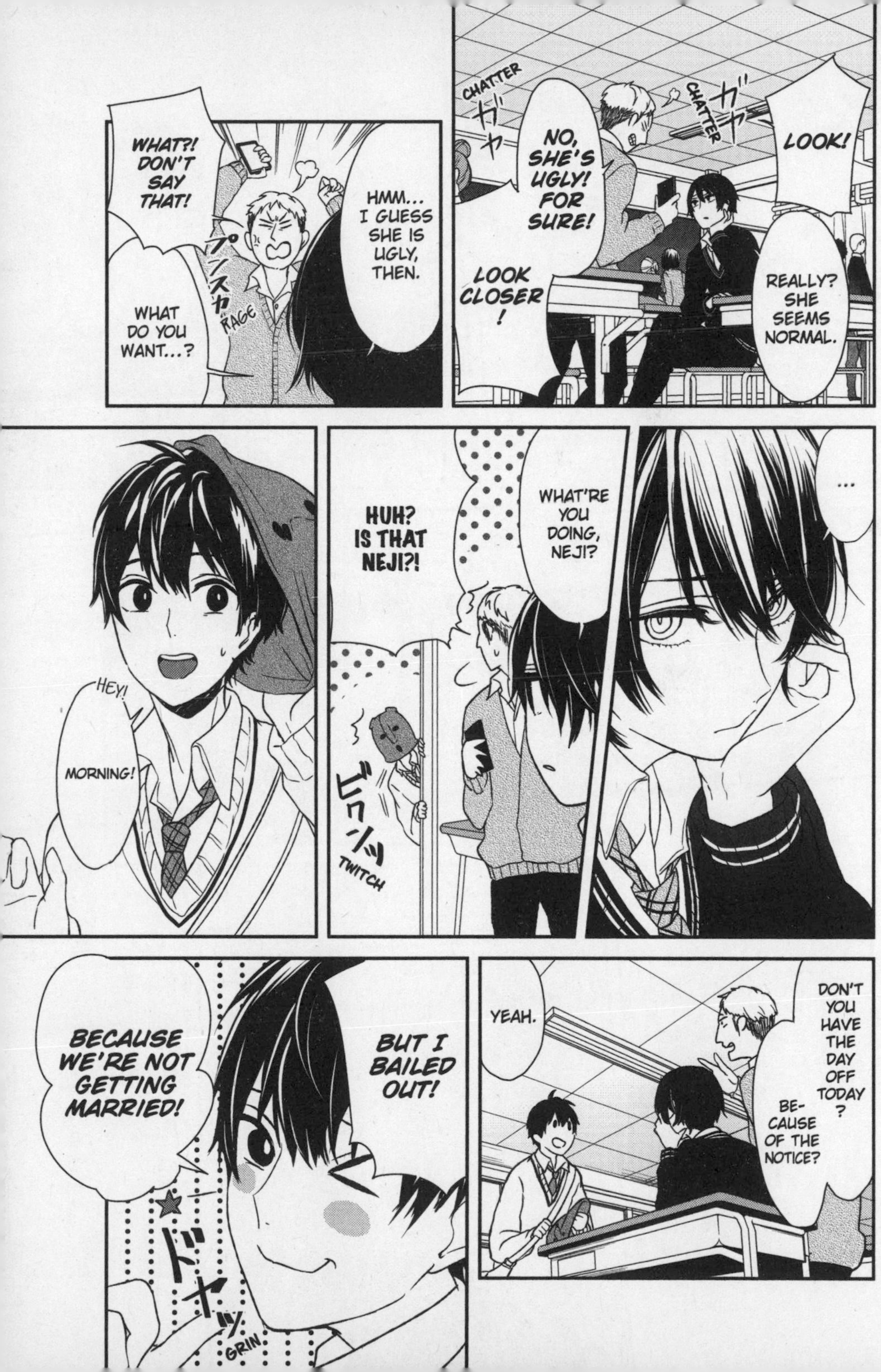
LOOK!
CHATTER
NO, SHE'S UGLY! FOR SURE!
CHATTER
REALLY? SHE SEEMS NORMAL.
LOOK CLOSER!
HMM... I GUESS SHE IS UGLY, THEN.
WHAT?! DON'T SAY THAT!
RAGE
WHAT DO YOU WANT...?
...
WHAT'RE YOU DOING, NEJI?
HUH? IS THAT NEJI?!
TWITCH
HEY!
MORNING!
DON'T YOU HAVE THE DAY OFF TODAY? BECAUSE OF THE NOTICE?
YEAH.
BUT I BAILED OUT!
BECAUSE WE'RE NOT GETTING MARRIED!
GRIN

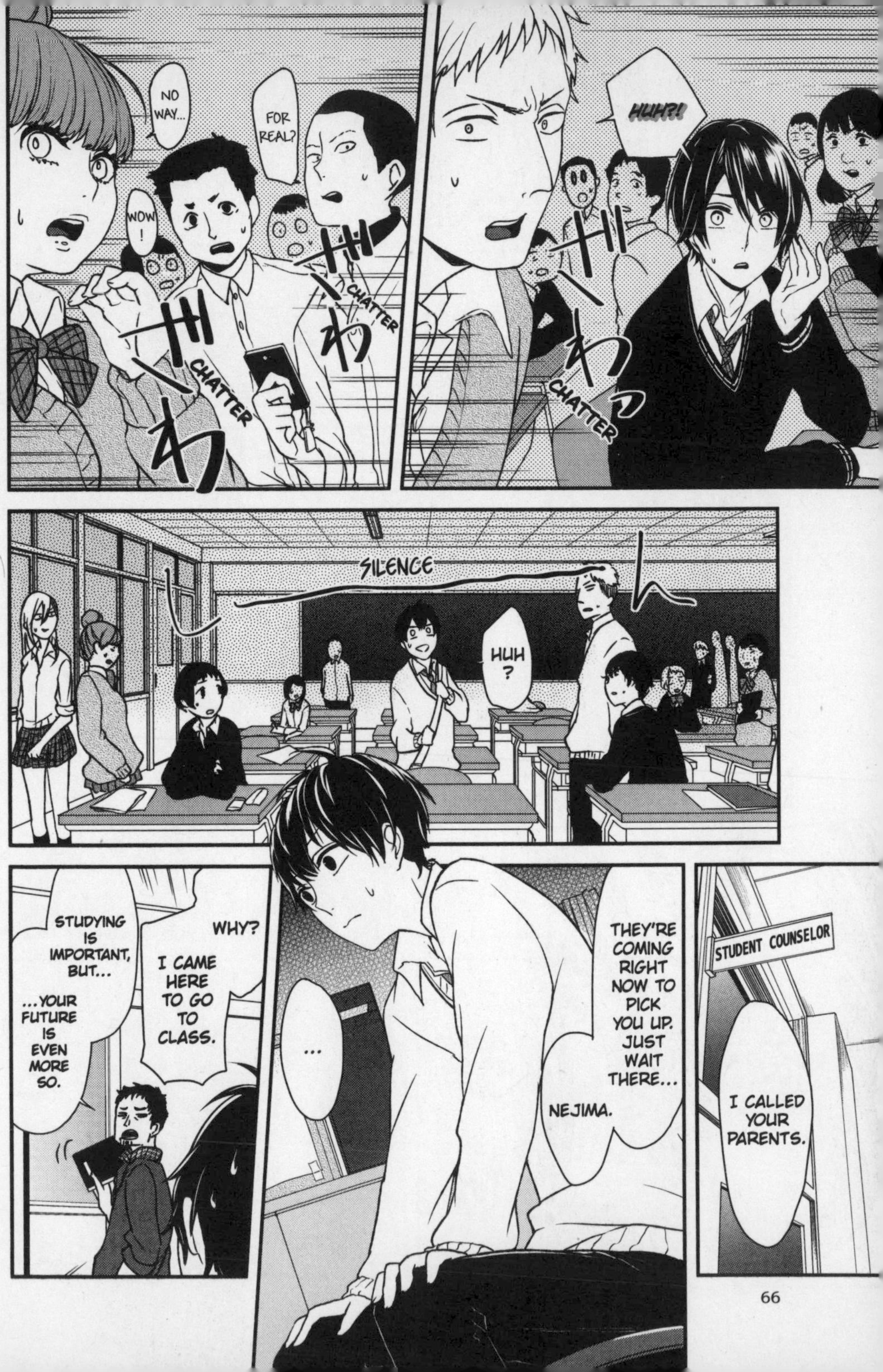
HUH?!
CHATTER
CHATTER
NO WAY...
FOR REAL?
WOW!
CHATTER
CHATTER
SILENCE
HUH?
STUDENT COUNSELOR
I CALLED YOUR PARENTS.
THEY'RE COMING RIGHT NOW TO PICK YOU UP. JUST WAIT THERE...
NEJIMA.
...
WHY?
I CAME HERE TO GO TO CLASS.
STUDYING IS IMPORTANT, BUT...
...YOUR FUTURE IS EVEN MORE SO.

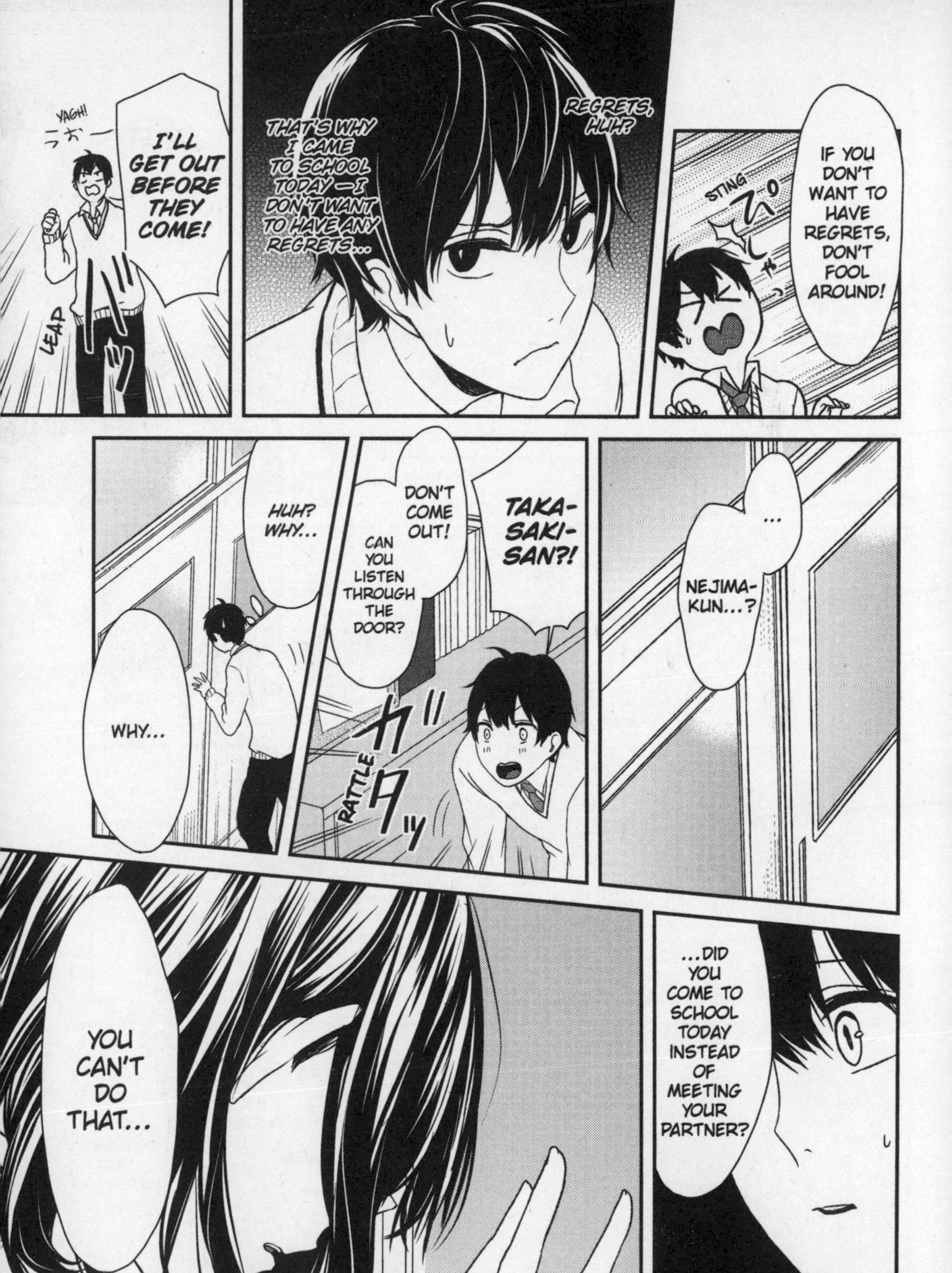
IF YOU DON'T WANT TO HAVE REGRETS, DON'T FOOL AROUND!
STING
REGRETS, HUH?
THAT'S WHY I CAME TO SCHOOL TODAY—I DON'T WANT TO HAVE ANY REGRETS...
YAGH!
I'LL GET OUT BEFORE THEY COME!
LEAP
...
NEJIMA-KUN...?
TAKA-SAKI-SAN?!
DON'T COME OUT!
CAN YOU LISTEN THROUGH THE DOOR?
RATTLE
HUH? WHY...
WHY...
...DID YOU COME TO SCHOOL TODAY INSTEAD OF MEETING YOUR PARTNER?
YOU CAN'T DO THAT...

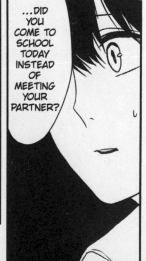

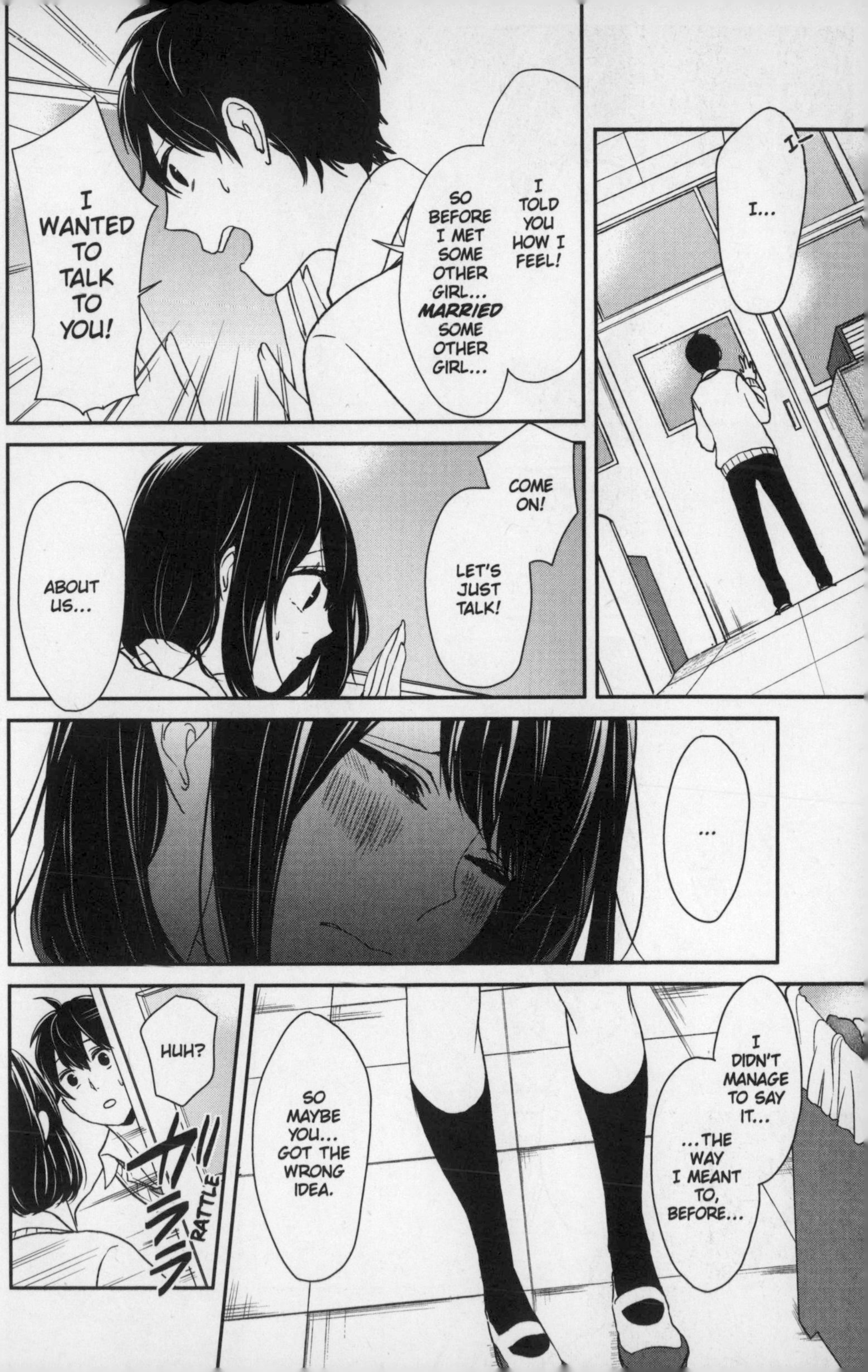
I—
I...
I TOLD YOU HOW I FEEL!
SO BEFORE I MET SOME OTHER GIRL... *MARRIED* SOME OTHER GIRL...
I WANTED TO TALK TO YOU!
COME ON!
LET'S JUST TALK!
ABOUT US...
...
I DIDN'T MANAGE TO SAY IT...
...THE WAY I MEANT TO, BEFORE...
SO MAYBE YOU... GOT THE WRONG IDEA.
HUH?
RATTLE

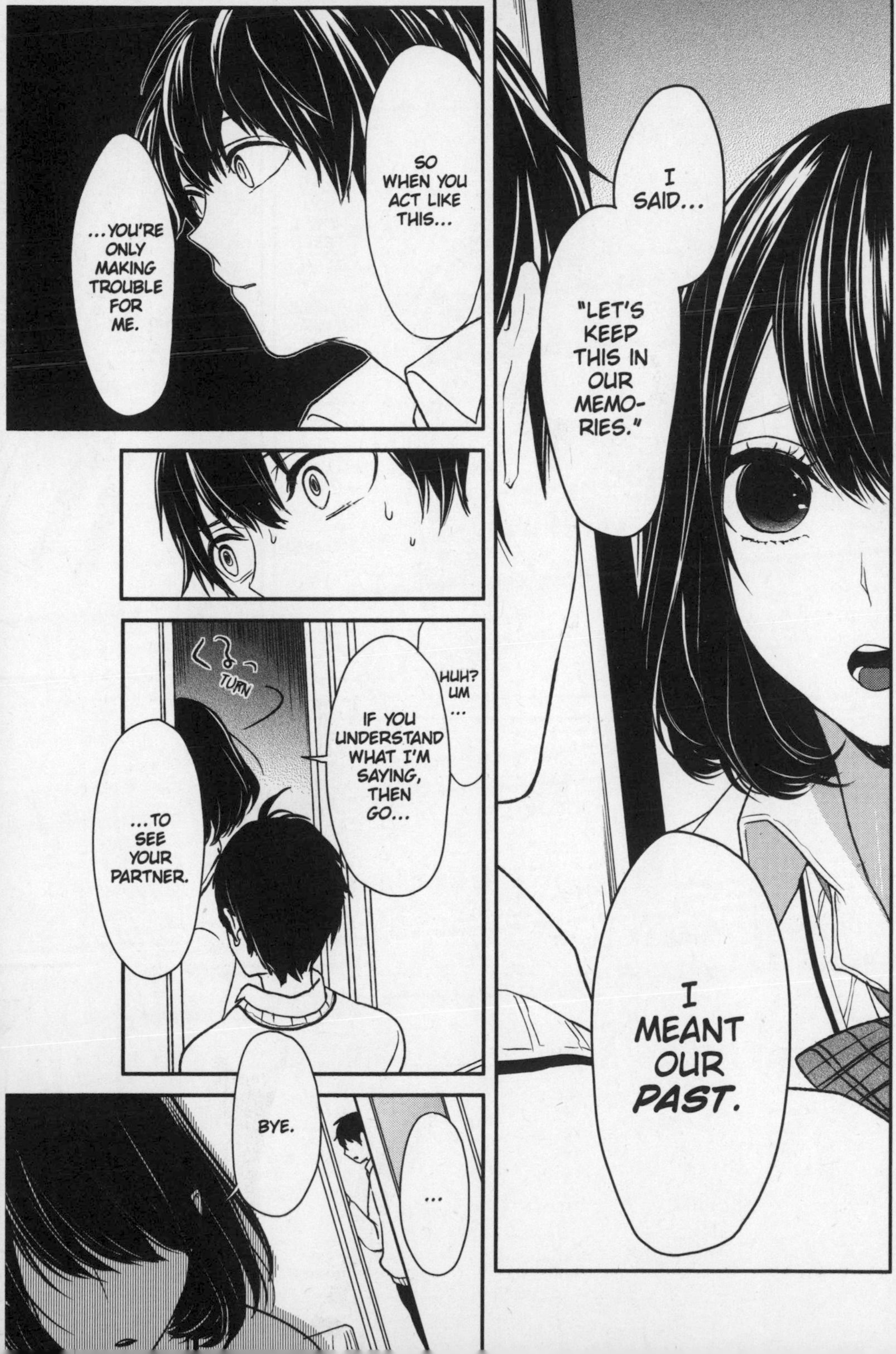
I SAID...
"LET'S KEEP THIS IN OUR MEMORIES."
I MEANT OUR ***PAST.***
SO WHEN YOU ACT LIKE THIS...
...YOU'RE ONLY MAKING TROUBLE FOR ME.
HUH? UM ...
IF YOU UNDERSTAND WHAT I'M SAYING, THEN GO...
TURN
...TO SEE YOUR PARTNER.
BYE.
...

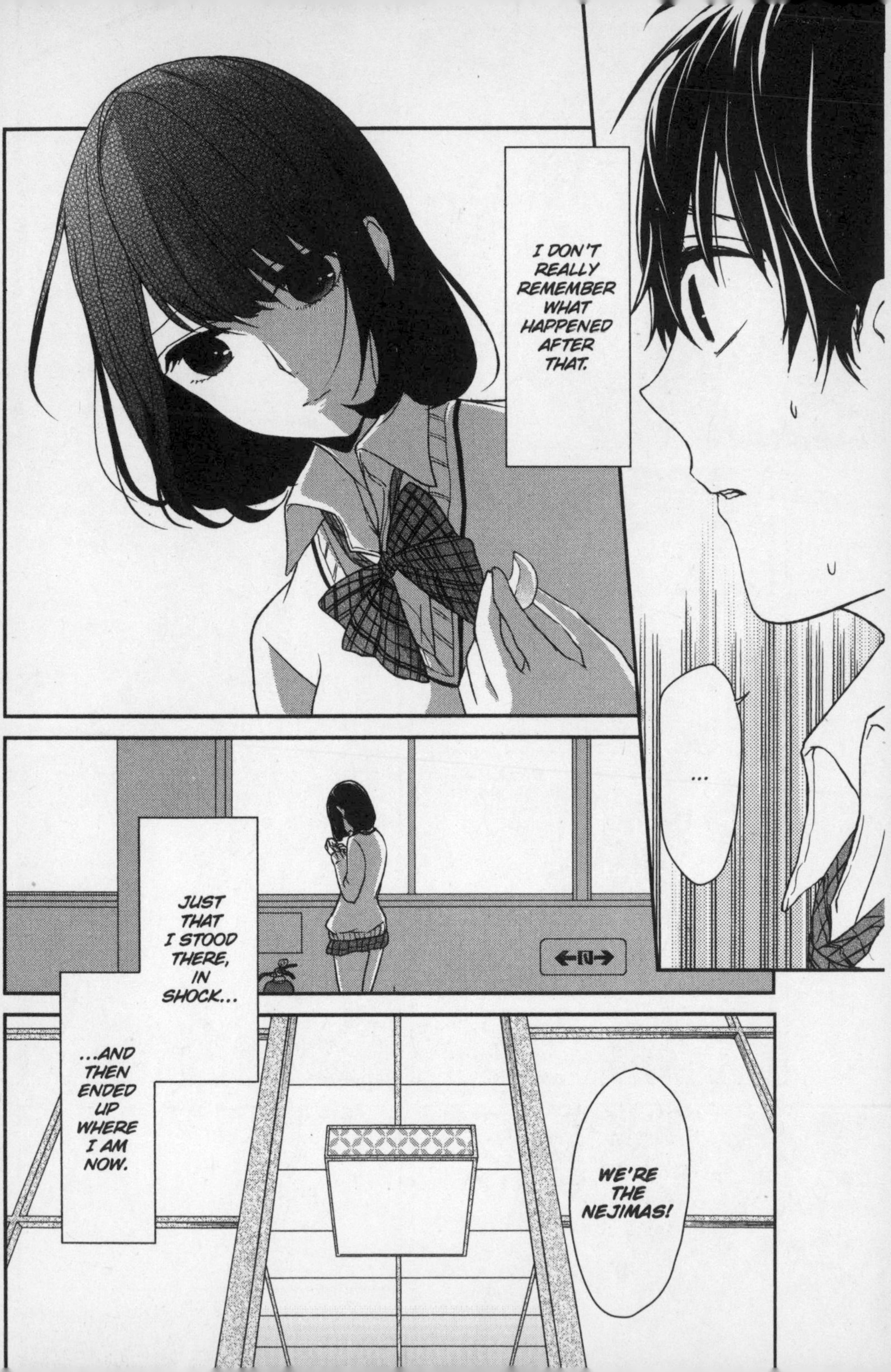
I DON'T REALLY REMEMBER WHAT HAPPENED AFTER THAT.
...
JUST THAT I STOOD THERE, IN SHOCK...
...AND THEN ENDED UP WHERE I AM NOW.
WE'RE THE NEJIMAS!

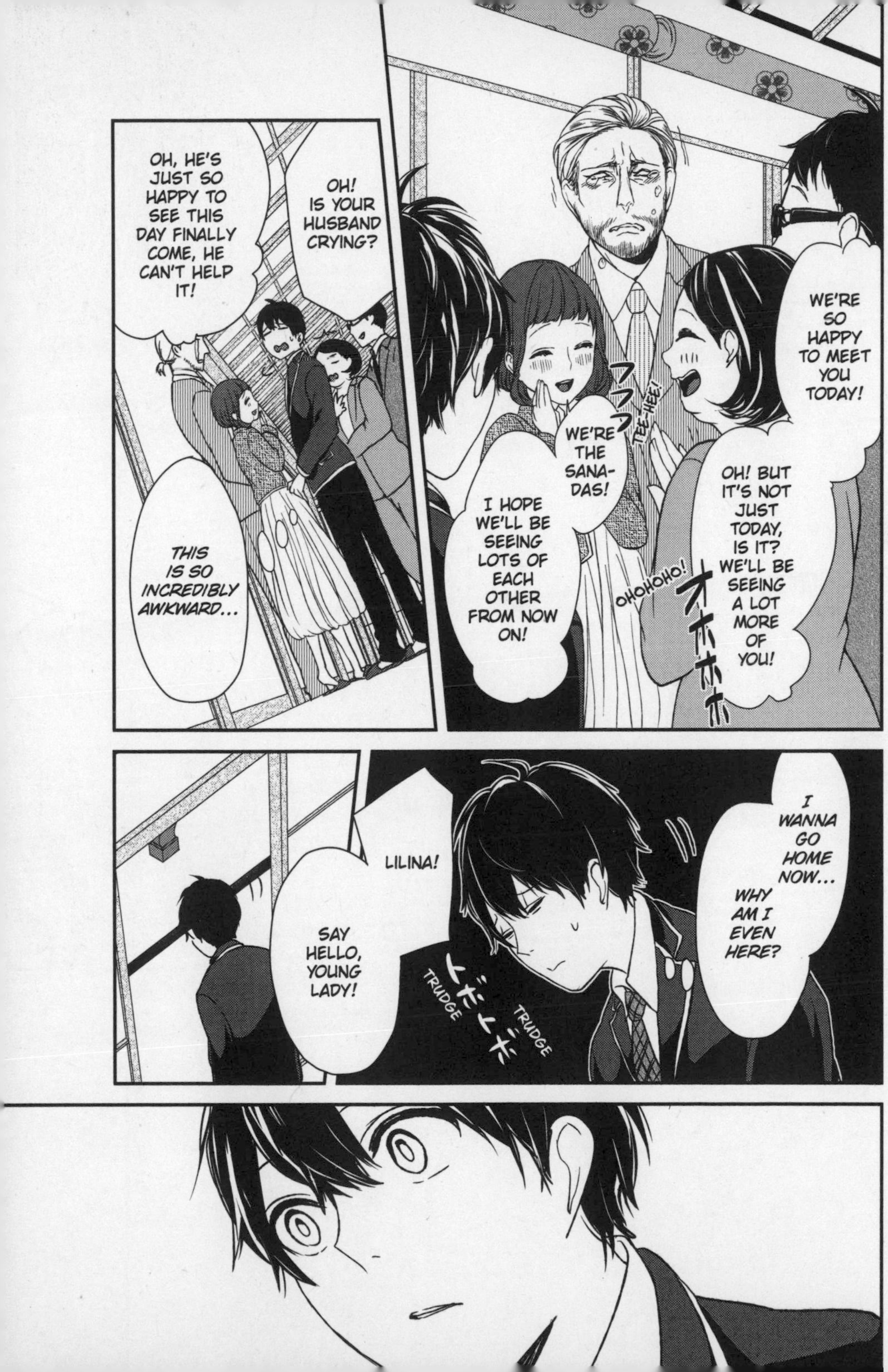
WE'RE SO HAPPY TO MEET YOU TODAY!
WE'RE THE SANADAS!
TEE-HEE!
OH! BUT IT'S NOT JUST TODAY, IS IT? WE'LL BE SEEING A LOT MORE OF YOU!
OHOHOHO!
I HOPE WE'LL BE SEEING LOTS OF EACH OTHER FROM NOW ON!
OH! IS YOUR HUSBAND CRYING?
OH, HE'S JUST SO HAPPY TO SEE THIS DAY FINALLY COME, HE CAN'T HELP IT!
THIS IS SO INCREDIBLY AWKWARD...
I WANNA GO HOME NOW... WHY AM I EVEN HERE?
TRUDGE
TRUDGE
LILINA!
SAY HELLO, YOUNG LADY!

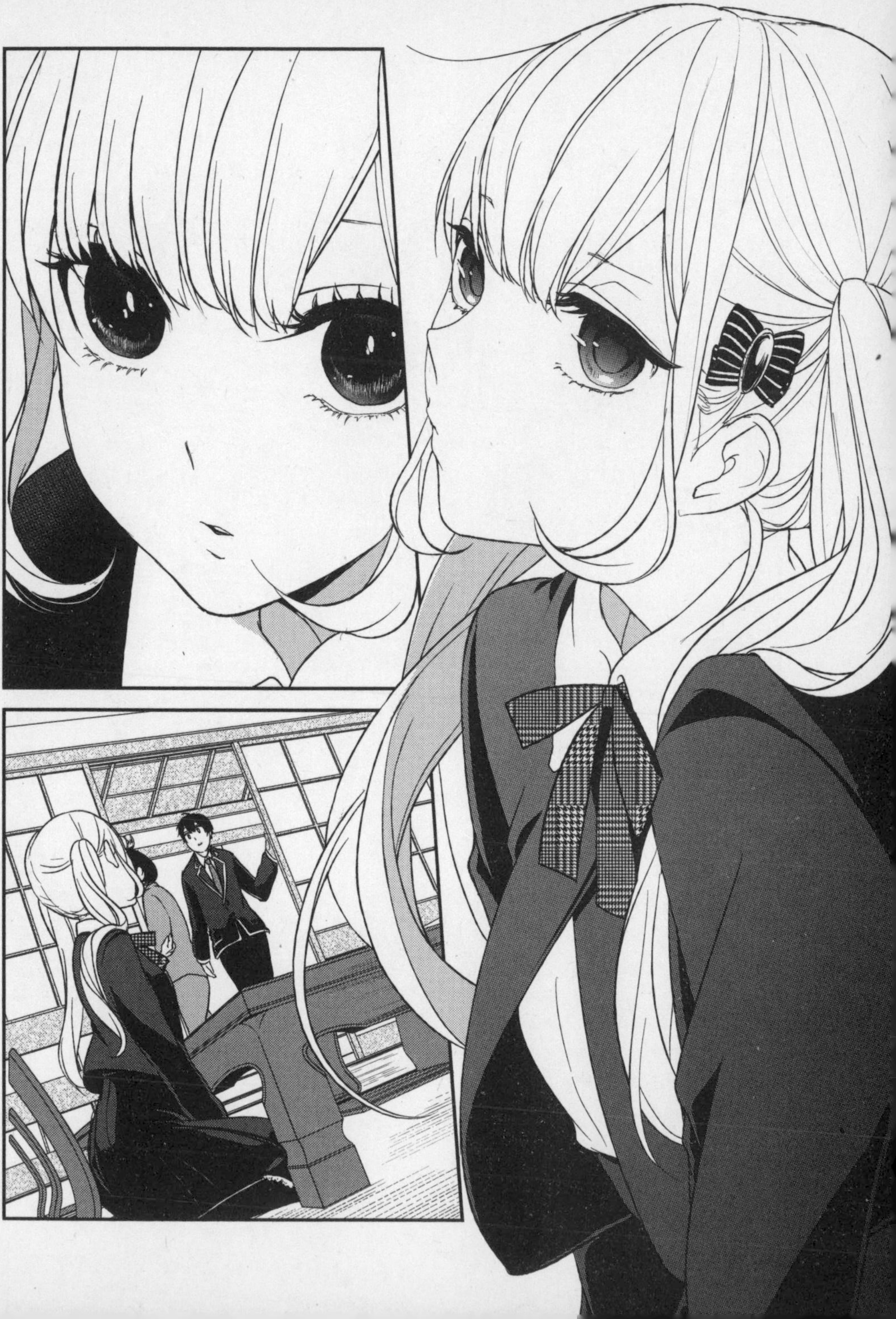

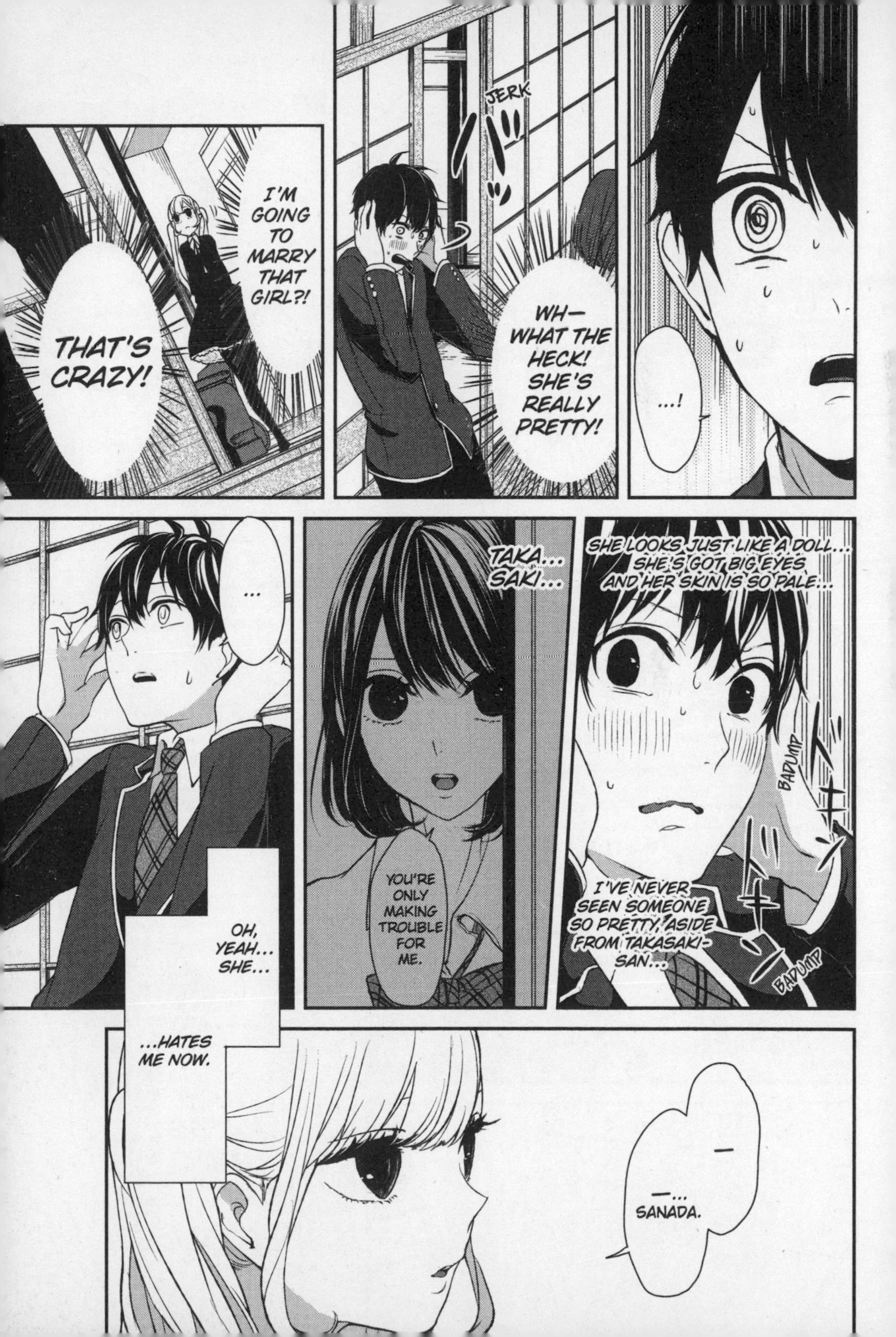
...!
JERK
WH—WHAT THE HECK! SHE'S REALLY PRETTY!
I'M GOING TO MARRY THAT GIRL?!
THAT'S CRAZY!
SHE LOOKS JUST LIKE A DOLL... SHE'S GOT BIG EYES AND HER SKIN IS SO PALE...
BADUMP
I'VE NEVER SEEN SOMEONE SO PRETTY, ASIDE FROM TAKASAKI-SAN...
BADUMP
TAKA... SAKI...
YOU'RE ONLY MAKING TROUBLE FOR ME.
...
OH, YEAH... SHE...
...HATES ME NOW.
—
—... SANADA.

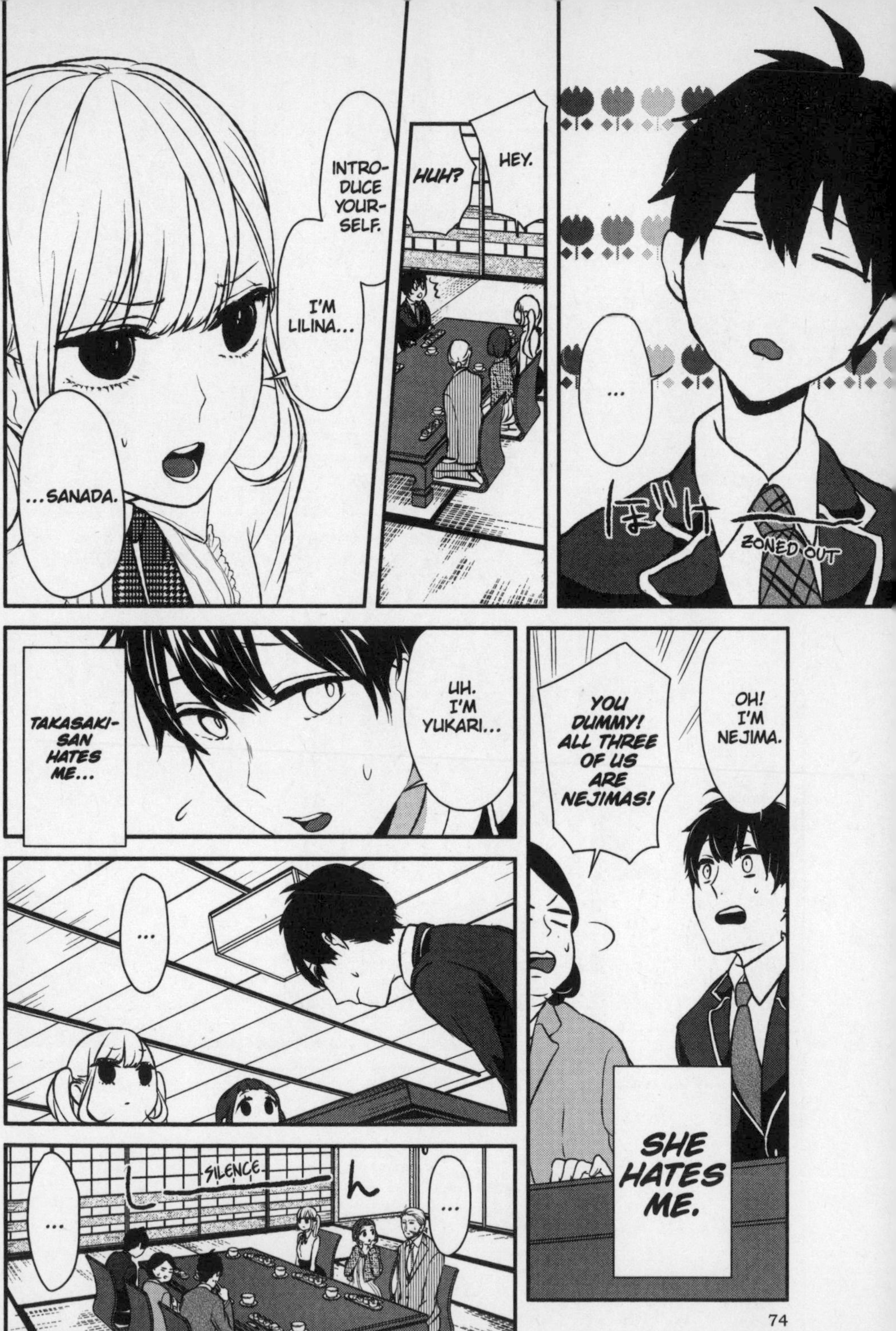
...
ぼけ
ZONED OUT
HEY.
HUH?
INTRO-DUCE YOUR-SELF.
I'M LILINA...
...SANADA.
OH! I'M NEJIMA.
YOU DUMMY! ALL THREE OF US ARE NEJIMAS!
SHE HATES ME.
UH. I'M YUKARI...
TAKASAKI-SAN HATES ME...
...
...
しーん
SILENCE
...

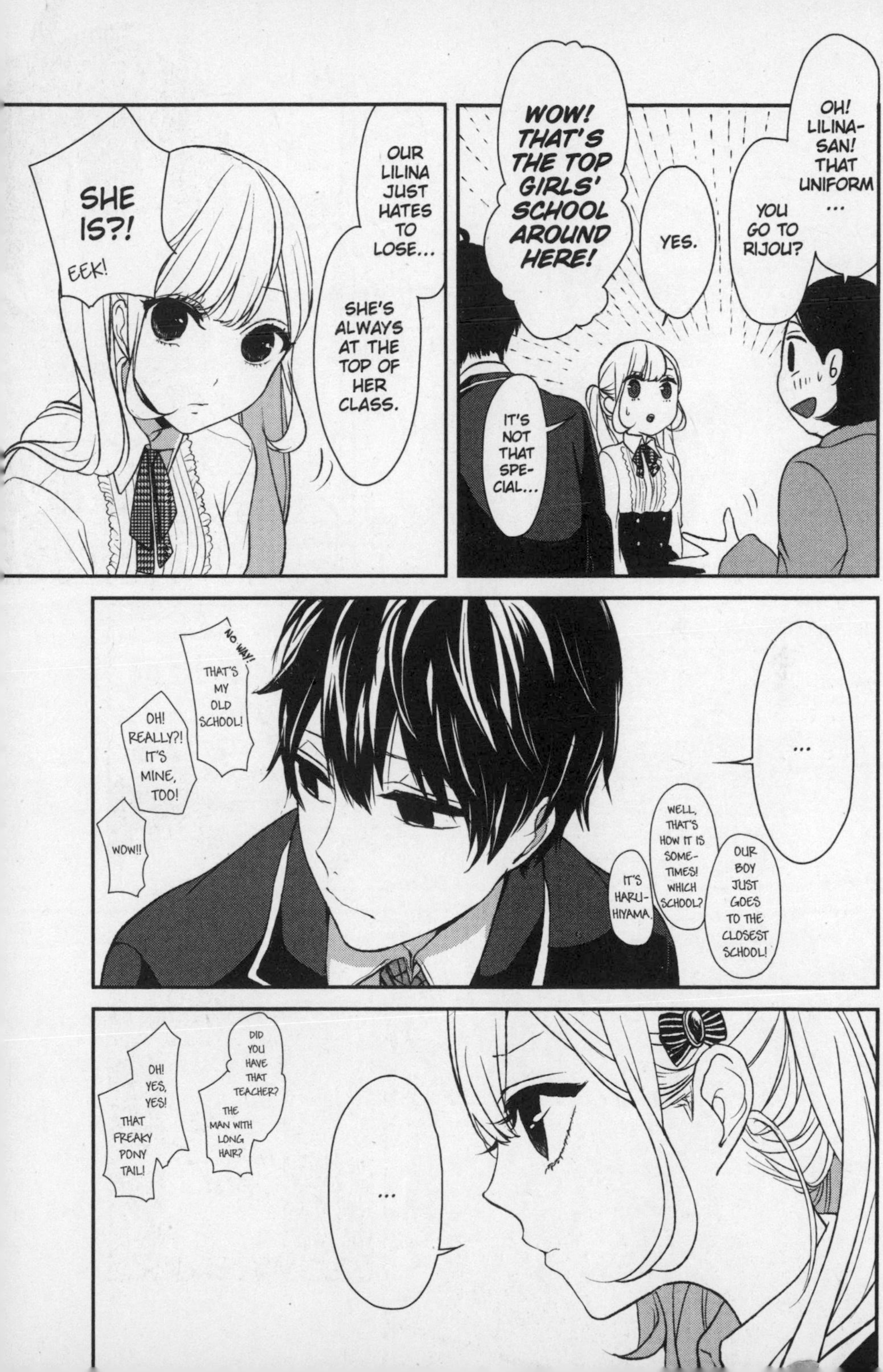
OH! LILINA-SAN! THAT UNIFORM ...
YOU GO TO RIJOU?
YES.
WOW! THAT'S THE TOP GIRLS' SCHOOL AROUND HERE!
IT'S NOT THAT SPE-CIAL...
OUR LILINA JUST HATES TO LOSE...
SHE'S ALWAYS AT THE TOP OF HER CLASS.
SHE IS?!
EEK!
...
OUR BOY JUST GOES TO THE CLOSEST SCHOOL!
WELL, THAT'S HOW IT IS SOME-TIMES! WHICH SCHOOL?
IT'S HARUHIYAMA.
NO WAY!
THAT'S MY OLD SCHOOL!
OH! REALLY?! IT'S MINE, TOO!
WOW!!
...
DID YOU HAVE THAT TEACHER?
THE MAN WITH LONG HAIR?
OH! YES, YES!
THAT FREAKY PONY TAIL!

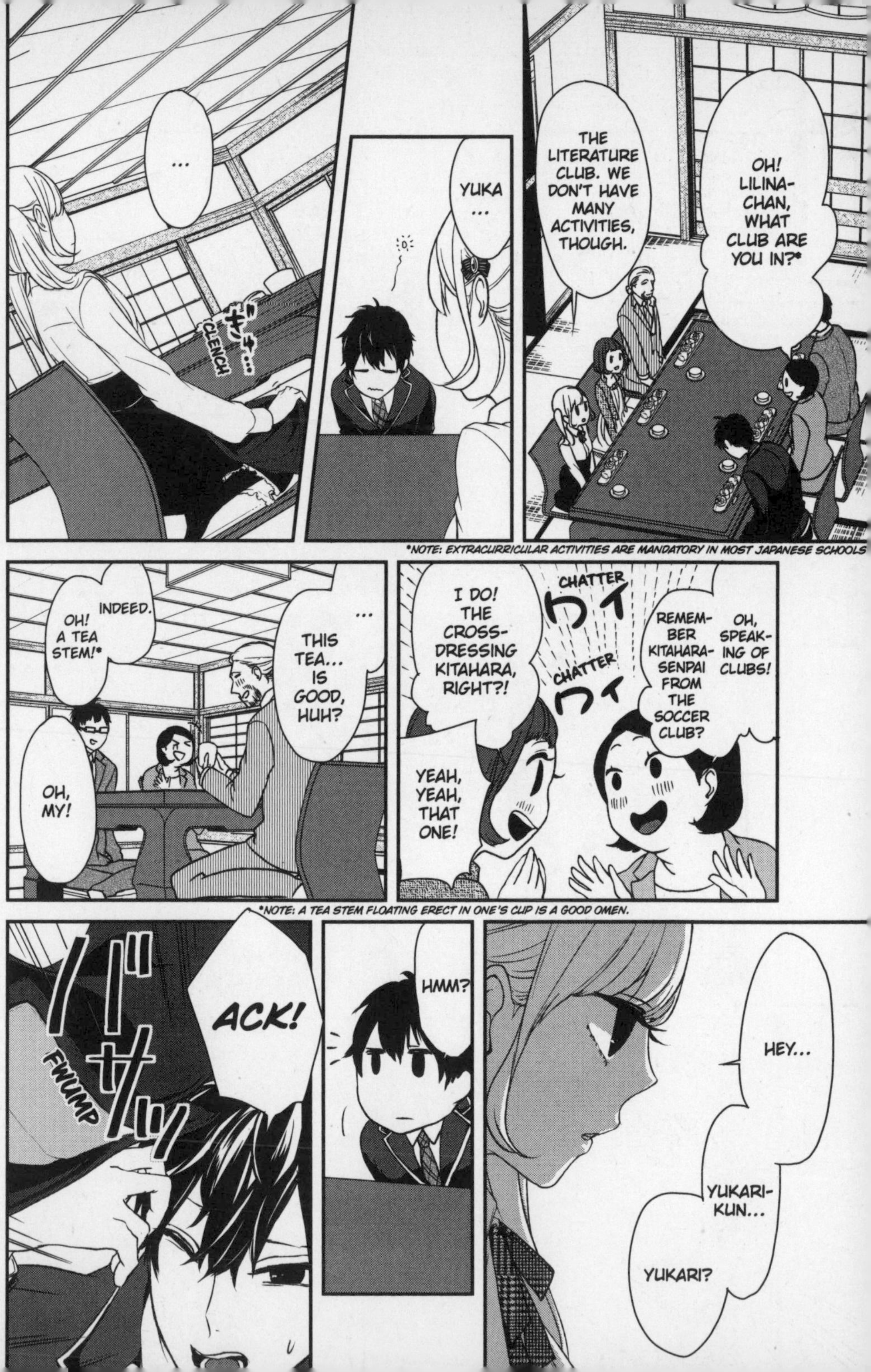
OH! LILINA-CHAN, WHAT CLUB ARE YOU IN?*
THE LITERATURE CLUB. WE DON'T HAVE MANY ACTIVITIES, THOUGH.
YUKA ...
...
ギュ… CLENCH
*NOTE: EXTRACURRICULAR ACTIVITIES ARE MANDATORY IN MOST JAPANESE SCHOOLS
OH, SPEAKING OF CLUBS!
REMEMBER KITAHARA-SENPAI FROM THE SOCCER CLUB?
ワイ CHATTER
ワイ CHATTER
I DO! THE CROSS-DRESSING KITAHARA, RIGHT?!
YEAH, YEAH, THAT ONE!
... THIS TEA... IS GOOD, HUH?
INDEED.
OH! A TEA STEM!*
OH, MY!
*NOTE: A TEA STEM FLOATING ERECT IN ONE'S CUP IS A GOOD OMEN.
HEY...
YUKARI-KUN...
YUKARI?
HMM?
ACK!
バサッ FWUMP

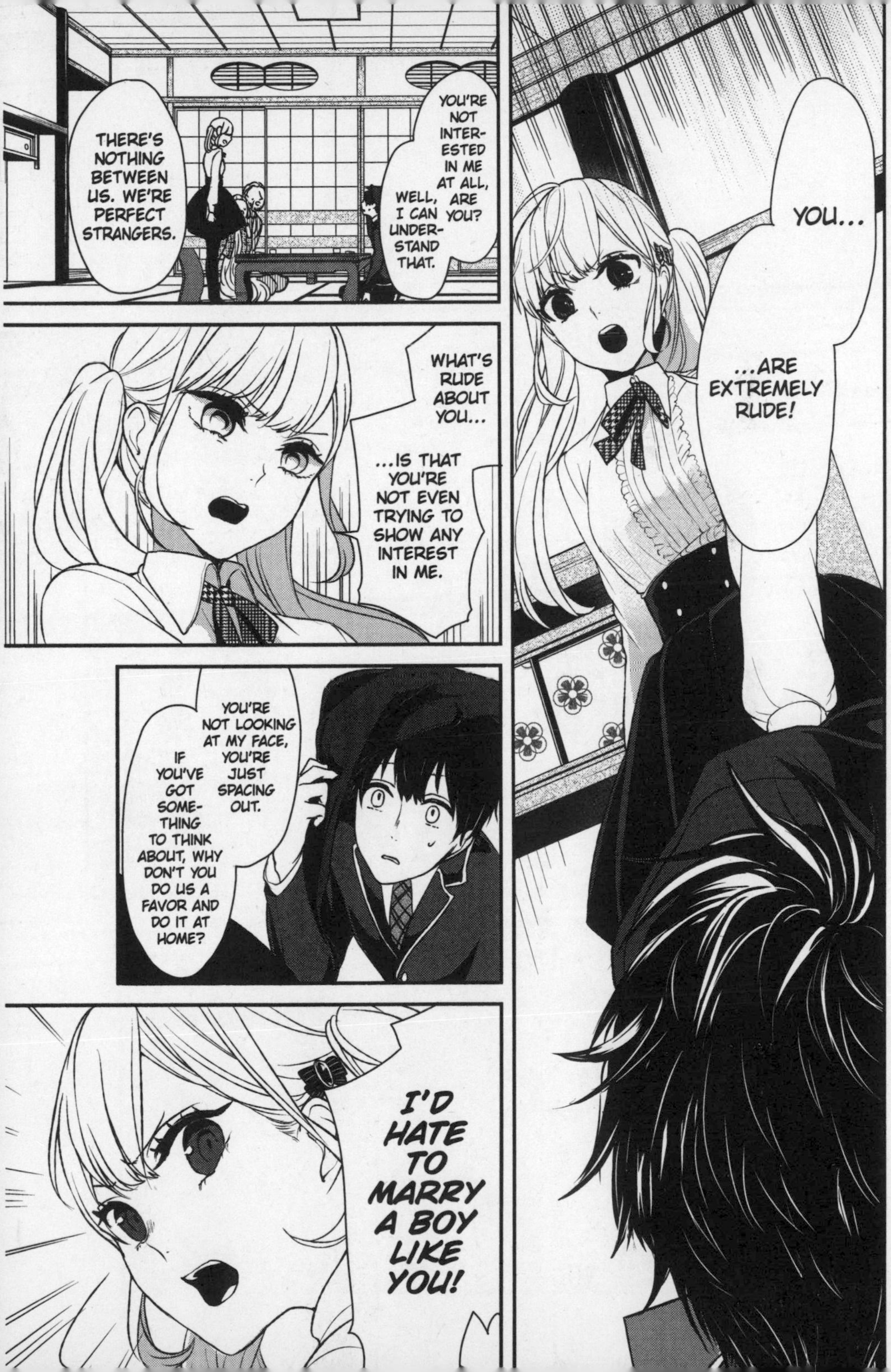
YOU...
...ARE EXTREMELY RUDE!
YOU'RE NOT INTERESTED IN ME AT ALL, ARE YOU?
WELL, I CAN UNDERSTAND THAT.
THERE'S NOTHING BETWEEN US. WE'RE PERFECT STRANGERS.
WHAT'S RUDE ABOUT YOU...
...IS THAT YOU'RE NOT EVEN TRYING TO SHOW ANY INTEREST IN ME.
YOU'RE NOT LOOKING AT MY FACE, YOU'RE JUST SPACING OUT.
IF YOU'VE GOT SOMETHING TO THINK ABOUT, WHY DON'T YOU DO US A FAVOR AND DO IT AT HOME?
I'D HATE TO MARRY A BOY LIKE YOU!

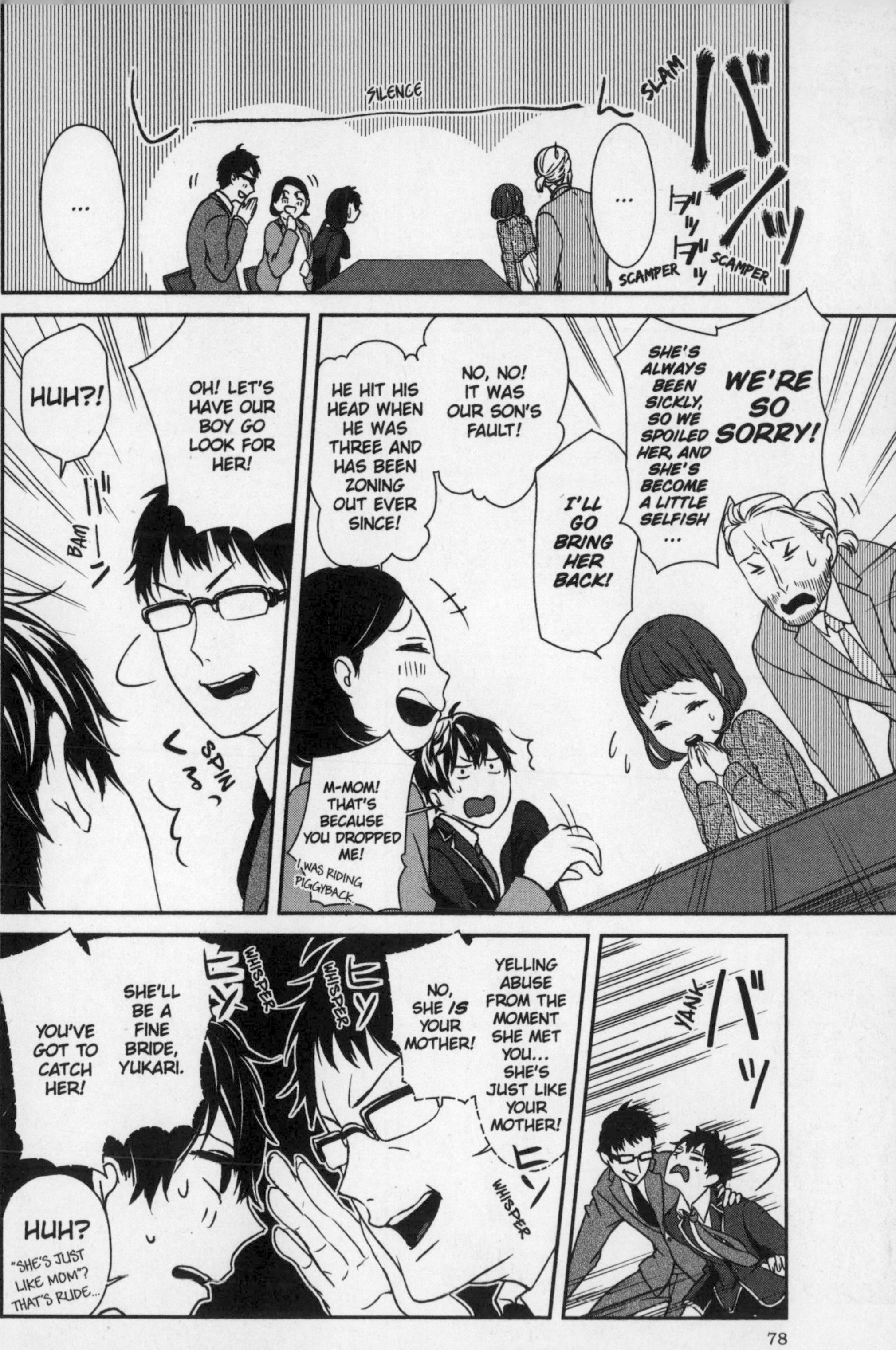
SLAM
SCAMPER
...
SCAMPER
SILENCE
...
WE'RE SO SORRY!
SHE'S ALWAYS BEEN SICKLY, SO WE SPOILED HER, AND SHE'S BECOME A LITTLE SELFISH...
I'LL GO BRING HER BACK!
NO, NO! IT WAS OUR SON'S FAULT!
HE HIT HIS HEAD WHEN HE WAS THREE AND HAS BEEN ZONING OUT EVER SINCE!
M-MOM! THAT'S BECAUSE YOU DROPPED ME!
I WAS RIDING PIGGYBACK.
OH! LET'S HAVE OUR BOY GO LOOK FOR HER!
HUH?!
BAM
SPIN
YANK
YELLING ABUSE FROM THE MOMENT SHE MET YOU... SHE'S JUST LIKE YOUR MOTHER!
NO, SHE *IS* YOUR MOTHER!
WHISPER
WHISPER
SHE'LL BE A FINE BRIDE, YUKARI.
YOU'VE GOT TO CATCH HER!
WHISPER
HUH?
"SHE'S JUST LIKE MOM"? THAT'S RUDE...

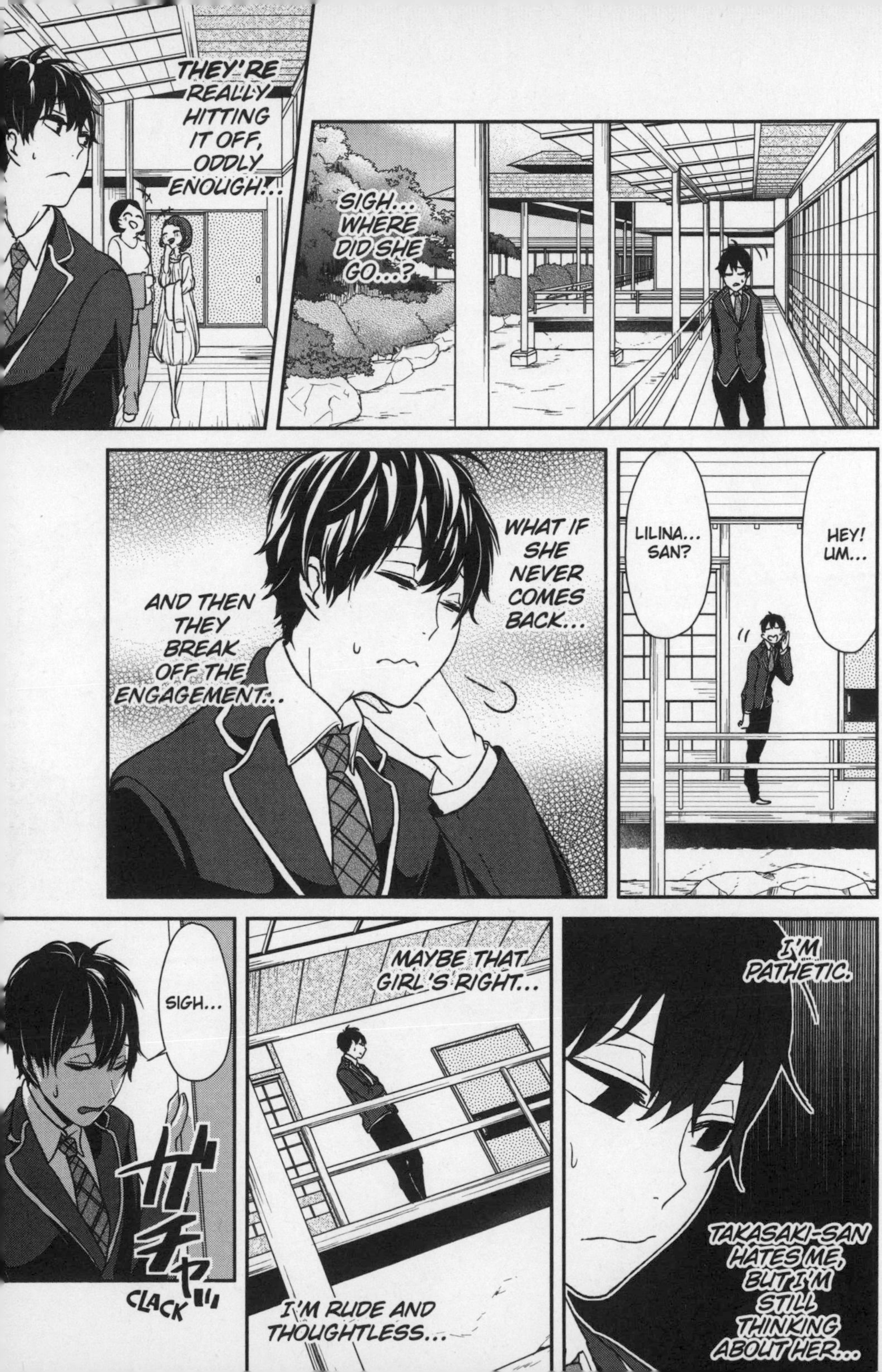
SIGH... WHERE DID SHE GO...?
THEY'RE REALLY HITTING IT OFF, ODDLY ENOUGH...
HEY! UM...
LILINA... SAN?
WHAT IF SHE NEVER COMES BACK...
AND THEN THEY BREAK OFF THE ENGAGEMENT...
I'M PATHETIC.
TAKASAKI-SAN HATES ME, BUT I'M STILL THINKING ABOUT HER...
MAYBE THAT GIRL'S RIGHT...
I'M RUDE AND THOUGHTLESS...
SIGH...
ガチャ
CLACK

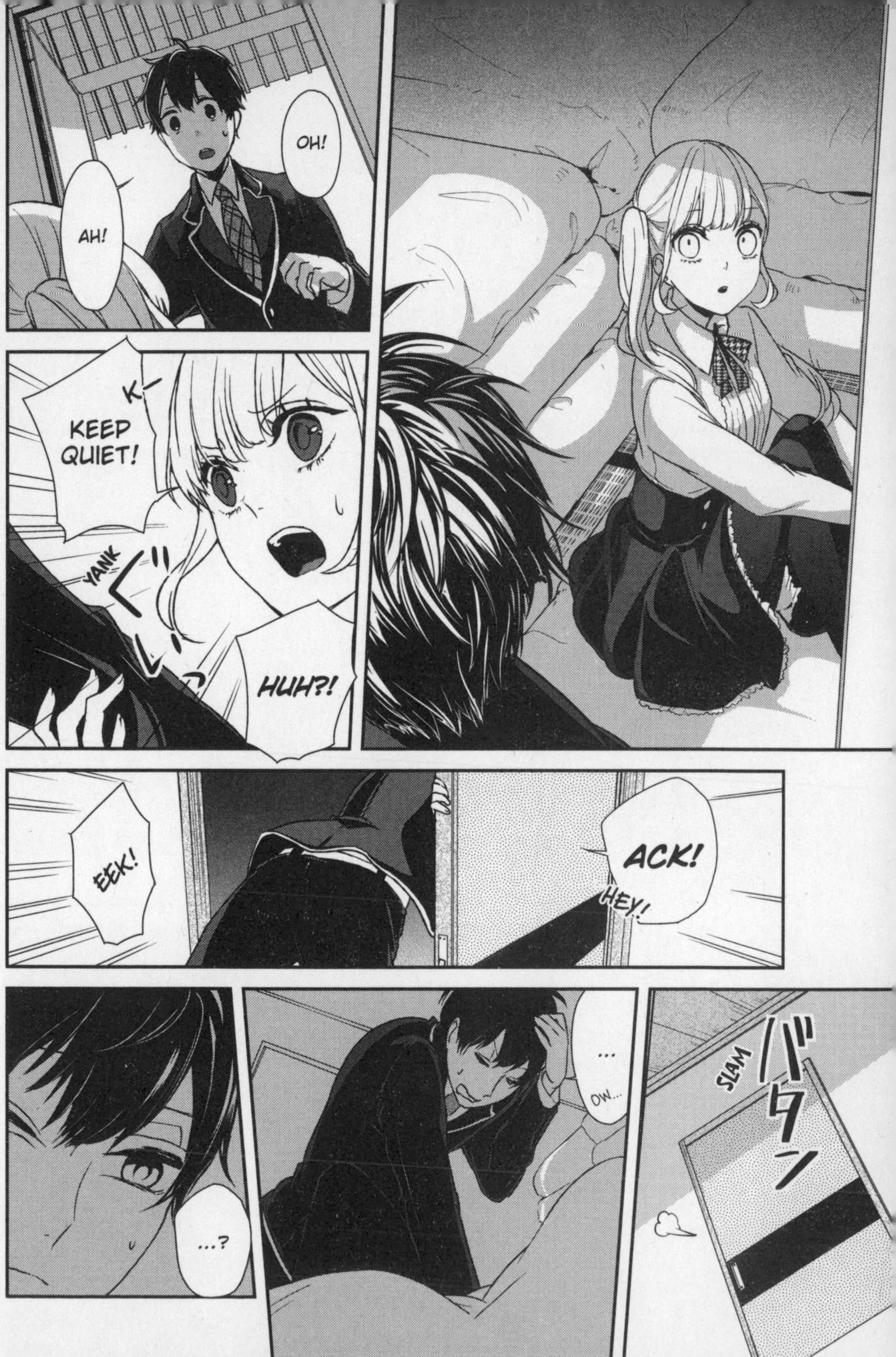
OH!
AH!
K- KEEP QUIET!
YANK
HUH?!
ACK!
HEY!
EEK!
SLAM
バタン
... OW...
...?

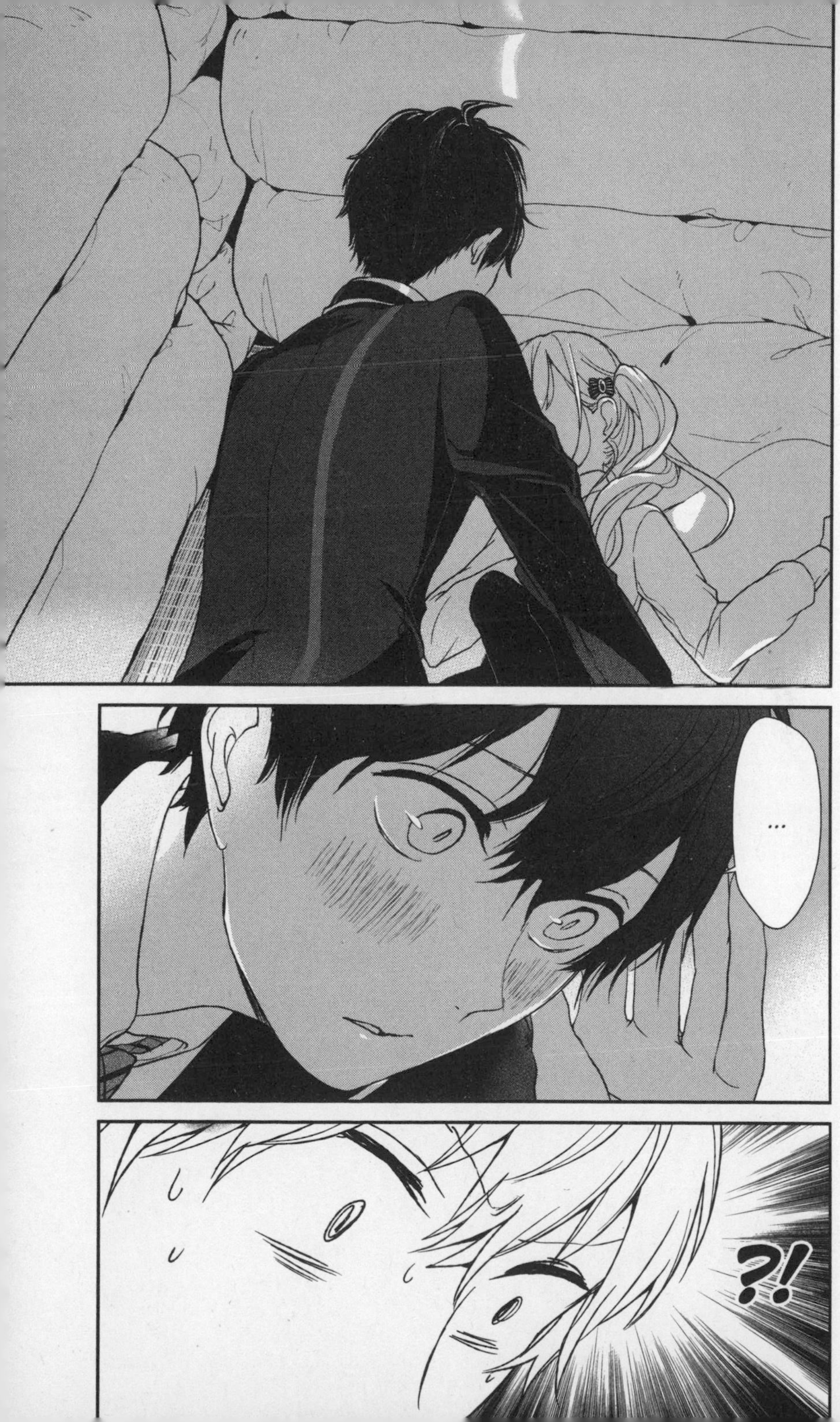
...
?!

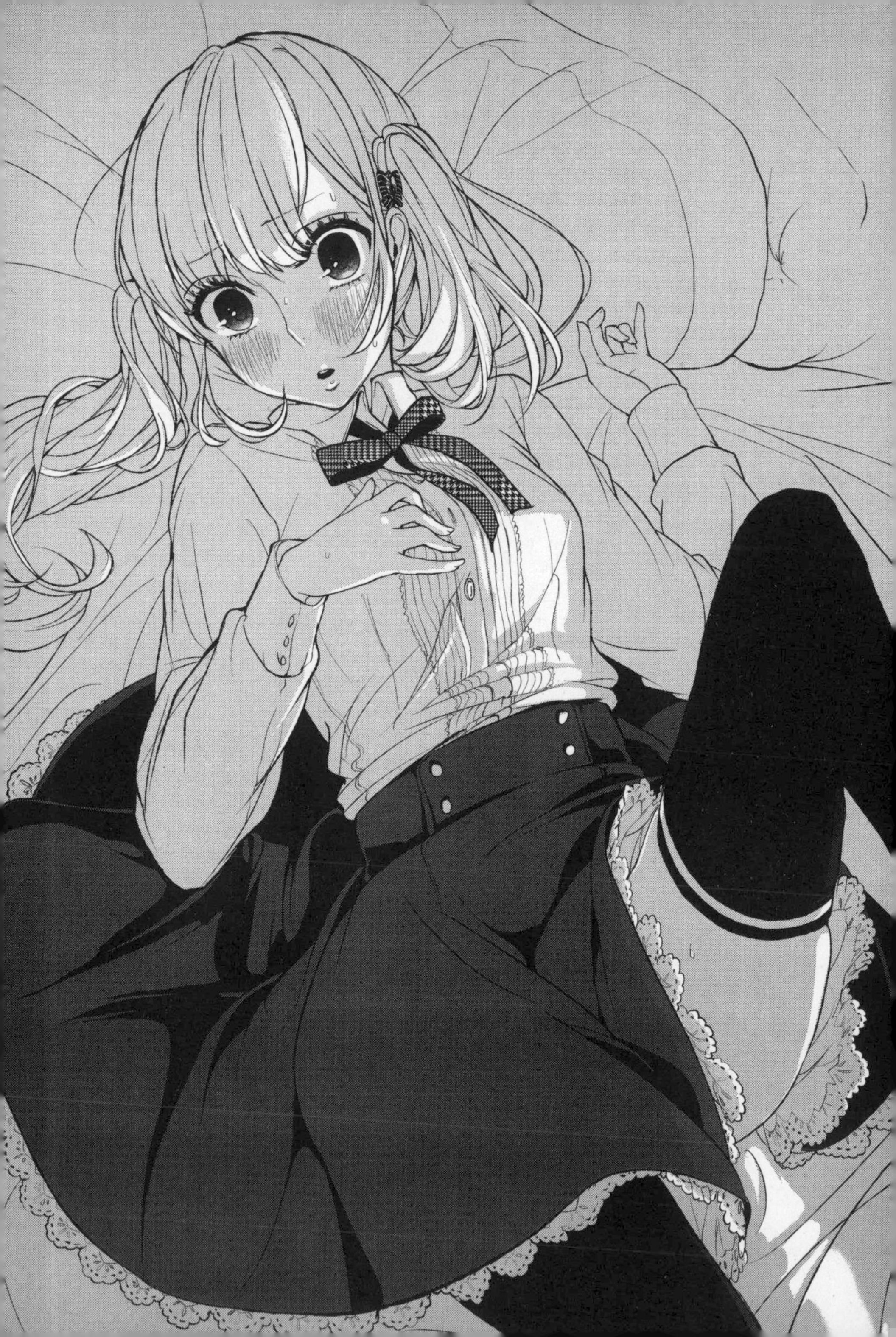

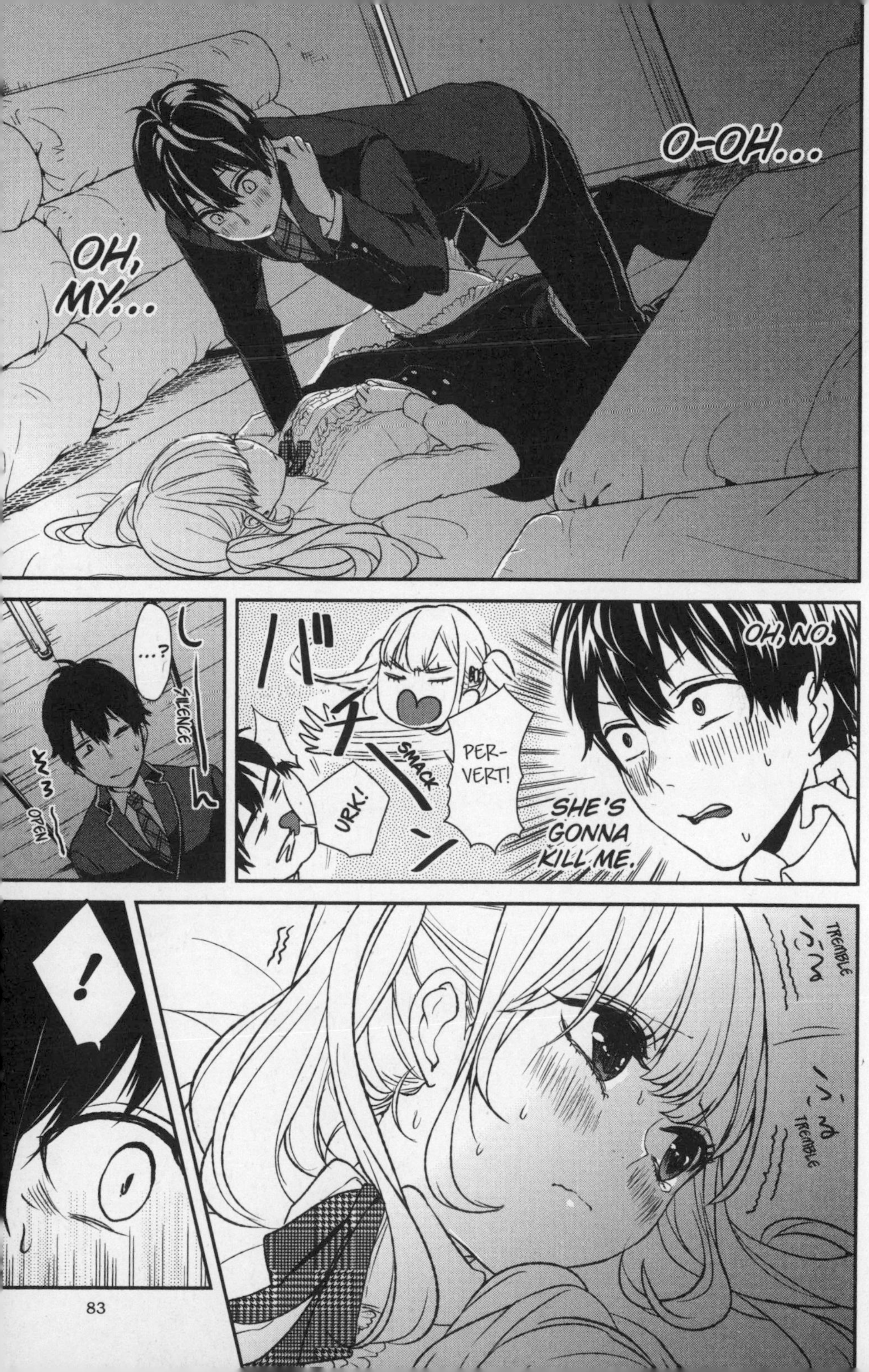
O-OH...
OH, MY...
OH, NO.
SHE'S GONNA KILL ME.
PER-VERT!
SMACK
URK!
...?
SILENCE
OPEN
TREMBLE
TREMBLE
!

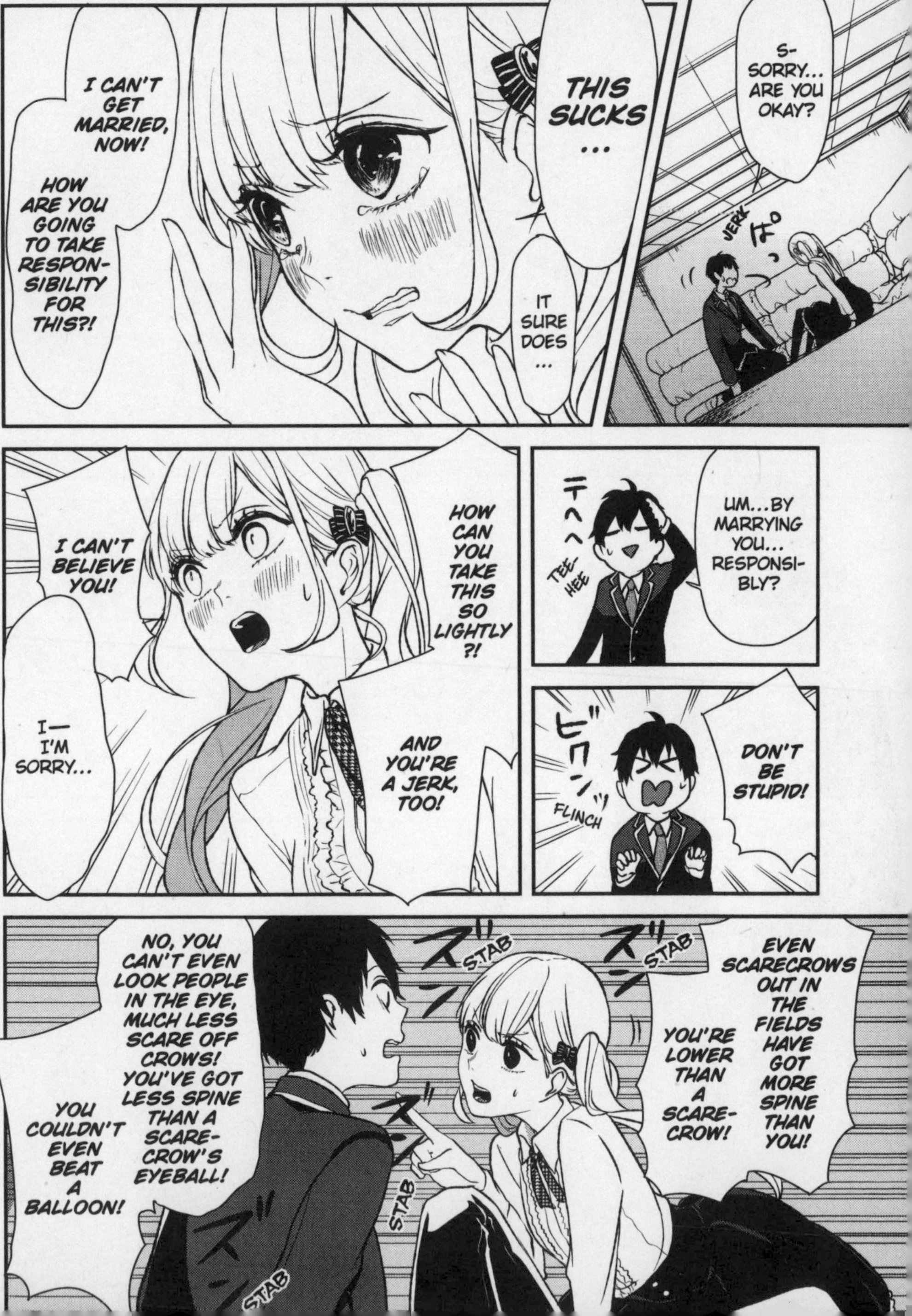
S-SORRY... ARE YOU OKAY?
JERK
THIS SUCKS...
IT SURE DOES...
I CAN'T GET MARRIED, NOW!
HOW ARE YOU GOING TO TAKE RESPONSIBILITY FOR THIS?!
UM...BY MARRYING YOU... RESPONSIBLY?
TEE HEE
DON'T BE STUPID!
FLINCH
HOW CAN YOU TAKE THIS SO LIGHTLY?!
I CAN'T BELIEVE YOU!
AND YOU'RE A JERK, TOO!
I— I'M SORRY...
EVEN SCARECROWS OUT IN THE FIELDS HAVE GOT MORE SPINE THAN YOU!
YOU'RE LOWER THAN A SCARE-CROW!
STAB
STAB
NO, YOU CAN'T EVEN LOOK PEOPLE IN THE EYE, MUCH LESS SCARE OFF CROWS! YOU'VE GOT LESS SPINE THAN A SCARE-CROW'S EYEBALL!
YOU COULDN'T EVEN BEAT A BALLOON!
STAB
STAB

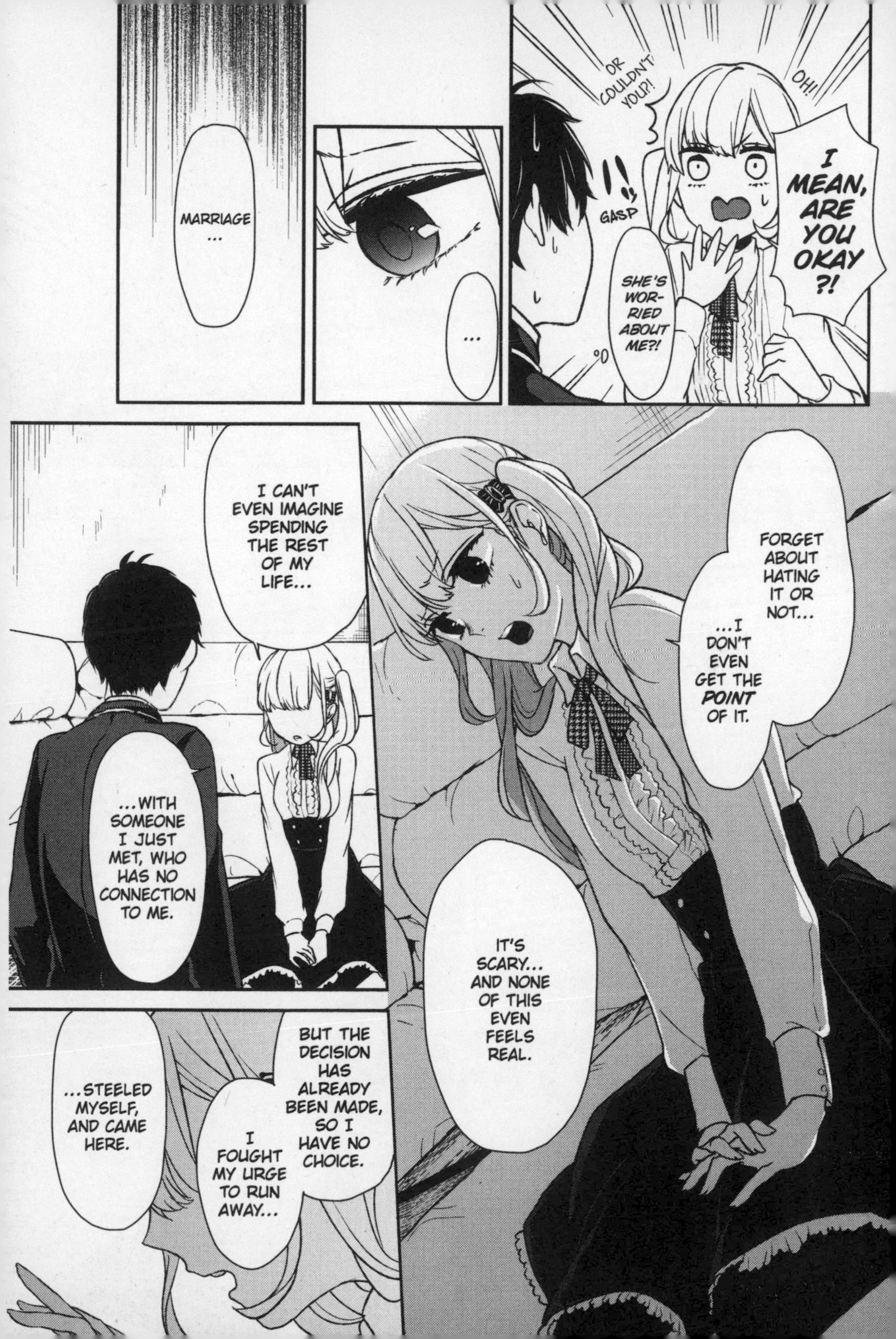
I MEAN, ARE YOU OKAY?!
OH!
OR COULDN'T YOU?!
GASP
SHE'S WORRIED ABOUT ME?!
...
MARRIAGE...
FORGET ABOUT HATING IT OR NOT...
...I DON'T EVEN GET THE *POINT* OF IT.
IT'S SCARY... AND NONE OF THIS EVEN FEELS REAL.
I CAN'T EVEN IMAGINE SPENDING THE REST OF MY LIFE...
...WITH SOMEONE I JUST MET, WHO HAS NO CONNECTION TO ME.
BUT THE DECISION HAS ALREADY BEEN MADE, SO I HAVE NO CHOICE.
I FOUGHT MY URGE TO RUN AWAY...
...STEELED MYSELF, AND CAME HERE.

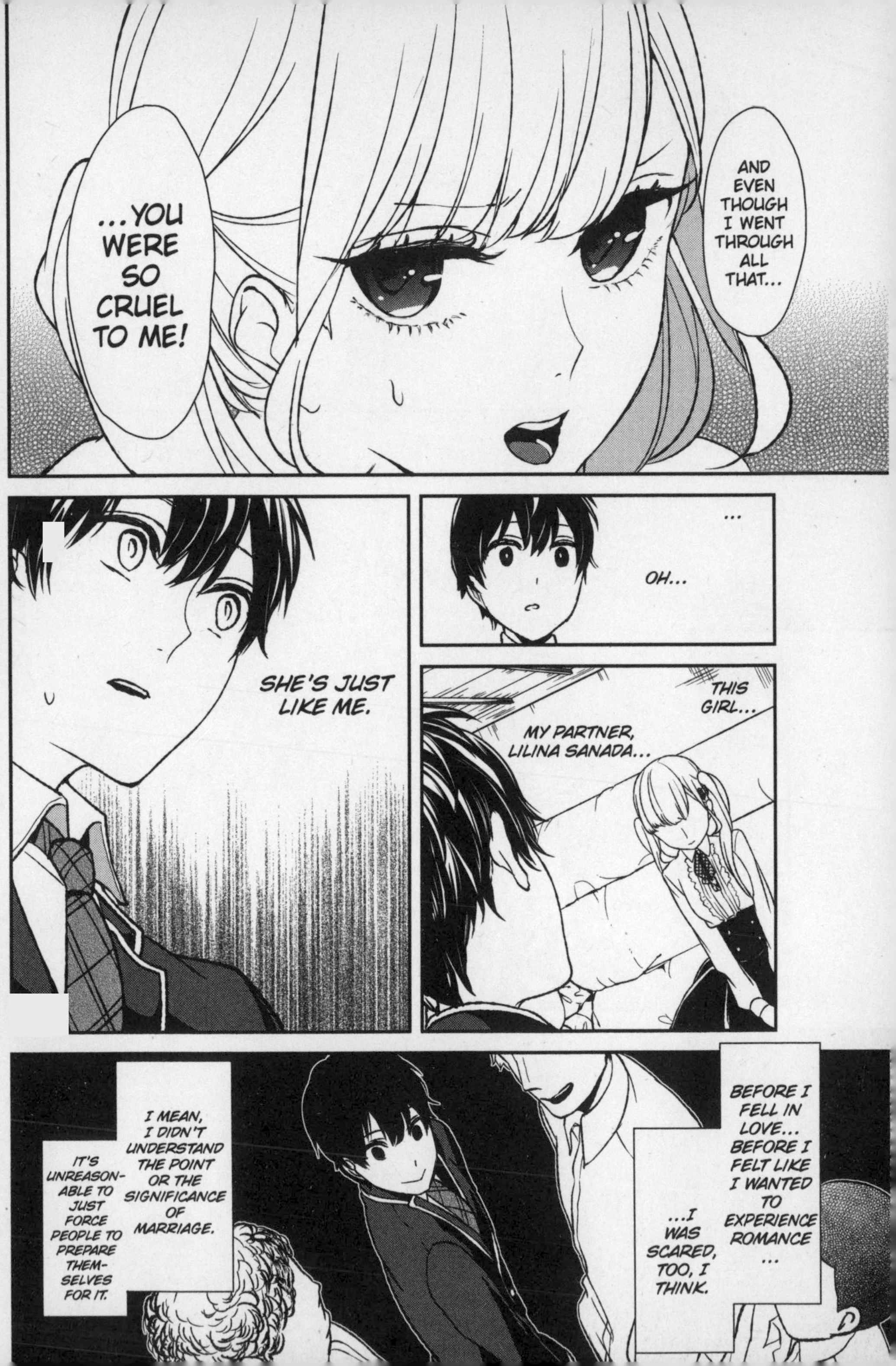
AND EVEN THOUGH I WENT THROUGH ALL THAT...
...YOU WERE SO CRUEL TO ME!
...
OH...
THIS GIRL...
MY PARTNER, LILINA SANADA...
SHE'S JUST LIKE ME.
BEFORE I FELL IN LOVE... BEFORE I FELT LIKE I WANTED TO EXPERIENCE ROMANCE...
...I WAS SCARED, TOO, I THINK.
I MEAN, I DIDN'T UNDERSTAND THE POINT OR THE SIGNIFICANCE OF MARRIAGE.
IT'S UNREASON-ABLE TO JUST FORCE PEOPLE TO PREPARE THEM-SELVES FOR IT.

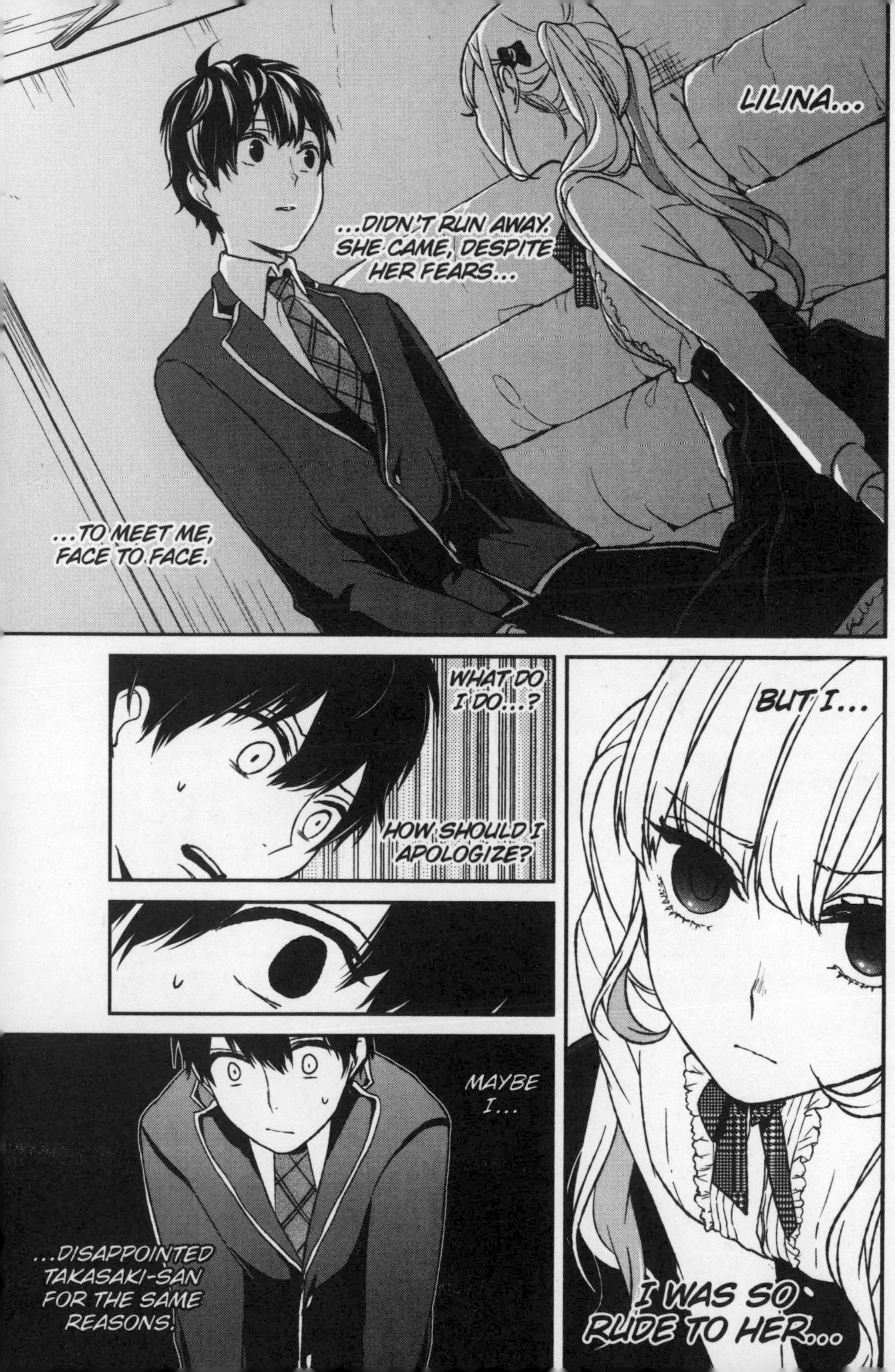
LILINA...
...DIDN'T RUN AWAY. SHE CAME, DESPITE HER FEARS...
...TO MEET ME, FACE TO FACE.
BUT I...
I WAS SO RUDE TO HER...
WHAT DO I DO...?
HOW SHOULD I APOLOGIZE?
MAYBE I...
...DISAPPOINTED TAKASAKI-SAN FOR THE SAME REASONS.

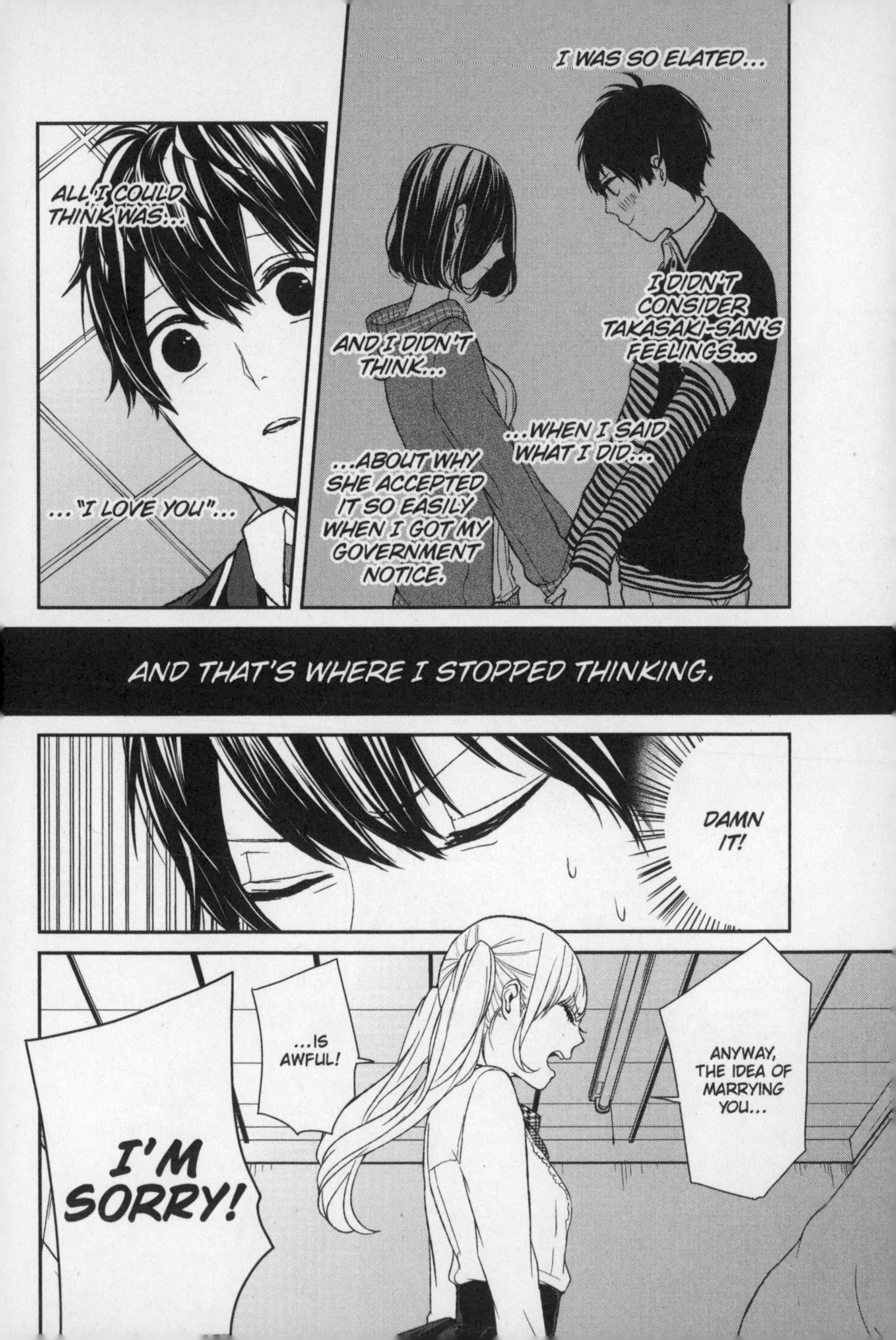
I WAS SO ELATED...
I DIDN'T CONSIDER TAKASAKI-SAN'S FEELINGS...
...WHEN I SAID WHAT I DID...
AND I DIDN'T THINK...
...ABOUT WHY SHE ACCEPTED IT SO EASILY WHEN I GOT MY GOVERNMENT NOTICE.
ALL I COULD THINK WAS...
..."I LOVE YOU"...
AND THAT'S WHERE I STOPPED THINKING.
DAMN IT!
ANYWAY, THE IDEA OF MARRYING YOU...
...IS AWFUL!
I'M SORRY!

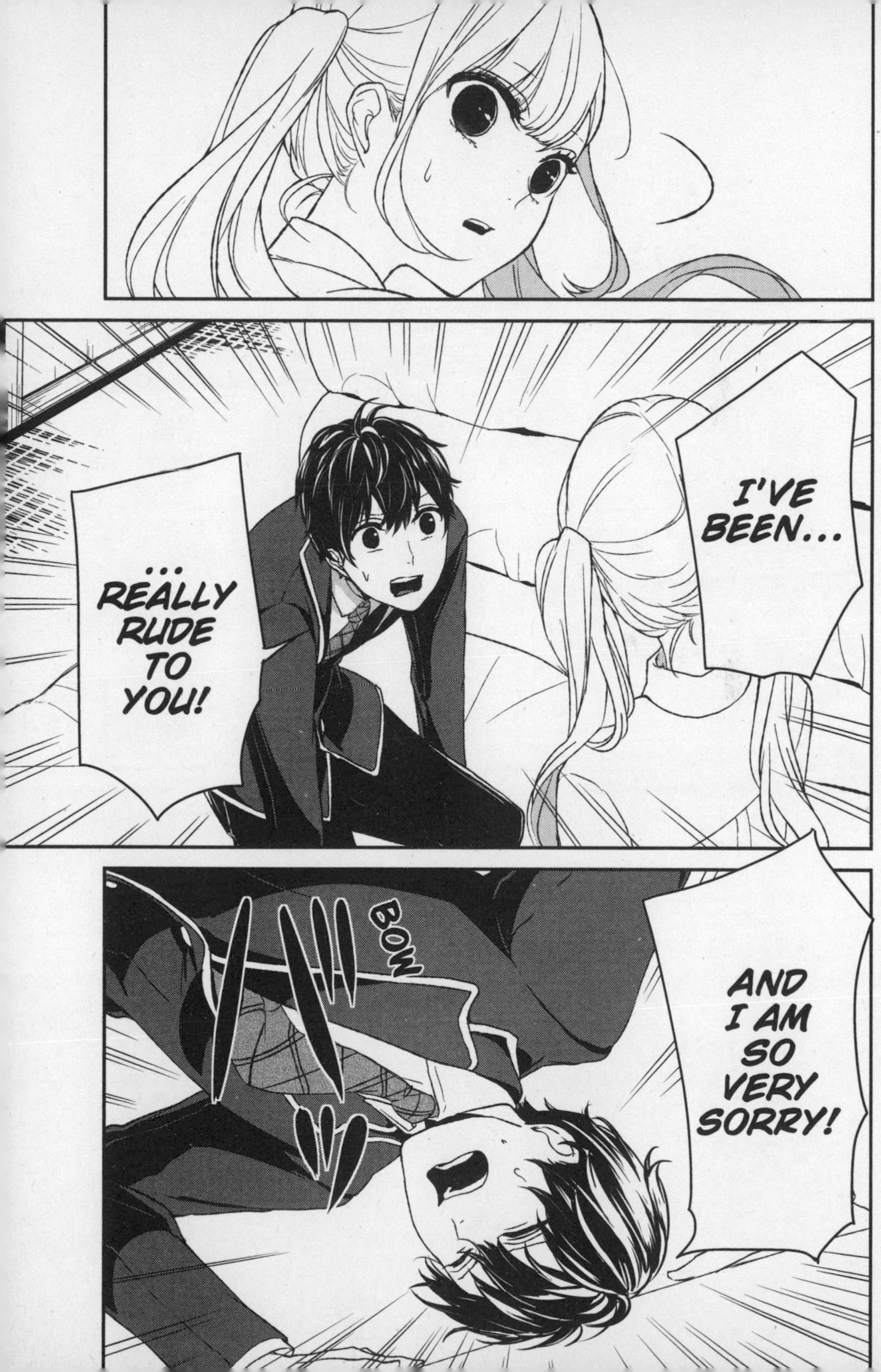
I'VE BEEN...
...REALLY RUDE TO YOU!
AND I AM SO VERY SORRY!
BOW

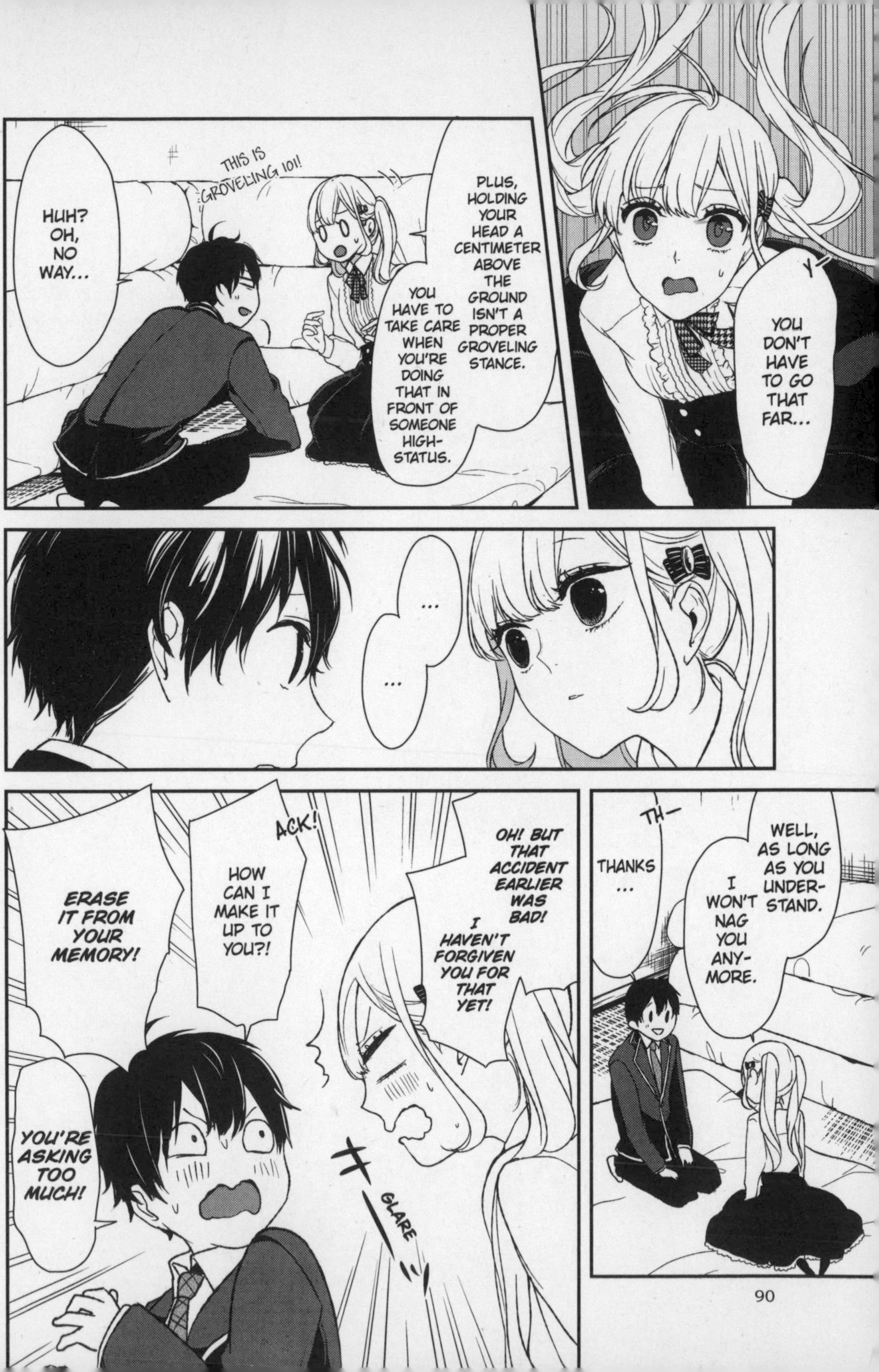

YOU DON'T HAVE TO GO THAT FAR...
PLUS, HOLDING YOUR HEAD A CENTIMETER ABOVE THE GROUND ISN'T A PROPER GROVELING STANCE.
YOU HAVE TO TAKE CARE WHEN YOU'RE DOING THAT IN FRONT OF SOMEONE HIGH-STATUS.
THIS IS GROVELING 101!
HUH? OH, NO WAY...
...
...
WELL, AS LONG AS YOU UNDER-STAND.
I WON'T NAG YOU ANY-MORE.
TH— THANKS...
OH! BUT THAT ACCIDENT EARLIER WAS BAD!
I HAVEN'T FORGIVEN YOU FOR THAT YET!
ACK!
HOW CAN I MAKE IT UP TO YOU?!
ERASE IT FROM YOUR MEMORY!
GLARE
YOU'RE ASKING TOO MUCH!

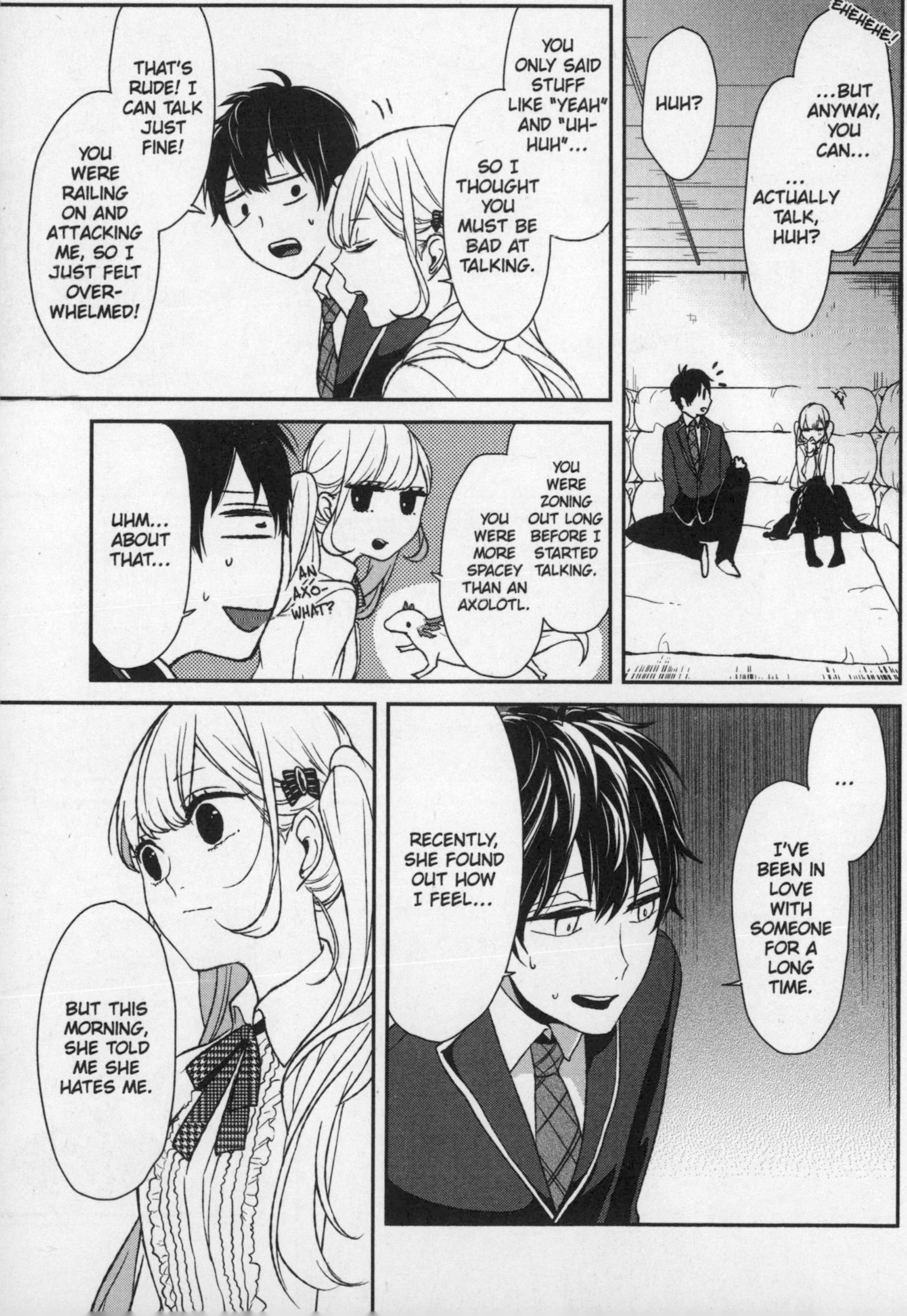
EHEHEHE!
...BUT ANYWAY, YOU CAN... ...ACTUALLY TALK, HUH?
HUH?
YOU ONLY SAID STUFF LIKE "YEAH" AND "UH-HUH"... SO I THOUGHT YOU MUST BE BAD AT TALKING.
THAT'S RUDE! I CAN TALK JUST FINE! YOU WERE RAILING ON AND ATTACKING ME, SO I JUST FELT OVER-WHELMED!
YOU WERE ZONING OUT LONG BEFORE I STARTED TALKING.
YOU WERE MORE SPACEY THAN AN AXOLOTL.
AN AXO-WHAT?
UHM... ABOUT THAT...
...
I'VE BEEN IN LOVE WITH SOMEONE FOR A LONG TIME.
RECENTLY, SHE FOUND OUT HOW I FEEL...
BUT THIS MORNING, SHE TOLD ME SHE HATES ME.

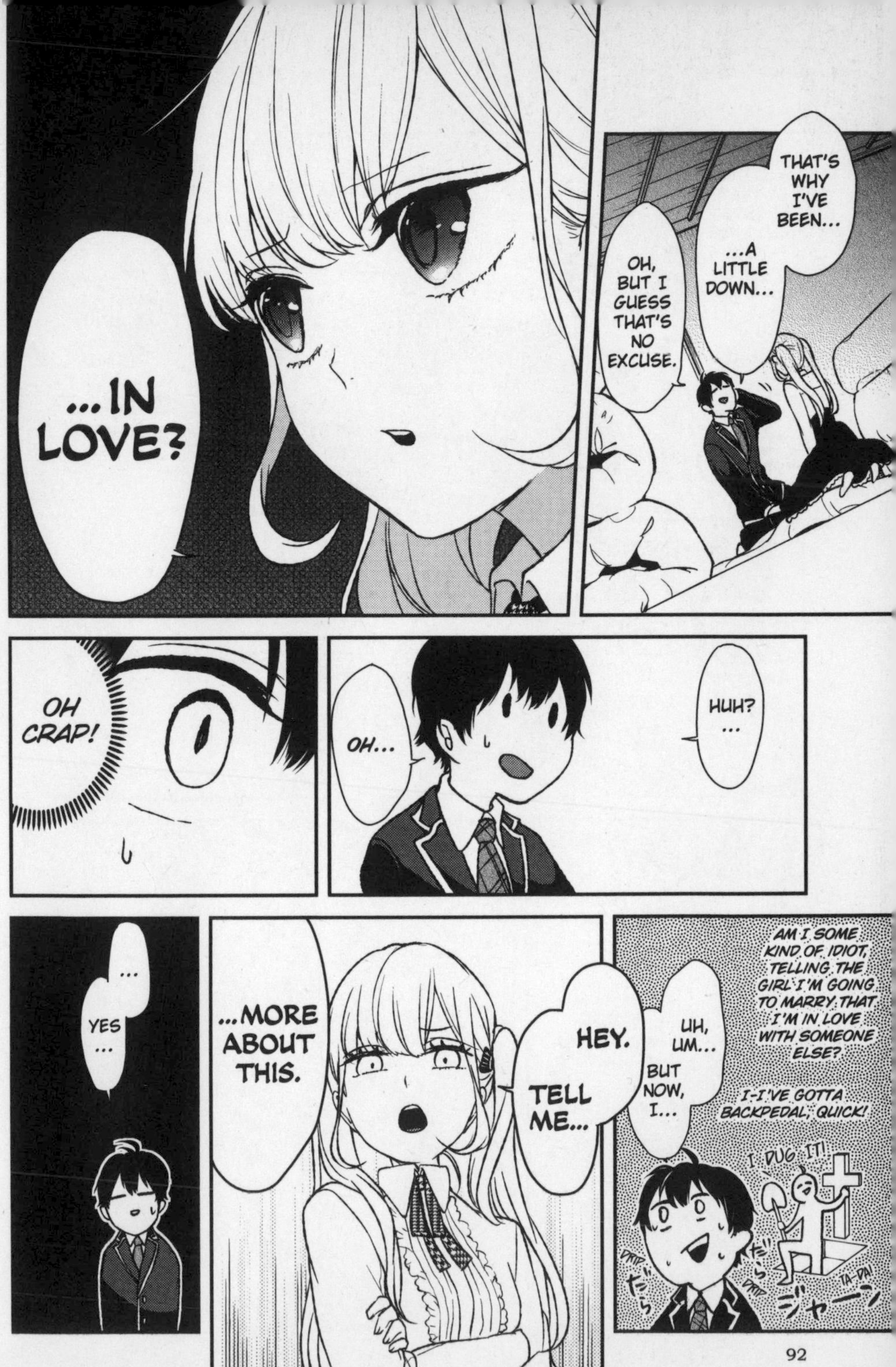
THAT'S WHY I'VE BEEN...
...A LITTLE DOWN...
OH, BUT I GUESS THAT'S NO EXCUSE.
...IN LOVE?
HUH? ...
OH...
OH CRAP!
AM I SOME KIND OF IDIOT, TELLING THE GIRL I'M GOING TO MARRY THAT I'M IN LOVE WITH SOMEONE ELSE?
UH, UM... BUT NOW, I...
I-I'VE GOTTA BACKPEDAL, QUICK!
I DUG IT!
DRIP
だら
DRIP
だら
TA-DA!
ジャーン
HEY.
TELL ME...
...MORE ABOUT THIS.
... YES ...

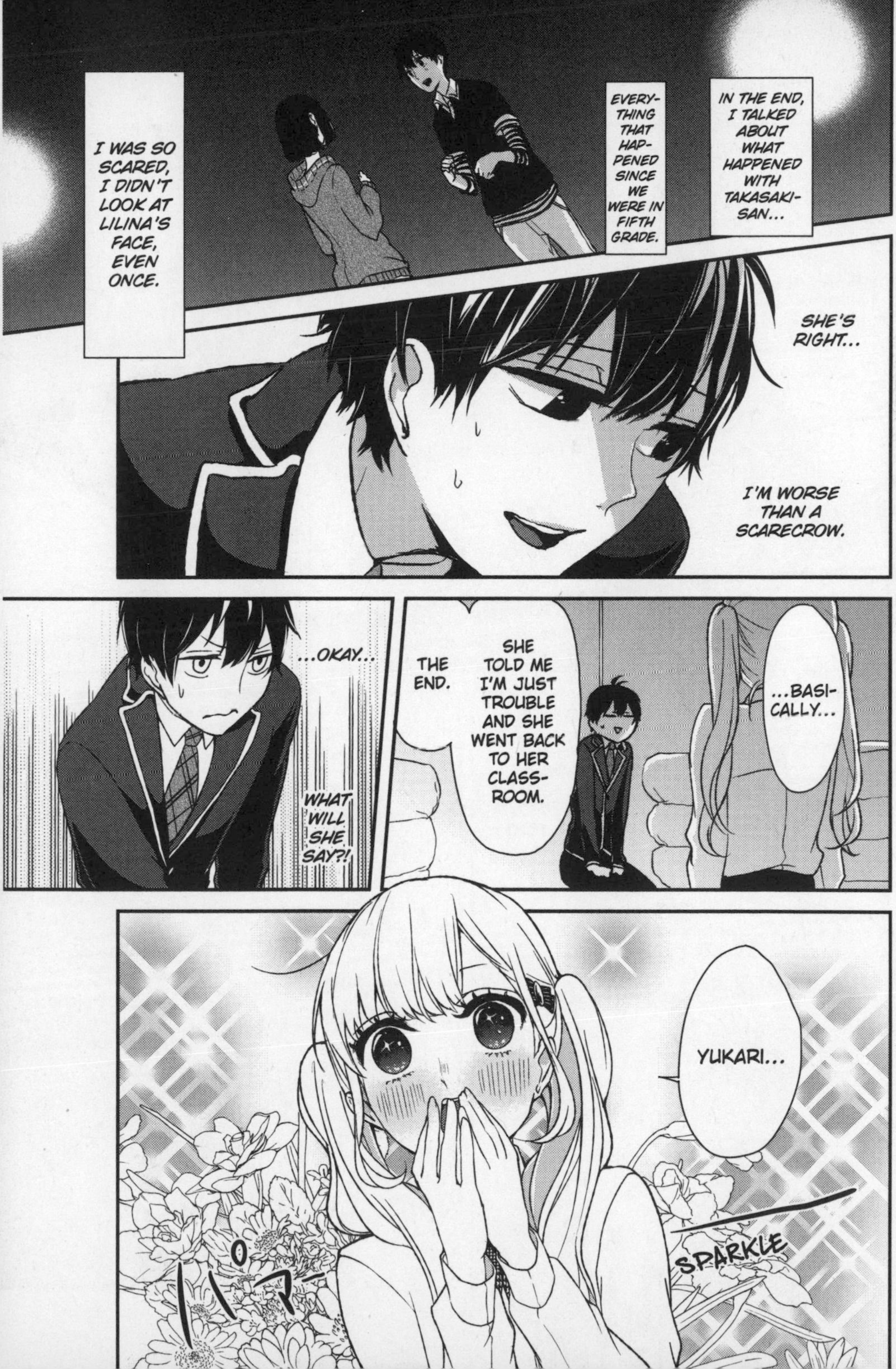
IN THE END, I TALKED ABOUT WHAT HAPPENED WITH TAKASAKI-SAN...
EVERYTHING THAT HAPPENED SINCE WE WERE IN FIFTH GRADE.
I WAS SO SCARED, I DIDN'T LOOK AT LILINA'S FACE, EVEN ONCE.
SHE'S RIGHT...
I'M WORSE THAN A SCARECROW.
...BASICALLY...
SHE TOLD ME I'M JUST TROUBLE AND SHE WENT BACK TO HER CLASSROOM.
THE END.
...OKAY...
WHAT WILL SHE SAY?!
YUKARI...
SPARKLE
パァー

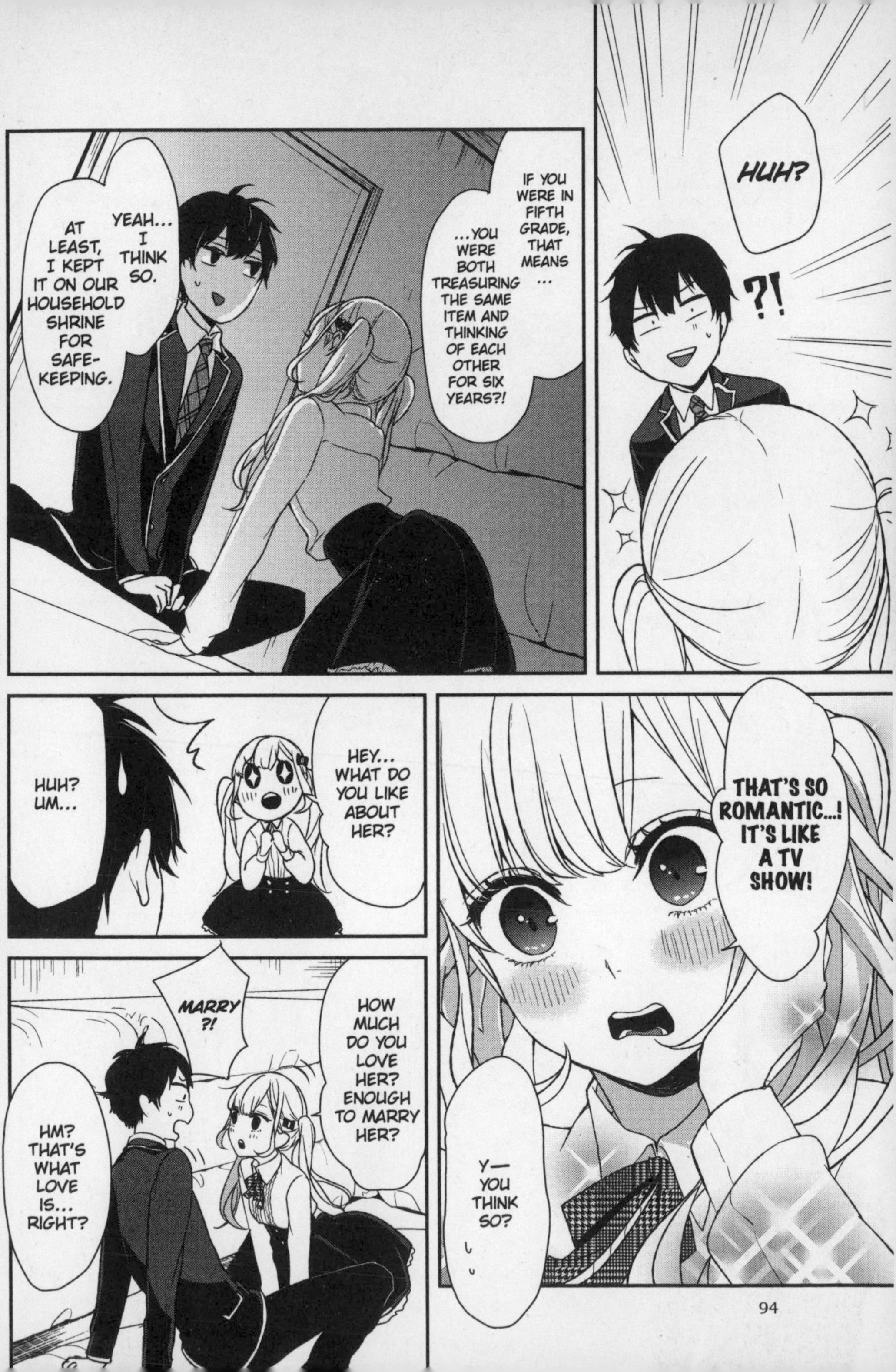
HUH?
?!
IF YOU WERE IN FIFTH GRADE, THAT MEANS... ...YOU WERE BOTH TREASURING THE SAME ITEM AND THINKING OF EACH OTHER FOR SIX YEARS?!
YEAH... I THINK SO. AT LEAST, I KEPT IT ON OUR HOUSEHOLD SHRINE FOR SAFE-KEEPING.
THAT'S SO ROMANTIC...! IT'S LIKE A TV SHOW!
Y— YOU THINK SO?
HEY... WHAT DO YOU LIKE ABOUT HER?
HUH? UM...
HOW MUCH DO YOU LOVE HER? ENOUGH TO MARRY HER?
MARRY ?!
HM? THAT'S WHAT LOVE IS... RIGHT?

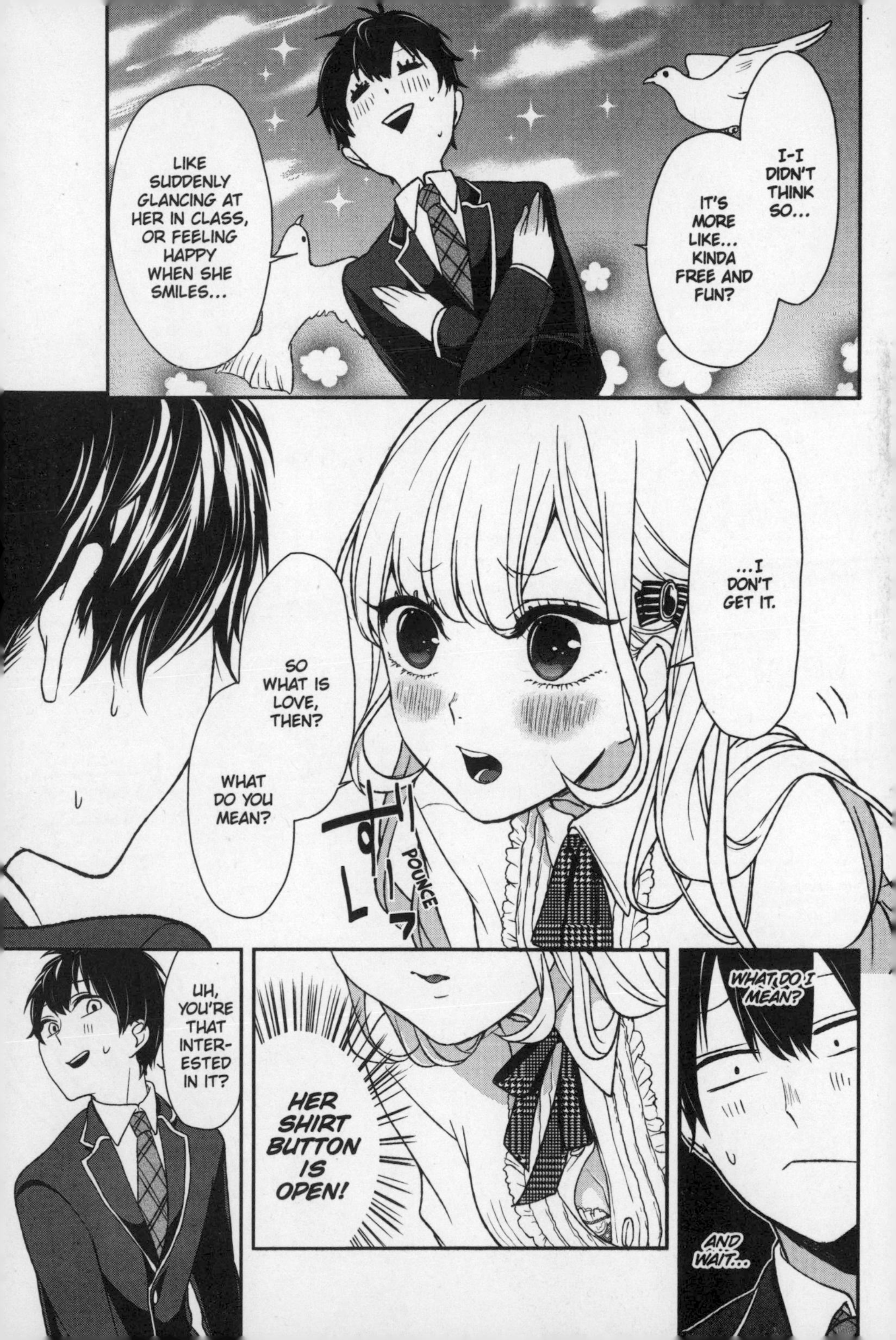
I-I DIDN'T THINK SO...
IT'S MORE LIKE... KINDA FREE AND FUN?
LIKE SUDDENLY GLANCING AT HER IN CLASS, OR FEELING HAPPY WHEN SHE SMILES...
...I DON'T GET IT.
SO WHAT IS LOVE, THEN?
WHAT DO YOU MEAN?
POUNCE
WHAT DO I MEAN?
AND WAIT...
HER SHIRT BUTTON IS OPEN!
UH, YOU'RE THAT INTERESTED IN IT?

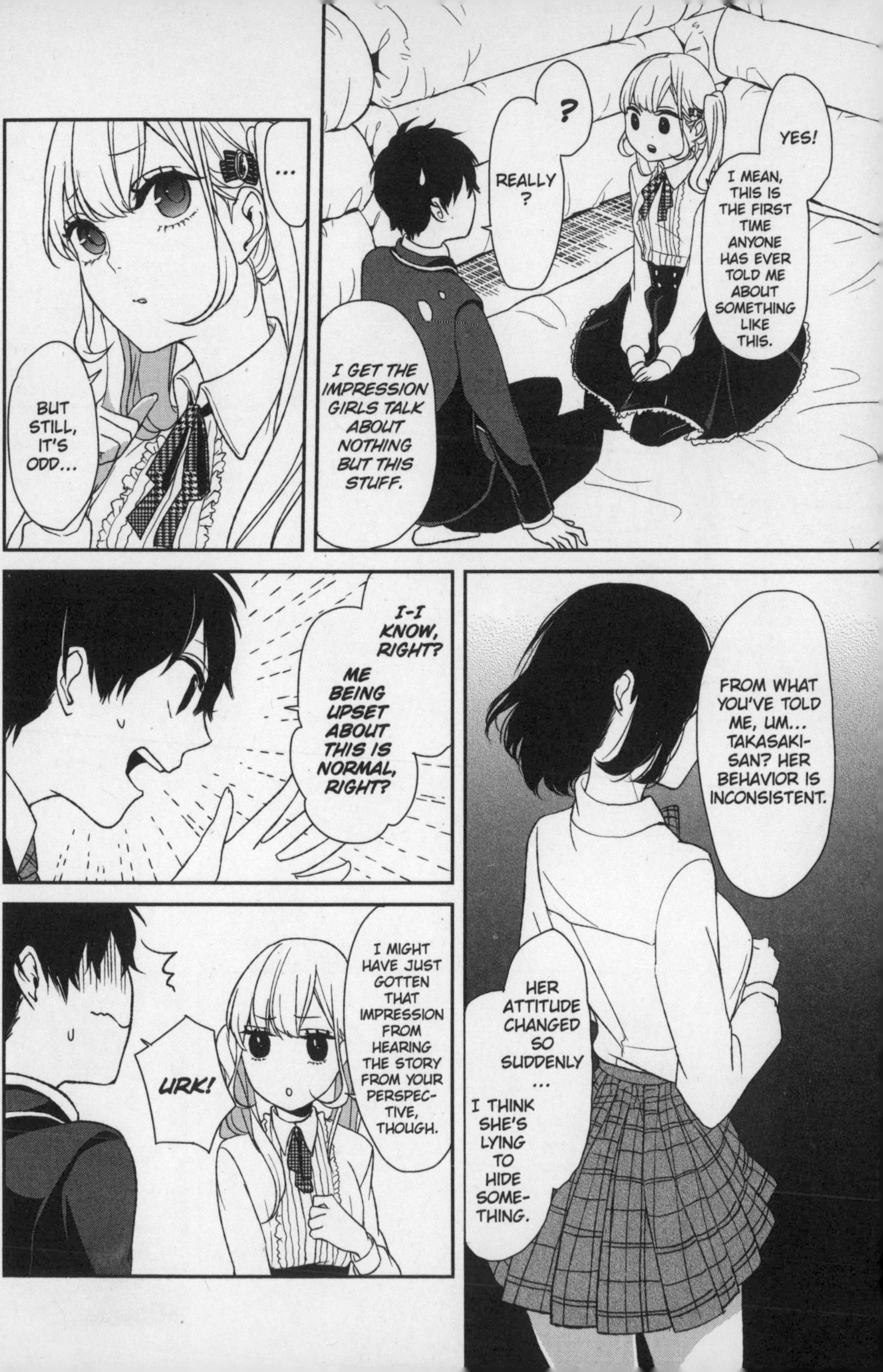
YES!
I MEAN, THIS IS THE FIRST TIME ANYONE HAS EVER TOLD ME ABOUT SOMETHING LIKE THIS.
?
REALLY?
I GET THE IMPRESSION GIRLS TALK ABOUT NOTHING BUT THIS STUFF.
...
BUT STILL, IT'S ODD...
FROM WHAT YOU'VE TOLD ME, UM... TAKASAKI-SAN? HER BEHAVIOR IS INCONSISTENT.
HER ATTITUDE CHANGED SO SUDDENLY...
I THINK SHE'S LYING TO HIDE SOME-THING.
I-I KNOW, RIGHT?
ME BEING UPSET ABOUT THIS IS NORMAL, RIGHT?
I MIGHT HAVE JUST GOTTEN THAT IMPRESSION FROM HEARING THE STORY FROM YOUR PERSPEC-TIVE, THOUGH.
URK!

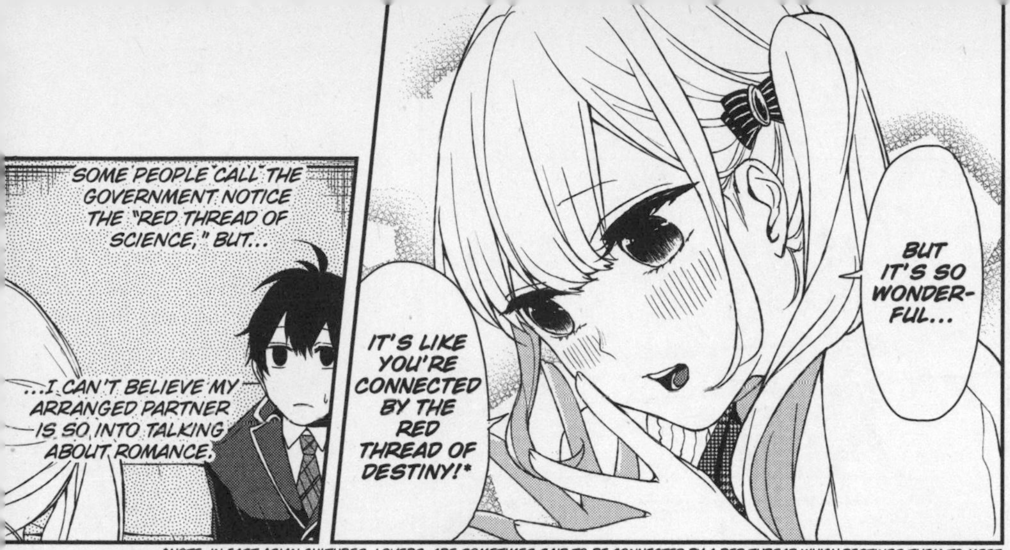
BUT IT'S SO WONDERFUL...
IT'S LIKE YOU'RE CONNECTED BY THE RED THREAD OF DESTINY!*
SOME PEOPLE CALL THE GOVERNMENT NOTICE THE "RED THREAD OF SCIENCE," BUT...
...I CAN'T BELIEVE MY ARRANGED PARTNER IS SO INTO TALKING ABOUT ROMANCE.

*NOTE: IN EAST ASIAN CULTURES, LOVERS ARE SOMETIMES SAID TO BE CONNECTED BY A RED THREAD WHICH DESTINES THEM TO MEET.

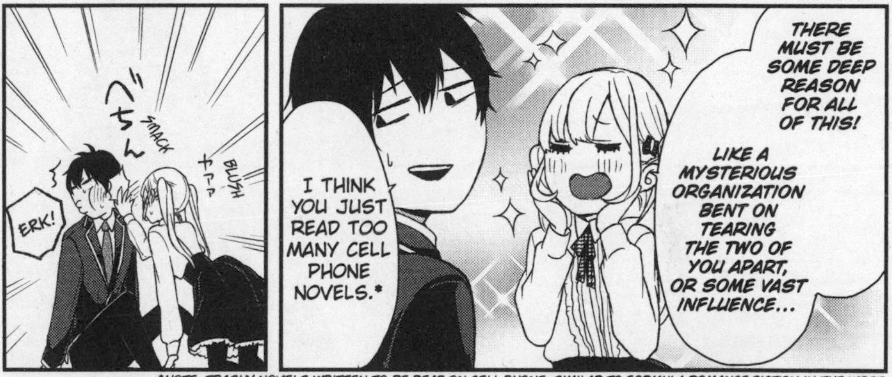
THERE MUST BE SOME DEEP REASON FOR ALL OF THIS!
LIKE A MYSTERIOUS ORGANIZATION BENT ON TEARING THE TWO OF YOU APART, OR SOME VAST INFLUENCE...
I THINK YOU JUST READ TOO MANY CELL PHONE NOVELS.*
べちん
SMACK
BLUSH
ERK!

*NOTE: TRASHY NOVELS WRITTEN TO BE READ ON CELL PHONE, SIMILAR TO FORMULA ROMANCE FICTION IN THE WEST.

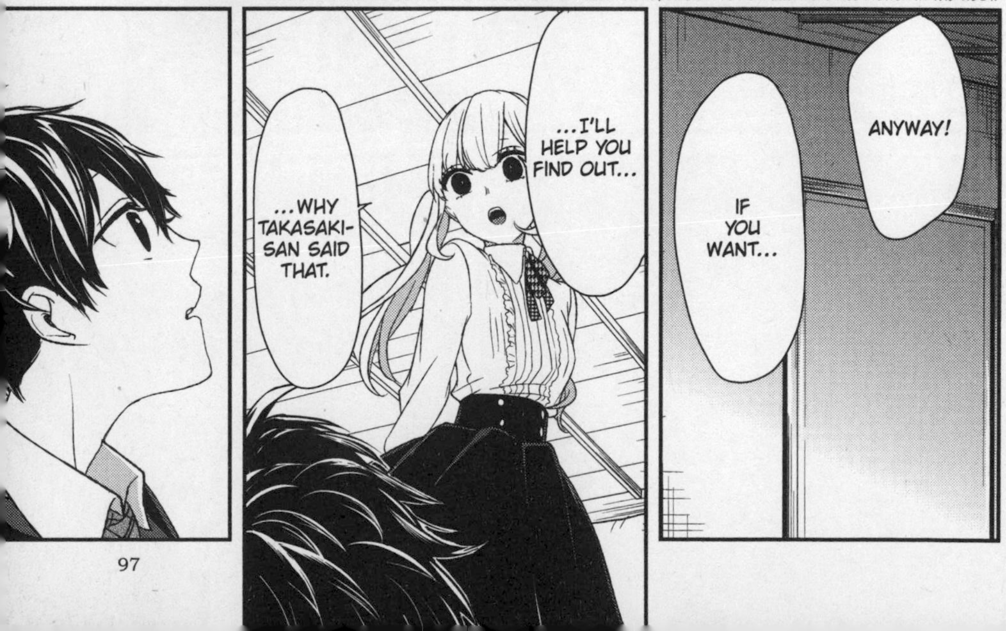
ANYWAY!
IF YOU WANT...
...I'LL HELP YOU FIND OUT...
...WHY TAKASAKI-SAN SAID THAT.

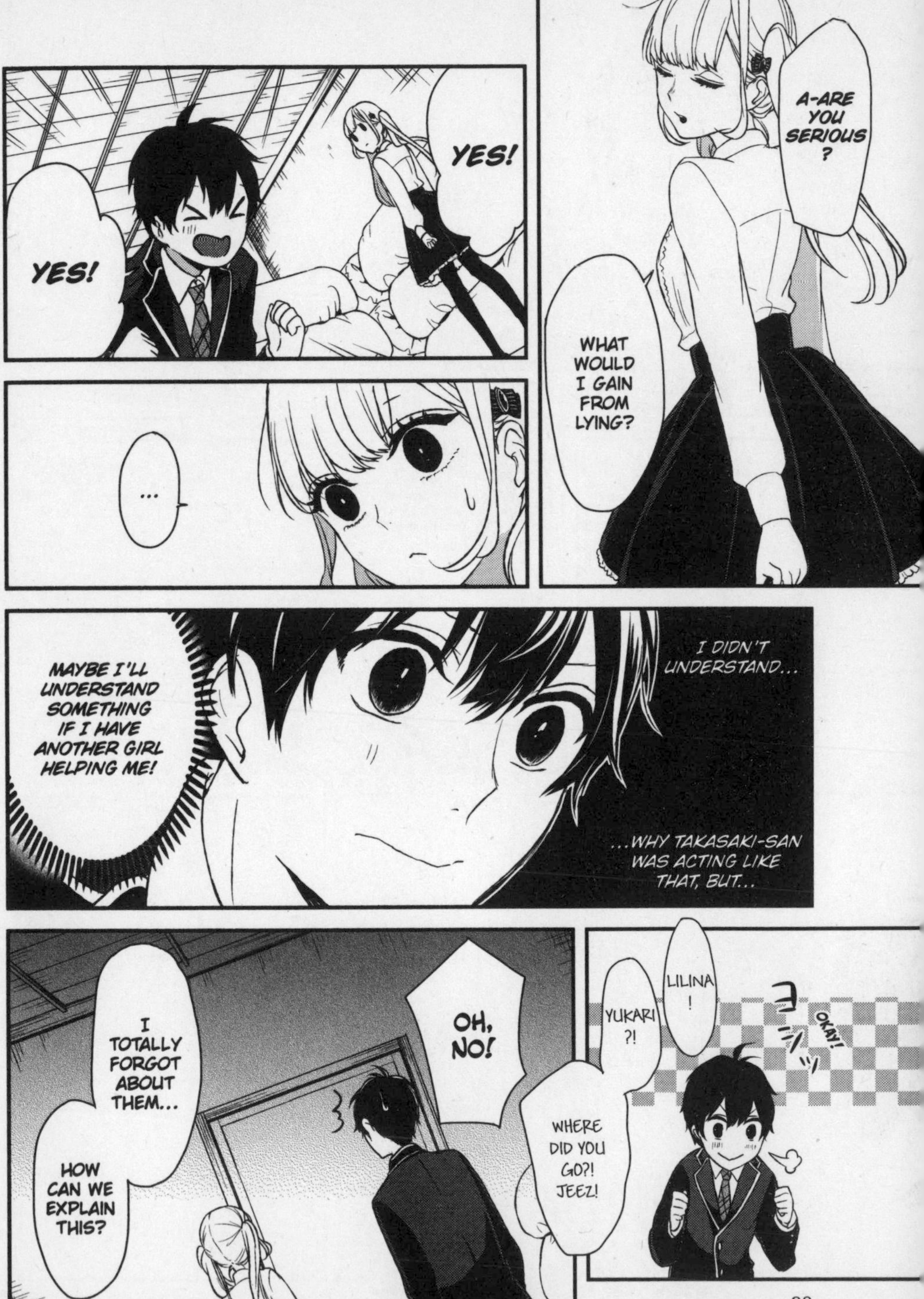
A-ARE YOU SERIOUS?
WHAT WOULD I GAIN FROM LYING?
YES!
YES!
...
I DIDN'T UNDERSTAND...
...WHY TAKASAKI-SAN WAS ACTING LIKE THAT, BUT...
MAYBE I'LL UNDERSTAND SOMETHING IF I HAVE ANOTHER GIRL HELPING ME!
OKAY!
LILINA!
YUKARI?!
WHERE DID YOU GO?! JEEZ!
OH, NO!
I TOTALLY FORGOT ABOUT THEM...
HOW CAN WE EXPLAIN THIS?

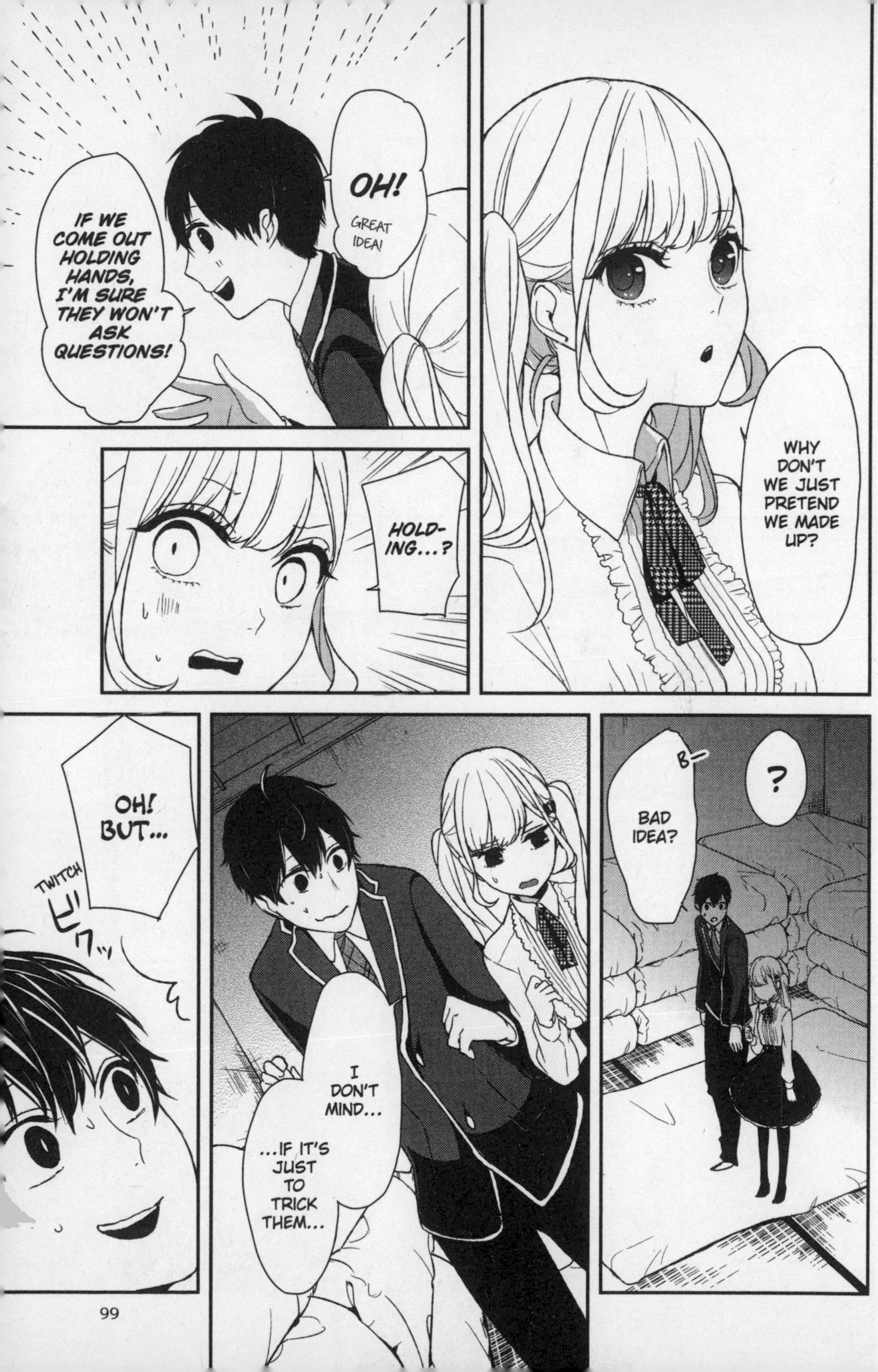
WHY DON'T WE JUST PRETEND WE MADE UP?
OH!
GREAT IDEA!
IF WE COME OUT HOLDING HANDS, I'M SURE THEY WON'T ASK QUESTIONS!
HOLD-ING...?
?
B—
BAD IDEA?
I DON'T MIND...
...IF IT'S JUST TO TRICK THEM...
OH! BUT...
TWITCH
ビクッ

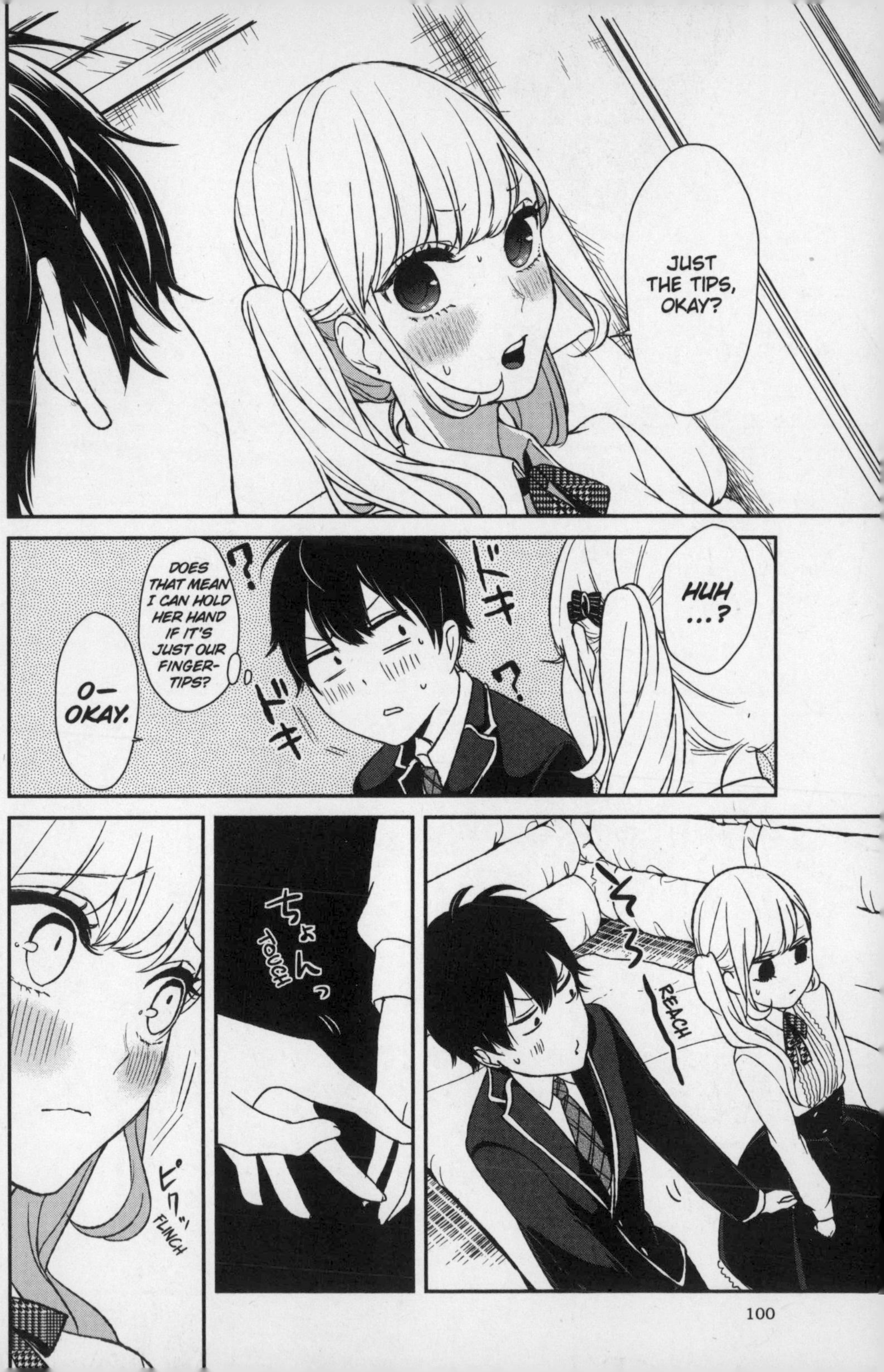
JUST THE TIPS, OKAY?
HUH ...?
ドキ
ドキ
DOES THAT MEAN I CAN HOLD HER HAND IF IT'S JUST OUR FINGER-TIPS?
O-OKAY.
REACH
ちょんっ
TOUCH
ピクッ
FLINCH

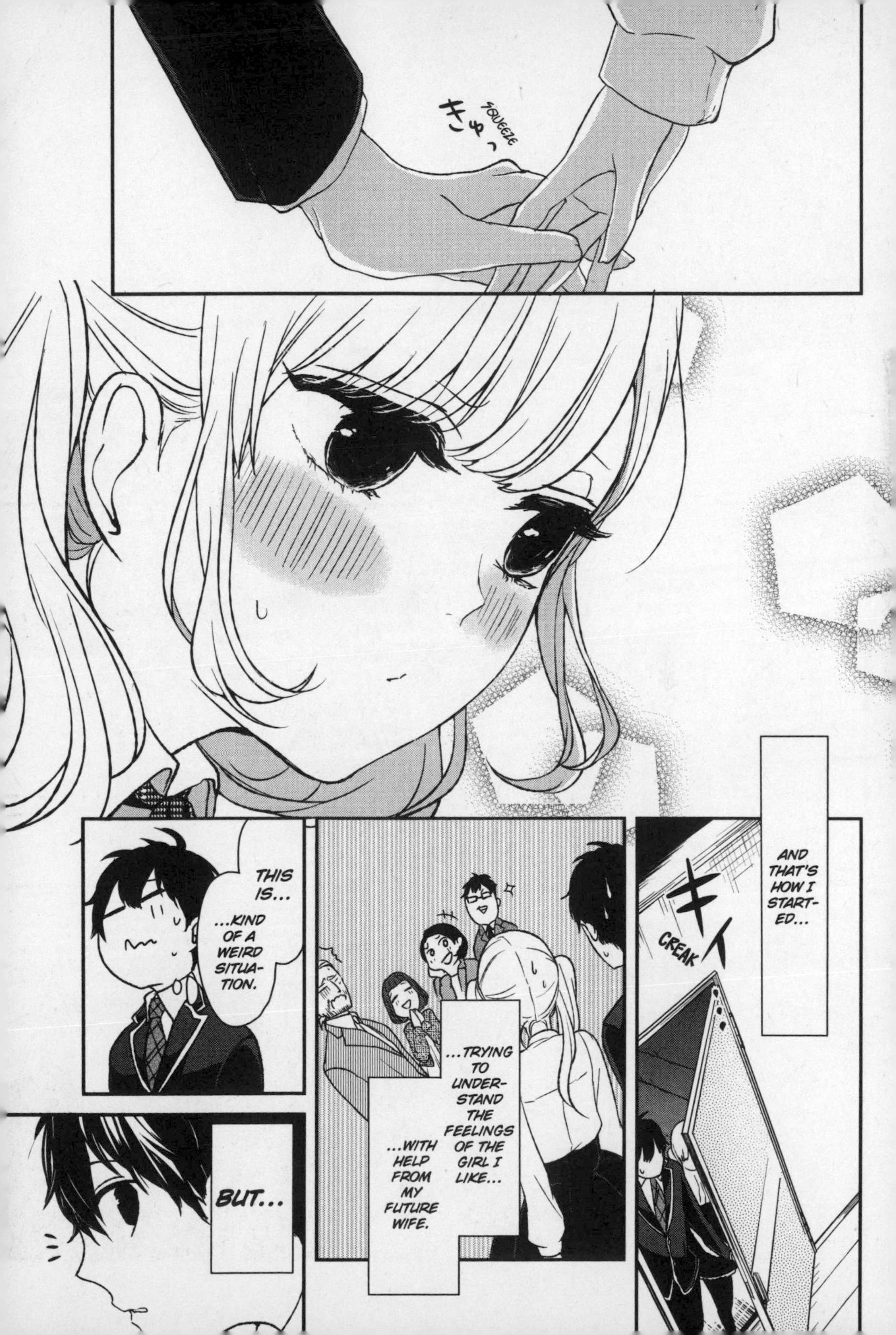
きゅっ
SQUEEZE
キイ
CREAK
AND THAT'S HOW I START-ED...
...TRYING TO UNDER-STAND THE FEELINGS OF THE GIRL I LIKE...
...WITH HELP FROM MY FUTURE WIFE.
THIS IS...
...KIND OF A WEIRD SITUA-TION.
BUT...

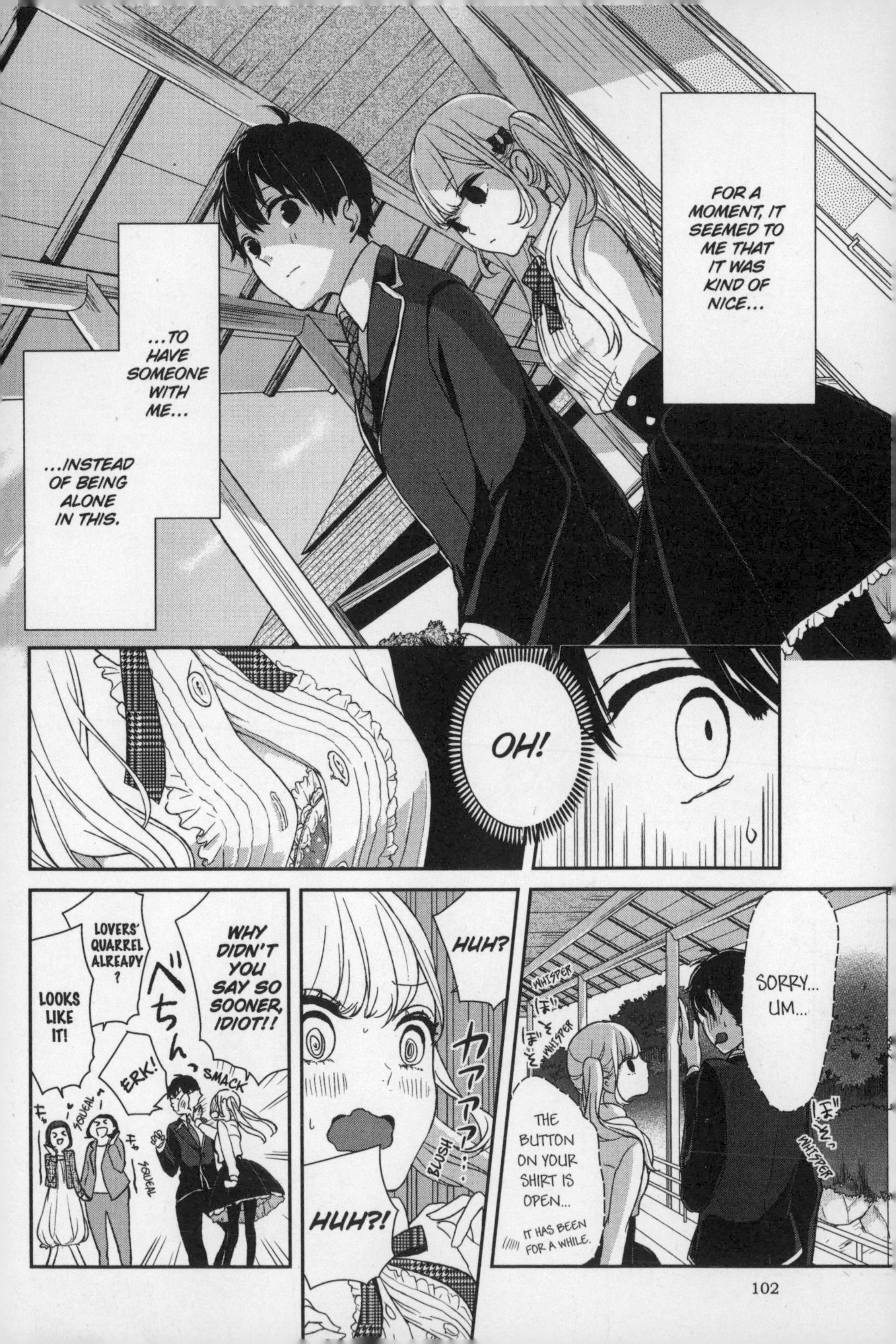
FOR A MOMENT, IT SEEMED TO ME THAT IT WAS KIND OF NICE...
...TO HAVE SOMEONE WITH ME...
...INSTEAD OF BEING ALONE IN THIS.
OH!
WHISPER
WHISPER
SORRY... UM...
WHISPER
THE BUTTON ON YOUR SHIRT IS OPEN...
IT HAS BEEN FOR A WHILE.
HUH?
BLUSH
HUH?!
WHY DIDN'T YOU SAY SO SOONER, IDIOT!!
LOVERS' QUARREL ALREADY?
LOOKS LIKE IT!
SMACK
ERK!
SQUEAL
SQUEAL

Chapter 3: Talk About Love

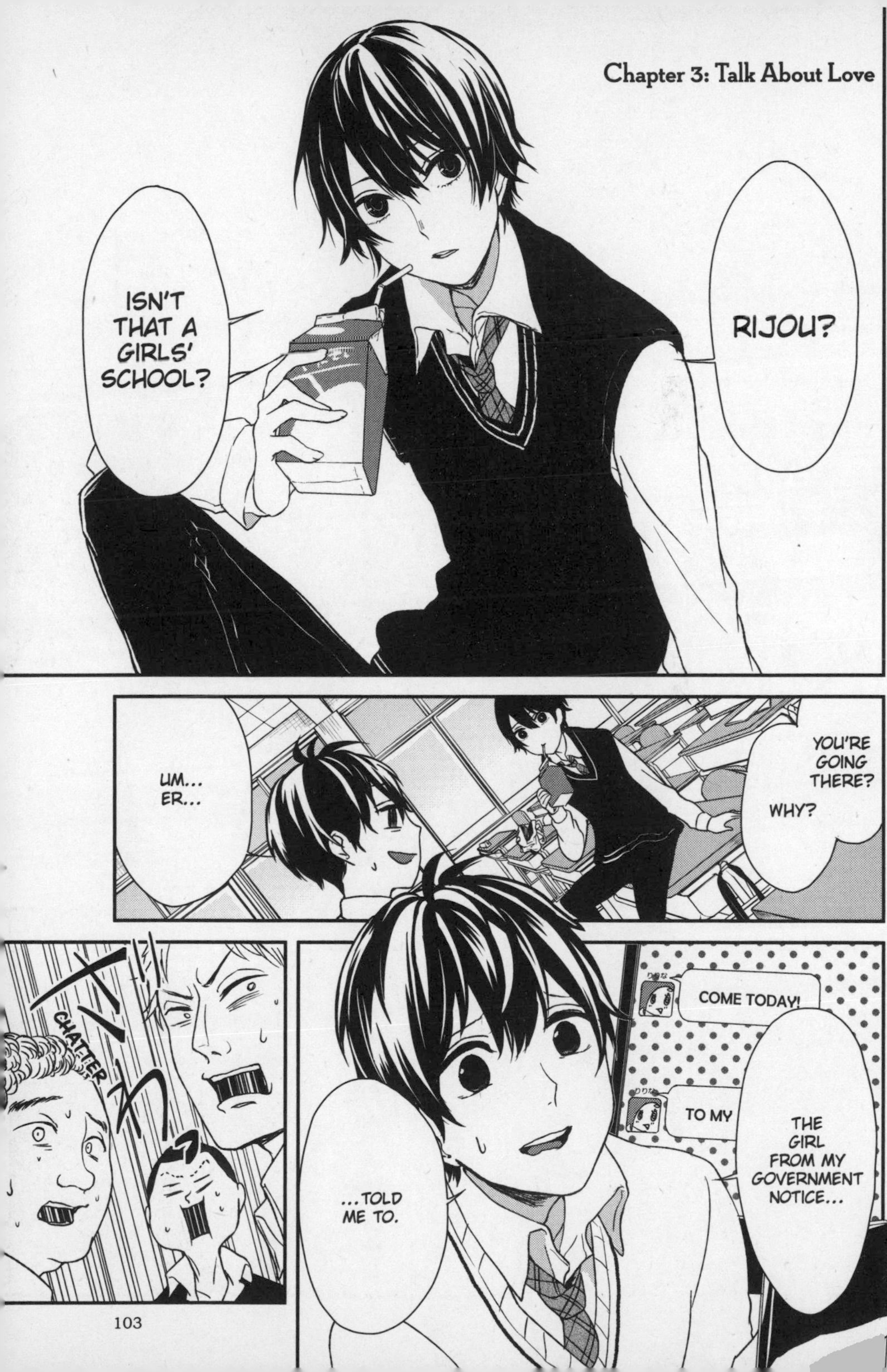
RIJOU?
ISN'T THAT A GIRLS' SCHOOL?
YOU'RE GOING THERE?
WHY?
UM... ER...
COME TODAY!
TO MY
THE GIRL FROM MY GOVERNMENT NOTICE...
...TOLD ME TO.
CHATTER

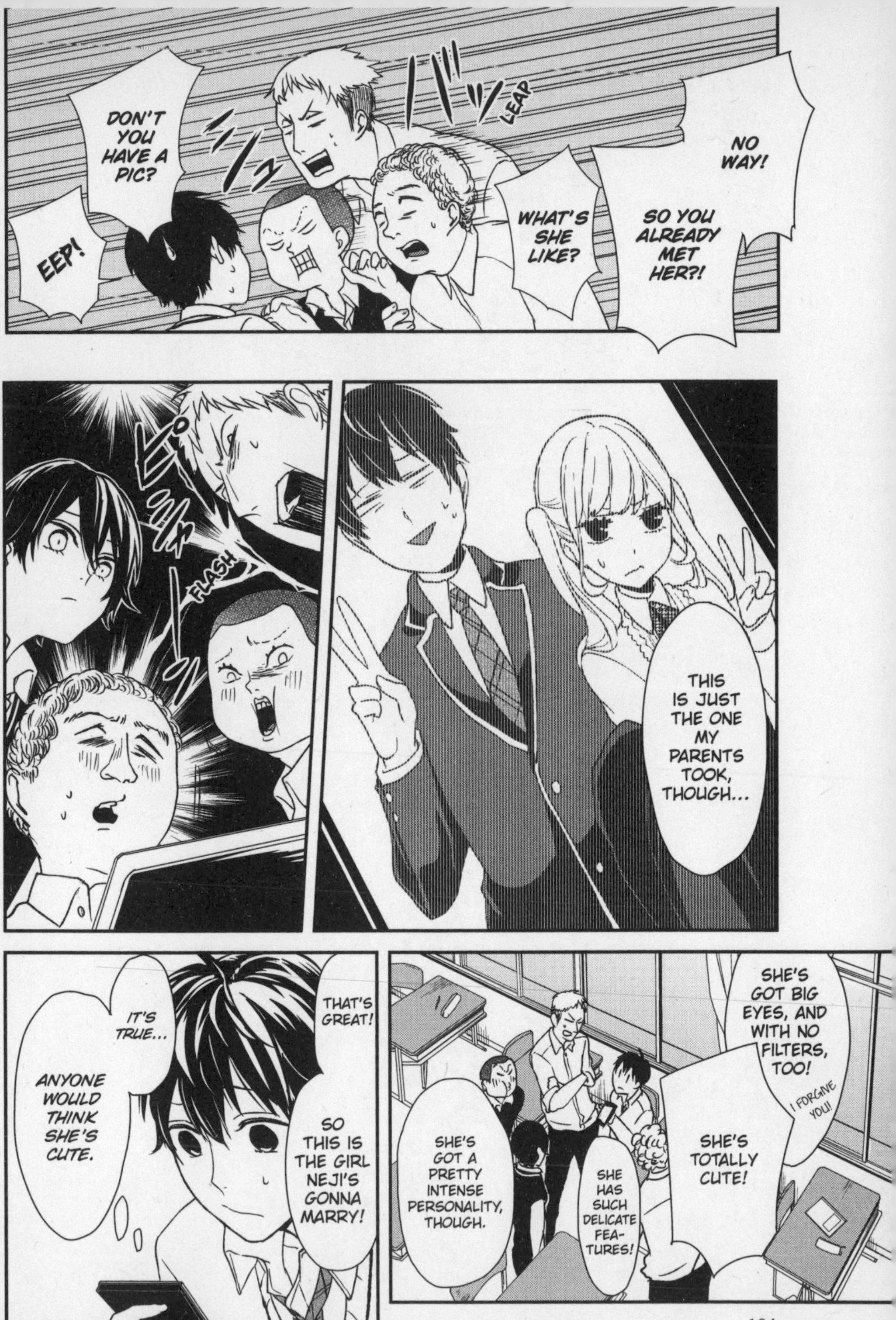
NO WAY!
SO YOU ALREADY MET HER?!
LEAP
WHAT'S SHE LIKE?
DON'T YOU HAVE A PIC?
EEP!
THIS IS JUST THE ONE MY PARENTS TOOK, THOUGH...
FLASH
SHE'S GOT BIG EYES, AND WITH NO FILTERS, TOO!
I FORGIVE YOU!
SHE'S TOTALLY CUTE!
SHE HAS SUCH DELICATE FEA-TURES!
SHE'S GOT A PRETTY INTENSE PERSONALITY, THOUGH.
THAT'S GREAT!
SO THIS IS THE GIRL NEJI'S GONNA MARRY!
IT'S TRUE...
ANYONE WOULD THINK SHE'S CUTE.

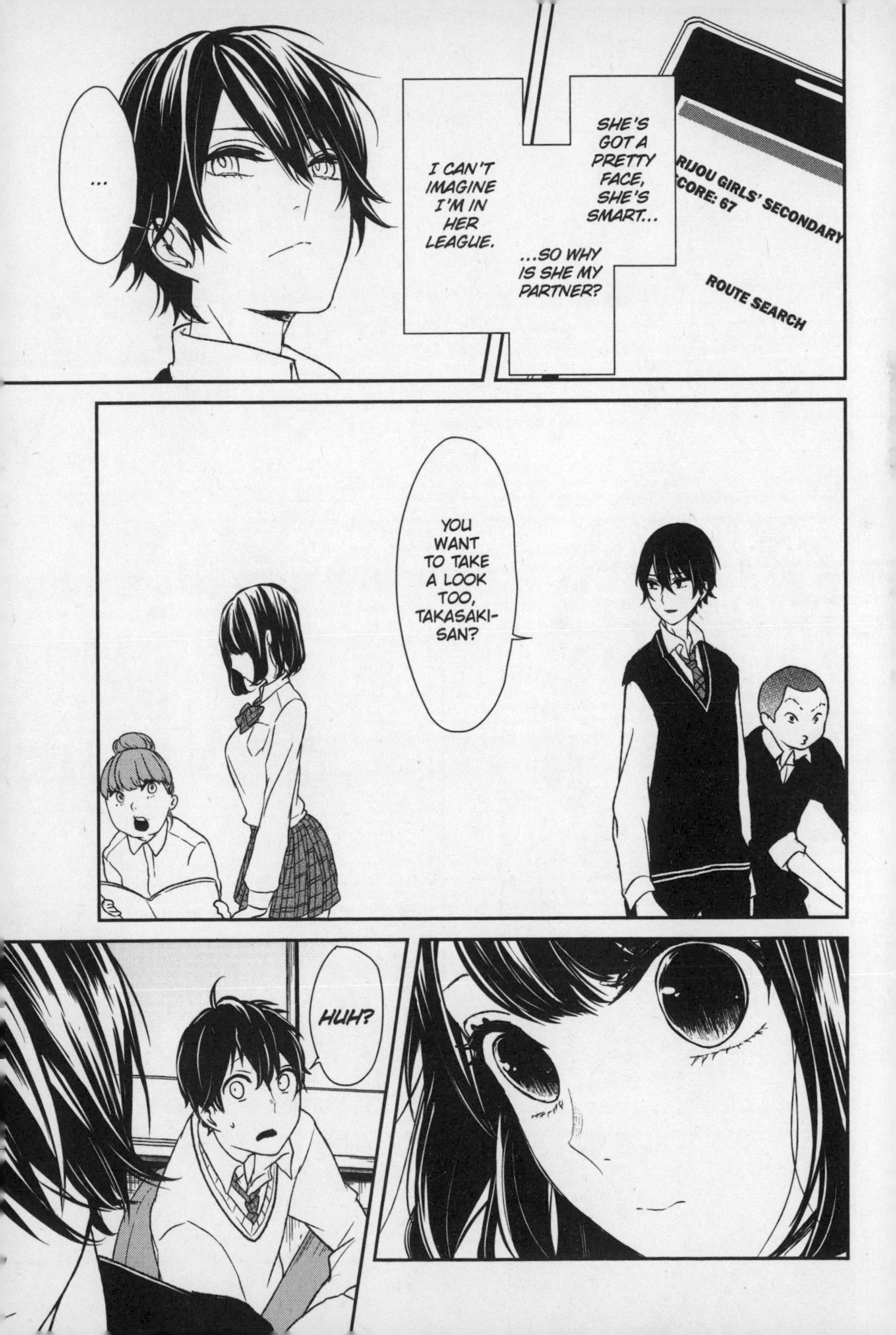
RIJOU GIRLS' SECONDARY
CORE: 67
ROUTE SEARCH
SHE'S GOT A PRETTY FACE, SHE'S SMART...
...SO WHY IS SHE MY PARTNER?
I CAN'T IMAGINE I'M IN HER LEAGUE.
...
YOU WANT TO TAKE A LOOK TOO, TAKASAKI-SAN?
HUH?

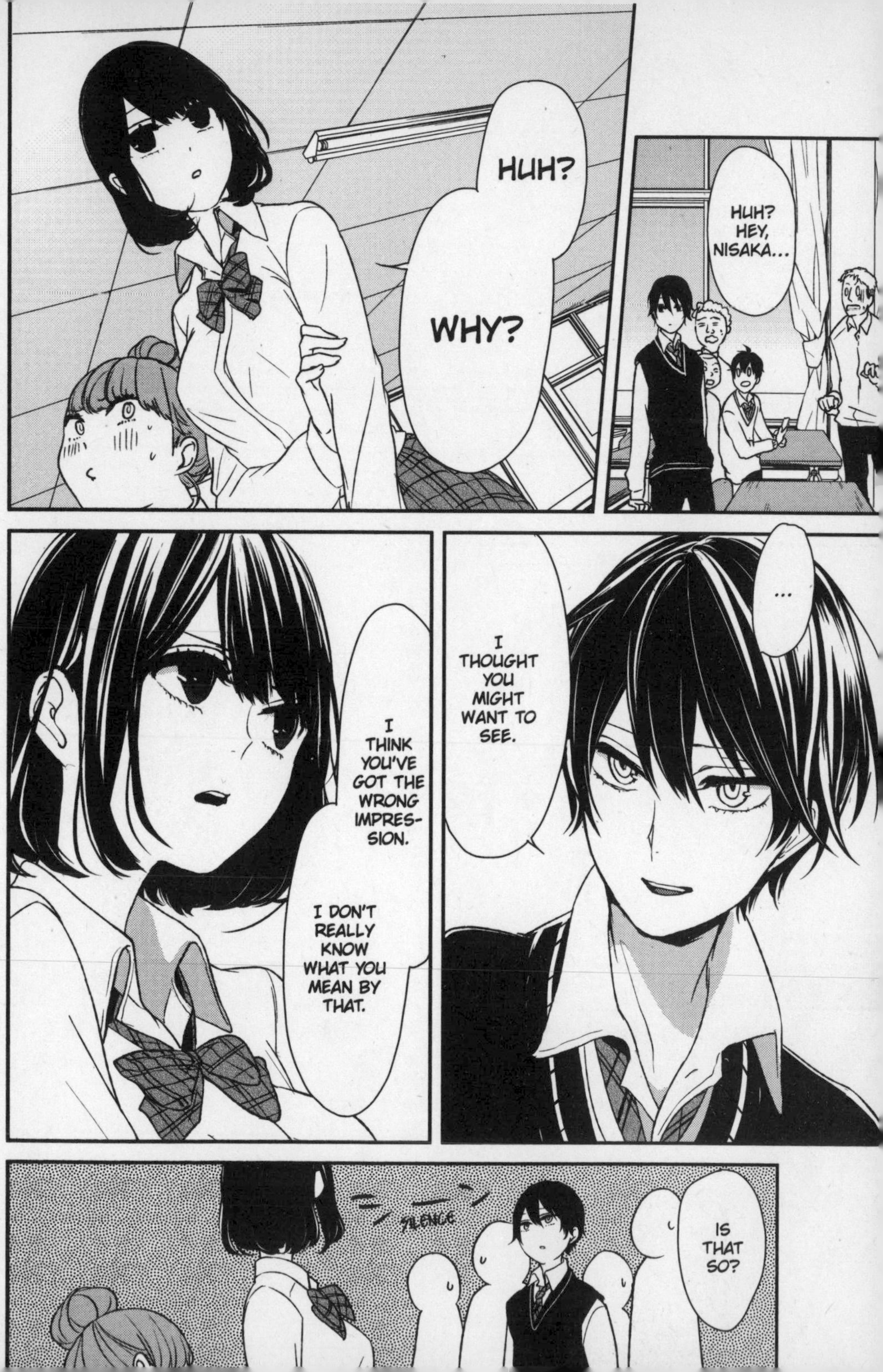
HUH? HEY, NISAKA...
HUH?
WHY?
...
I THOUGHT YOU MIGHT WANT TO SEE.
I THINK YOU'VE GOT THE WRONG IMPRES-SION.
I DON'T REALLY KNOW WHAT YOU MEAN BY THAT.
IS THAT SO?
SILENCE

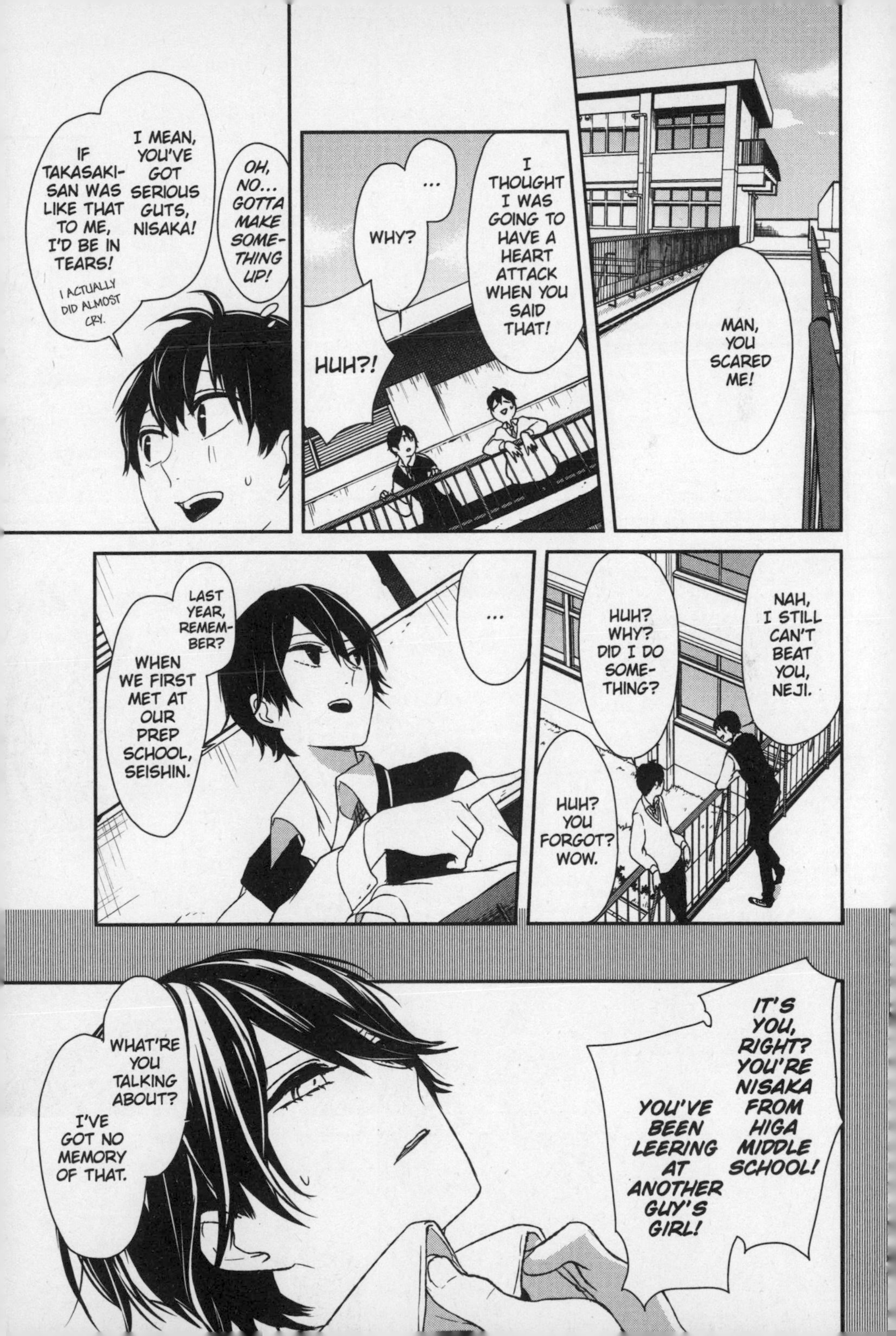
MAN, YOU SCARED ME!
I THOUGHT I WAS GOING TO HAVE A HEART ATTACK WHEN YOU SAID THAT!
...
WHY?
HUH?!
OH, NO... GOTTA MAKE SOMETHING UP!
I MEAN, YOU'VE GOT SERIOUS GUTS, NISAKA!
IF TAKASAKI-SAN WAS LIKE THAT TO ME, I'D BE IN TEARS!
I ACTUALLY DID ALMOST CRY.
NAH, I STILL CAN'T BEAT YOU, NEJI.
HUH? WHY? DID I DO SOMETHING?
HUH? YOU FORGOT? WOW.
...
LAST YEAR, REMEMBER?
WHEN WE FIRST MET AT OUR PREP SCHOOL, SEISHIN.
IT'S YOU, RIGHT? YOU'RE NISAKA FROM HIGA MIDDLE SCHOOL!
YOU'VE BEEN LEERING AT ANOTHER GUY'S GIRL!
WHAT'RE YOU TALKING ABOUT?
I'VE GOT NO MEMORY OF THAT.

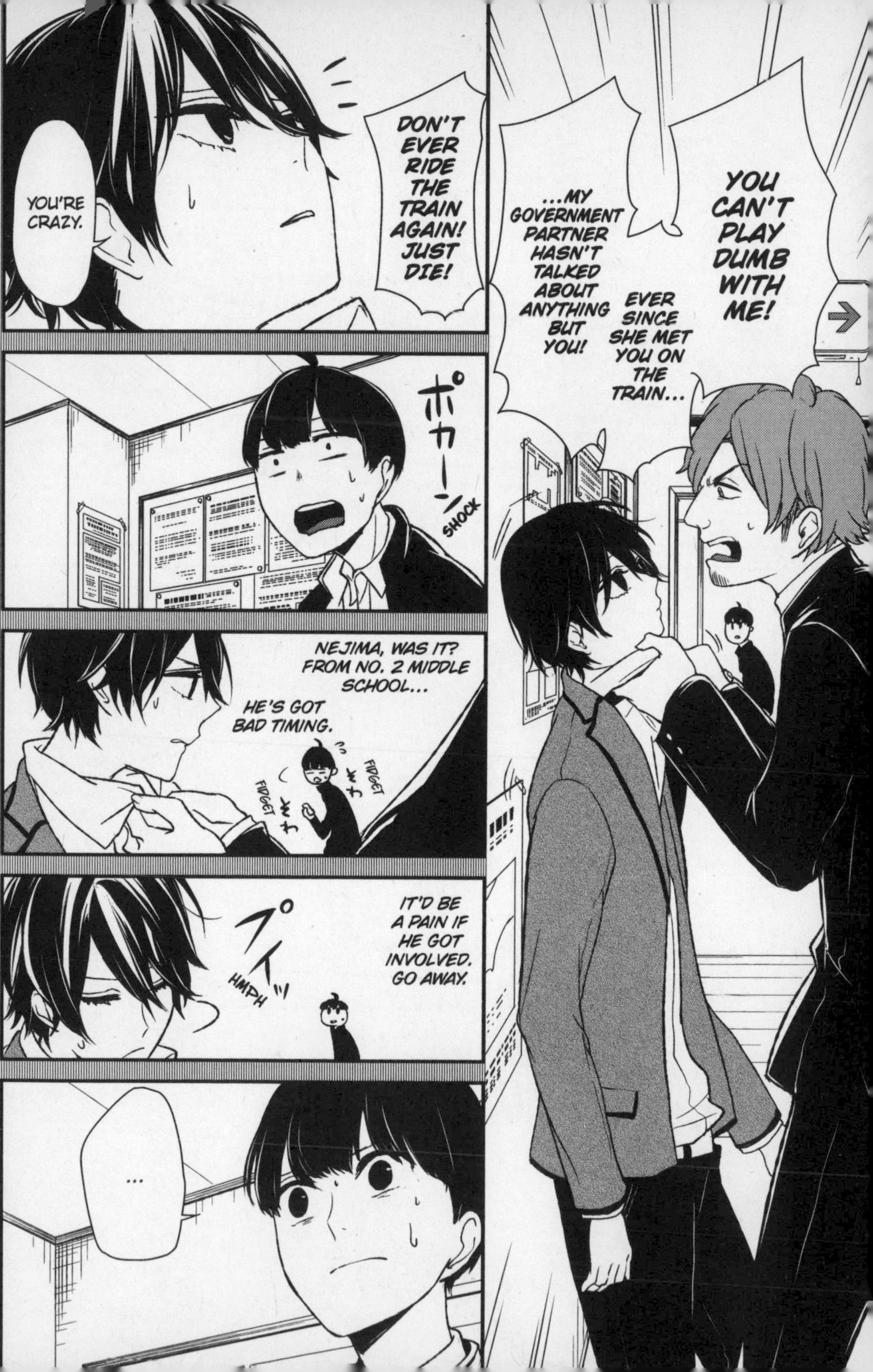
YOU CAN'T PLAY DUMB WITH ME!
EVER SINCE SHE MET YOU ON THE TRAIN...
...MY GOVERNMENT PARTNER HASN'T TALKED ABOUT ANYTHING BUT YOU!
DON'T EVER RIDE THE TRAIN AGAIN! JUST DIE!
YOU'RE CRAZY.
ポカーン
SHOCK
NEJIMA, WAS IT? FROM NO. 2 MIDDLE SCHOOL...
HE'S GOT BAD TIMING.
そわ
FIDGET
そわ
FIDGET
IT'D BE A PAIN IF HE GOT INVOLVED. GO AWAY.
プイッ
HMPH
...

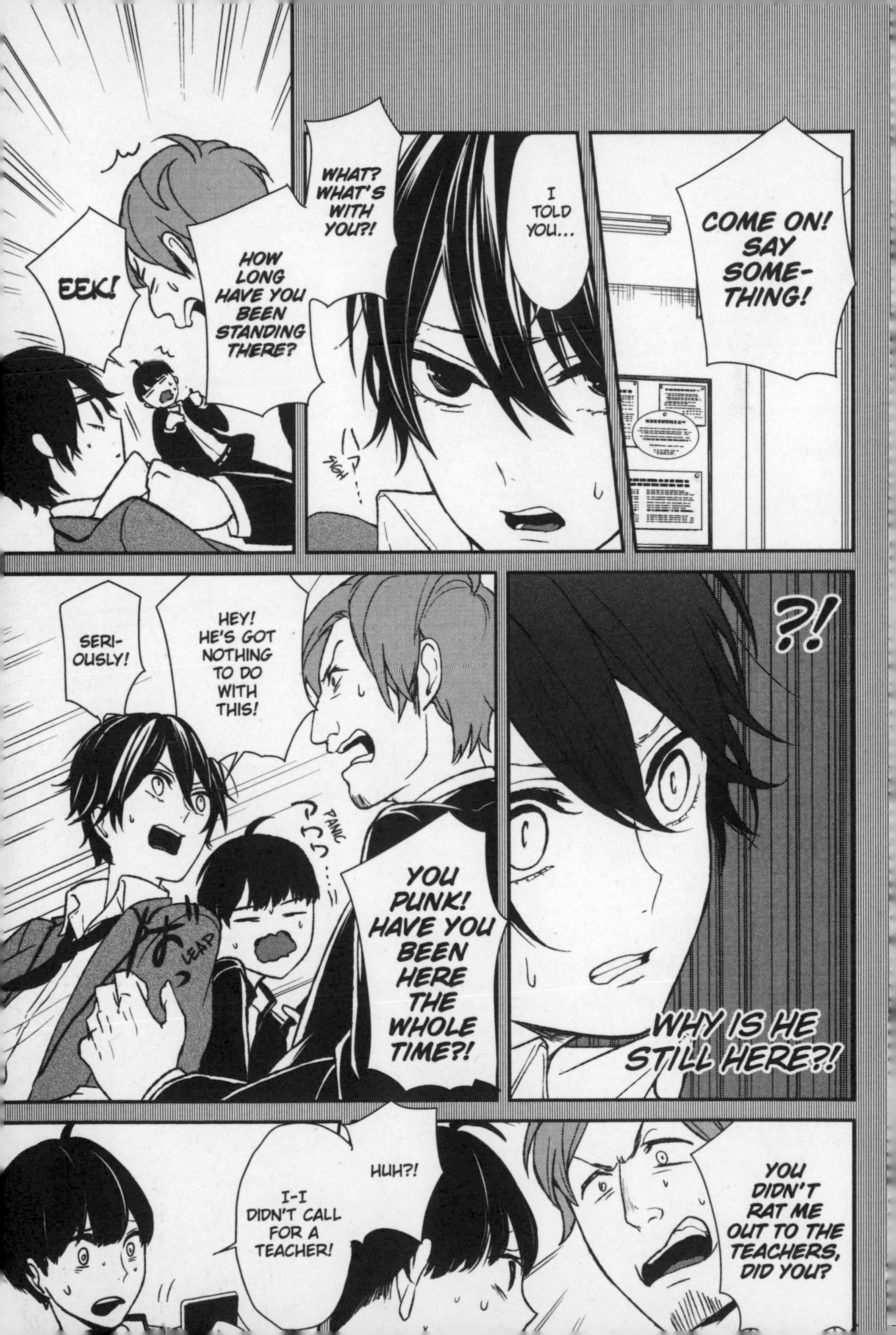
COME ON! SAY SOME-THING!
I TOLD YOU...
SIGH
WHAT? WHAT'S WITH YOU?!
HOW LONG HAVE YOU BEEN STANDING THERE?
EEK!
?!
WHY IS HE STILL HERE?!
YOU PUNK! HAVE YOU BEEN HERE THE WHOLE TIME?!
PANIC
HEY! HE'S GOT NOTHING TO DO WITH THIS!
SERI-OUSLY!
LEAP
YOU DIDN'T RAT ME OUT TO THE TEACHERS, DID YOU?
HUH?!
I-I DIDN'T CALL FOR A TEACHER!

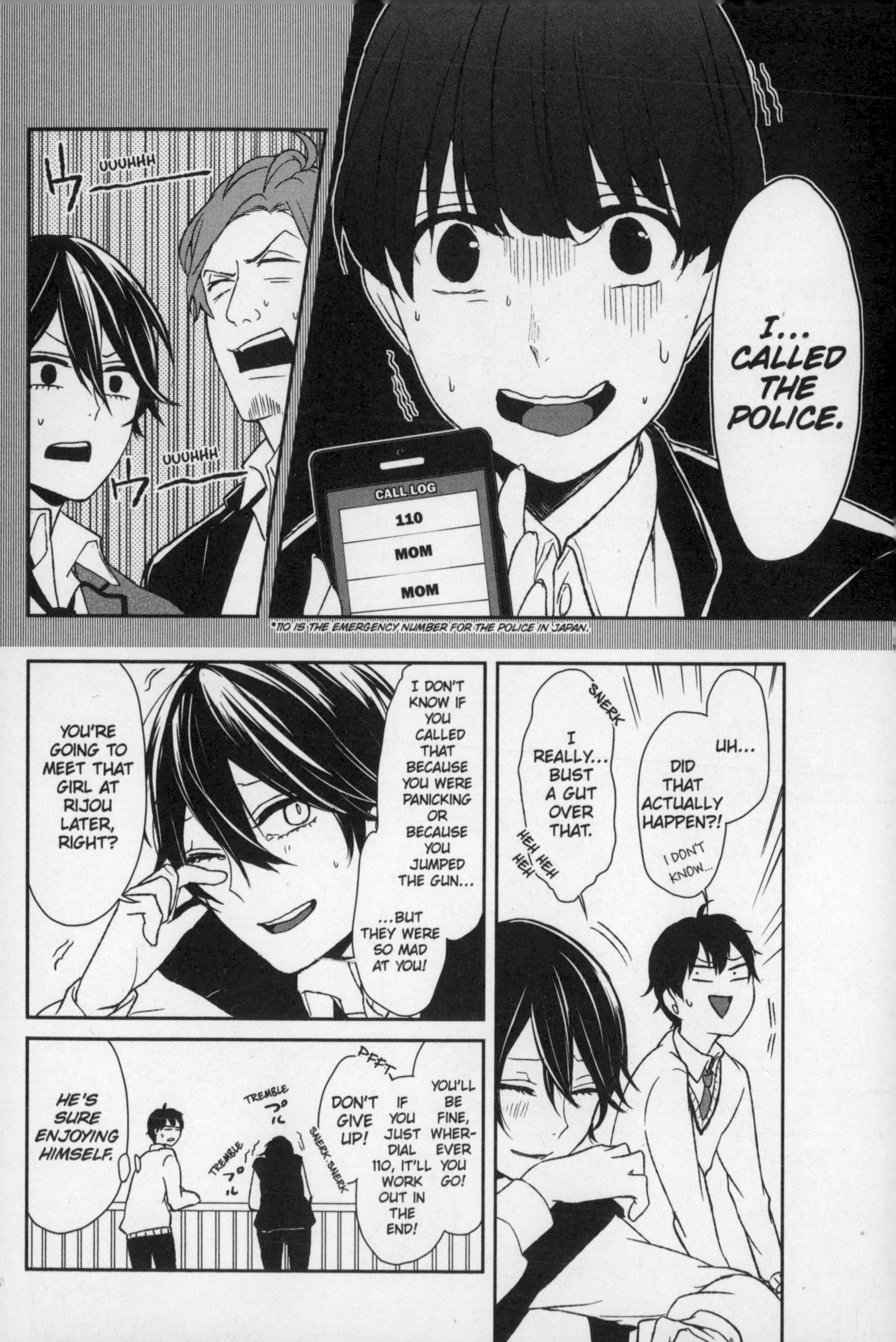
I... CALLED THE POLICE.
CALL LOG
110
MOM
MOM
UUUHHH
UUUHHH
*110 IS THE EMERGENCY NUMBER FOR THE POLICE IN JAPAN.
UH...
DID THAT ACTUALLY HAPPEN?!
I DON'T KNOW...
SNERK
I REALLY... BUST A GUT OVER THAT.
HEH HEH HEH
I DON'T KNOW IF YOU CALLED THAT BECAUSE YOU WERE PANICKING OR BECAUSE YOU JUMPED THE GUN...
...BUT THEY WERE SO MAD AT YOU!
YOU'RE GOING TO MEET THAT GIRL AT RIJOU LATER, RIGHT?
PFFT
YOU'LL BE FINE, WHER-EVER YOU GO!
IF YOU JUST DIAL 110, IT'LL WORK OUT IN THE END!
DON'T GIVE UP!
SNERK SNERK
TREMBLE
TREMBLE
HE'S SURE ENJOYING HIMSELF.

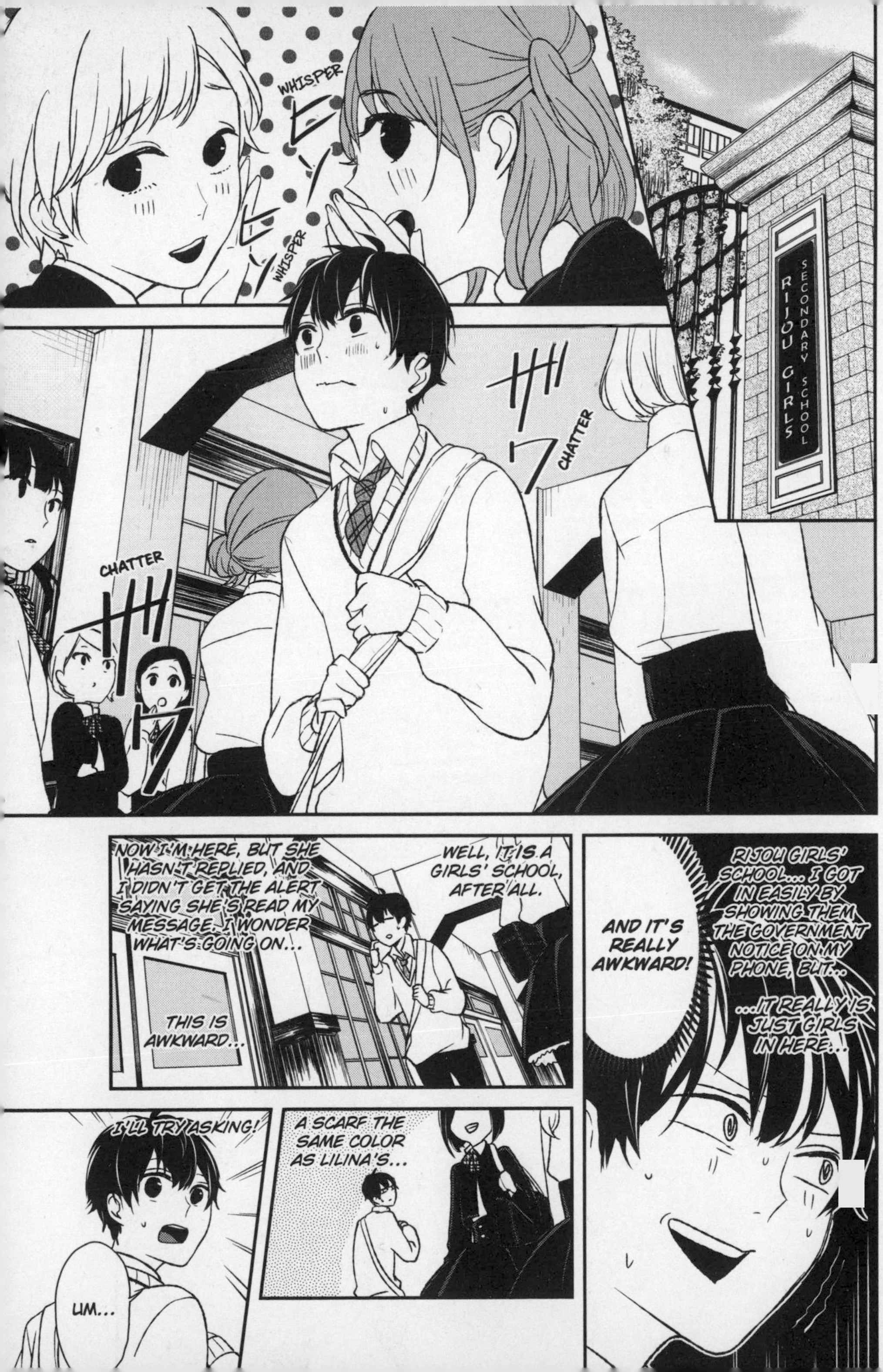

RIJOU GIRLS
SECONDARY SCHOOL
WHISPER
WHISPER
CHATTER
CHATTER
RIJOU GIRLS' SCHOOL... I GOT IN EASILY BY SHOWING THEM THE GOVERNMENT NOTICE ON MY PHONE, BUT...
...IT REALLY IS JUST GIRLS IN HERE...
AND IT'S REALLY AWKWARD!
WELL, IT IS A GIRLS' SCHOOL, AFTER ALL.
NOW I'M HERE, BUT SHE HASN'T REPLIED, AND I DIDN'T GET THE ALERT SAYING SHE'S READ MY MESSAGE. I WONDER WHAT'S GOING ON...
THIS IS AWKWARD...
A SCARF THE SAME COLOR AS LILINA'S...
I'LL TRY ASKING!
UM...

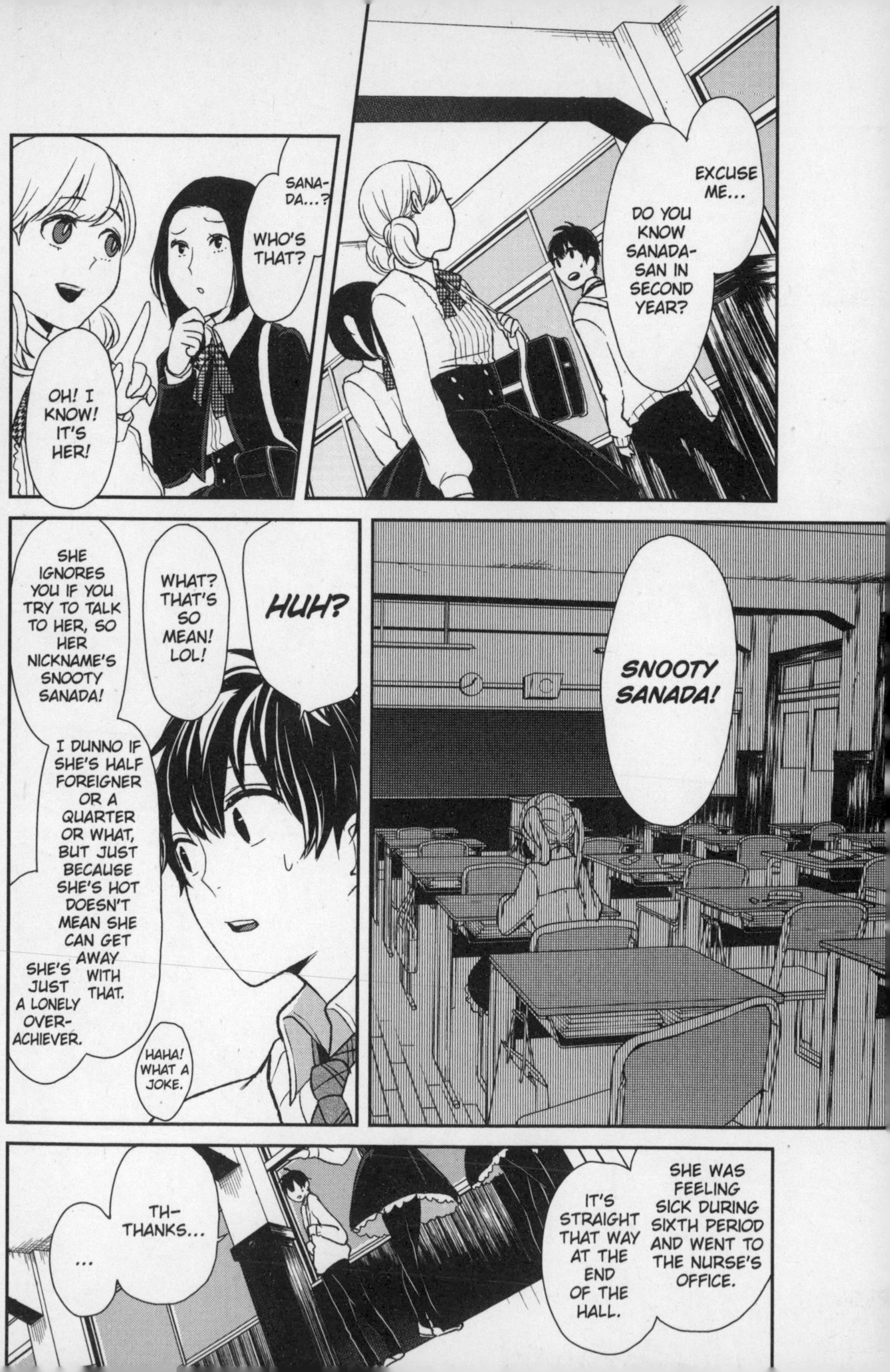
EXCUSE ME...
DO YOU KNOW SANADA-SAN IN SECOND YEAR?
SANADA...?
WHO'S THAT?
OH! I KNOW! IT'S HER!
SNOOTY SANADA!
HUH?
WHAT? THAT'S SO MEAN! LOL!
SHE IGNORES YOU IF YOU TRY TO TALK TO HER, SO HER NICKNAME'S SNOOTY SANADA!
I DUNNO IF SHE'S HALF FOREIGNER OR A QUARTER OR WHAT, BUT JUST BECAUSE SHE'S HOT DOESN'T MEAN SHE CAN GET AWAY WITH THAT.
SHE'S JUST A LONELY OVER-ACHIEVER.
HAHA! WHAT A JOKE.
SHE WAS FEELING SICK DURING SIXTH PERIOD AND WENT TO THE NURSE'S OFFICE.
IT'S STRAIGHT THAT WAY AT THE END OF THE HALL.
TH-THANKS...
...

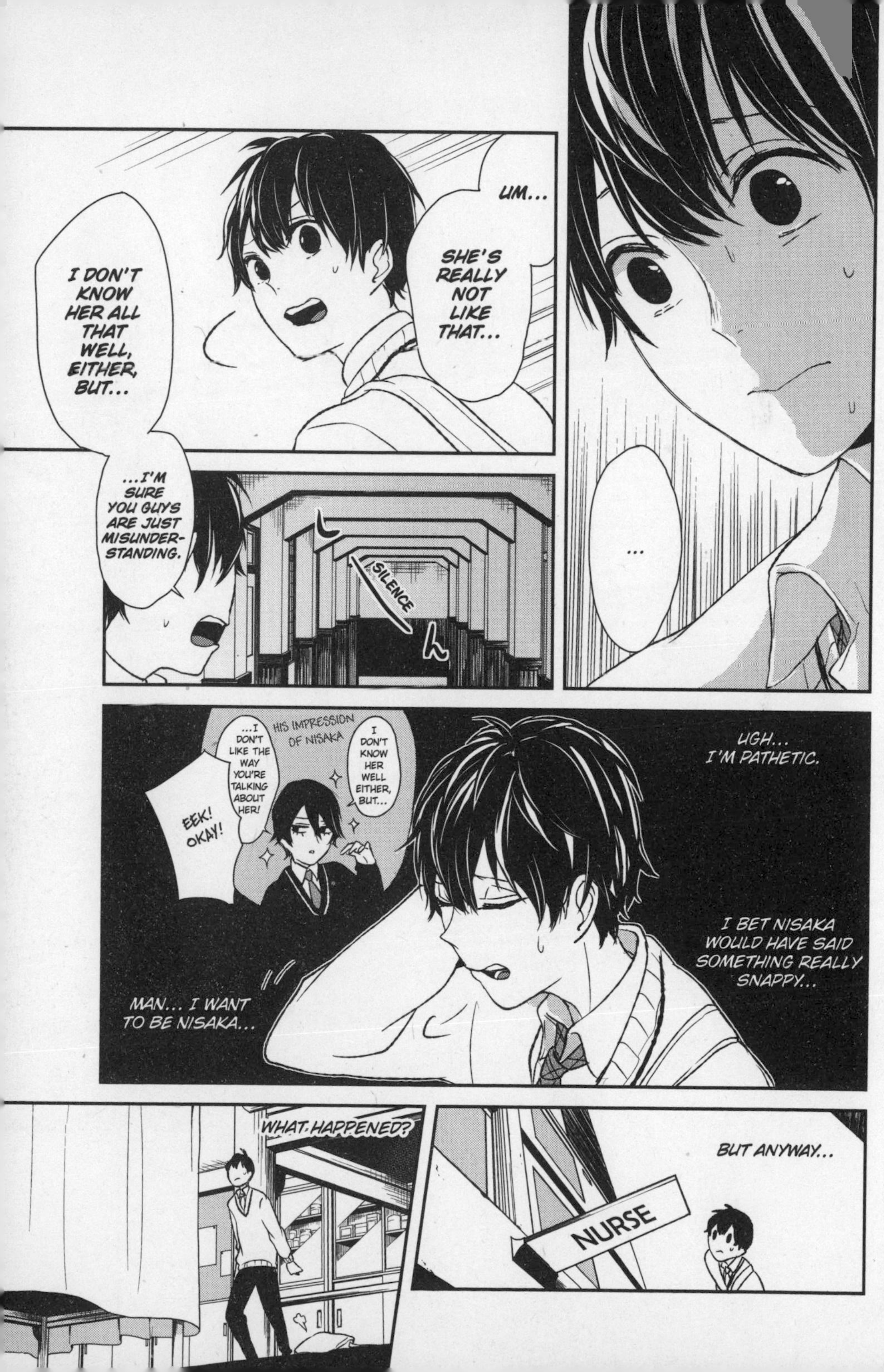
...
UM...
SHE'S REALLY NOT LIKE THAT...
I DON'T KNOW HER ALL THAT WELL, EITHER, BUT...
...I'M SURE YOU GUYS ARE JUST MISUNDERSTANDING.
SILENCE
UGH... I'M PATHETIC.
HIS IMPRESSION OF NISAKA
I DON'T KNOW HER WELL EITHER, BUT...
...I DON'T LIKE THE WAY YOU'RE TALKING ABOUT HER!
EEK! OKAY!
I BET NISAKA WOULD HAVE SAID SOMETHING REALLY SNAPPY...
MAN... I WANT TO BE NISAKA...
BUT ANYWAY...
NURSE
WHAT HAPPENED?

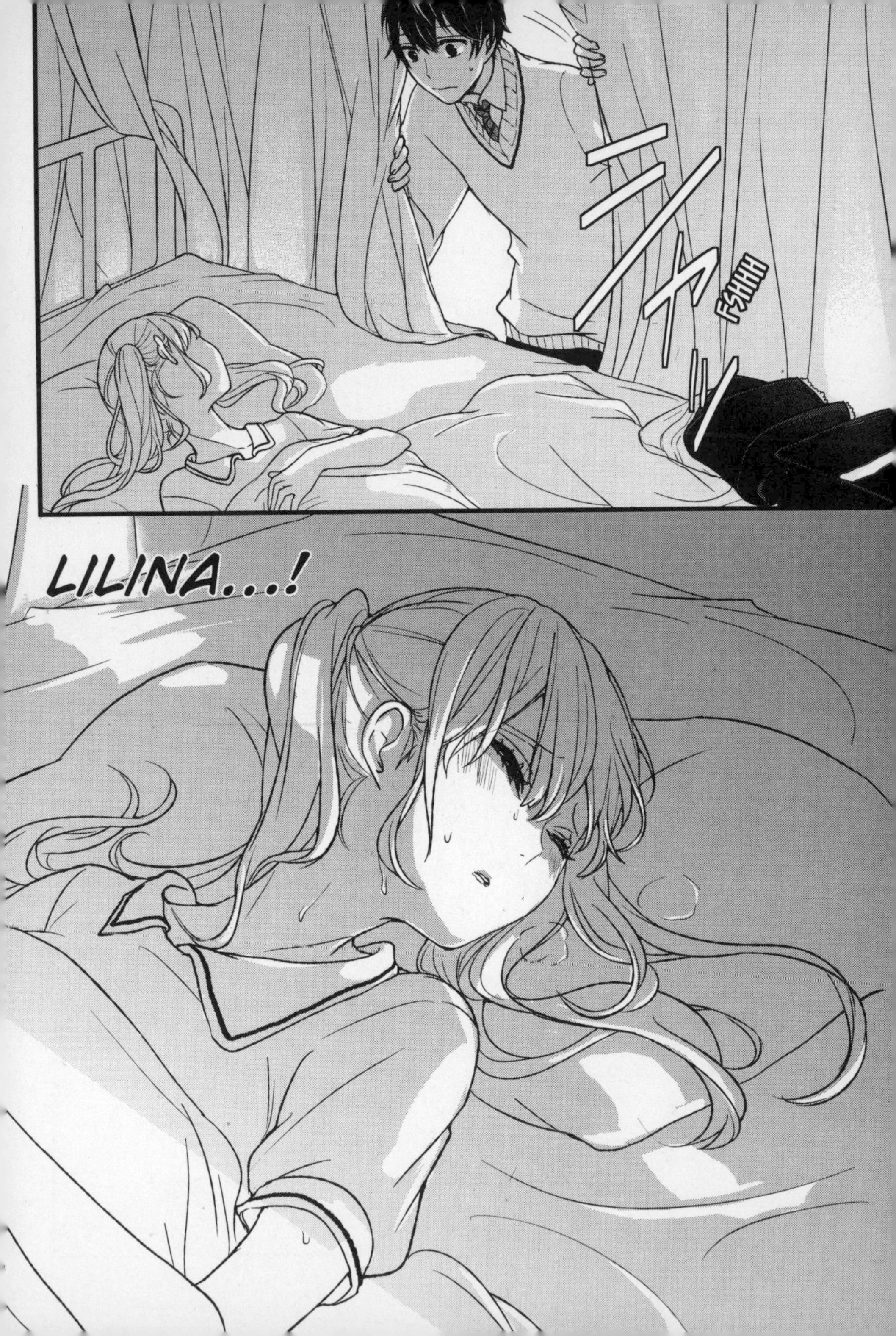
FSHHH
LILINA...!

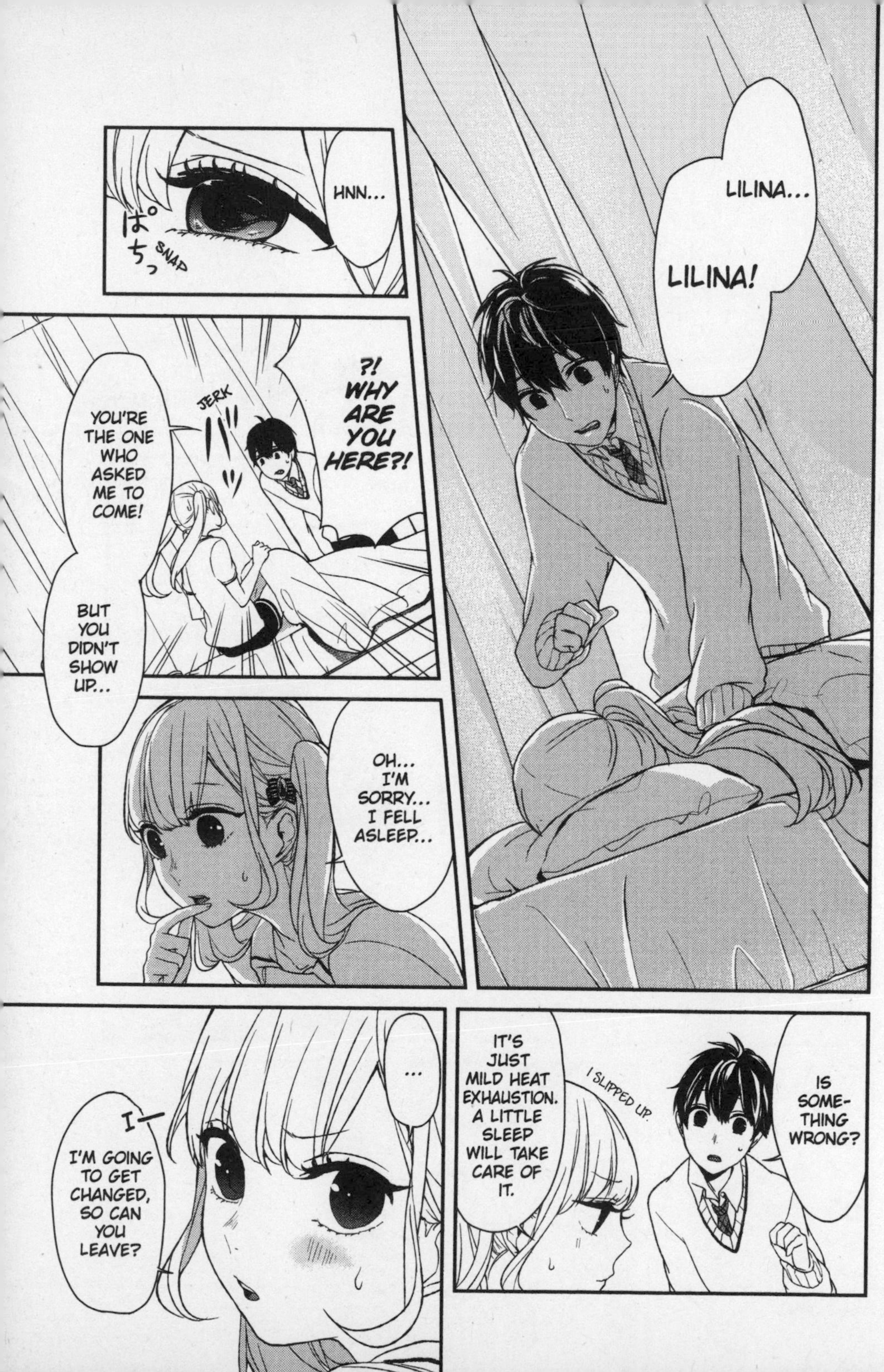
LILINA...
LILINA!
HNN...
ぱちっ
SNAP
?! WHY ARE YOU HERE?!
JERK
YOU'RE THE ONE WHO ASKED ME TO COME!
BUT YOU DIDN'T SHOW UP...
OH... I'M SORRY... I FELL ASLEEP...
IS SOME-THING WRONG?
I SLIPPED UP.
IT'S JUST MILD HEAT EXHAUSTION. A LITTLE SLEEP WILL TAKE CARE OF IT.
...
I—
I'M GOING TO GET CHANGED, SO CAN YOU LEAVE?

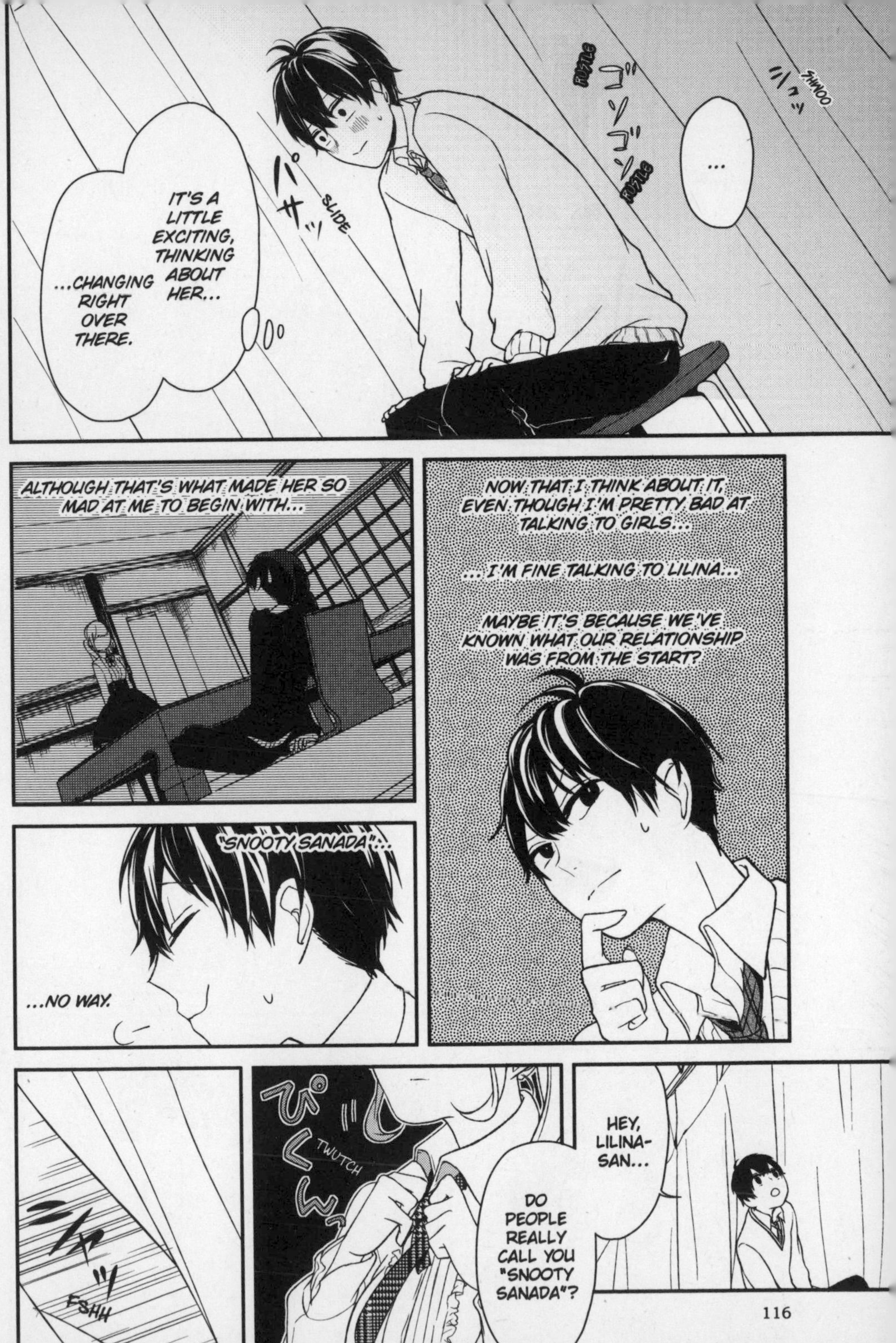
SHWOO
...
FUSTLE
FUSTLE
SLIDE
IT'S A LITTLE EXCITING, THINKING ABOUT HER...
...CHANGING RIGHT OVER THERE.
NOW THAT I THINK ABOUT IT, EVEN THOUGH I'M PRETTY BAD AT TALKING TO GIRLS...
... I'M FINE TALKING TO LILINA...
MAYBE IT'S BECAUSE WE'VE KNOWN WHAT OUR RELATIONSHIP WAS FROM THE START?
ALTHOUGH THAT'S WHAT MADE HER SO MAD AT ME TO BEGIN WITH...
"SNOOTY SANADA"...
...NO WAY.
HEY, LILINA-SAN...
DO PEOPLE REALLY CALL YOU "SNOOTY SANADA"?
TWUTCH
FSHH

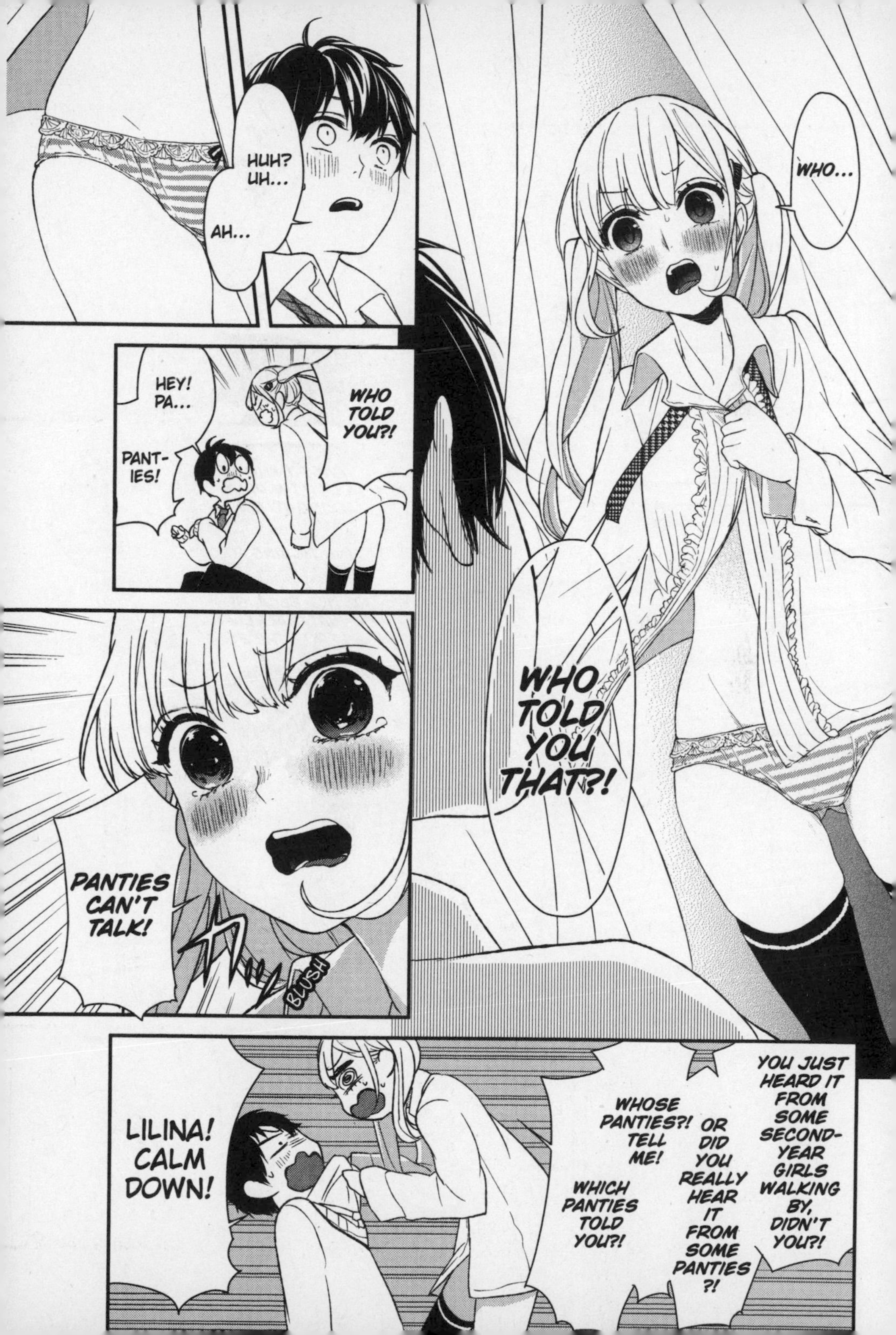
WHO…
WHO TOLD YOU THAT?!
HUH? UH…
AH…
WHO TOLD YOU?!
HEY! PA…
PANT-IES!
PANTIES CAN'T TALK!
BLUSH
YOU JUST HEARD IT FROM SOME SECOND-YEAR GIRLS WALKING BY, DIDN'T YOU?!
OR DID YOU REALLY HEAR IT FROM SOME PANTIES ?!
WHOSE PANTIES?! TELL ME!
WHICH PANTIES TOLD YOU?!
LILINA! CALM DOWN!

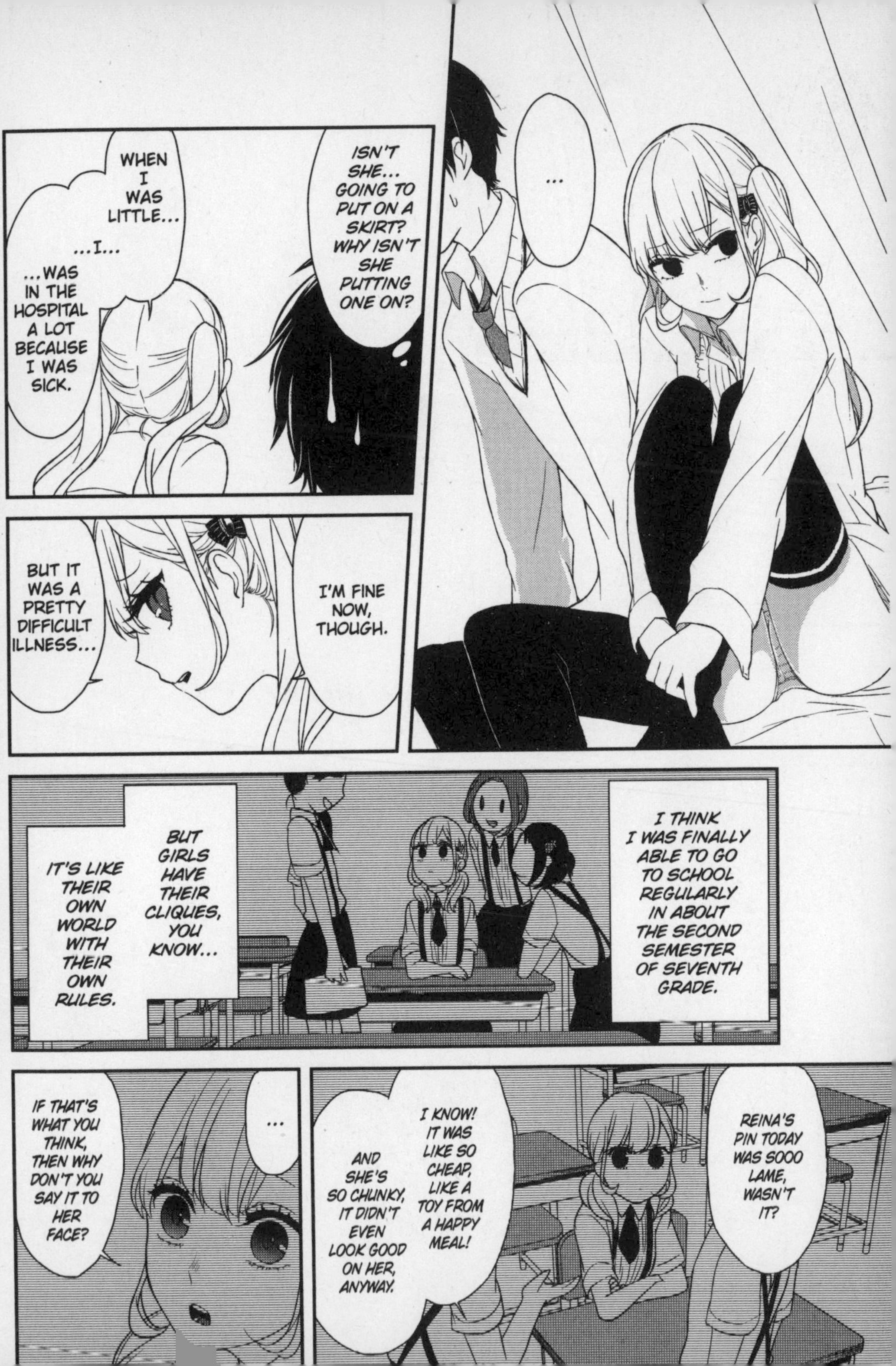
...
ISN'T SHE... GOING TO PUT ON A SKIRT? WHY ISN'T SHE PUTTING ONE ON?
WHEN I WAS LITTLE...
...I...
...WAS IN THE HOSPITAL A LOT BECAUSE I WAS SICK.
I'M FINE NOW, THOUGH.
BUT IT WAS A PRETTY DIFFICULT ILLNESS...
I THINK I WAS FINALLY ABLE TO GO TO SCHOOL REGULARLY IN ABOUT THE SECOND SEMESTER OF SEVENTH GRADE.
BUT GIRLS HAVE THEIR CLIQUES, YOU KNOW...
IT'S LIKE THEIR OWN WORLD WITH THEIR OWN RULES.
REINA'S PIN TODAY WAS SOOO LAME, WASN'T IT?
I KNOW! IT WAS LIKE SO CHEAP, LIKE A TOY FROM A HAPPY MEAL!
AND SHE'S SO CHUNKY, IT DIDN'T EVEN LOOK GOOD ON HER, ANYWAY.
...
IF THAT'S WHAT YOU THINK, THEN WHY DON'T YOU SAY IT TO HER FACE?

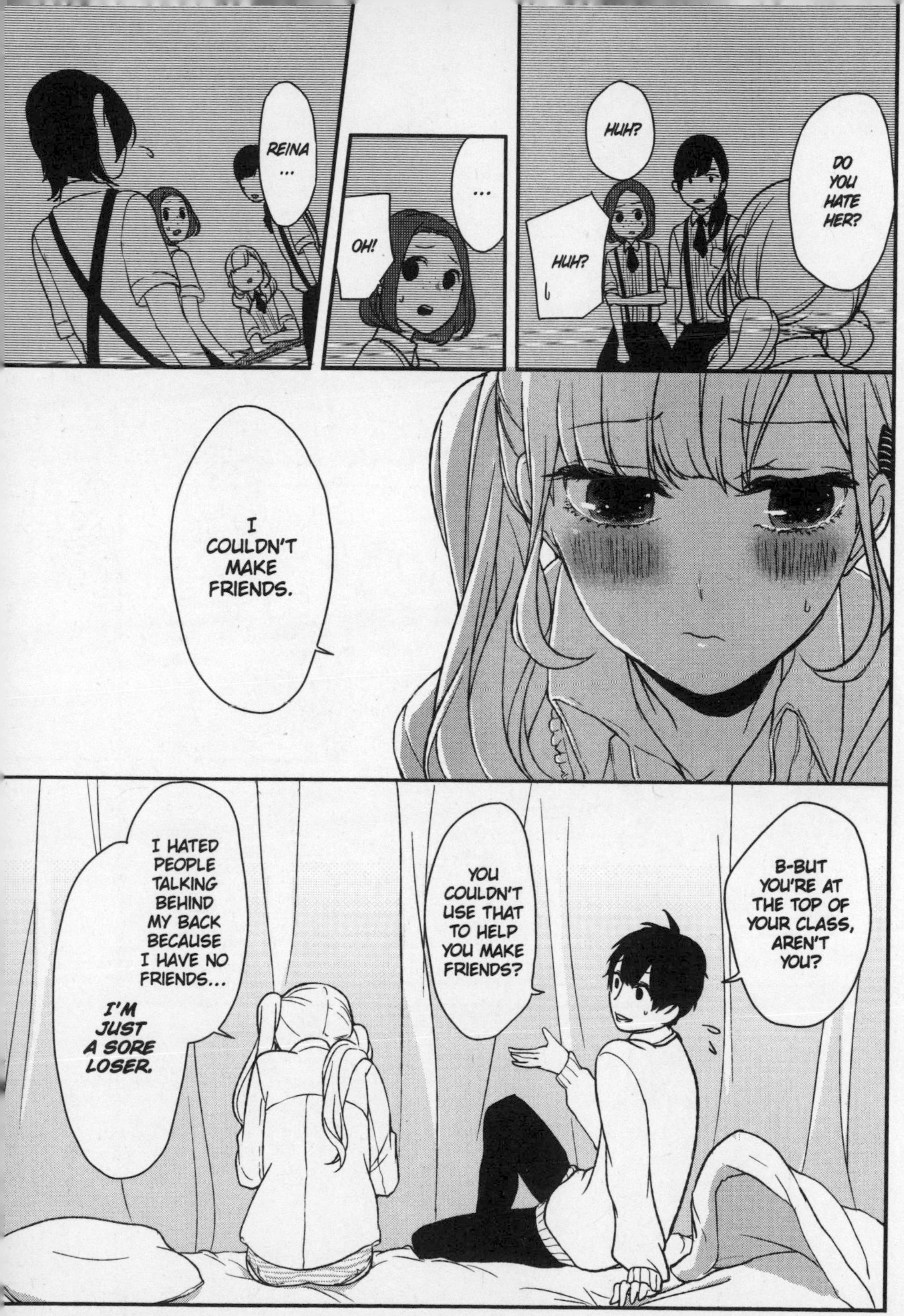
DO YOU HATE HER?
HUH?
HUH?
...
OH!
REINA ...
I COULDN'T MAKE FRIENDS.
B-BUT YOU'RE AT THE TOP OF YOUR CLASS, AREN'T YOU?
YOU COULDN'T USE THAT TO HELP YOU MAKE FRIENDS?
I HATED PEOPLE TALKING BEHIND MY BACK BECAUSE I HAVE NO FRIENDS...
I'M JUST A SORE LOSER.

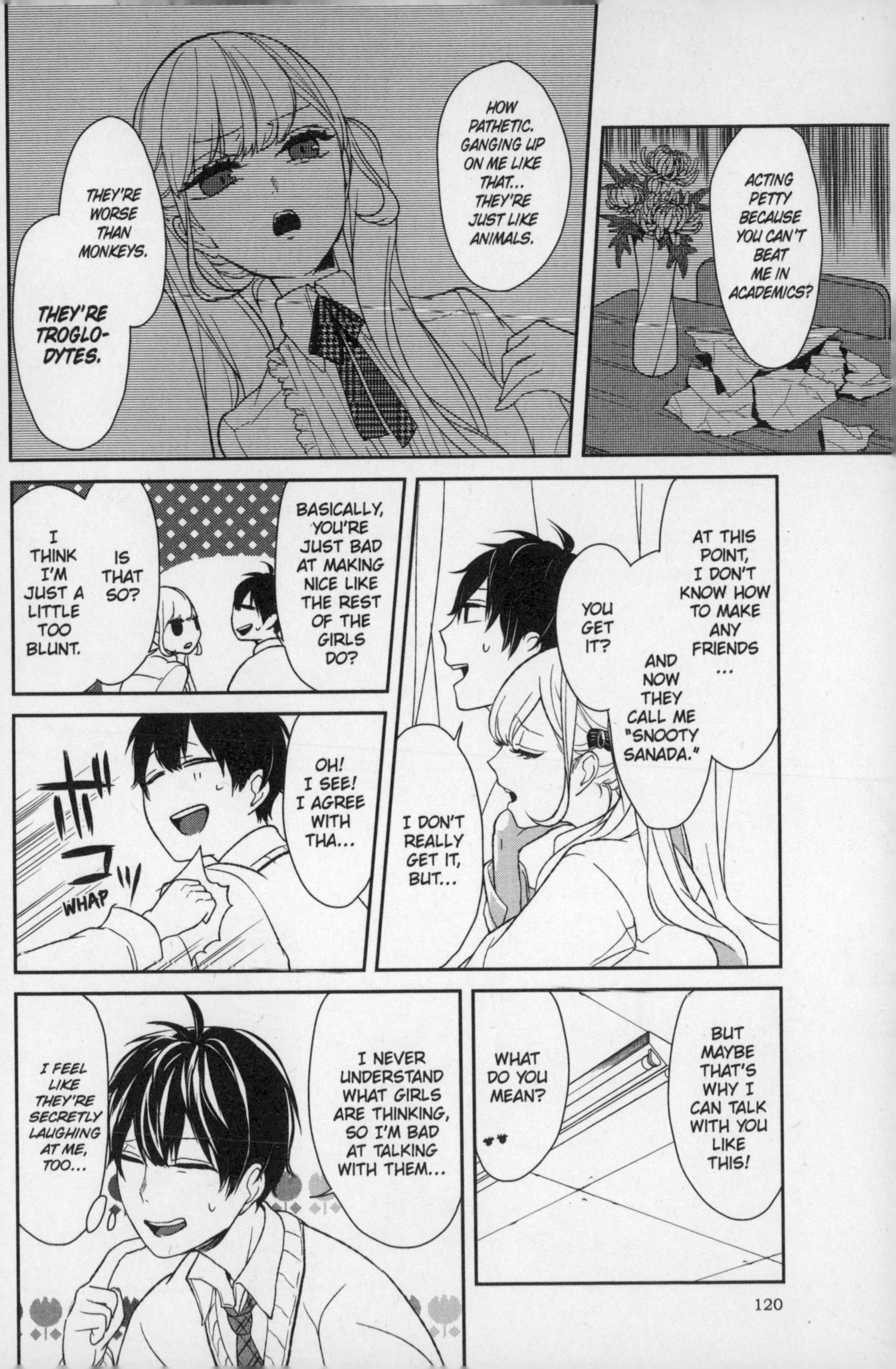

ACTING PETTY BECAUSE YOU CAN'T BEAT ME IN ACADEMICS?
HOW PATHETIC. GANGING UP ON ME LIKE THAT... THEY'RE JUST LIKE ANIMALS.
THEY'RE WORSE THAN MONKEYS.
THEY'RE TROGLO-DYTES.
AT THIS POINT, I DON'T KNOW HOW TO MAKE ANY FRIENDS...
AND NOW THEY CALL ME "SNOOTY SANADA."
YOU GET IT?
I DON'T REALLY GET IT, BUT...
BASICALLY, YOU'RE JUST BAD AT MAKING NICE LIKE THE REST OF THE GIRLS DO?
IS THAT SO?
I THINK I'M JUST A LITTLE TOO BLUNT.
OH! I SEE! I AGREE WITH THA...
WHAP
BUT MAYBE THAT'S WHY I CAN TALK WITH YOU LIKE THIS!
WHAT DO YOU MEAN?
I NEVER UNDERSTAND WHAT GIRLS ARE THINKING, SO I'M BAD AT TALKING WITH THEM...
I FEEL LIKE THEY'RE SECRETLY LAUGHING AT ME, TOO...

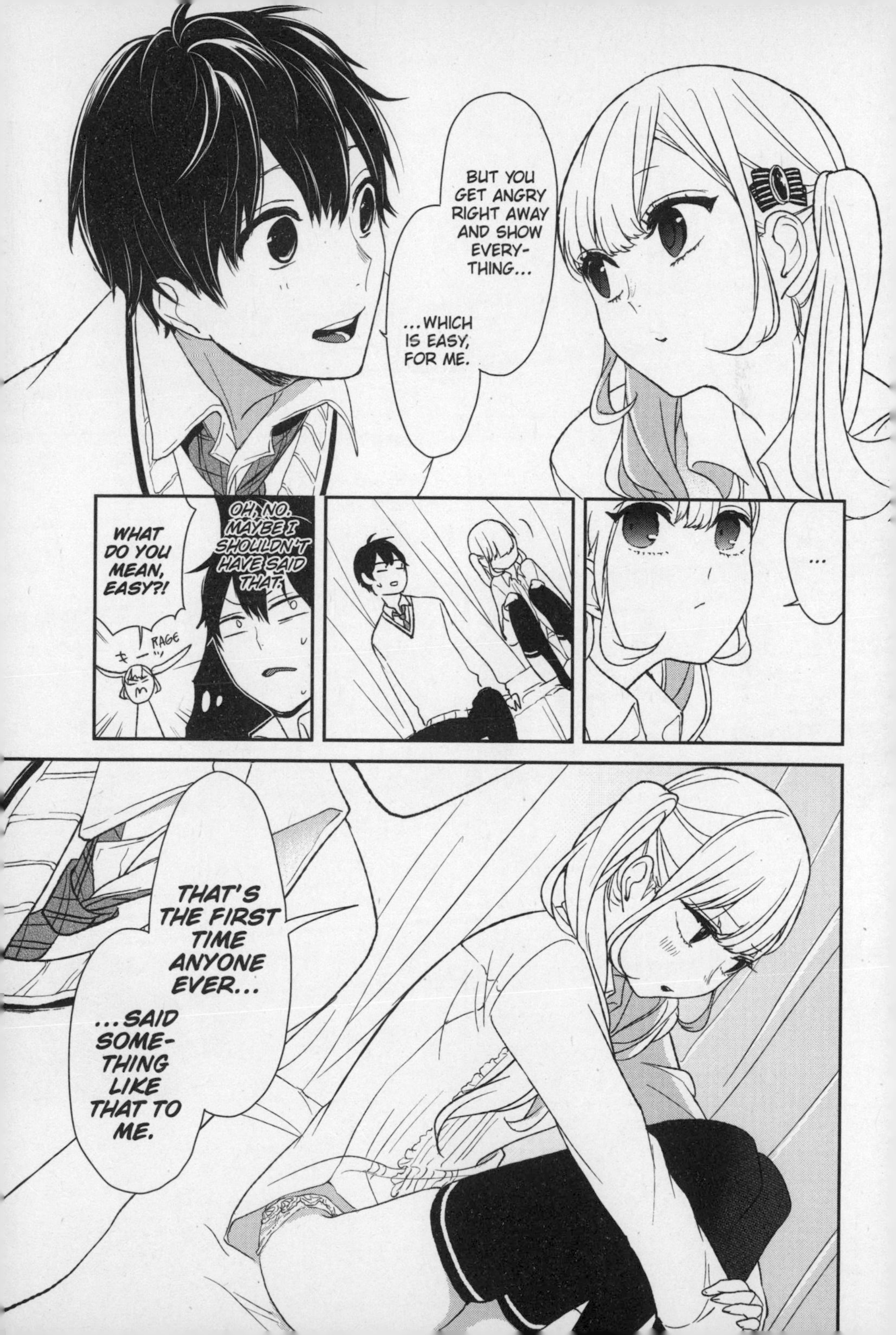
BUT YOU GET ANGRY RIGHT AWAY AND SHOW EVERY-THING...
...WHICH IS EASY, FOR ME.
...
OH, NO. MAYBE I SHOULDN'T HAVE SAID THAT.
WHAT DO YOU MEAN, EASY?!
キーッ
RAGE
THAT'S THE FIRST TIME ANYONE EVER...
...SAID SOME-THING LIKE THAT TO ME.

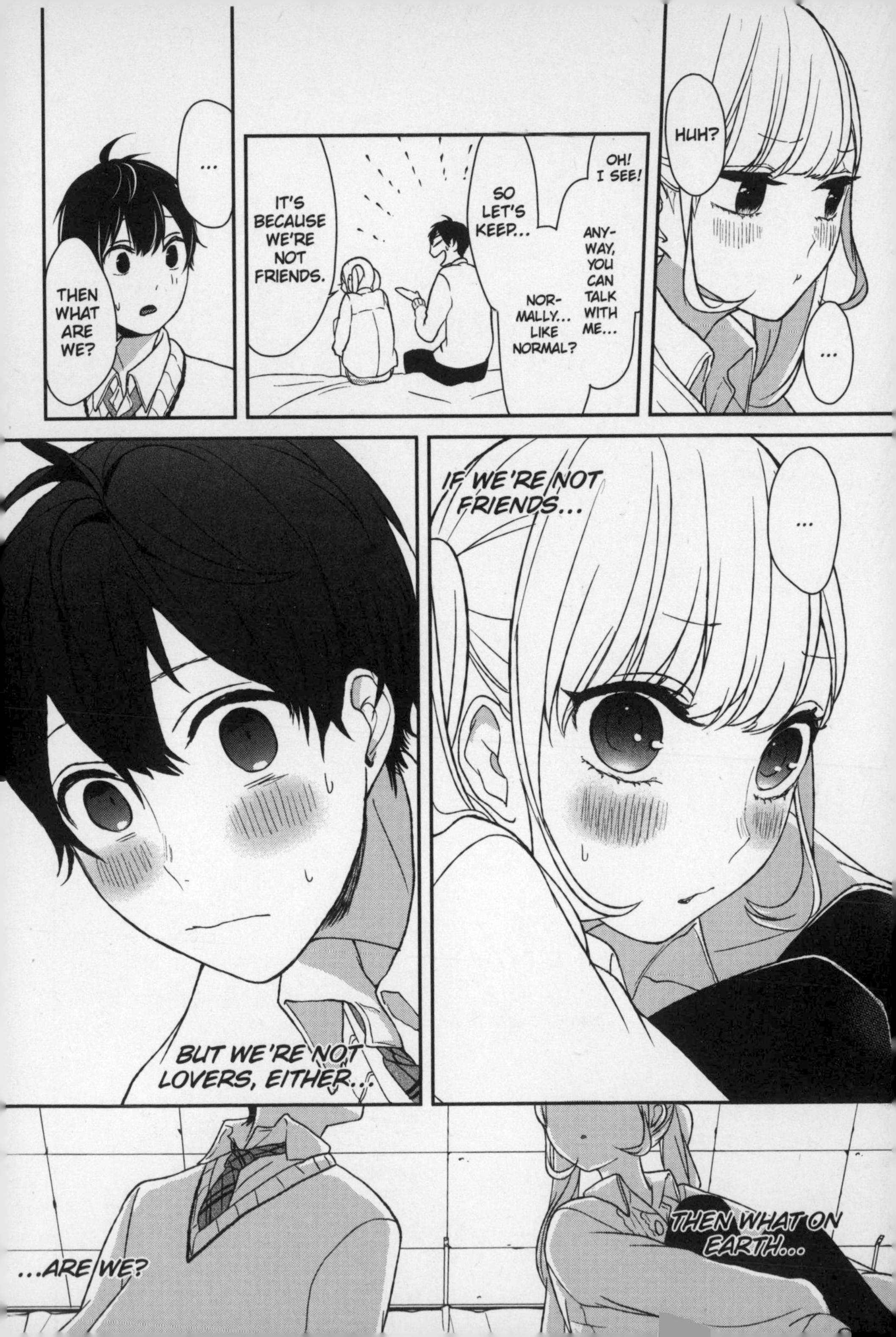
HUH?
...
OH! I SEE!
ANY-WAY, YOU CAN TALK WITH ME...
NOR-MALLY... LIKE NORMAL?
SO LET'S KEEP...
IT'S BECAUSE WE'RE NOT FRIENDS.
...
THEN WHAT ARE WE?
...
IF WE'RE NOT FRIENDS...
BUT WE'RE NOT LOVERS, EITHER...
THEN WHAT ON EARTH...
...ARE WE?

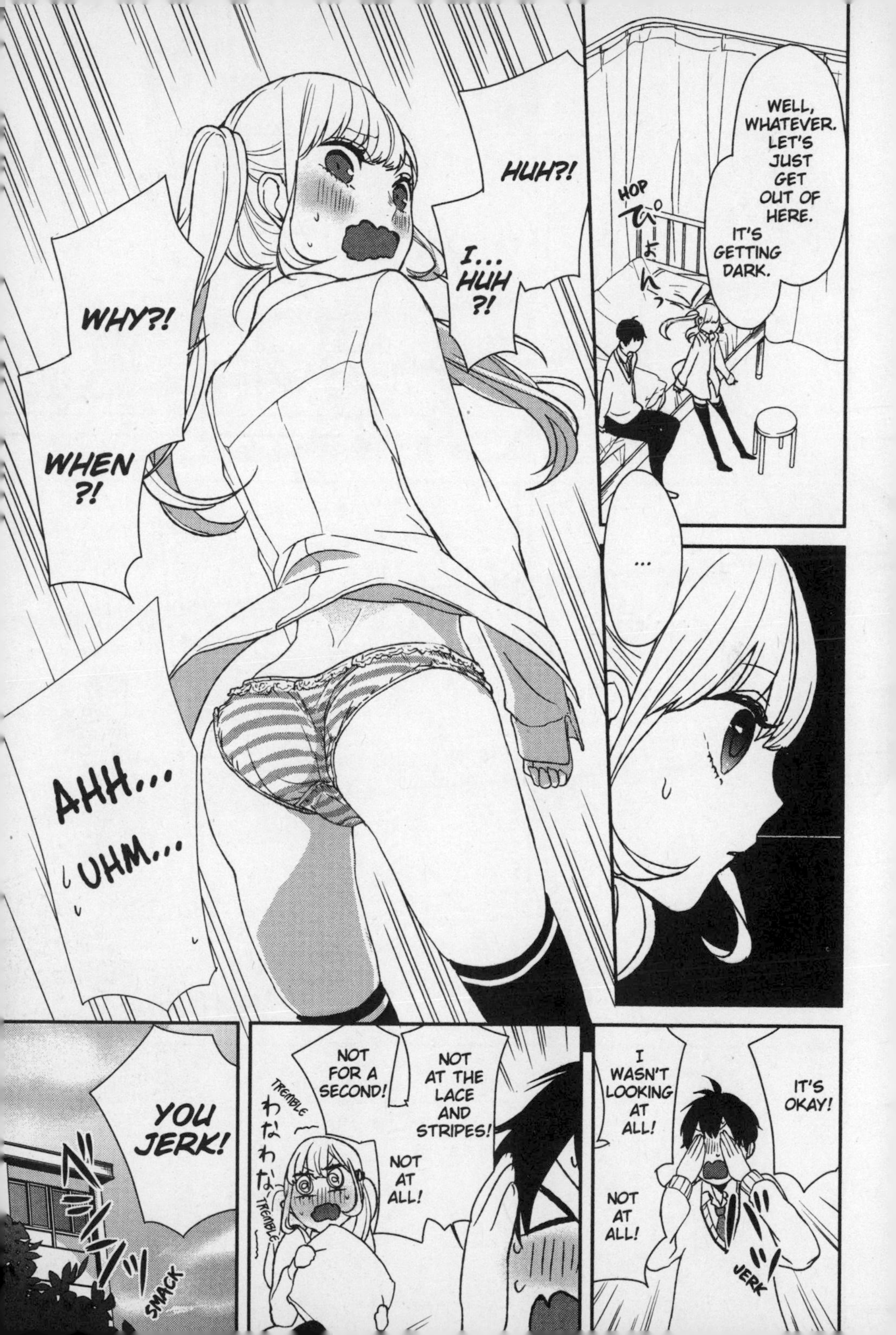
WELL, WHATEVER. LET'S JUST GET OUT OF HERE.
IT'S GETTING DARK.
HOP
...
HUH?!
I... HUH?!
WHY?!
WHEN?!
AHH... UHM...
IT'S OKAY!
I WASN'T LOOKING AT ALL!
NOT AT ALL!
JERK
NOT AT THE LACE AND STRIPES!
NOT FOR A SECOND!
NOT AT ALL!
TREMBLE
TREMBLE
YOU JERK!
SMACK

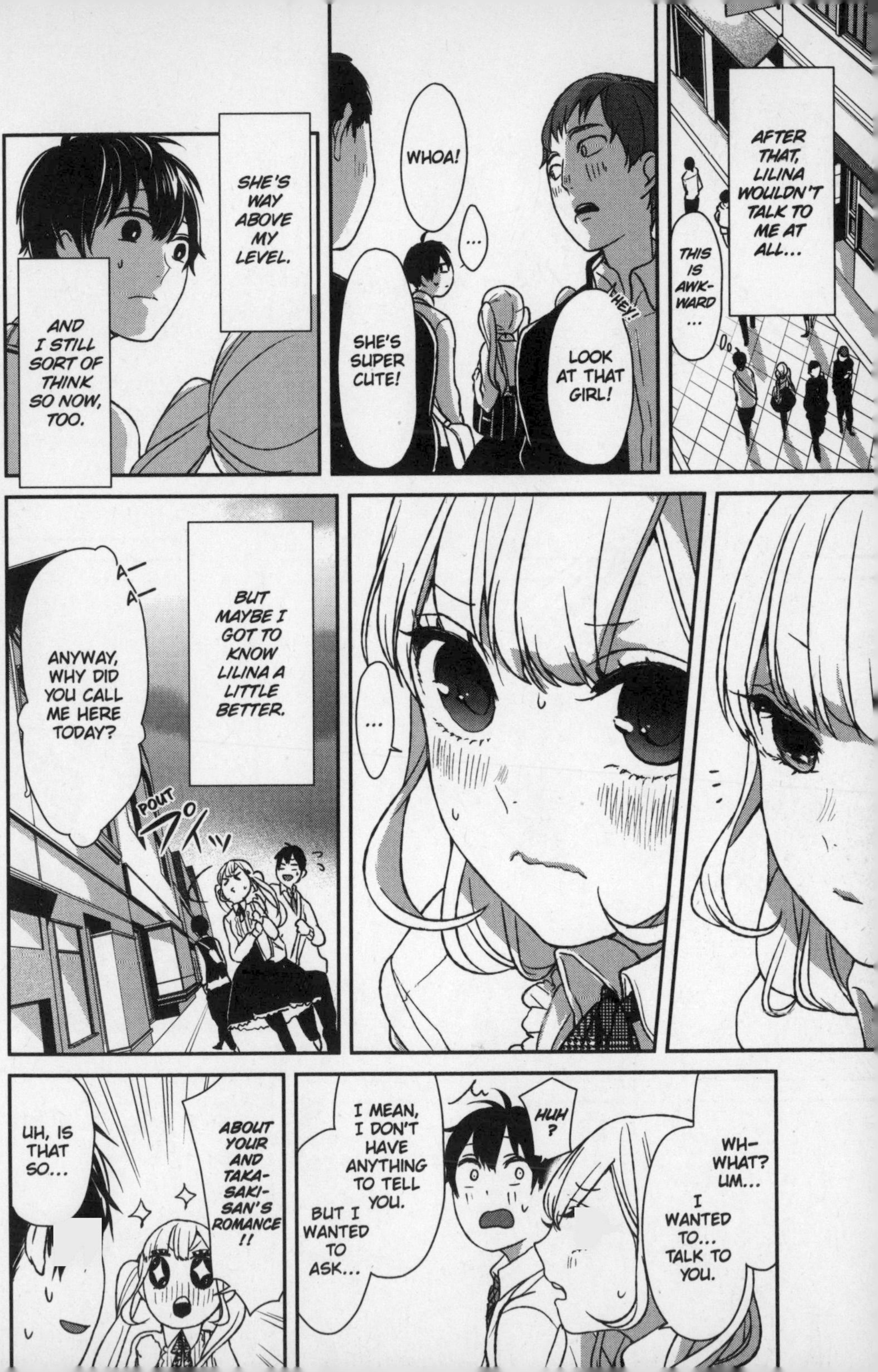
AFTER THAT, LILINA WOULDN'T TALK TO ME AT ALL…
THIS IS AWK-WARD…
WHOA!
…
HEY!
LOOK AT THAT GIRL!
SHE'S SUPER CUTE!
SHE'S WAY ABOVE MY LEVEL.
AND I STILL SORT OF THINK SO NOW, TOO.
…
BUT MAYBE I GOT TO KNOW LILINA A LITTLE BETTER.
ANYWAY, WHY DID YOU CALL ME HERE TODAY?
POUT
WH-WHAT? UM… I WANTED TO… TALK TO YOU.
HUH?
I MEAN, I DON'T HAVE ANYTHING TO TELL YOU. BUT I WANTED TO ASK…
ABOUT YOUR AND TAKA-SAKI-SAN'S ROMANCE!!
UH, IS THAT SO…

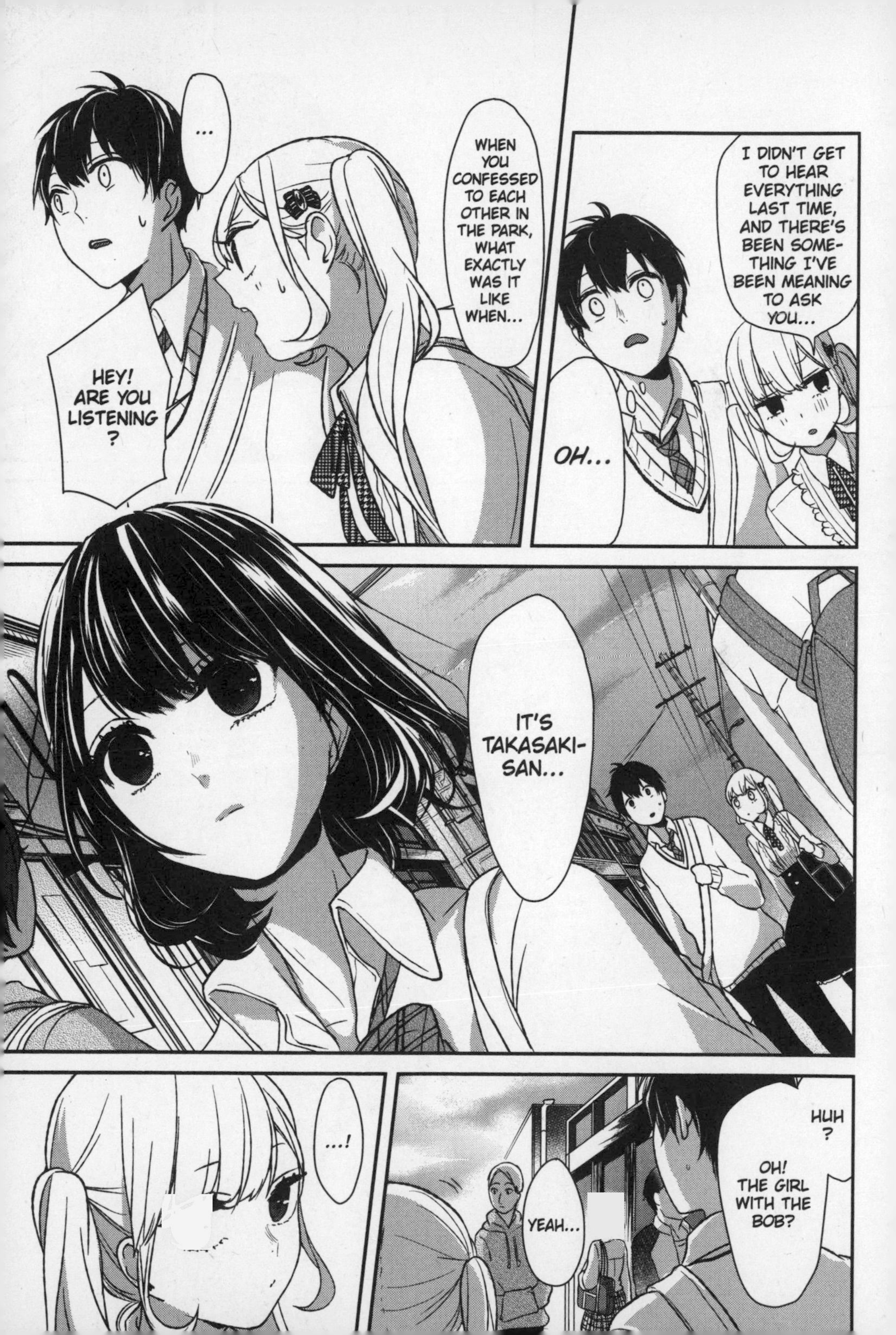
I DIDN'T GET TO HEAR EVERYTHING LAST TIME, AND THERE'S BEEN SOME-THING I'VE BEEN MEANING TO ASK YOU...
OH...
WHEN YOU CONFESSED TO EACH OTHER IN THE PARK, WHAT EXACTLY WAS IT LIKE WHEN...
...
HEY! ARE YOU LISTENING ?
IT'S TAKASAKI-SAN...
HUH ?
OH! THE GIRL WITH THE BOB?
YEAH...
...!

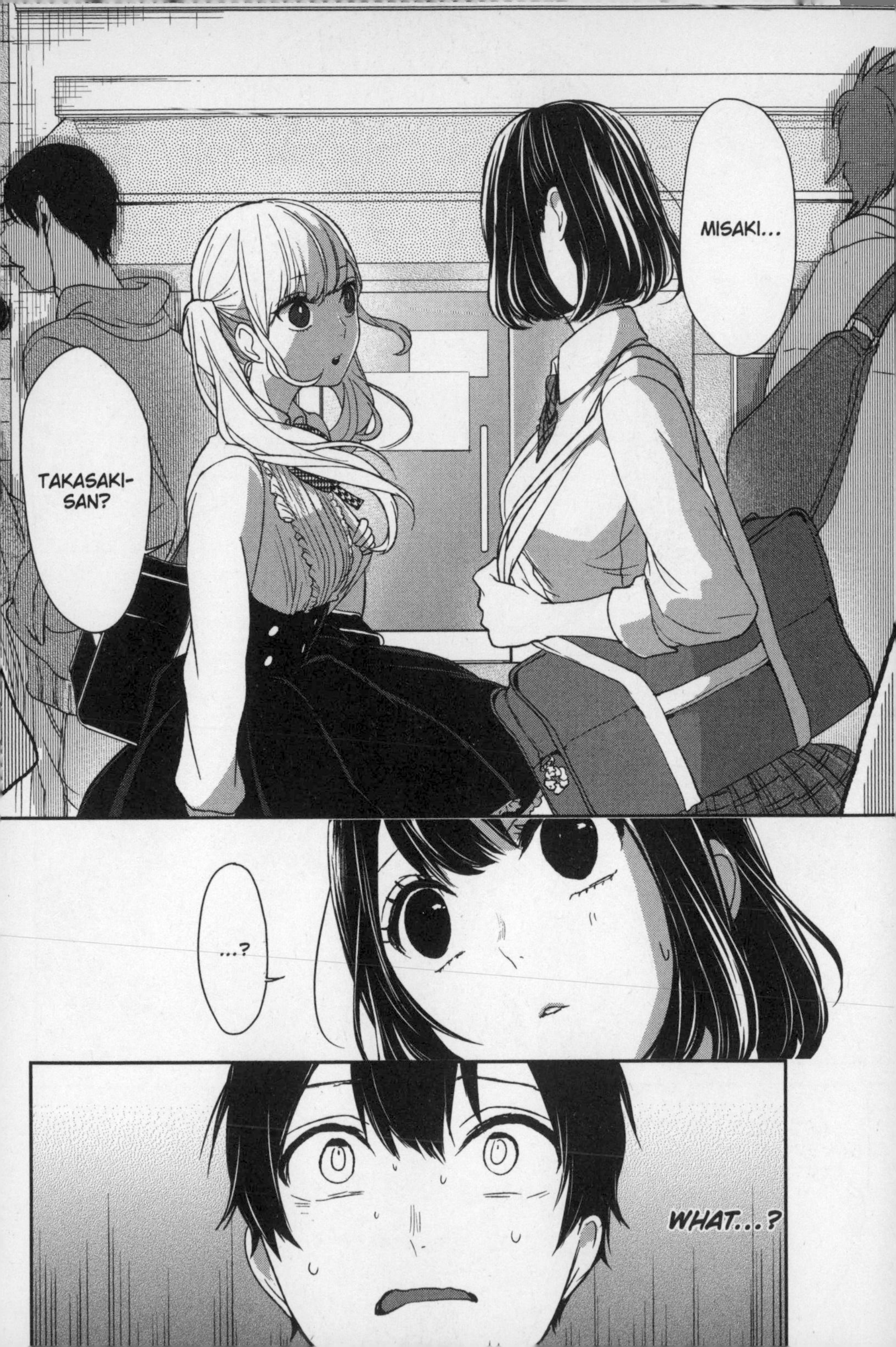
MISAKI...
TAKASAKI-SAN?
...?
WHAT...?

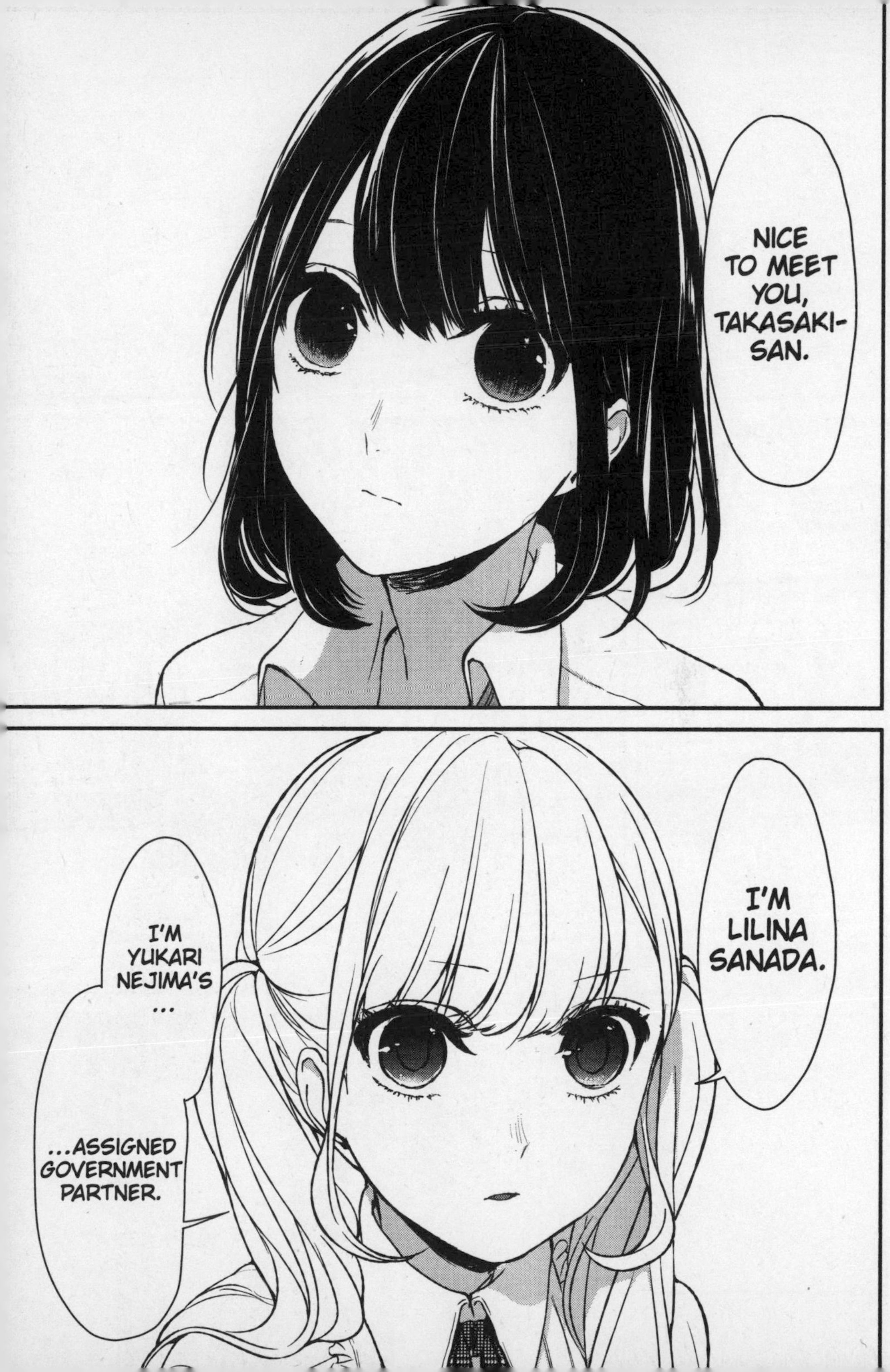
NICE TO MEET YOU, TAKASAKI-SAN.
I'M LILINA SANADA.
I'M YUKARI NEJIMA'S ...
...ASSIGNED GOVERNMENT PARTNER.

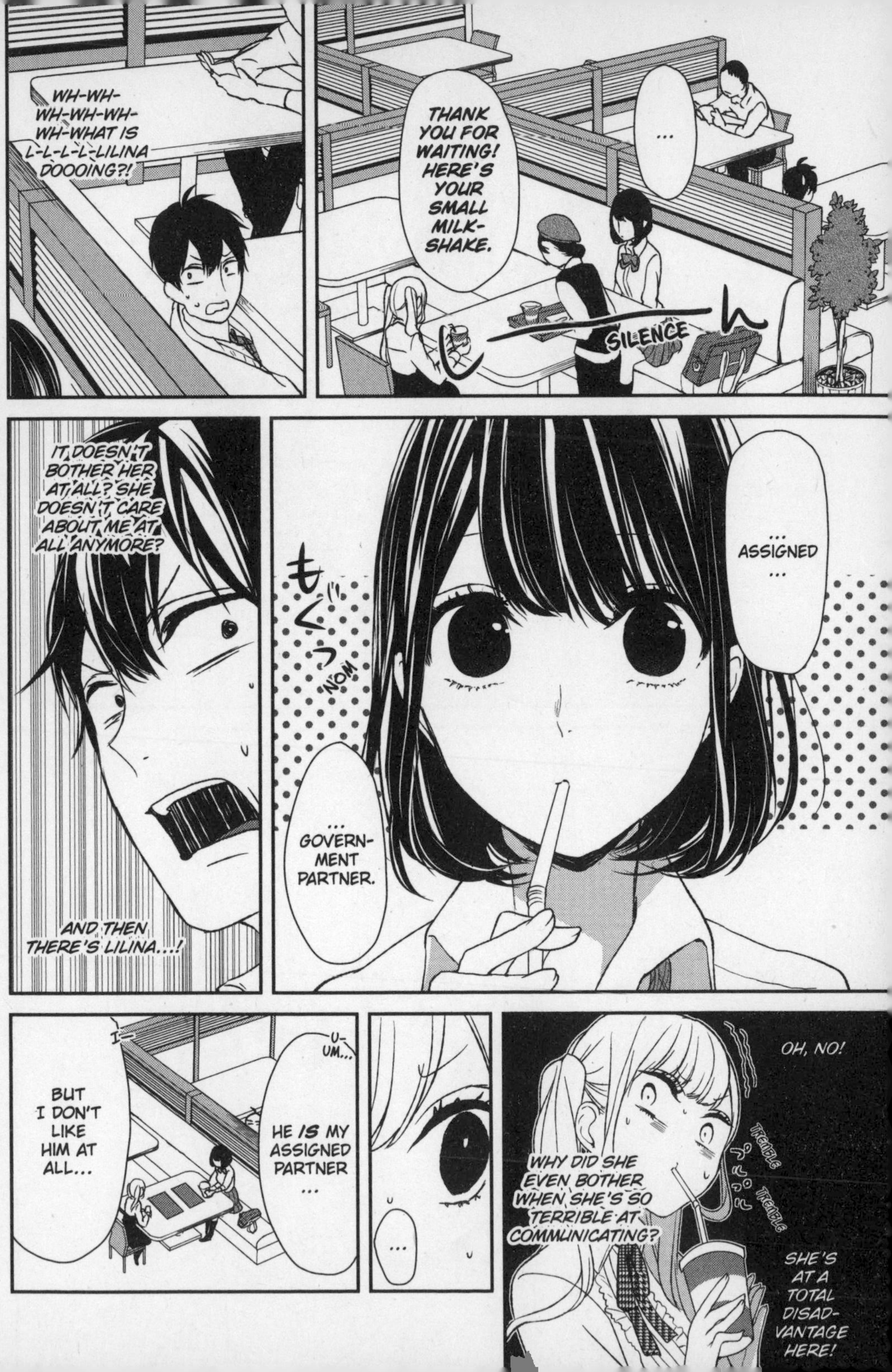
...
THANK YOU FOR WAITING! HERE'S YOUR SMALL MILK-SHAKE.
SILENCE
WH-WH-WH-WH-WH-WH-WHAT IS L-L-L-L-LILINA DOOOING?!
... ASSIGNED ...
もぐっ
NOM
... GOVERNMENT PARTNER.
IT DOESN'T BOTHER HER AT ALL? SHE DOESN'T CARE ABOUT ME AT ALL ANYMORE?
AND THEN THERE'S LILINA...!
OH, NO!
TREMBLE TREMBLE
WHY DID SHE EVEN BOTHER WHEN SHE'S SO TERRIBLE AT COMMUNICATING?
SHE'S AT A TOTAL DISADVANTAGE HERE!
...
U-UM...
HE *IS* MY ASSIGNED PARTNER ...
I—
BUT I DON'T LIKE HIM AT ALL...

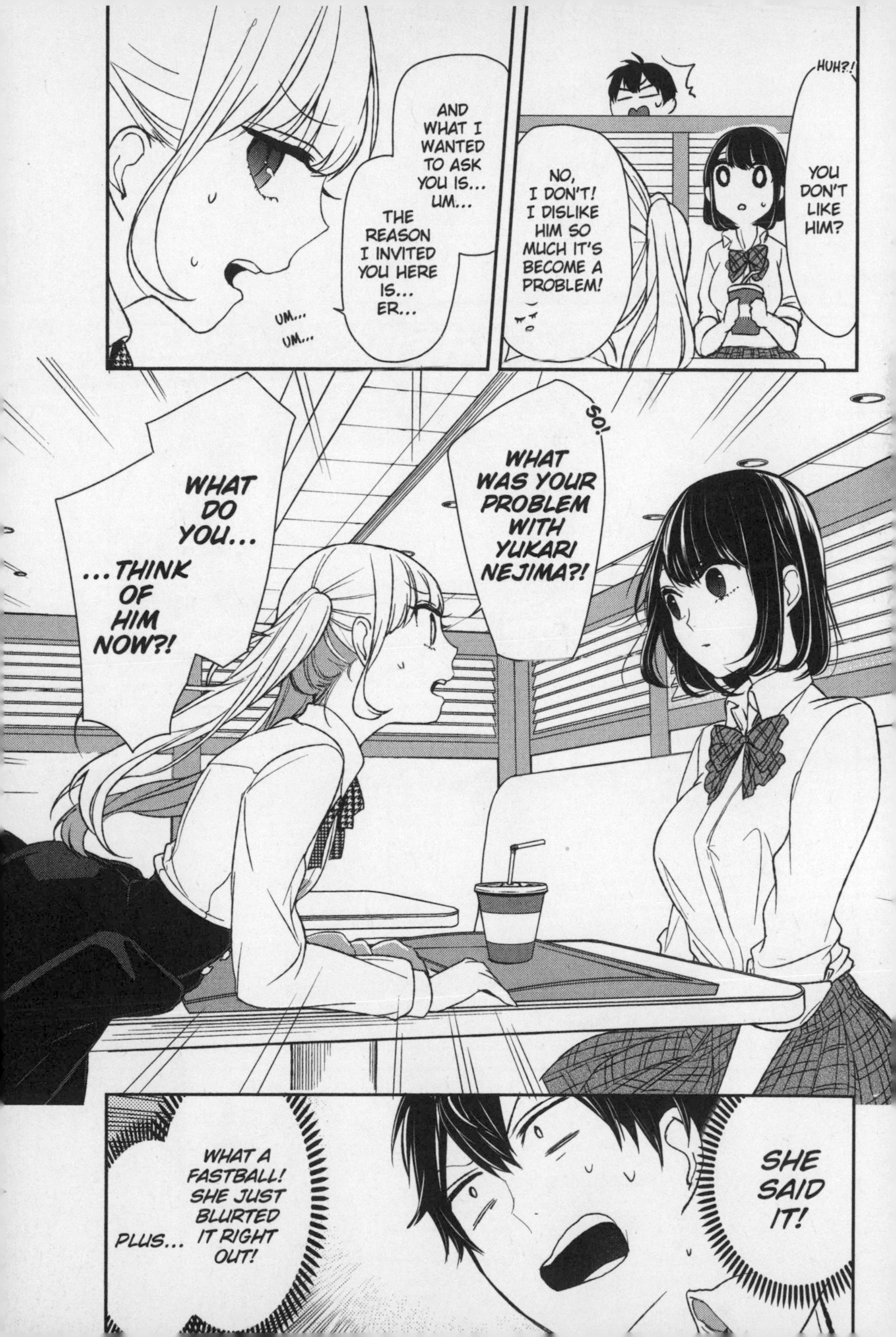
HUH?!
YOU DON'T LIKE HIM?
NO, I DON'T! I DISLIKE HIM SO MUCH IT'S BECOME A PROBLEM!
AND WHAT I WANTED TO ASK YOU IS... UM...
THE REASON I INVITED YOU HERE IS... ER...
UM... UM...
SO!
WHAT WAS YOUR PROBLEM WITH YUKARI NEJIMA?!
WHAT DO YOU...
...THINK OF HIM NOW?!
SHE SAID IT!
WHAT A FASTBALL! SHE JUST BLURTED IT RIGHT OUT!
PLUS...

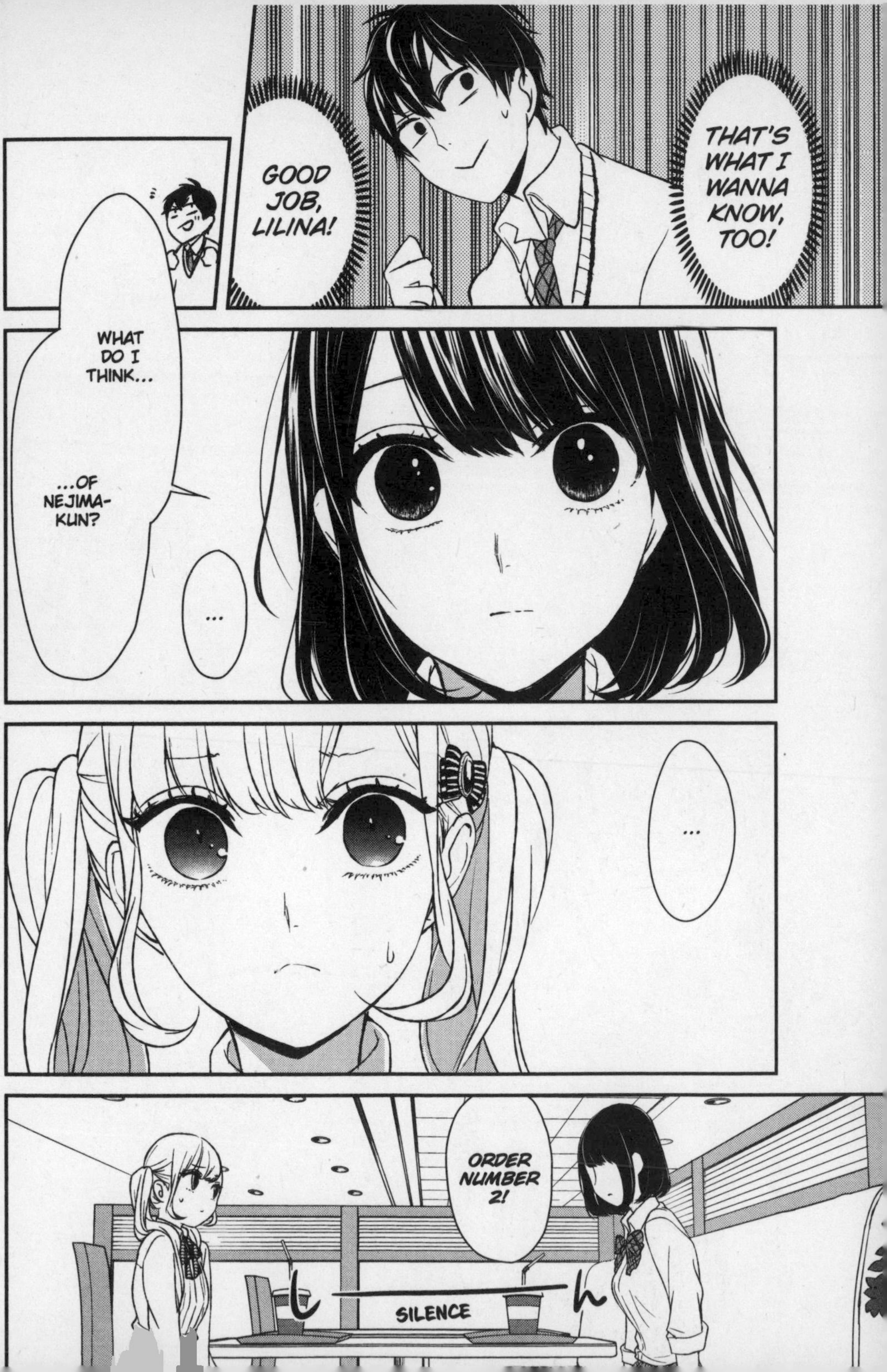
THAT'S WHAT I WANNA KNOW, TOO!
GOOD JOB, LILINA!
WHAT DO I THINK...
...OF NEJIMA-KUN?
...
...
ORDER NUMBER 2!
SILENCE

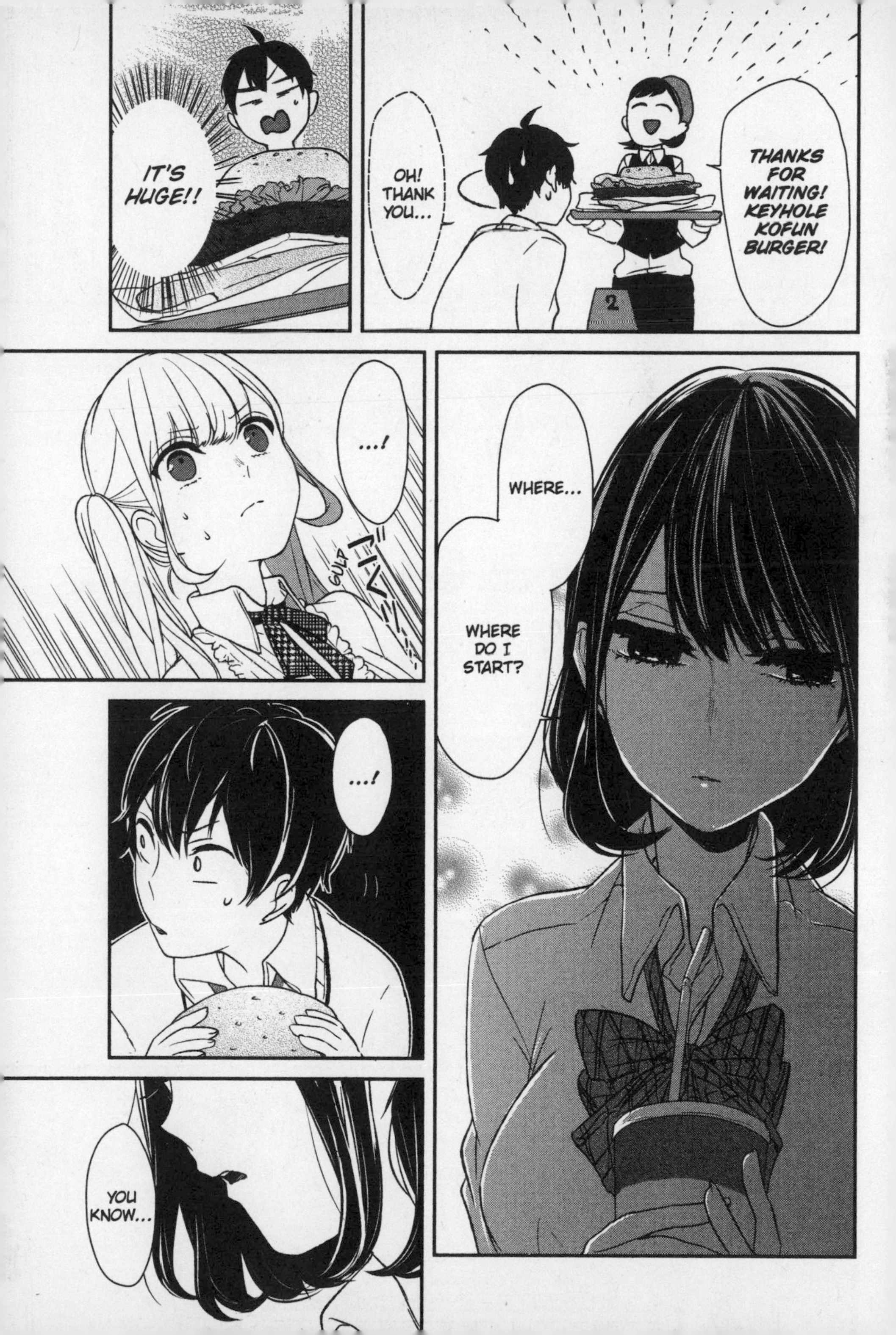
THANKS FOR WAITING! KEYHOLE KOFUN BURGER!
OH! THANK YOU...
IT'S HUGE!!
WHERE...
WHERE DO I START?
...!
GULP
...!
YOU KNOW...

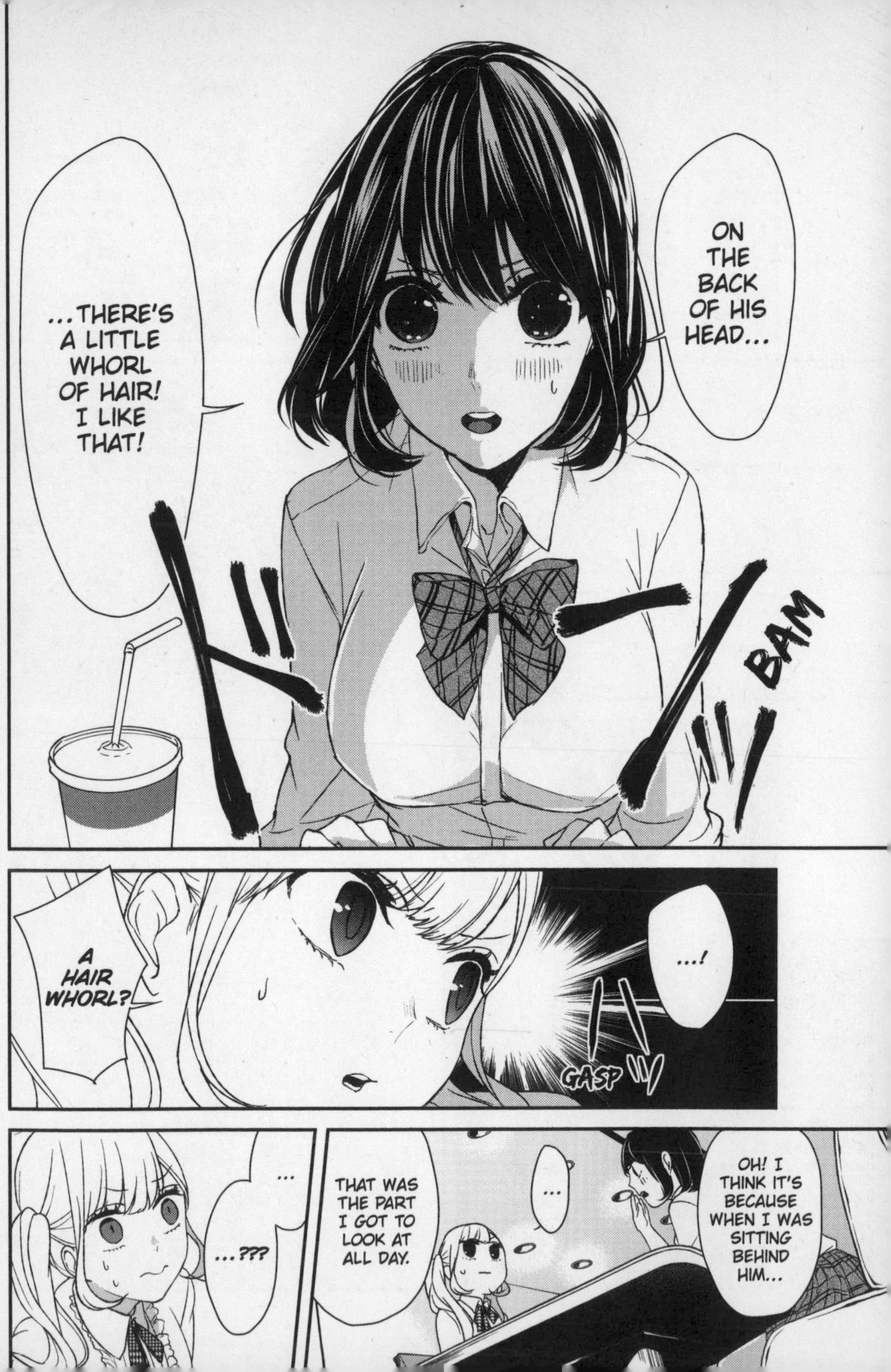
ON THE BACK OF HIS HEAD...
...THERE'S A LITTLE WHORL OF HAIR! I LIKE THAT!
BAM
...!
GASP
A HAIR WHORL?
OH! I THINK IT'S BECAUSE WHEN I WAS SITTING BEHIND HIM...
...
THAT WAS THE PART I GOT TO LOOK AT ALL DAY.
...
...???

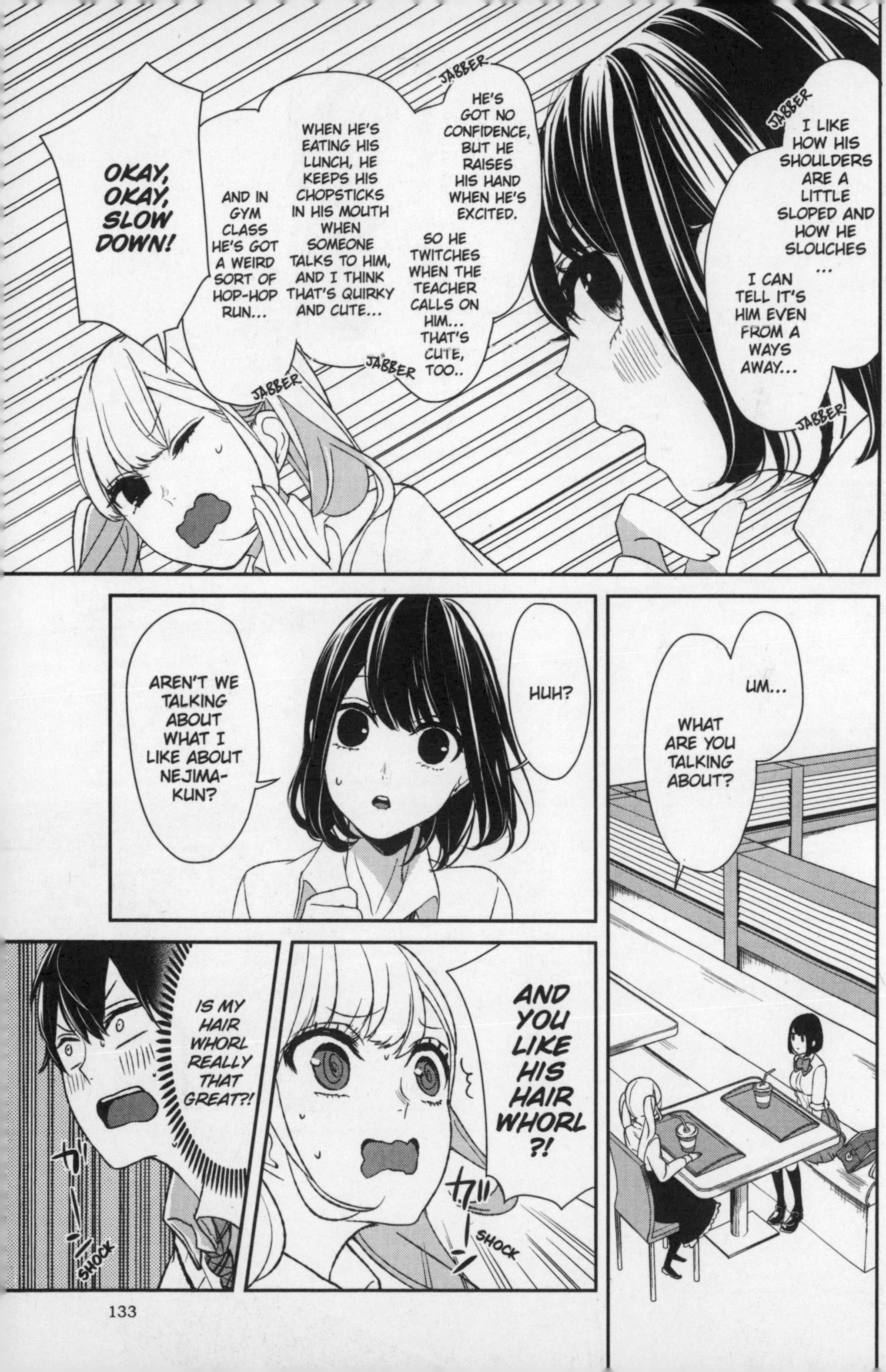
JABBER
I LIKE HOW HIS SHOULDERS ARE A LITTLE SLOPED AND HOW HE SLOUCHES...
I CAN TELL IT'S HIM EVEN FROM A WAYS AWAY...
JABBER
JABBER
HE'S GOT NO CONFIDENCE, BUT HE RAISES HIS HAND WHEN HE'S EXCITED.
SO HE TWITCHES WHEN THE TEACHER CALLS ON HIM... THAT'S CUTE, TOO..
JABBER
WHEN HE'S EATING HIS LUNCH, HE KEEPS HIS CHOPSTICKS IN HIS MOUTH WHEN SOMEONE TALKS TO HIM, AND I THINK THAT'S QUIRKY AND CUTE...
AND IN GYM CLASS HE'S GOT A WEIRD SORT OF HOP-HOP RUN...
JABBER
OKAY, OKAY, SLOW DOWN!
UM...
WHAT ARE YOU TALKING ABOUT?
HUH?
AREN'T WE TALKING ABOUT WHAT I LIKE ABOUT NEJIMA-KUN?
AND YOU LIKE HIS HAIR WHORL?!
SHOCK
IS MY HAIR WHORL REALLY THAT GREAT?!
SHOCK

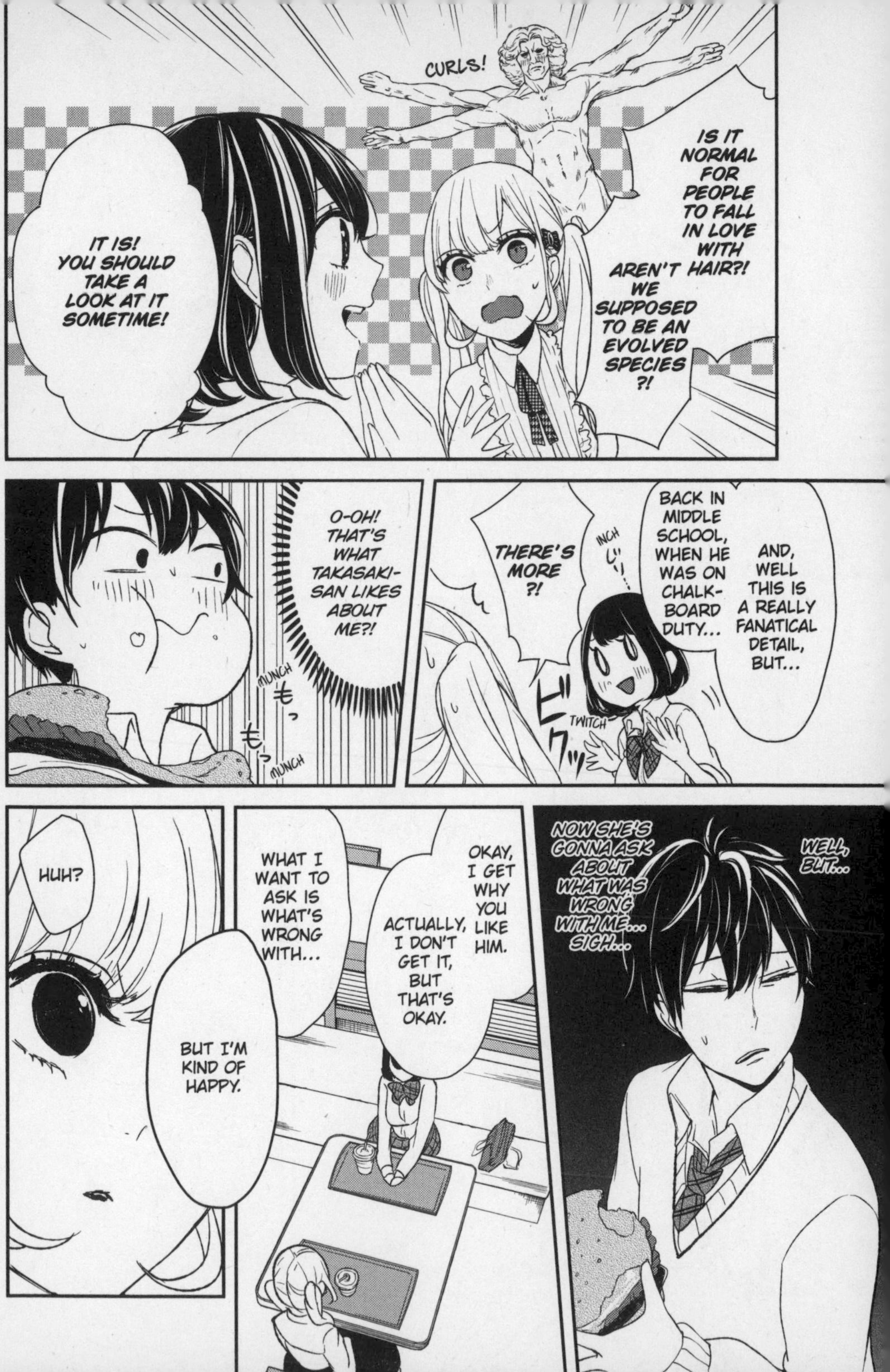
IS IT NORMAL FOR PEOPLE TO FALL IN LOVE WITH HAIR?!
AREN'T WE SUPPOSED TO BE AN EVOLVED SPECIES?!
CURLS!
IT IS! YOU SHOULD TAKE A LOOK AT IT SOMETIME!
AND, WELL THIS IS A REALLY FANATICAL DETAIL, BUT...
BACK IN MIDDLE SCHOOL, WHEN HE WAS ON CHALK-BOARD DUTY...
INCH
THERE'S MORE?!
TWITCH
O-OH! THAT'S WHAT TAKASAKI-SAN LIKES ABOUT ME?!
MUNCH
MUNCH
WELL, BUT...
NOW SHE'S GONNA ASK ABOUT WHAT WAS WRONG WITH ME... SIGH...
OKAY, I GET WHY YOU LIKE HIM.
ACTUALLY, I DON'T GET IT, BUT THAT'S OKAY.
WHAT I WANT TO ASK IS WHAT'S WRONG WITH...
HUH?
BUT I'M KIND OF HAPPY.

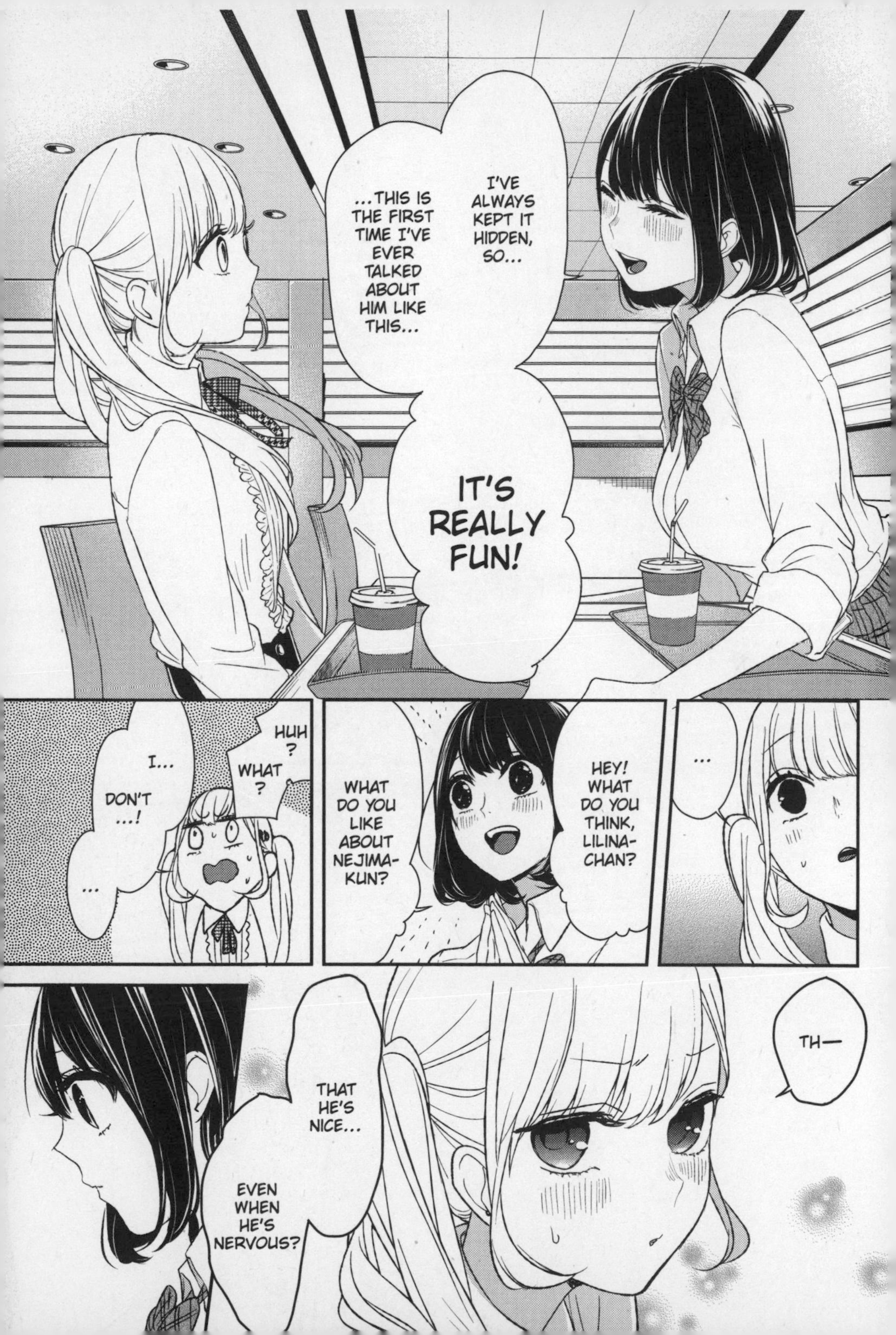
I'VE ALWAYS KEPT IT HIDDEN, SO...
...THIS IS THE FIRST TIME I'VE EVER TALKED ABOUT HIM LIKE THIS...
IT'S REALLY FUN!
...
HEY! WHAT DO YOU THINK, LILINA-CHAN?
WHAT DO YOU LIKE ABOUT NEJIMA-KUN?
HUH? WHAT?
I... DON'T ...! ...
TH—
THAT HE'S NICE...
EVEN WHEN HE'S NERVOUS?

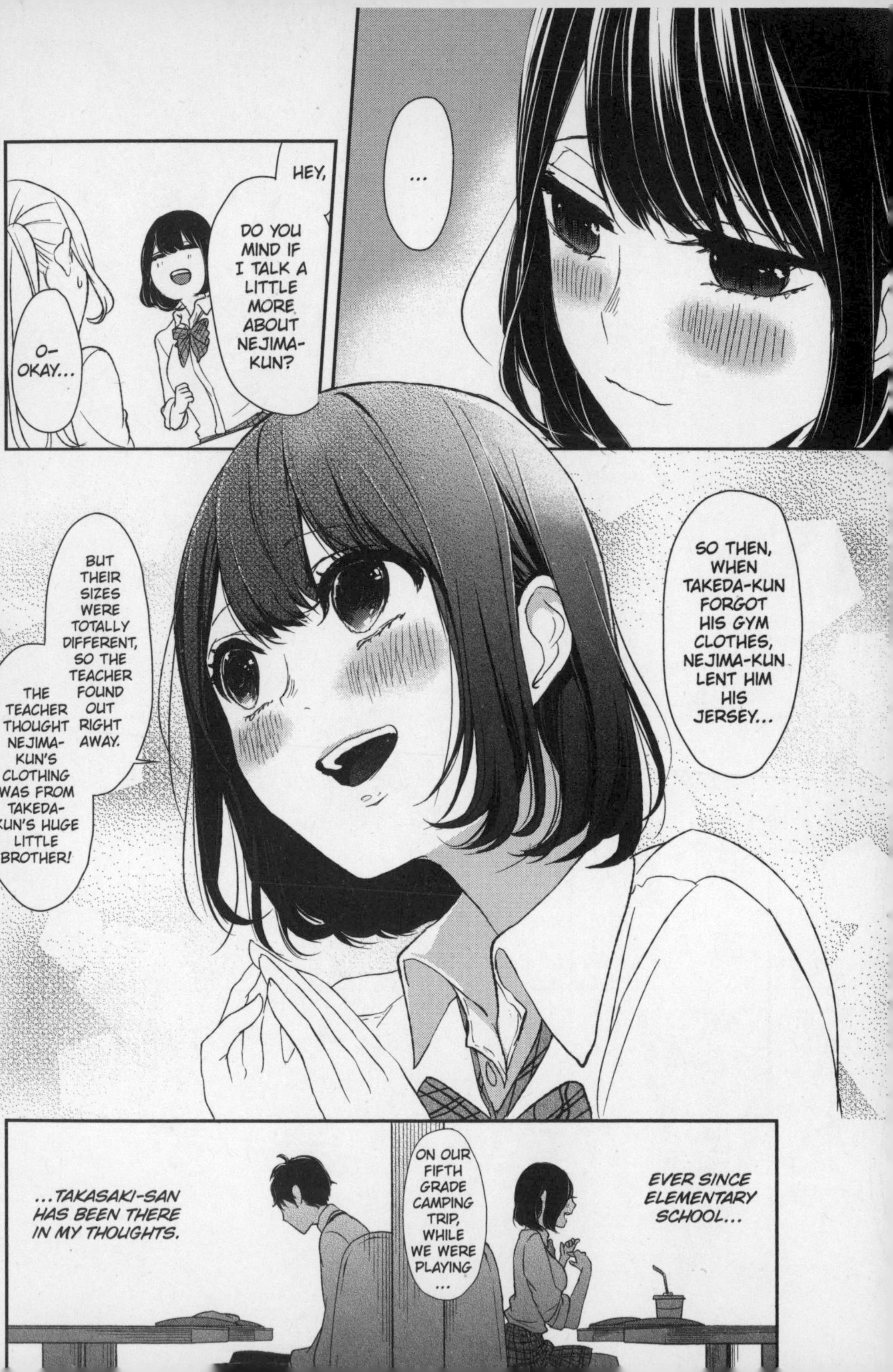
...
HEY, DO YOU MIND IF I TALK A LITTLE MORE ABOUT NEJIMA-KUN?
O-OKAY...
SO THEN, WHEN TAKEDA-KUN FORGOT HIS GYM CLOTHES, NEJIMA-KUN LENT HIM HIS JERSEY...
THE TEACHER THOUGHT NEJIMA-KUN'S CLOTHING WAS FROM TAKEDA-KUN'S HUGE LITTLE BROTHER! BUT THEIR SIZES WERE TOTALLY DIFFERENT, SO THE TEACHER FOUND OUT RIGHT AWAY.
EVER SINCE ELEMENTARY SCHOOL...
ON OUR FIFTH GRADE CAMPING TRIP, WHILE WE WERE PLAYING ...
...TAKASAKI-SAN HAS BEEN THERE IN MY THOUGHTS.

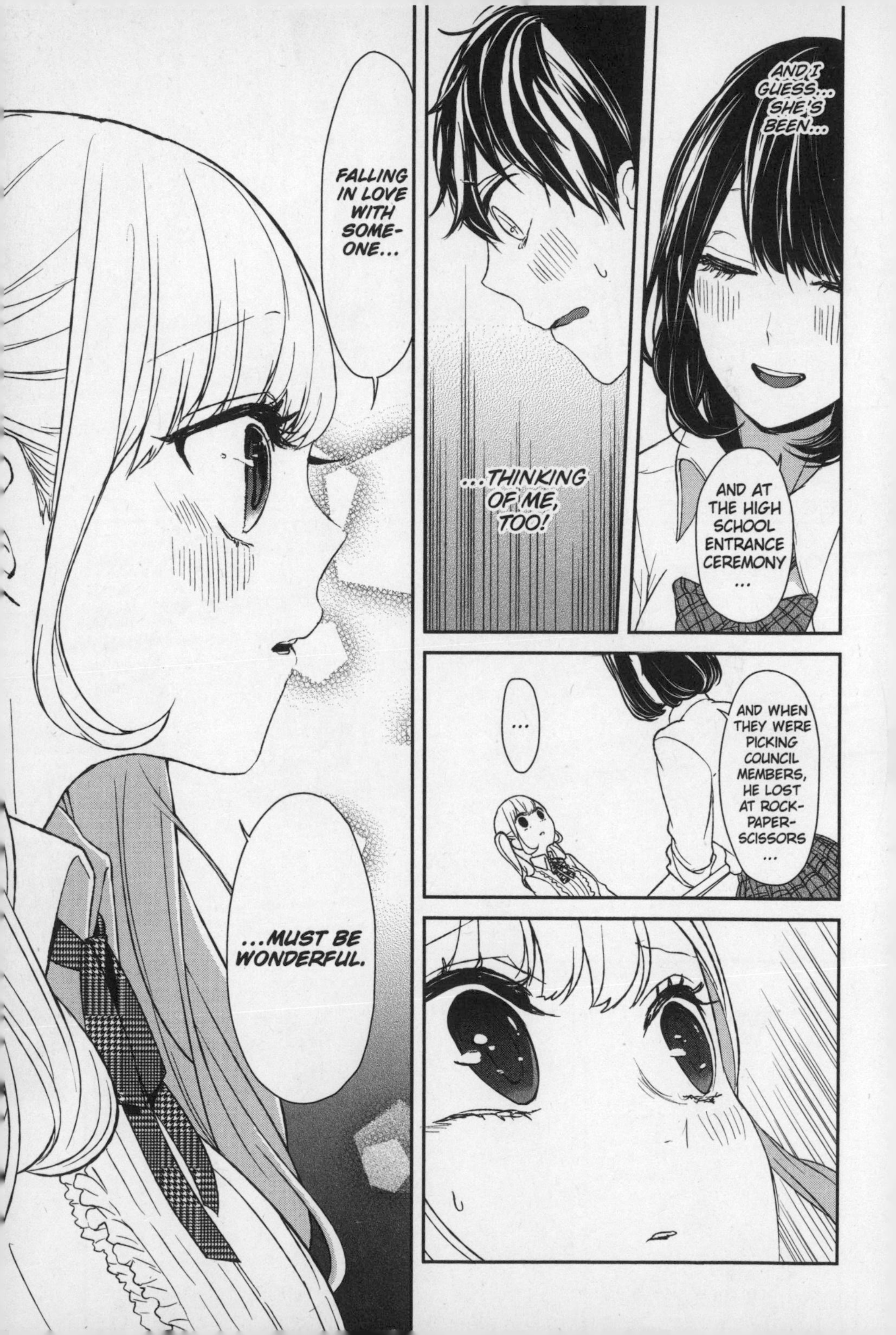

AND I GUESS... SHE'S BEEN...
AND AT THE HIGH SCHOOL ENTRANCE CEREMONY ...
...THINKING OF ME, TOO!
AND WHEN THEY WERE PICKING COUNCIL MEMBERS, HE LOST AT ROCK-PAPER-SCISSORS ...
...
FALLING IN LOVE WITH SOME-ONE...
...MUST BE WONDERFUL.

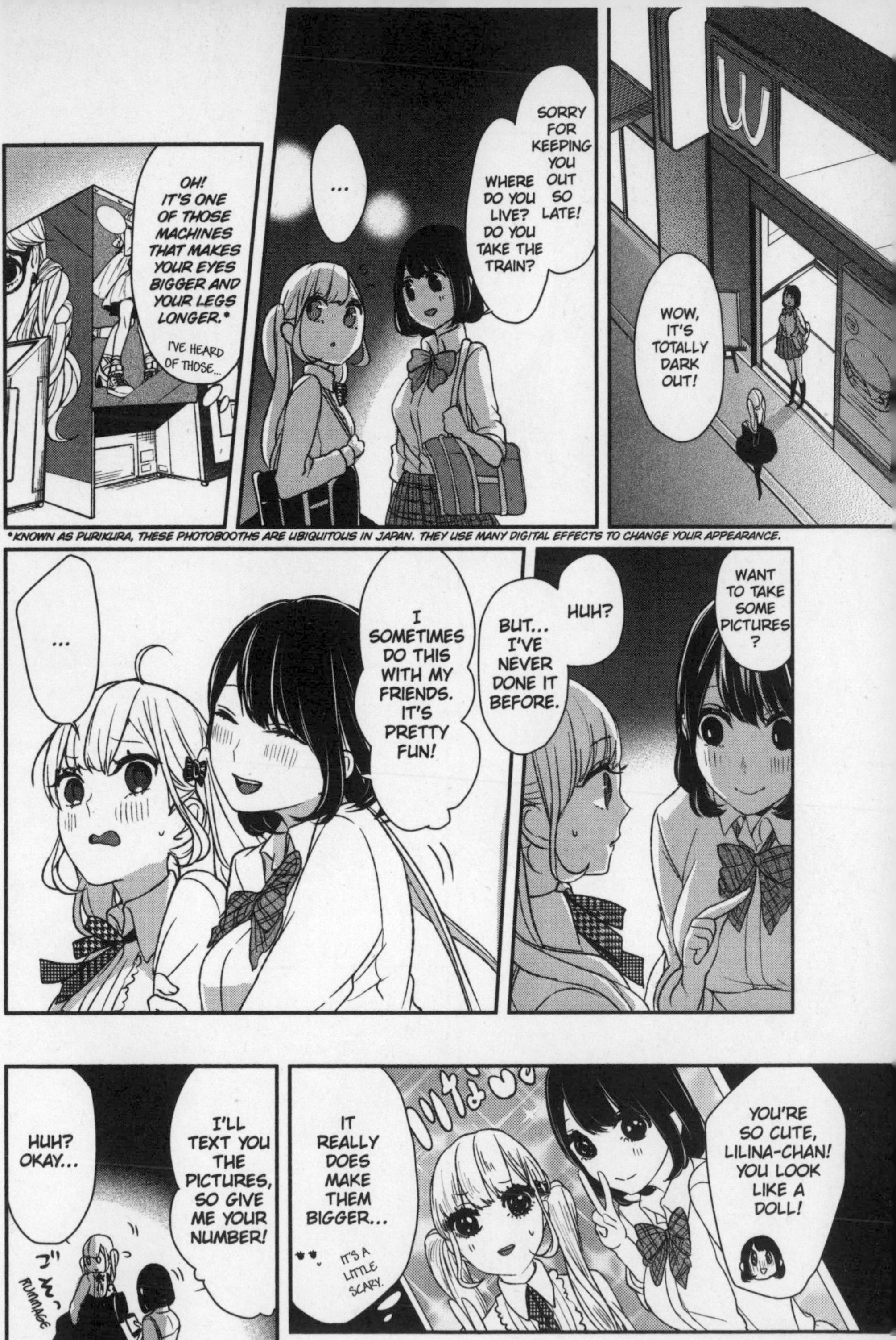
WOW, IT'S TOTALLY DARK OUT!
SORRY FOR KEEPING YOU OUT SO LATE!
WHERE DO YOU LIVE? DO YOU TAKE THE TRAIN?
...
OH! IT'S ONE OF THOSE MACHINES THAT MAKES YOUR EYES BIGGER AND YOUR LEGS LONGER.*
I'VE HEARD OF THOSE...
WANT TO TAKE SOME PICTURES?
HUH?
BUT... I'VE NEVER DONE IT BEFORE.
I SOMETIMES DO THIS WITH MY FRIENDS. IT'S PRETTY FUN!
...
YOU'RE SO CUTE, LILINA-CHAN! YOU LOOK LIKE A DOLL!
IT REALLY DOES MAKE THEM BIGGER...
IT'S A LITTLE SCARY.
I'LL TEXT YOU THE PICTURES, SO GIVE ME YOUR NUMBER!
HUH? OKAY...
RUMMAGE

*KNOWN AS PURIKURA, THESE PHOTOBOOTHS ARE UBIQUITOUS IN JAPAN. THEY USE MANY DIGITAL EFFECTS TO CHANGE YOUR APPEARANCE.

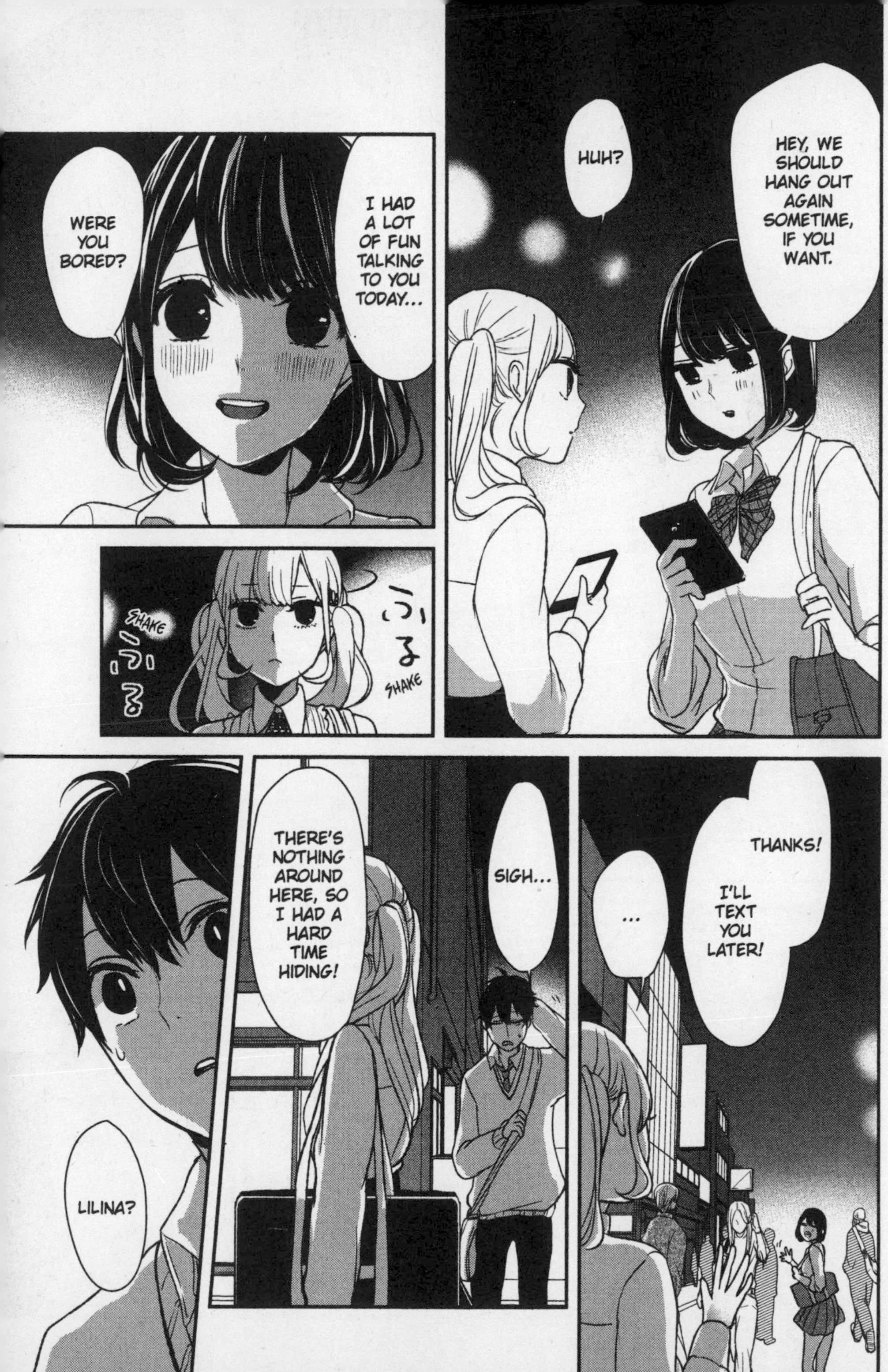
HEY, WE SHOULD HANG OUT AGAIN SOMETIME, IF YOU WANT.
HUH?
I HAD A LOT OF FUN TALKING TO YOU TODAY...
WERE YOU BORED?
ふる SHAKE
ふる SHAKE
THANKS!
I'LL TEXT YOU LATER!
...
SIGH...
THERE'S NOTHING AROUND HERE, SO I HAD A HARD TIME HIDING!
LILINA?

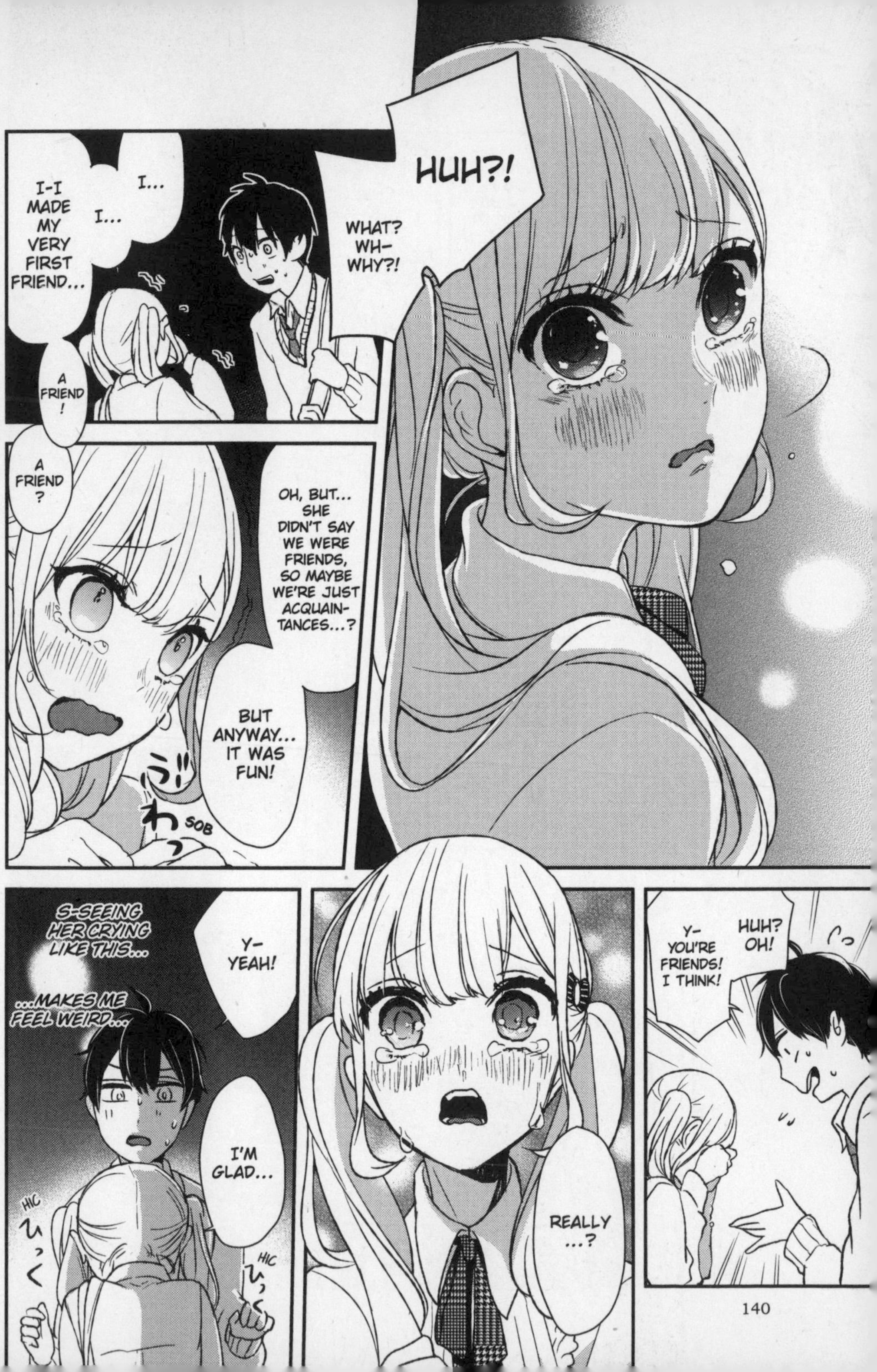
HUH?!
WHAT? WH-WHY?!
I...
I...
I-I MADE MY VERY FIRST FRIEND...
A FRIEND!
A FRIEND?
OH, BUT... SHE DIDN'T SAY WE WERE FRIENDS, SO MAYBE WE'RE JUST ACQUAIN-TANCES...?
BUT ANYWAY... IT WAS FUN!
SOB
HUH? OH!
Y-YOU'RE FRIENDS! I THINK!
REALLY...?
Y-YEAH!
S-SEEING HER CRYING LIKE THIS...
...MAKES ME FEEL WEIRD...
I'M GLAD...
HIC
HIC

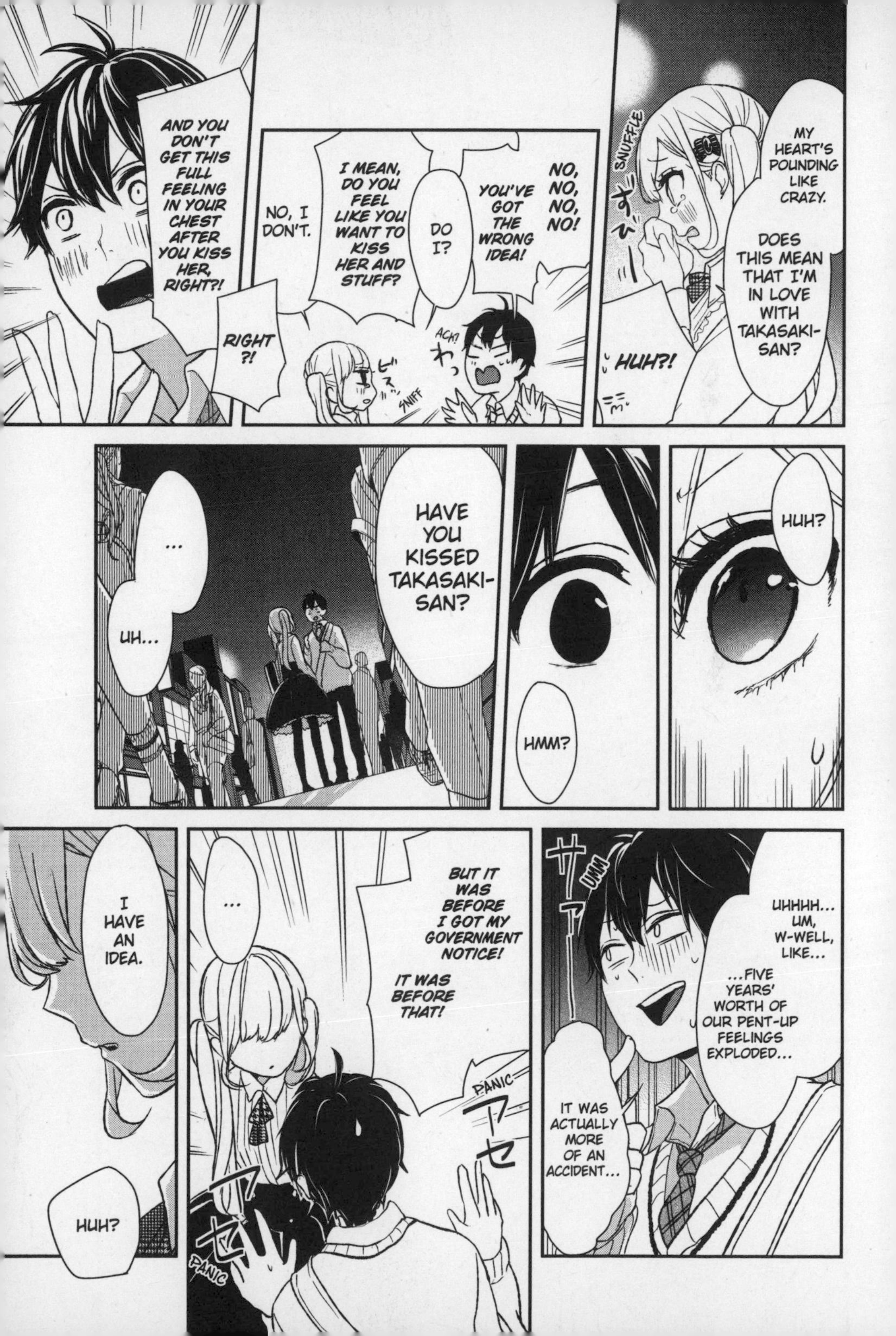
SNUFFLE
MY HEART'S POUNDING LIKE CRAZY.
DOES THIS MEAN THAT I'M IN LOVE WITH TAKASAKI-SAN?
HUH?!
NO, NO, NO, NO!
YOU'VE GOT THE WRONG IDEA!
DO I?
I MEAN, DO YOU FEEL LIKE YOU WANT TO KISS HER AND STUFF?
NO, I DON'T.
ACK!
SNIFF
AND YOU DON'T GET THIS FULL FEELING IN YOUR CHEST AFTER YOU KISS HER, RIGHT?!
RIGHT?!
HUH?
HMM?
HAVE YOU KISSED TAKASAKI-SAN?
...
UH...
UMM
UHHHH... UM, W-WELL, LIKE...
...FIVE YEARS' WORTH OF OUR PENT-UP FEELINGS EXPLODED...
IT WAS ACTUALLY MORE OF AN ACCIDENT...
BUT IT WAS BEFORE I GOT MY GOVERNMENT NOTICE!
IT WAS BEFORE THAT!
...
PANIC
PANIC
I HAVE AN IDEA.
HUH?

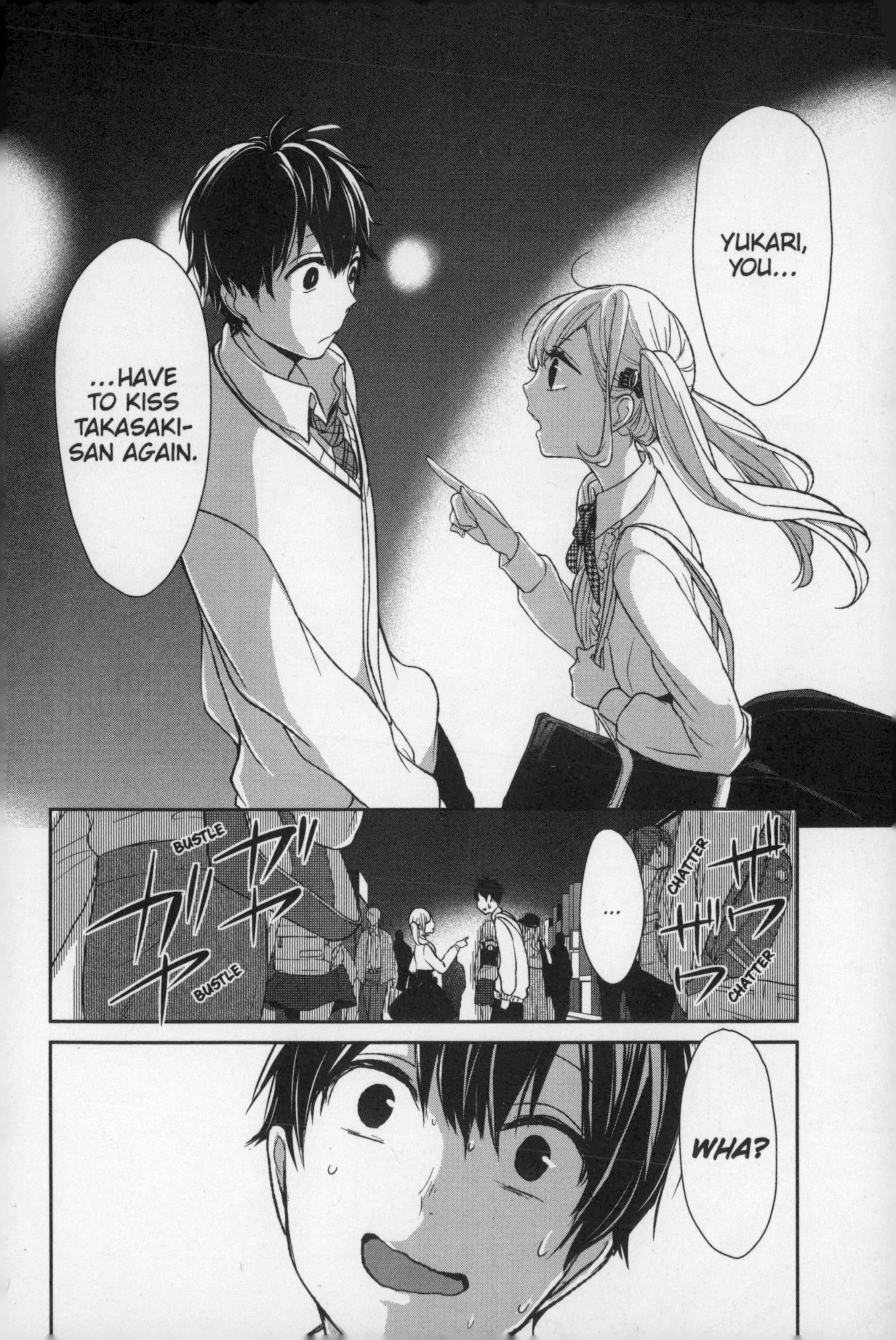
YUKARI, YOU...
...HAVE TO KISS TAKASAKI-SAN AGAIN.
ザワ
ザワ
CHATTER
CHATTER
...
ガヤ
ガヤ
BUSTLE
BUSTLE
WHA?

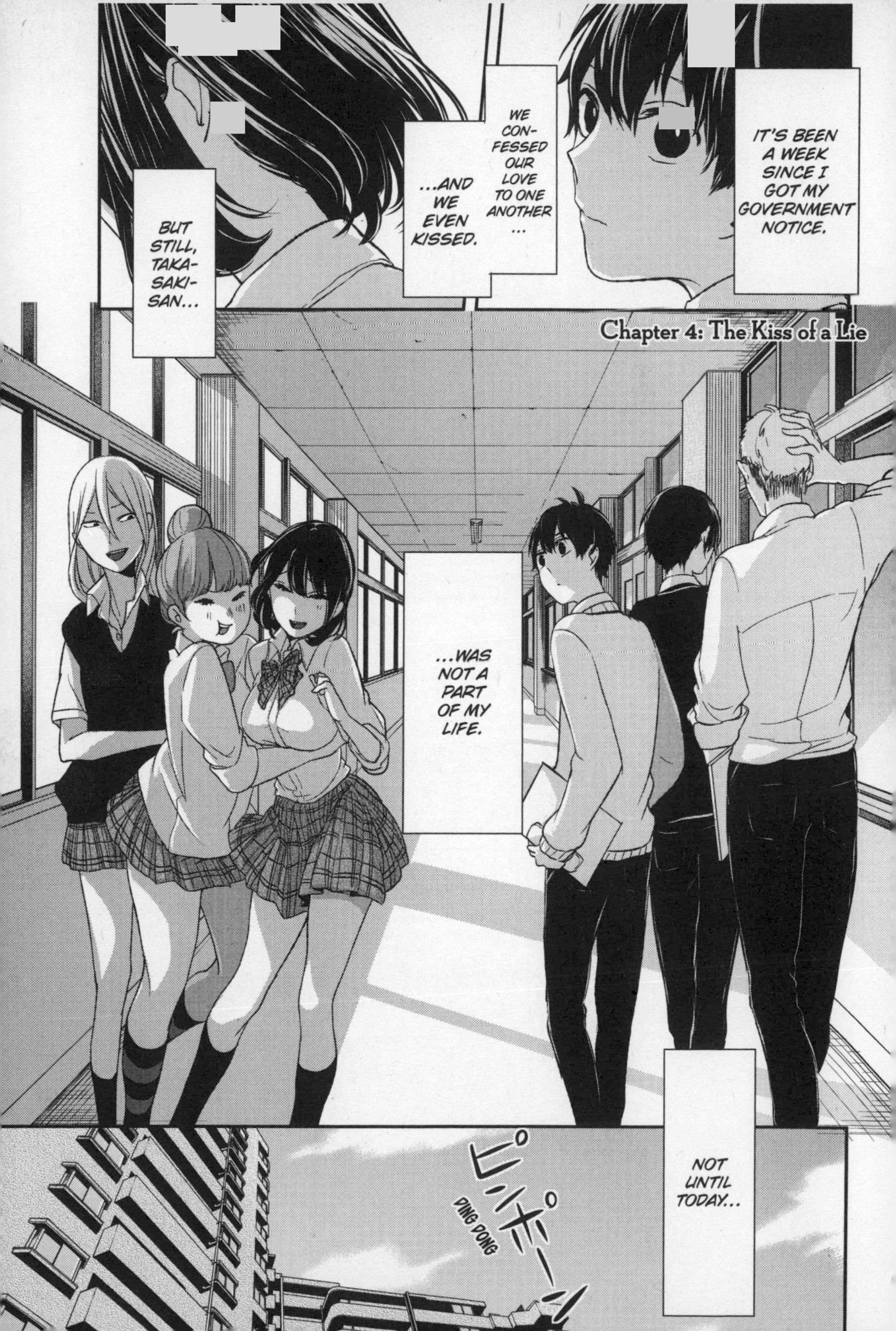
IT'S BEEN A WEEK SINCE I GOT MY GOVERNMENT NOTICE.
WE CON-FESSED OUR LOVE TO ONE ANOTHER ...
...AND WE EVEN KISSED.
BUT STILL, TAKA-SAKI-SAN...
Chapter 4: The Kiss of a Lie
...WAS NOT A PART OF MY LIFE.
NOT UNTIL TODAY...
DING DONG

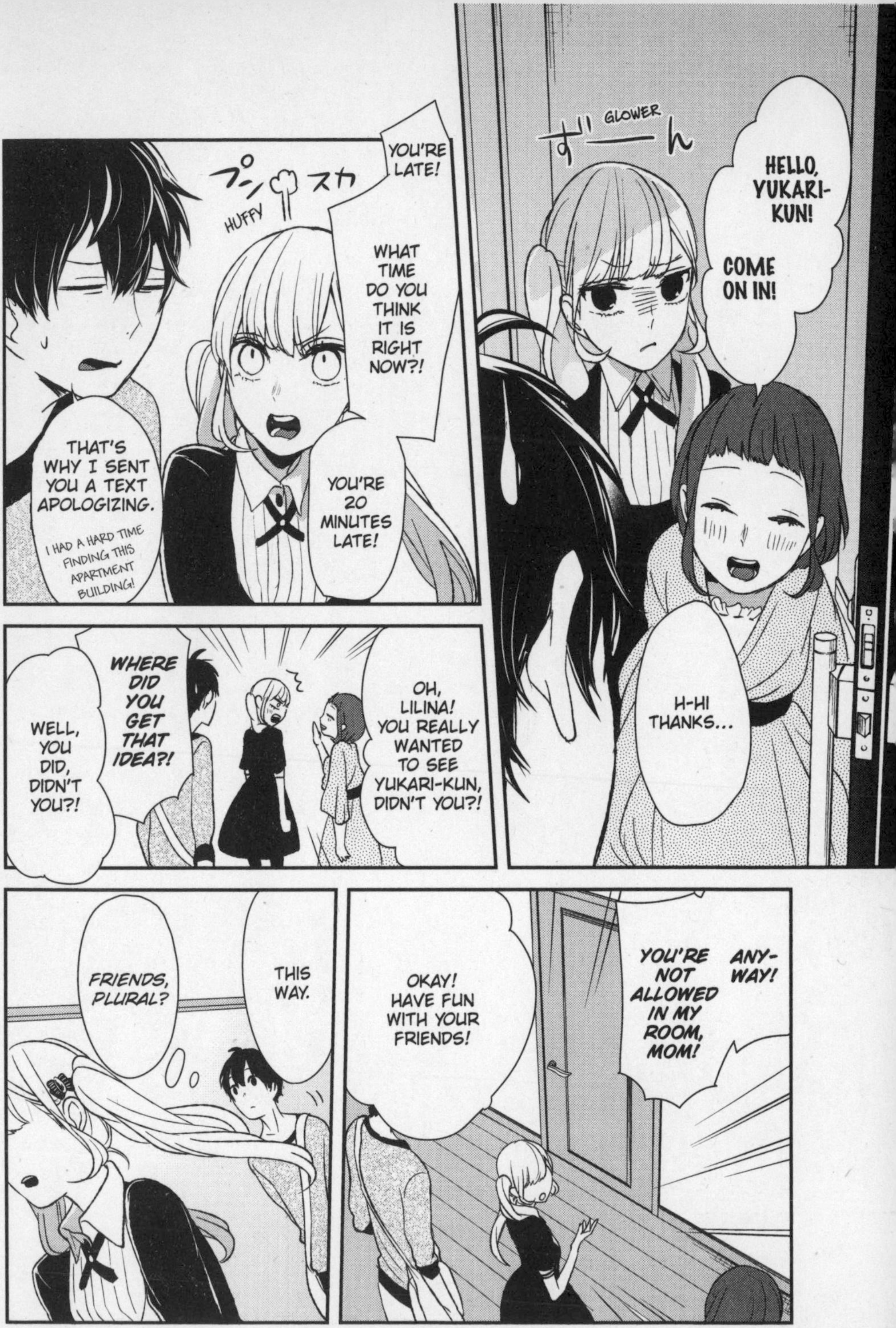
ずーん
GLOWER
HELLO, YUKARI-KUN!
COME ON IN!
H-HI THANKS...
YOU'RE LATE!
プン スカ
HUFFY
WHAT TIME DO YOU THINK IT IS RIGHT NOW?!
YOU'RE 20 MINUTES LATE!
THAT'S WHY I SENT YOU A TEXT APOLOGIZING.
I HAD A HARD TIME FINDING THIS APARTMENT BUILDING!
OH, LILINA! YOU REALLY WANTED TO SEE YUKARI-KUN, DIDN'T YOU?!
WHERE DID YOU GET THAT IDEA?!
WELL, YOU DID, DIDN'T YOU?!
ANY-WAY!
YOU'RE NOT ALLOWED IN MY ROOM, MOM!
OKAY! HAVE FUN WITH YOUR FRIENDS!
THIS WAY.
FRIENDS, PLURAL?

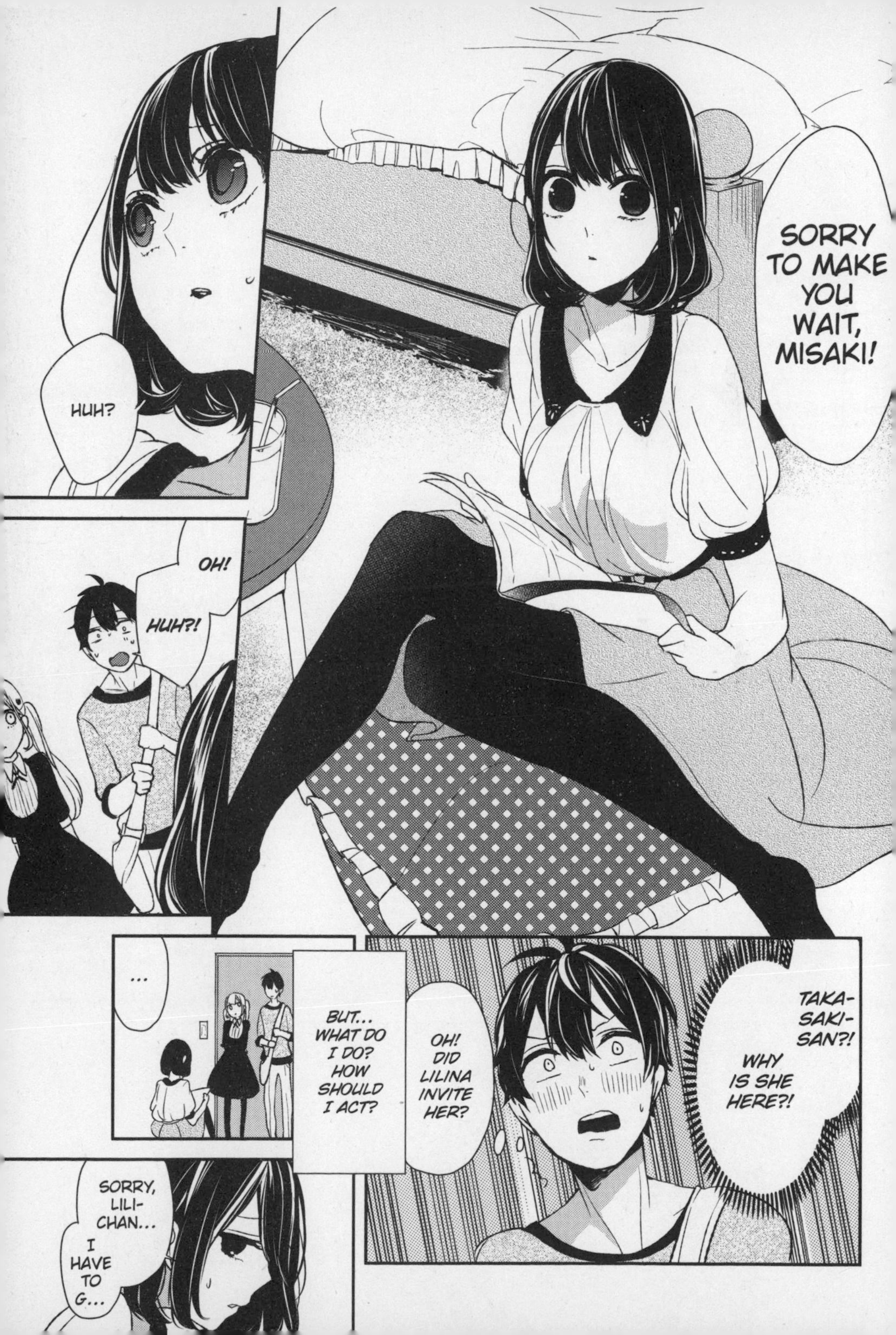
SORRY TO MAKE YOU WAIT, MISAKI!
HUH?
OH!
HUH?!
TAKA-SAKI-SAN?!
WHY IS SHE HERE?!
OH! DID LILINA INVITE HER?
BUT... WHAT DO I DO? HOW SHOULD I ACT?
...
SORRY, LILI-CHAN...
I HAVE TO G...

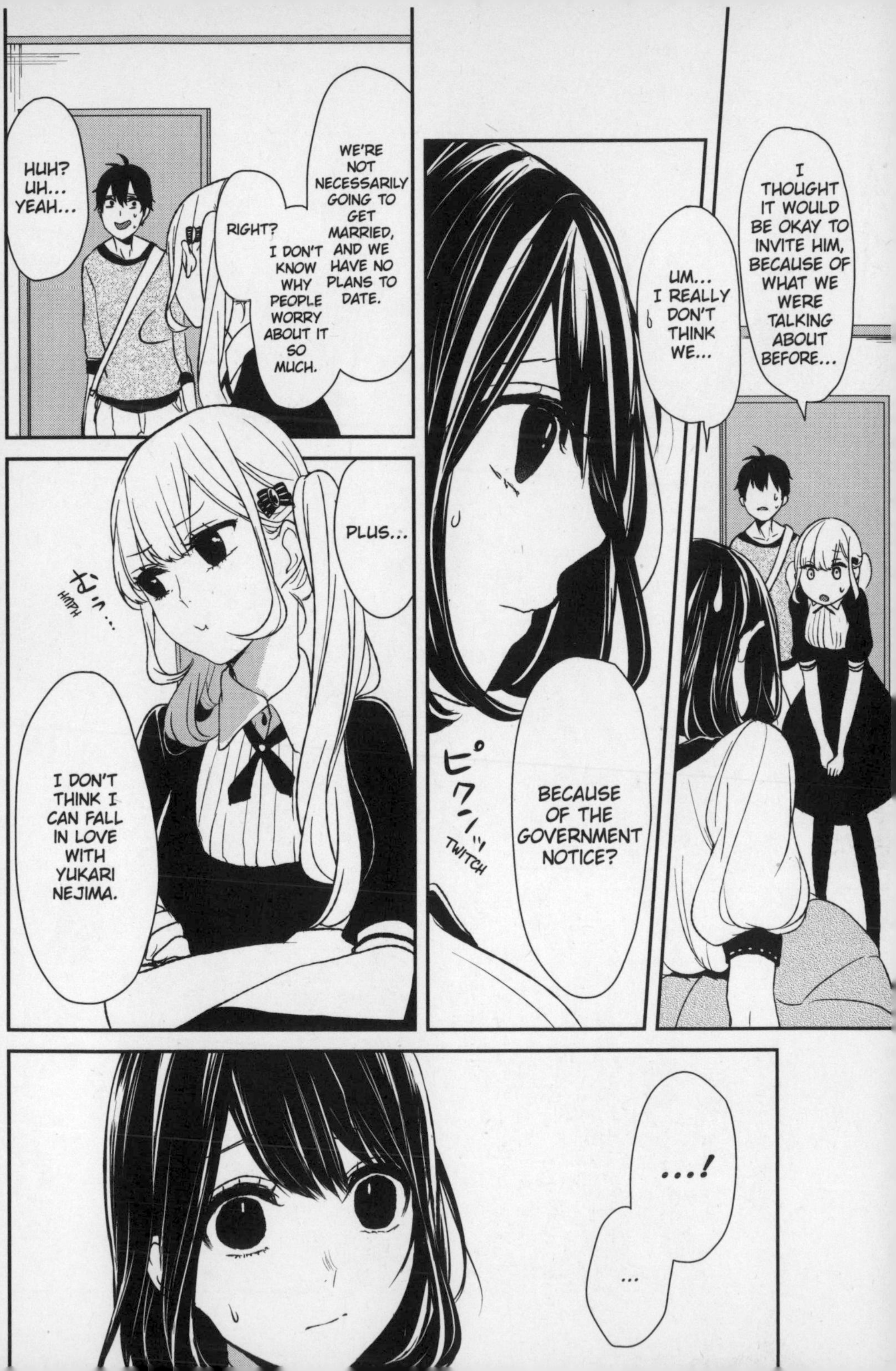

I THOUGHT IT WOULD BE OKAY TO INVITE HIM, BECAUSE OF WHAT WE WERE TALKING ABOUT BEFORE...
UM... I REALLY DON'T THINK WE...
BECAUSE OF THE GOVERNMENT NOTICE?
TWITCH
WE'RE NOT NECESSARILY GOING TO GET MARRIED, AND WE HAVE NO PLANS TO DATE.
RIGHT? I DON'T KNOW WHY PEOPLE WORRY ABOUT IT SO MUCH.
HUH? UH... YEAH...
PLUS...
HMPH
I DON'T THINK I CAN FALL IN LOVE WITH YUKARI NEJIMA.
...!
...

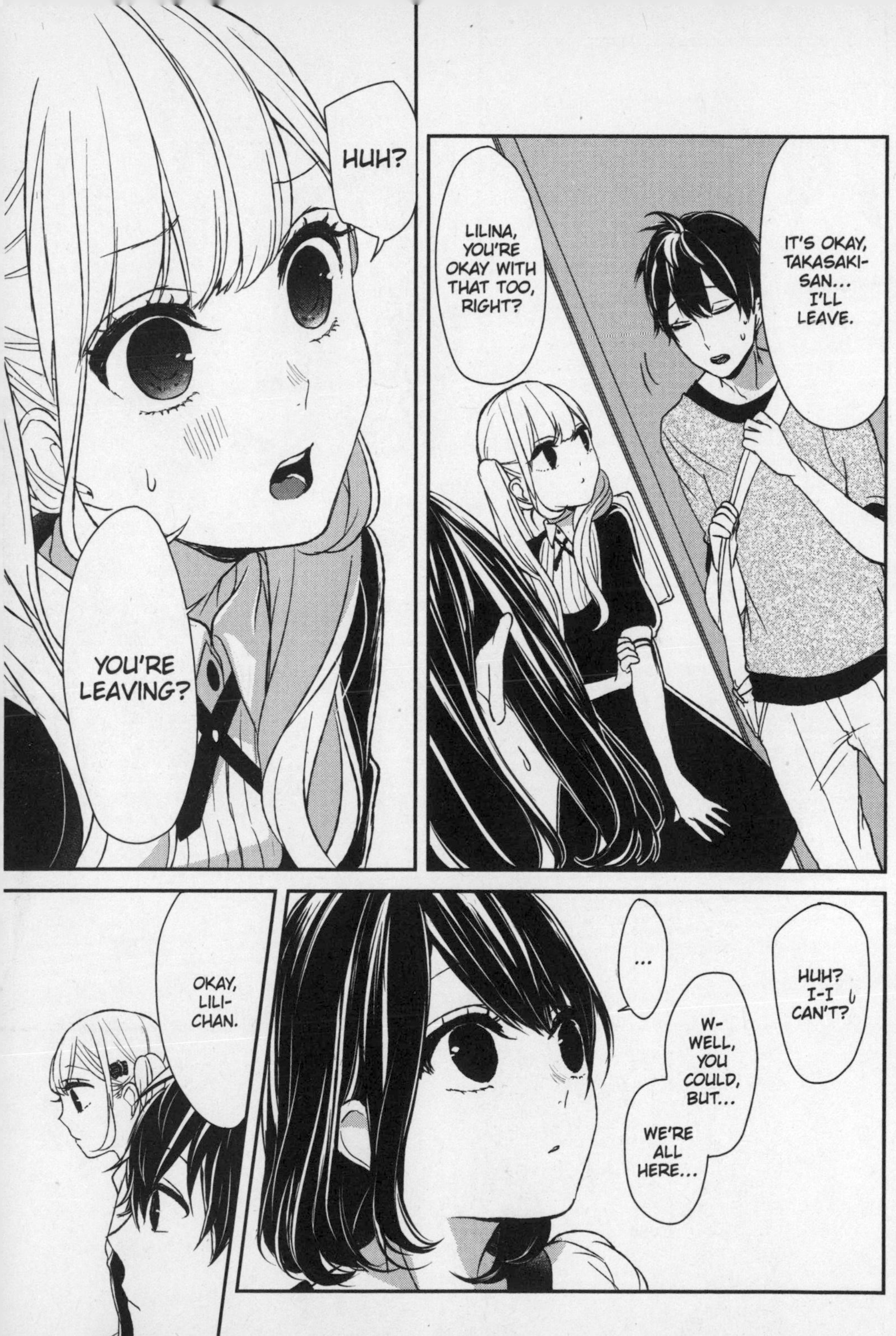
IT'S OKAY, TAKASAKI-SAN... I'LL LEAVE.
LILINA, YOU'RE OKAY WITH THAT TOO, RIGHT?
HUH?
YOU'RE LEAVING?
HUH? I-I CAN'T?
...
W-WELL, YOU COULD, BUT...
WE'RE ALL HERE...
OKAY, LILI-CHAN.

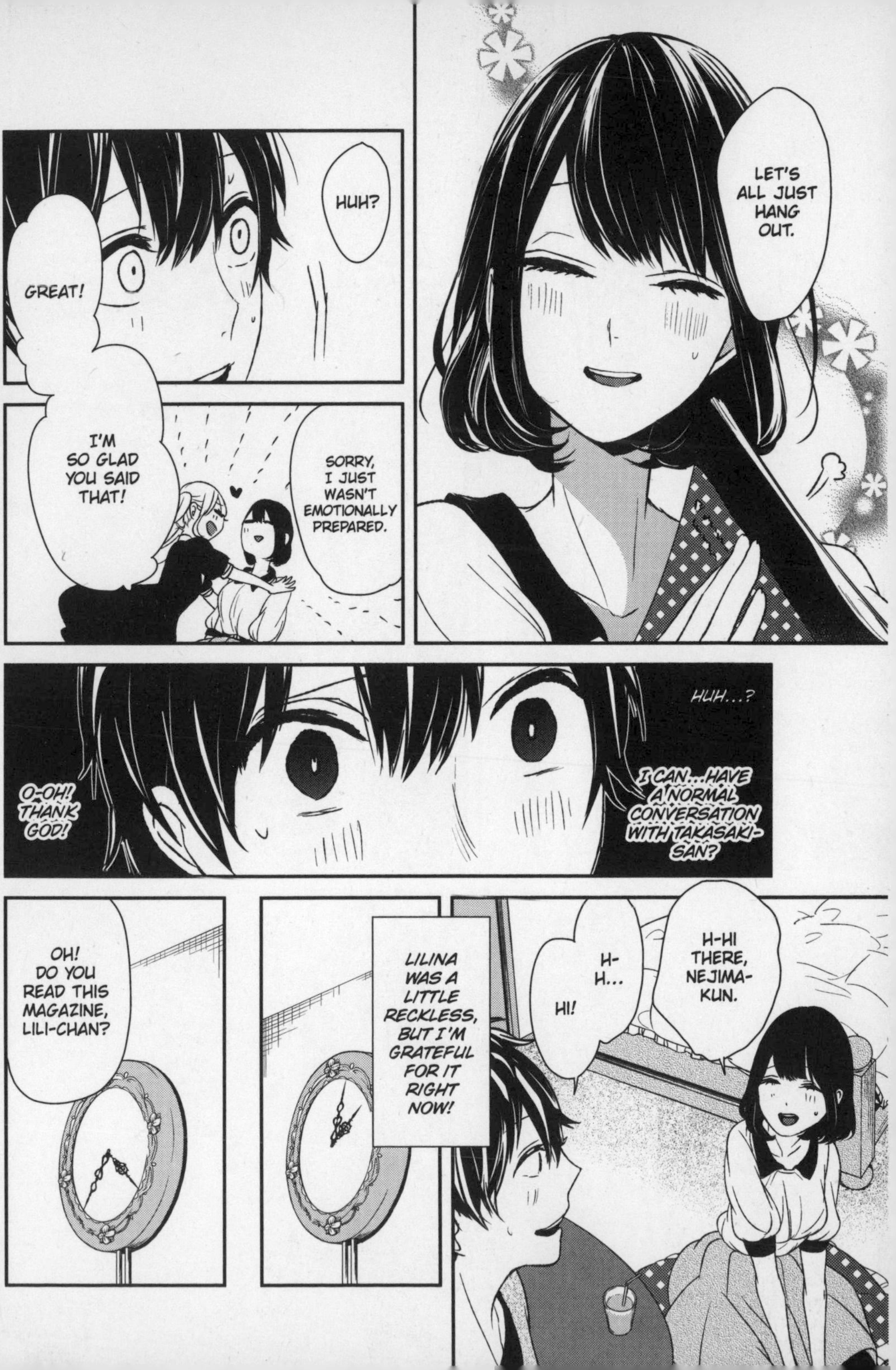
LET'S ALL JUST HANG OUT.
HUH?
GREAT!
SORRY, I JUST WASN'T EMOTIONALLY PREPARED.
I'M SO GLAD YOU SAID THAT!
HUH...?
I CAN...HAVE A NORMAL CONVERSATION WITH TAKASAKI-SAN?
O-OH! THANK GOD!
H-HI THERE, NEJIMA-KUN.
H- H... HI!
LILINA WAS A LITTLE RECKLESS, BUT I'M GRATEFUL FOR IT RIGHT NOW!
OH! DO YOU READ THIS MAGAZINE, LILI-CHAN?

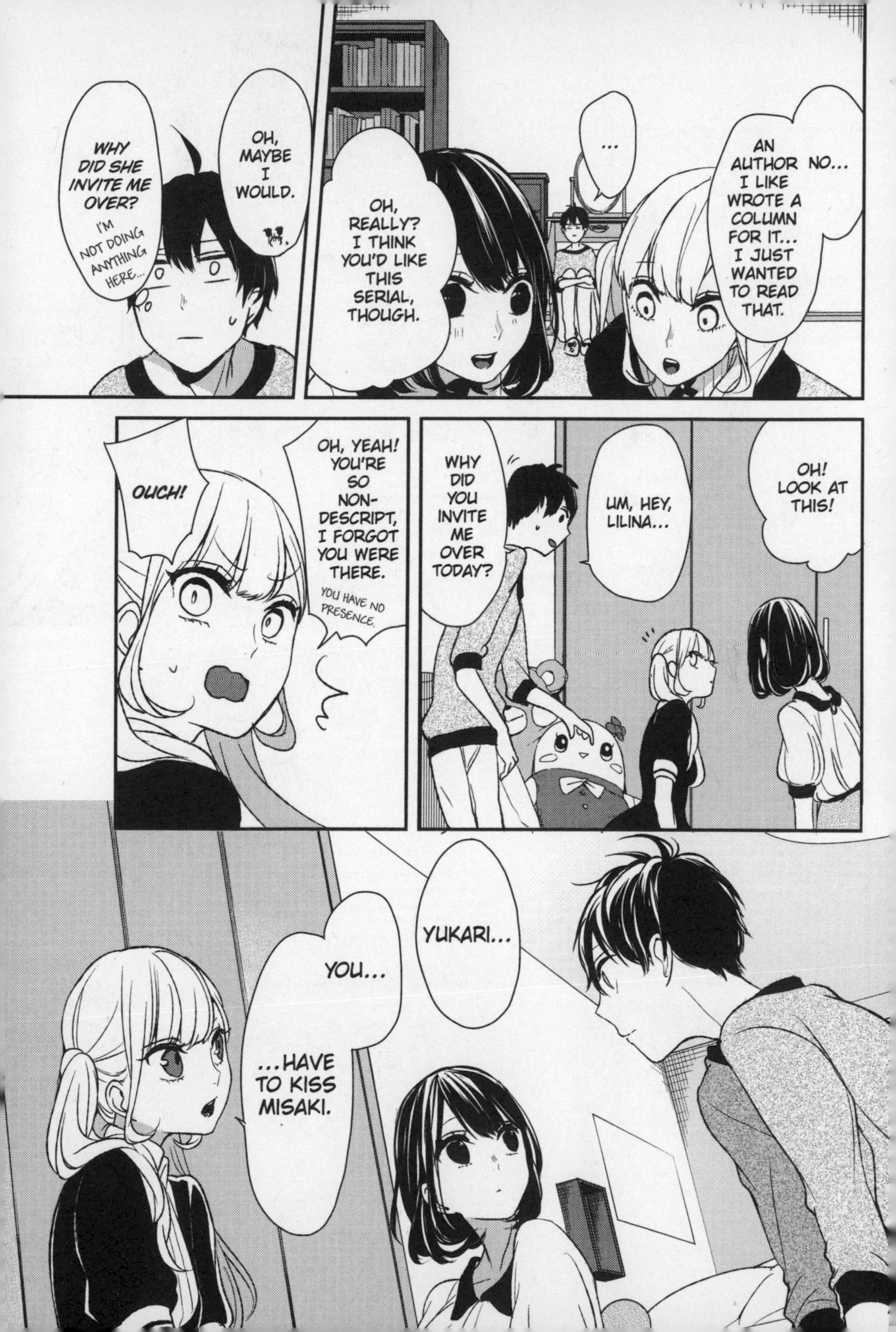
NO...
AN AUTHOR I LIKE WROTE A COLUMN FOR IT... I JUST WANTED TO READ THAT.
...
OH, REALLY? I THINK YOU'D LIKE THIS SERIAL, THOUGH.
OH, MAYBE I WOULD.
WHY DID SHE INVITE ME OVER?
I'M NOT DOING ANYTHING HERE...
OH! LOOK AT THIS!
UM, HEY, LILINA...
WHY DID YOU INVITE ME OVER TODAY?
OH, YEAH! YOU'RE SO NON-DESCRIPT, I FORGOT YOU WERE THERE.
YOU HAVE NO PRESENCE.
OUCH!
YUKARI...
YOU...
...HAVE TO KISS MISAKI.

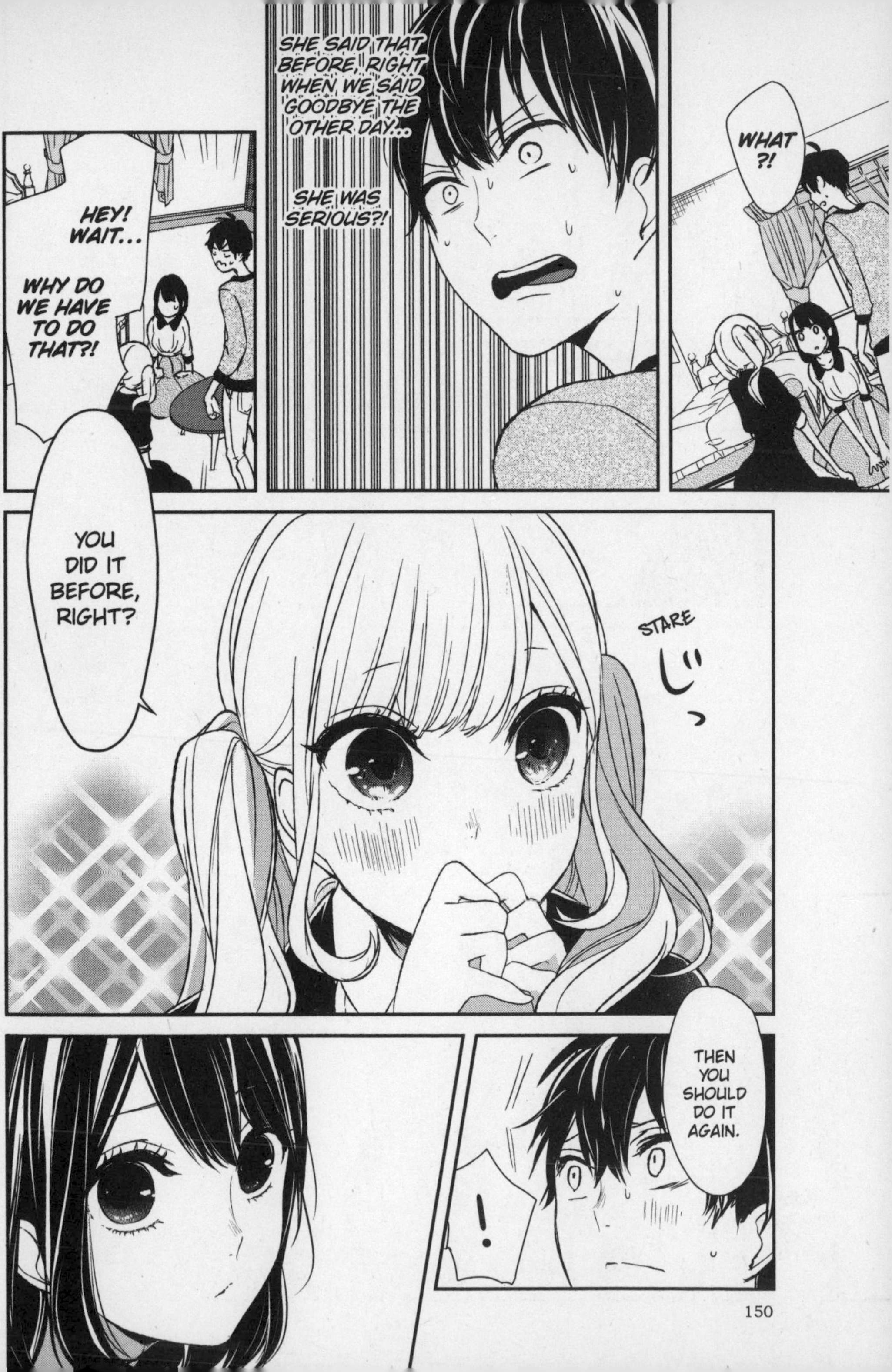
WHAT?!
SHE SAID THAT BEFORE, RIGHT WHEN WE SAID GOODBYE THE OTHER DAY...
SHE WAS SERIOUS?!
HEY! WAIT...
WHY DO WE HAVE TO DO THAT?!
STARE
じっ
YOU DID IT BEFORE, RIGHT?
THEN YOU SHOULD DO IT AGAIN.
!

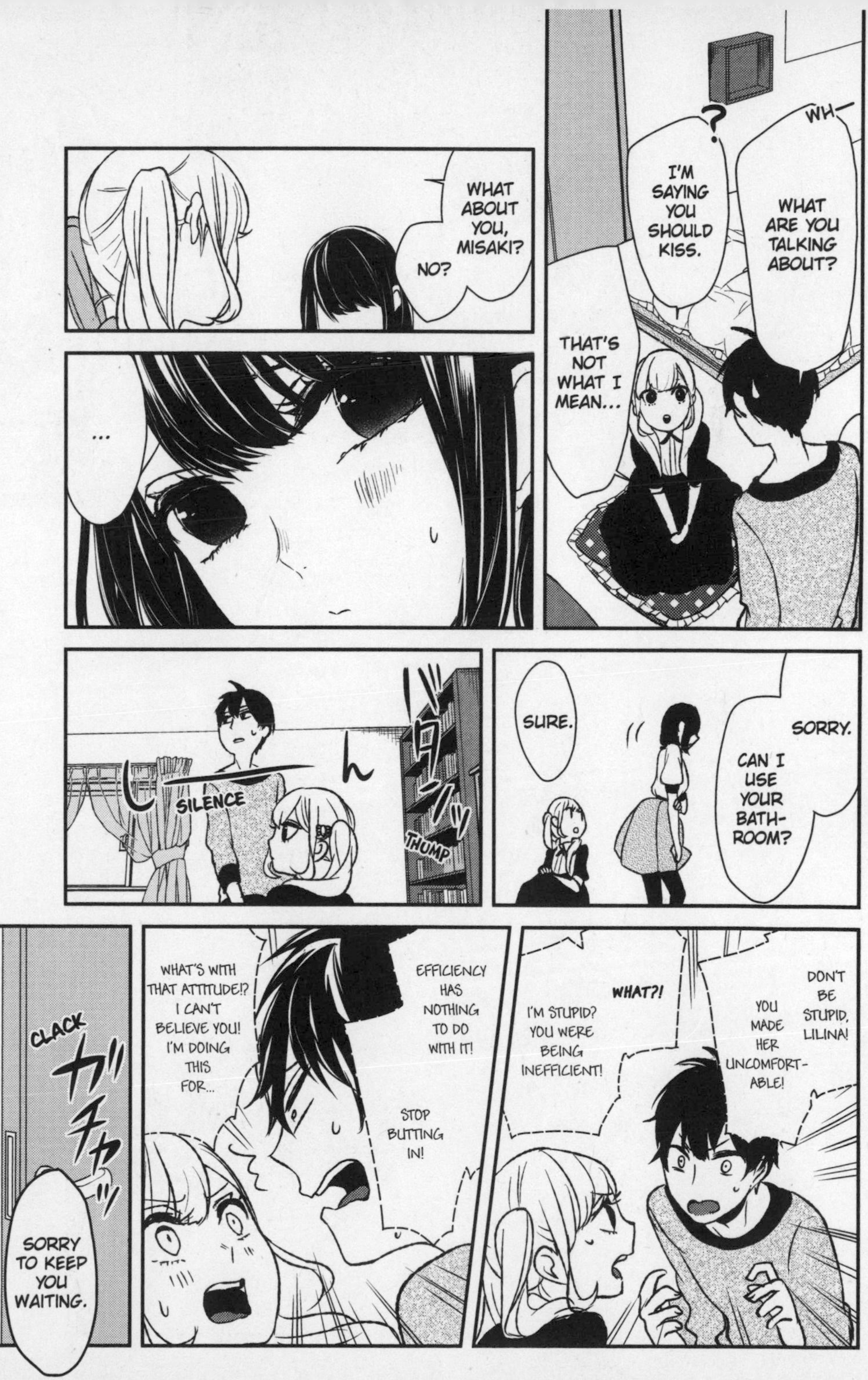
WH—
WHAT ARE YOU TALKING ABOUT?
?
I'M SAYING YOU SHOULD KISS.
THAT'S NOT WHAT I MEAN...
WHAT ABOUT YOU, MISAKI?
NO?
...
SORRY.
CAN I USE YOUR BATHROOM?
SURE.
THUMP
SILENCE
DON'T BE STUPID, LILINA!
YOU MADE HER UNCOMFORT-ABLE!
WHAT?!
I'M STUPID? YOU WERE BEING INEFFICIENT!
EFFICIENCY HAS NOTHING TO DO WITH IT!
WHAT'S WITH THAT ATTITUDE!? I CAN'T BELIEVE YOU! I'M DOING THIS FOR...
STOP BUTTING IN!
CLACK
SORRY TO KEEP YOU WAITING.

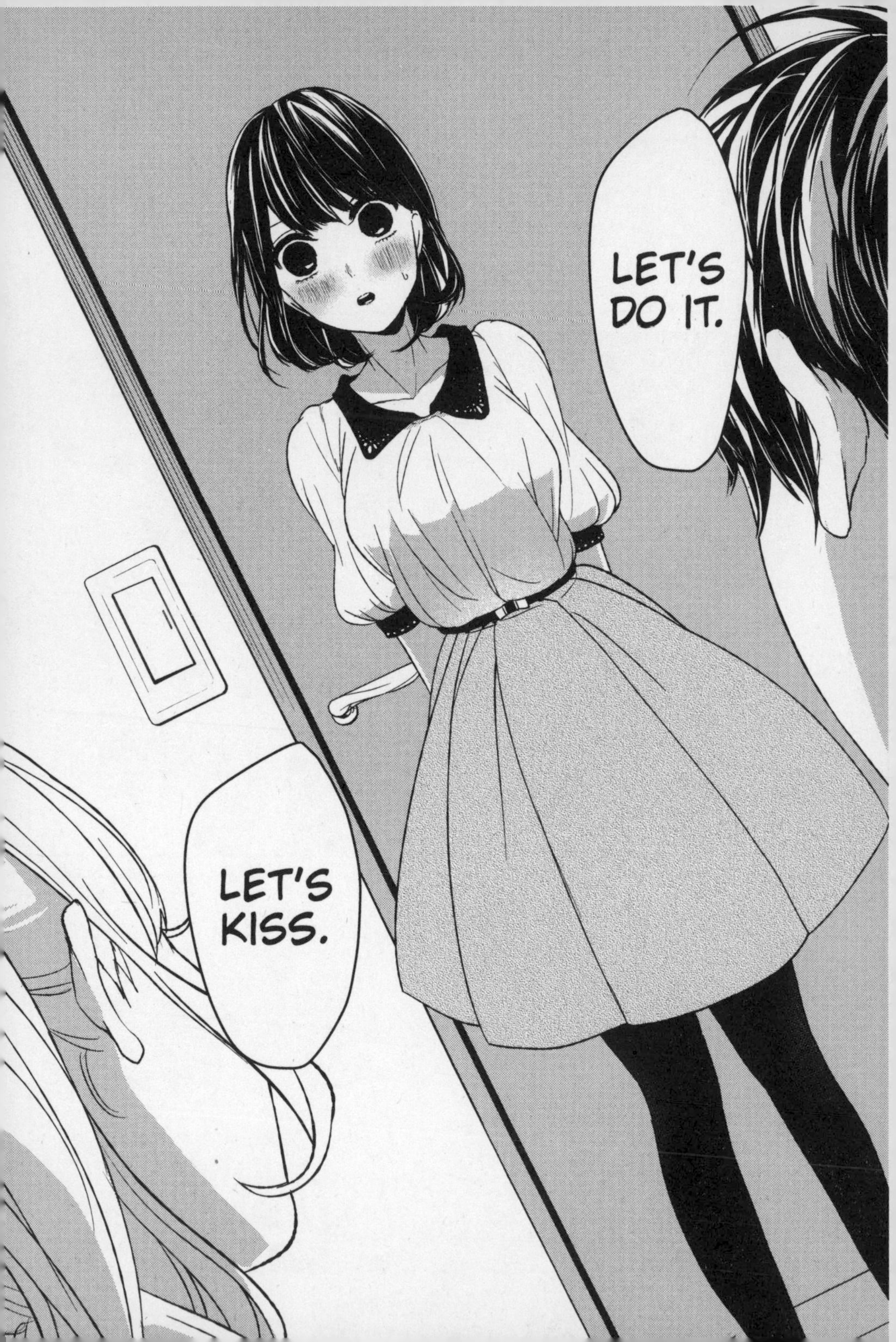
LET'S DO IT.
LET'S KISS.

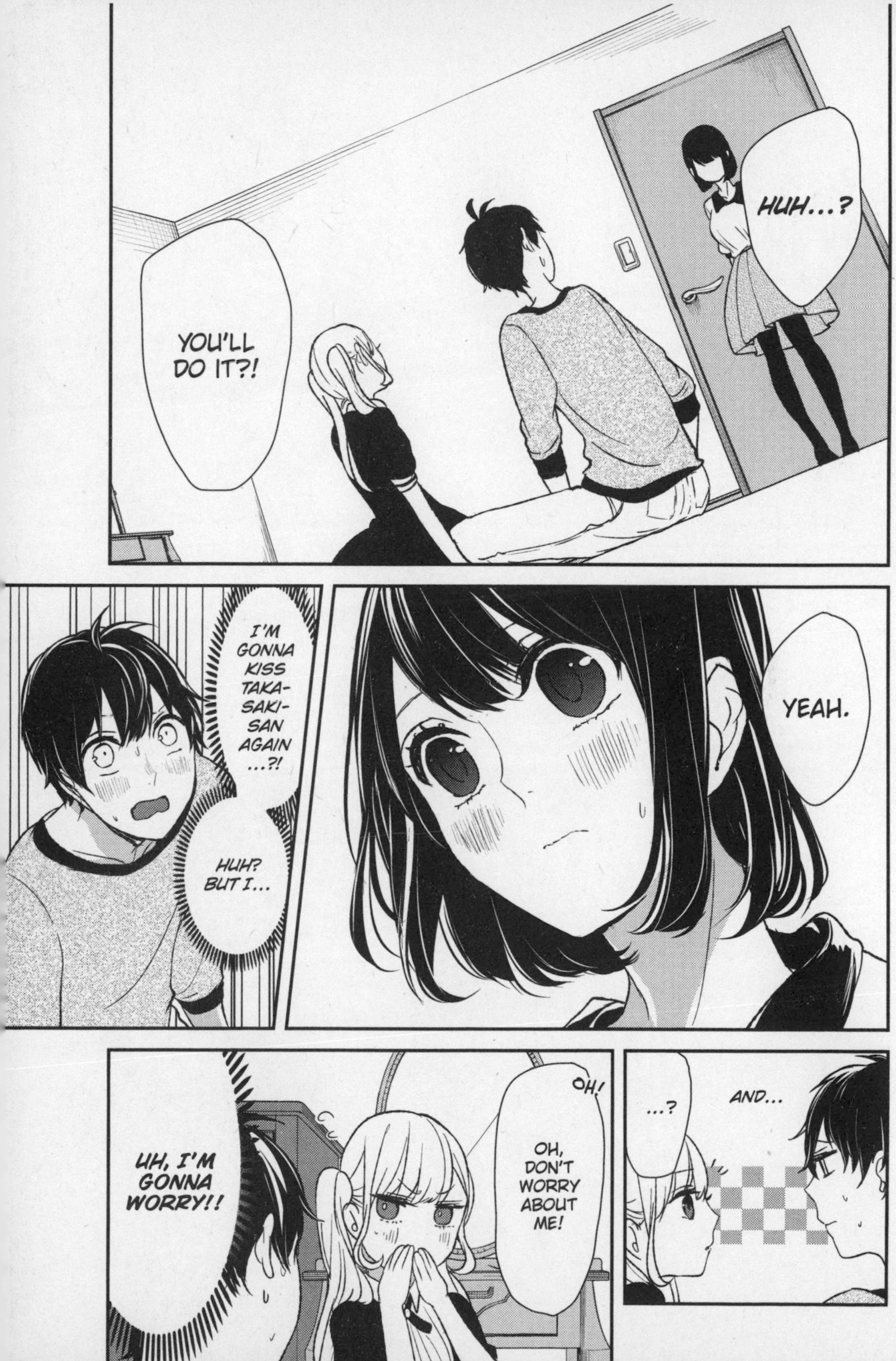
HUH...?
YOU'LL DO IT?!
YEAH.
I'M GONNA KISS TAKA-SAKI-SAN AGAIN ...?!
HUH? BUT I...
AND...
...?
OH!
OH, DON'T WORRY ABOUT ME!
UH, I'M GONNA WORRY!!

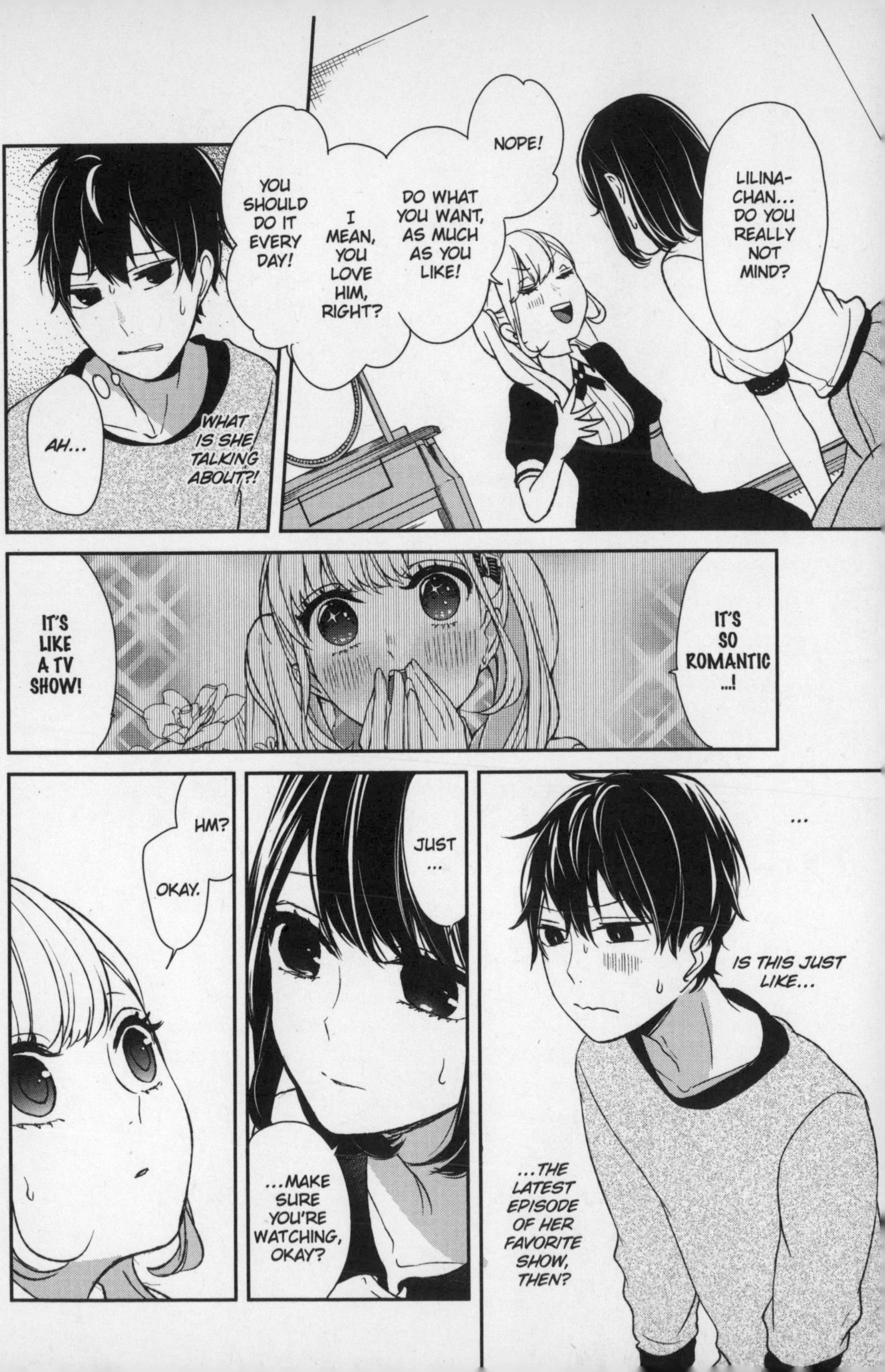
LILINA-CHAN... DO YOU REALLY NOT MIND?
NOPE!
DO WHAT YOU WANT, AS MUCH AS YOU LIKE!
I MEAN, YOU LOVE HIM, RIGHT?
YOU SHOULD DO IT EVERY DAY!
WHAT IS SHE TALKING ABOUT?!
AH...
IT'S SO ROMANTIC ...!
IT'S LIKE A TV SHOW!
...
IS THIS JUST LIKE...
...THE LATEST EPISODE OF HER FAVORITE SHOW, THEN?
JUST ...
...MAKE SURE YOU'RE WATCHING, OKAY?
HM?
OKAY.

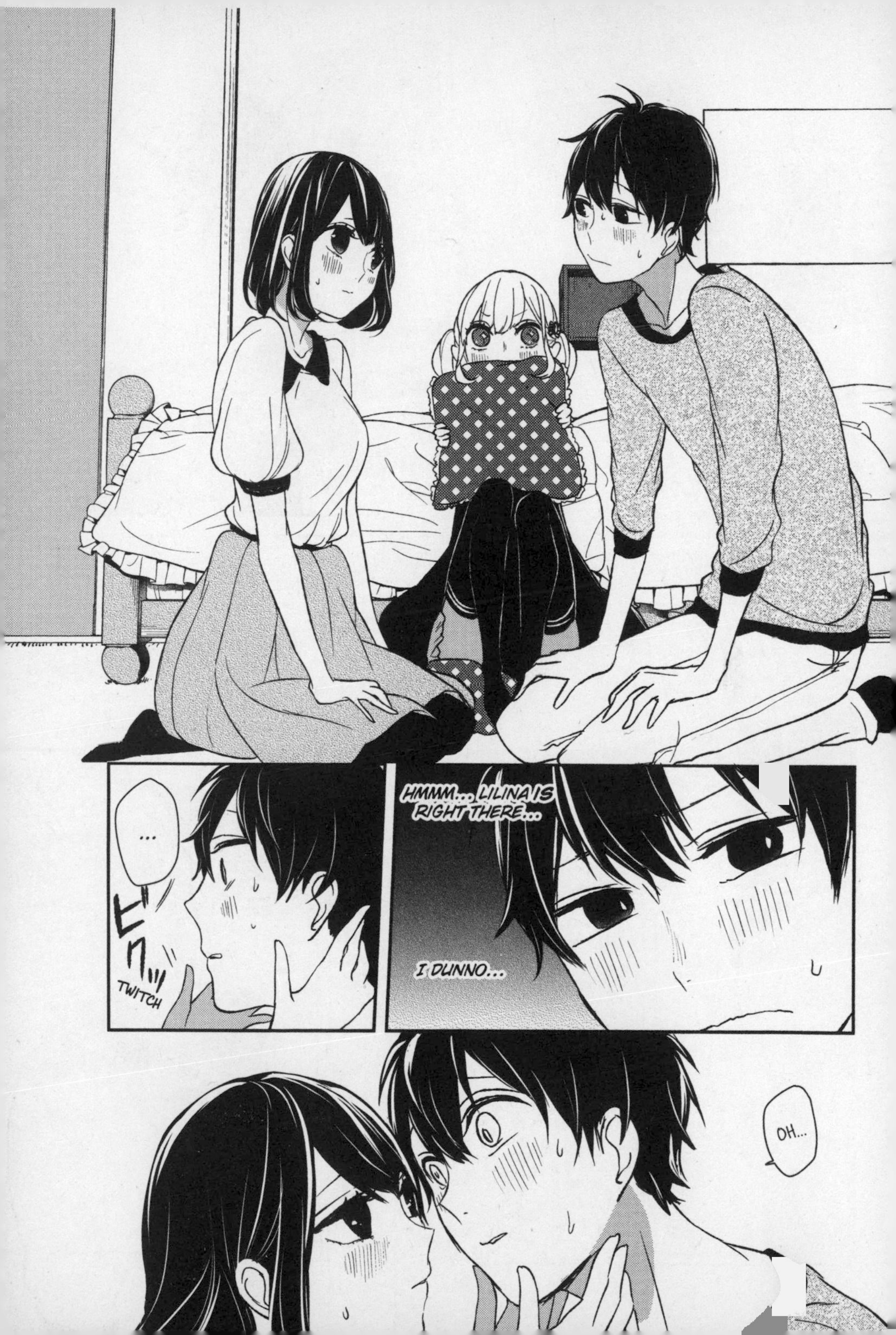
HMMM... LILINA IS RIGHT THERE...
I DUNNO...
...
ビクッ
TWITCH
OH...

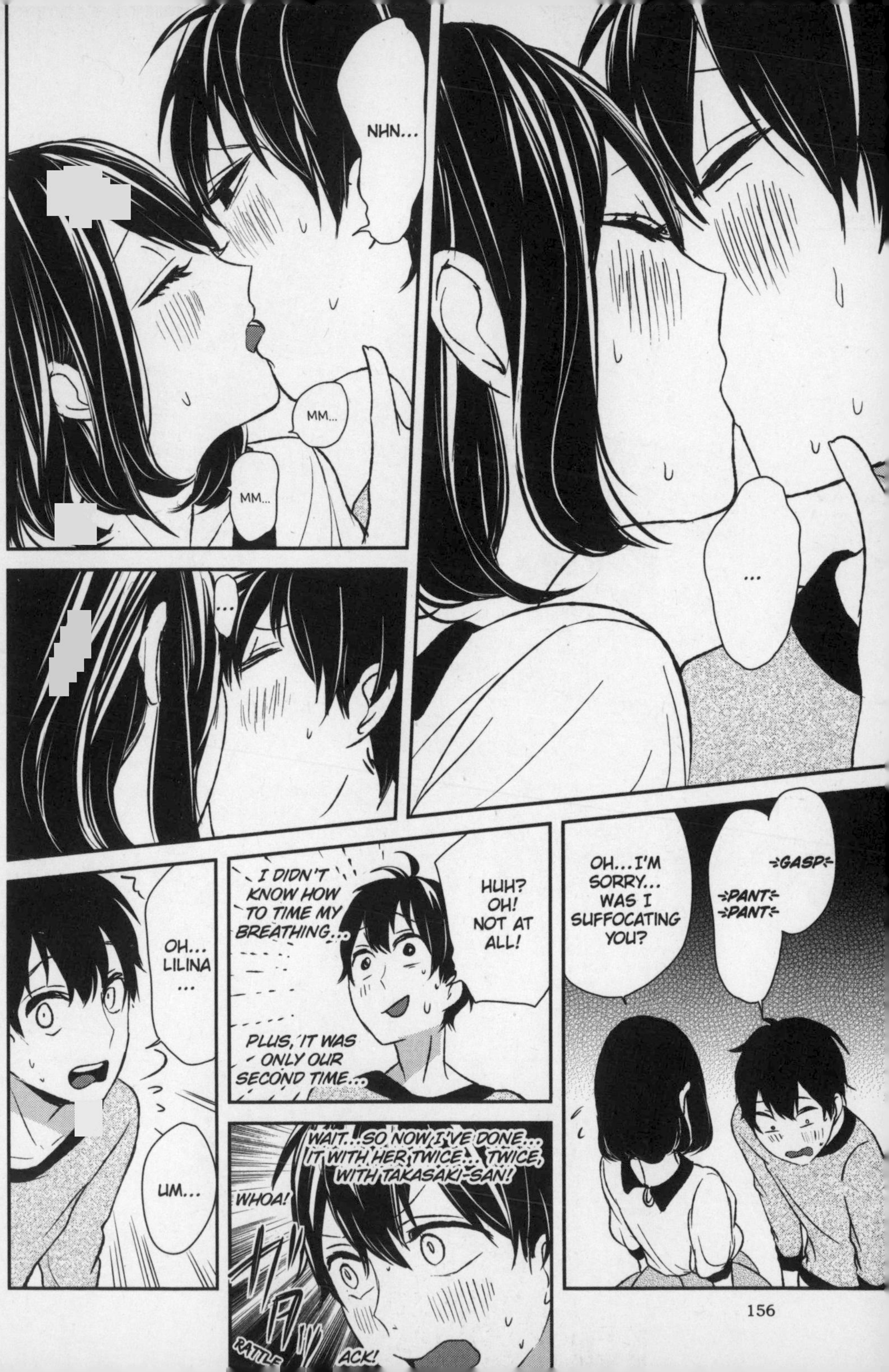
...
NHN...
MM...
MM...
...
GASP
PANT PANT
OH...I'M SORRY... WAS I SUFFOCATING YOU?
HUH? OH! NOT AT ALL!
I DIDN'T KNOW HOW TO TIME MY BREATHING...
PLUS, IT WAS ONLY OUR SECOND TIME...
WAIT...SO NOW I'VE DONE... IT WITH HER TWICE... TWICE, WITH TAKASAKI-SAN!
WHOA!
RATTLE
ACK!
OH... LILINA ...
UM...

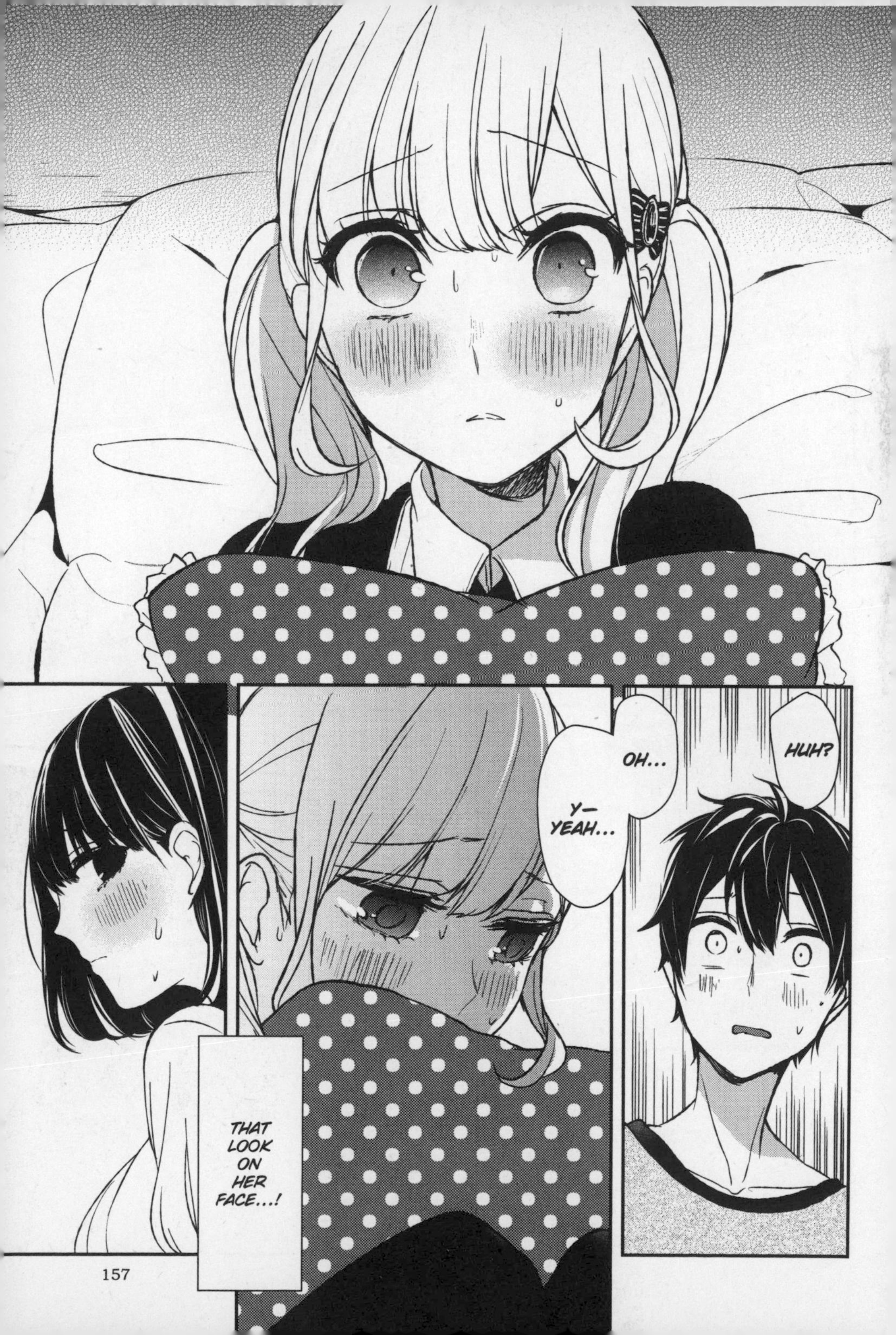
HUH?
OH... Y— YEAH...
THAT LOOK ON HER FACE...!

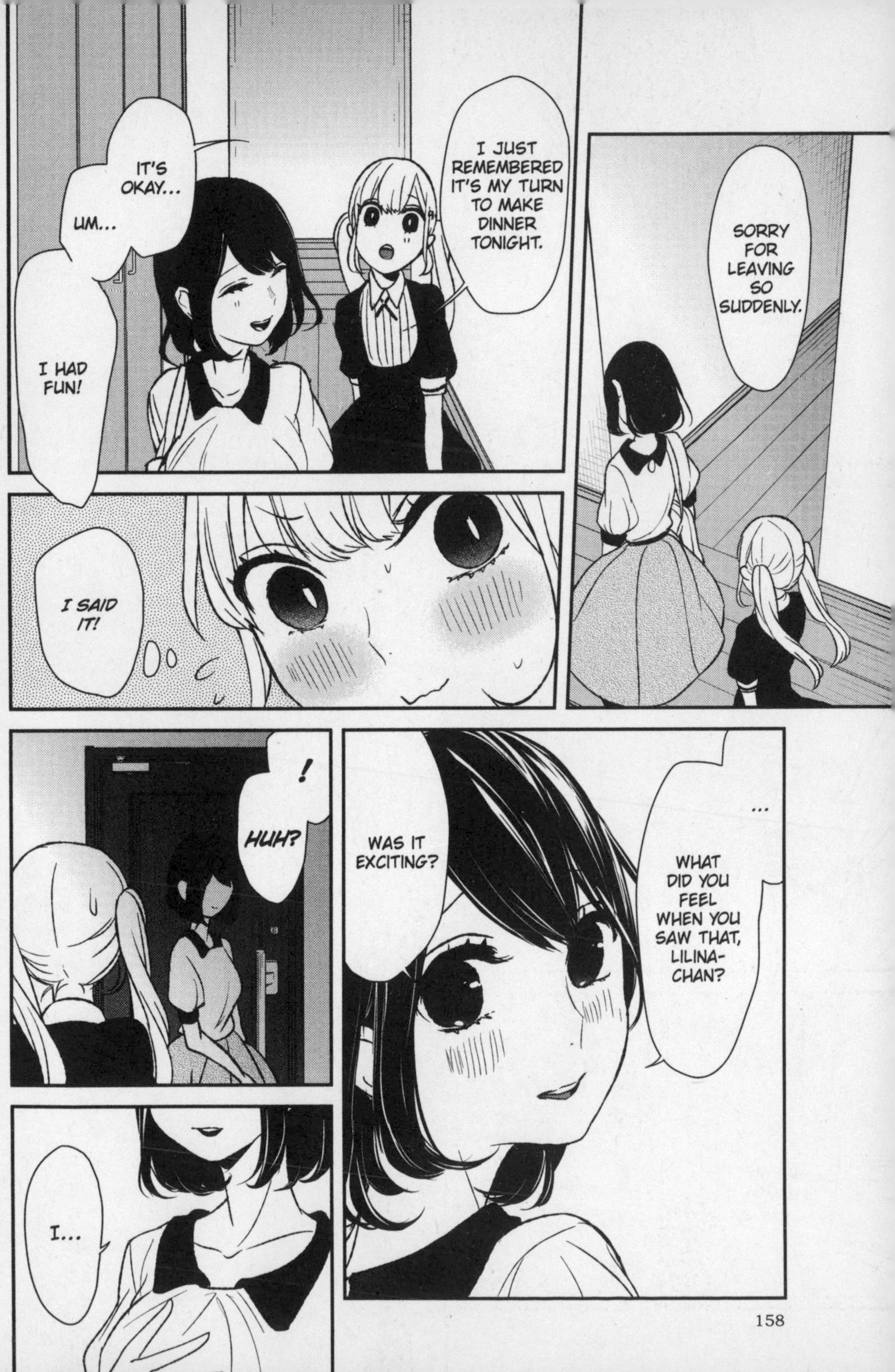
SORRY FOR LEAVING SO SUDDENLY.
I JUST REMEMBERED IT'S MY TURN TO MAKE DINNER TONIGHT.
IT'S OKAY... UM...
I HAD FUN!
I SAID IT!
...
WHAT DID YOU FEEL WHEN YOU SAW THAT, LILINA-CHAN?
WAS IT EXCITING?
! HUH?
I...

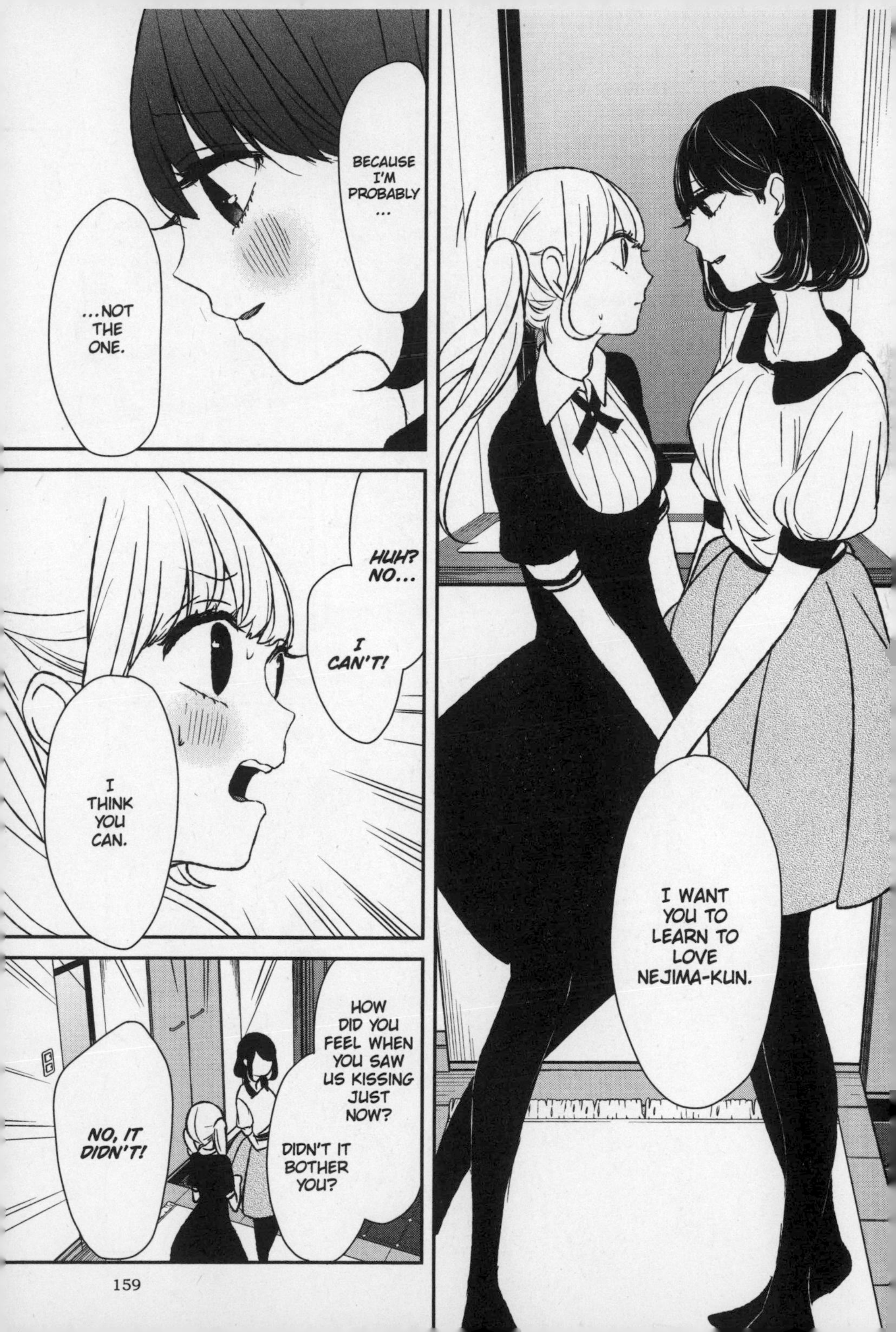
I WANT YOU TO LEARN TO LOVE NEJIMA-KUN.
BECAUSE I'M PROBABLY ...
...NOT THE ONE.
HUH? NO...
I CAN'T!
I THINK YOU CAN.
HOW DID YOU FEEL WHEN YOU SAW US KISSING JUST NOW?
DIDN'T IT BOTHER YOU?
NO, IT DIDN'T!

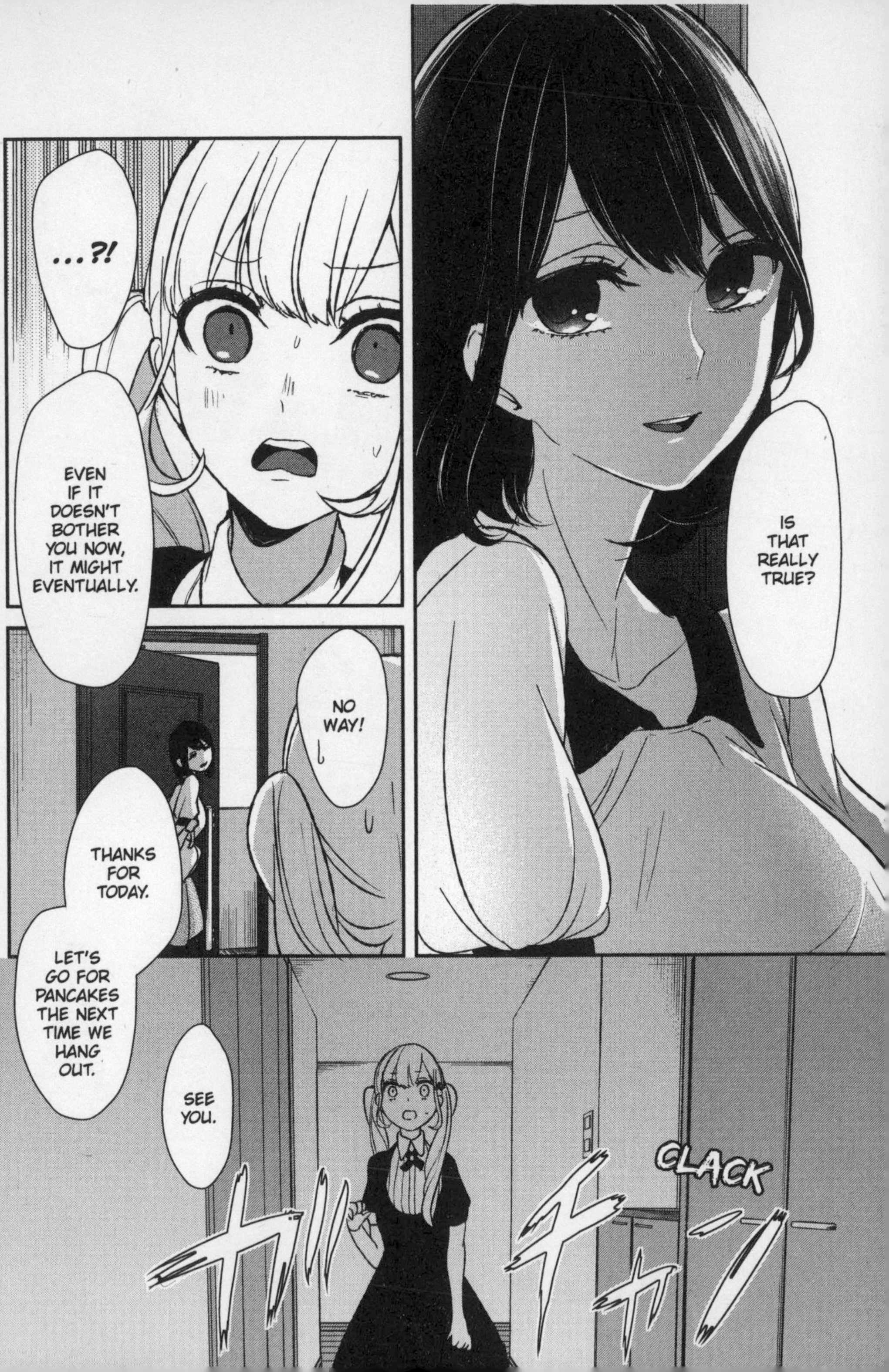
IS THAT REALLY TRUE?
...?!
EVEN IF IT DOESN'T BOTHER YOU NOW, IT MIGHT EVENTUALLY.
NO WAY!
THANKS FOR TODAY.
LET'S GO FOR PANCAKES THE NEXT TIME WE HANG OUT.
SEE YOU.
CLACK
ガチャン

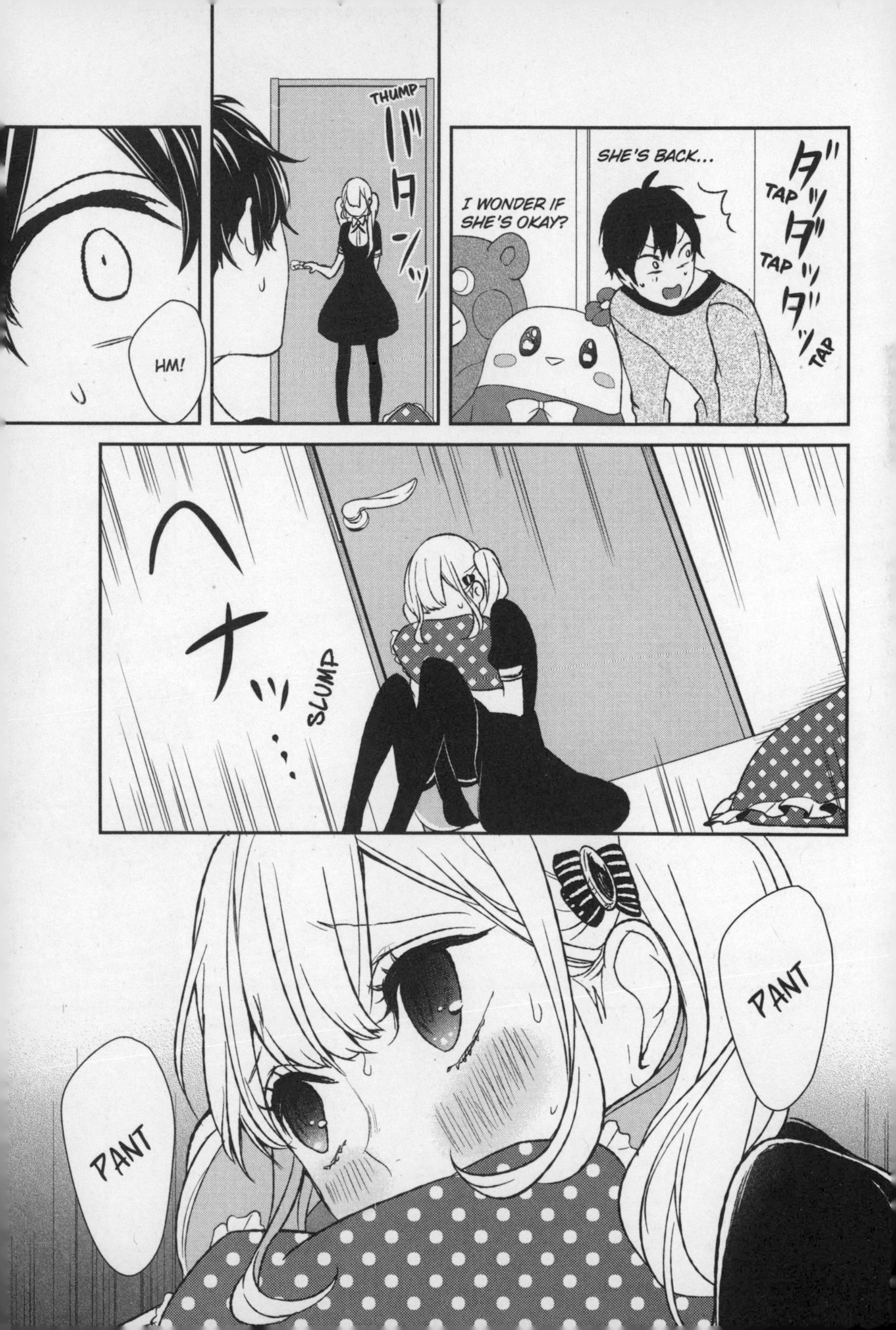
ダッダッダッ
TAP
TAP
TAP
TAP
SHE'S BACK...
I WONDER IF SHE'S OKAY?
THUMP
バタンッ
HM!
へナッ…
SLUMP
PANT
PANT

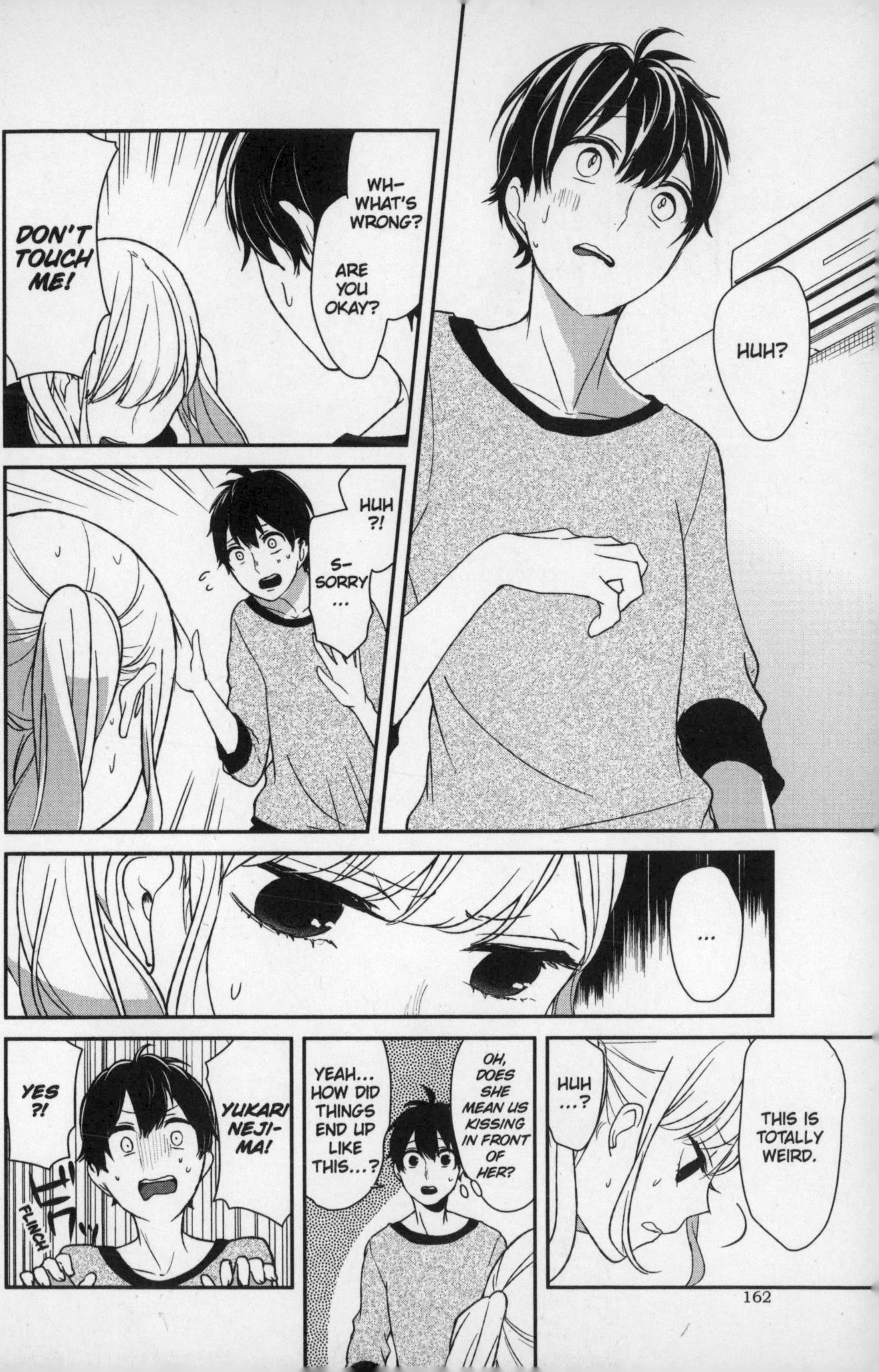
HUH?
WH- WHAT'S WRONG?
ARE YOU OKAY?
DON'T TOUCH ME!
HUH ?!
S- SORRY ...
...
THIS IS TOTALLY WEIRD.
HUH ...?
OH, DOES SHE MEAN US KISSING IN FRONT OF HER?
YEAH... HOW DID THINGS END UP LIKE THIS...?
YUKARI NEJI- MA!
YES ?!
FLINCH

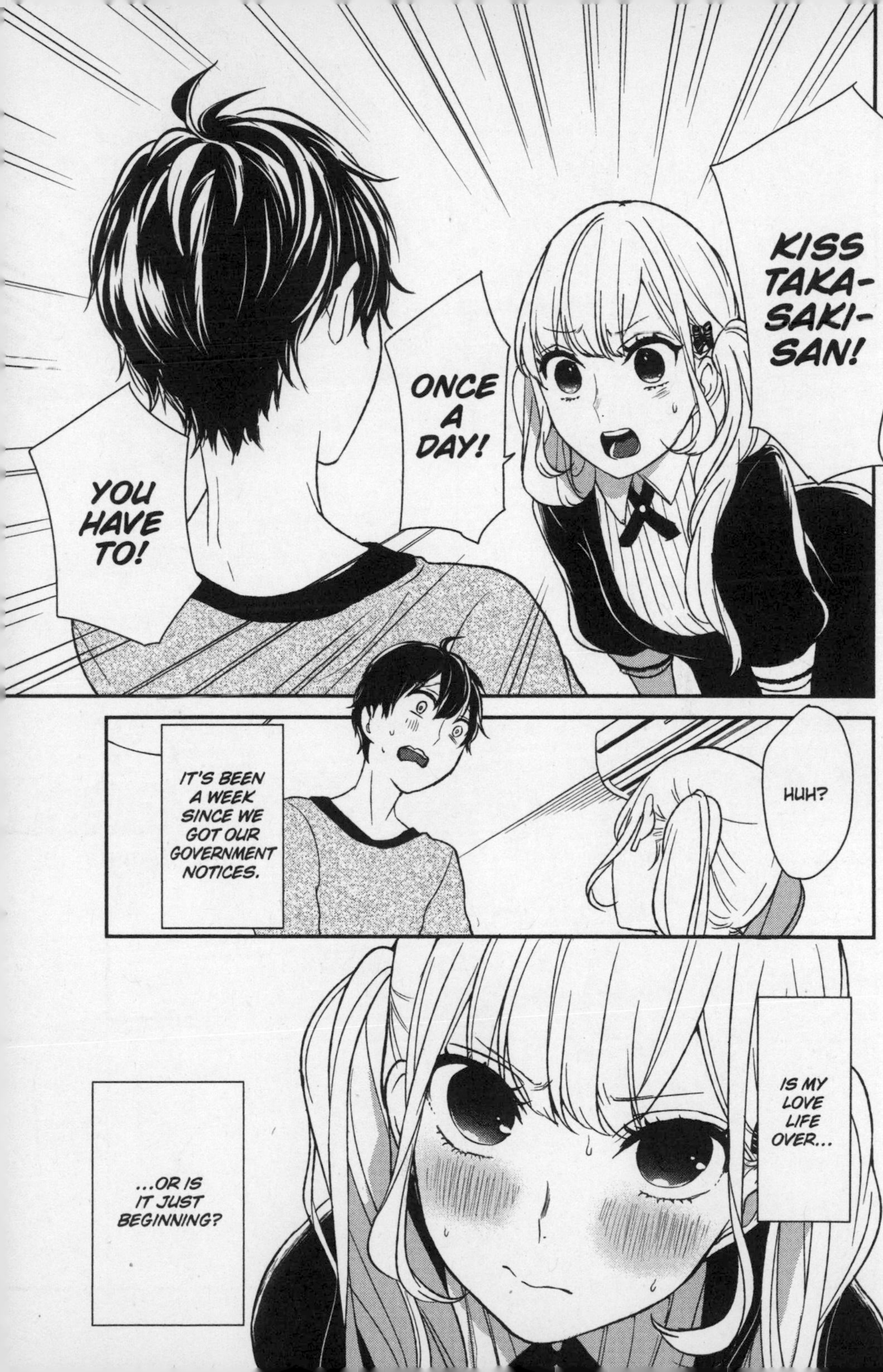
KISS TAKASAKI-SAN!
ONCE A DAY!
YOU HAVE TO!
HUH?
IT'S BEEN A WEEK SINCE WE GOT OUR GOVERNMENT NOTICES.
IS MY LOVE LIFE OVER...
...OR IS IT JUST BEGINNING?

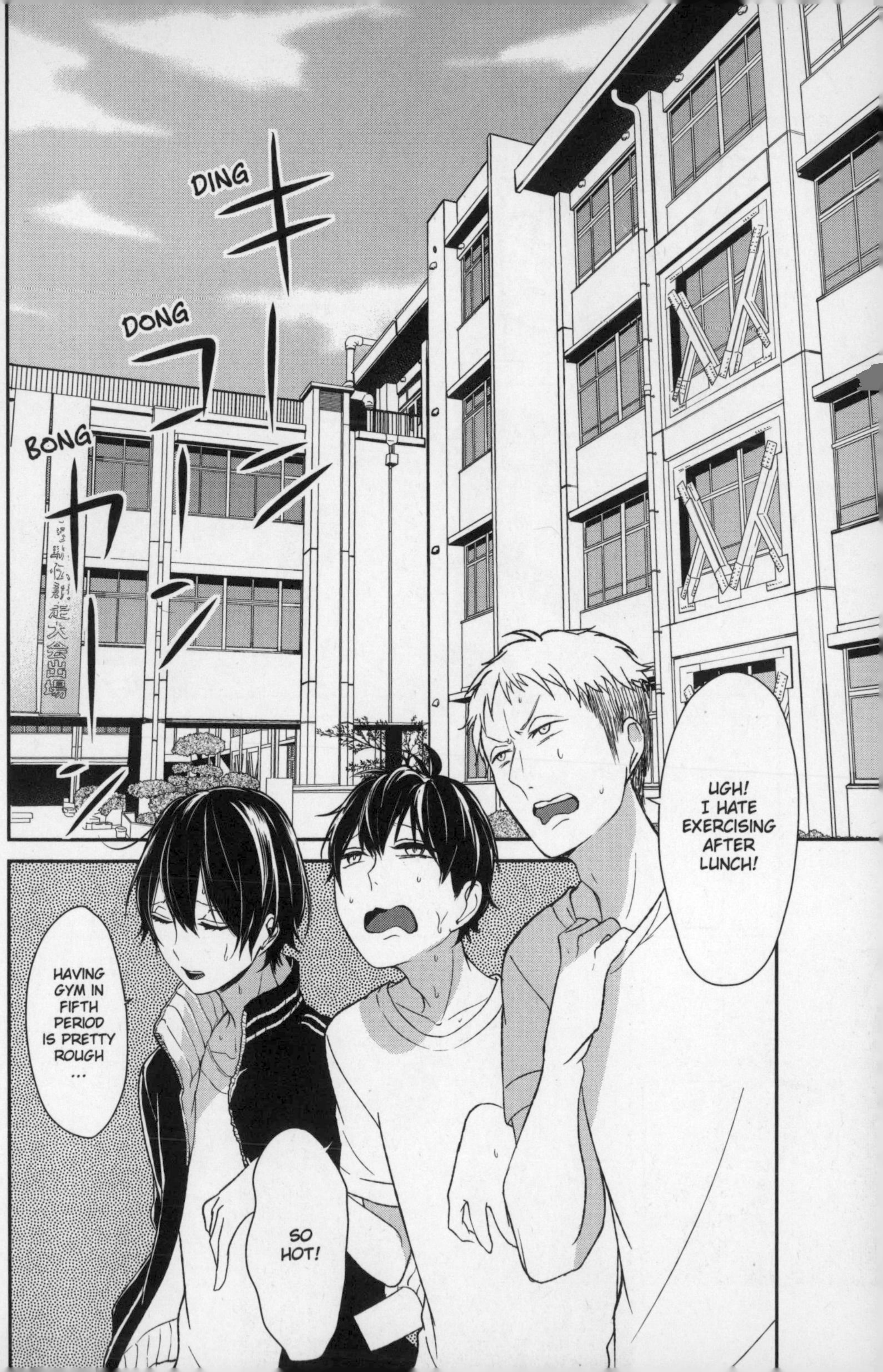
DING
DONG
BONG
UGH! I HATE EXERCISING AFTER LUNCH!
SO HOT!
HAVING GYM IN FIFTH PERIOD IS PRETTY ROUGH...

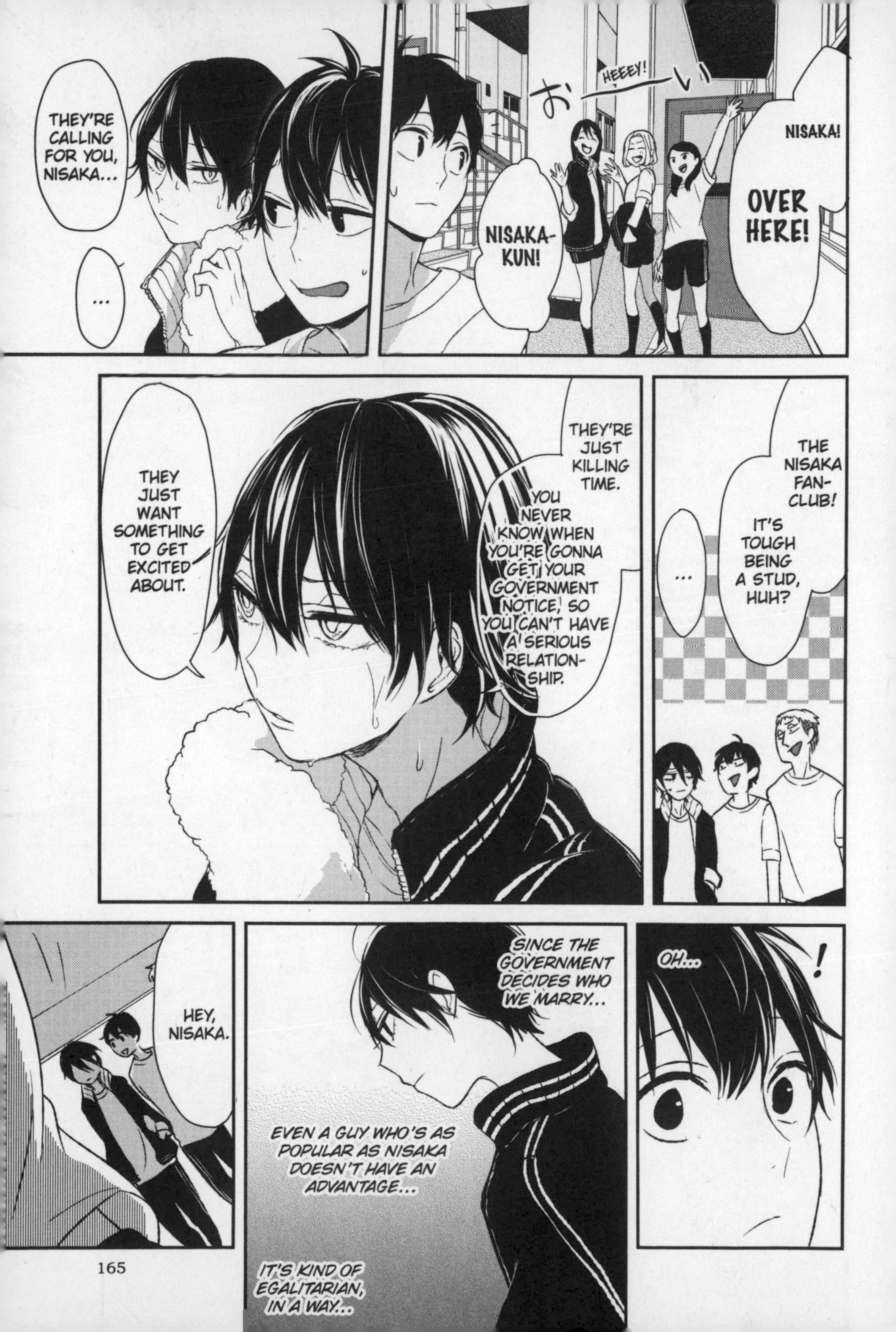
NISAKA!
OVER HERE!
HEEEY!
NISAKA-KUN!
THEY'RE CALLING FOR YOU, NISAKA...
...
THE NISAKA FAN-CLUB!
IT'S TOUGH BEING A STUD, HUH?
...
THEY'RE JUST KILLING TIME.
YOU NEVER KNOW WHEN YOU'RE GONNA GET YOUR GOVERNMENT NOTICE, SO YOU CAN'T HAVE A SERIOUS RELATION-SHIP.
THEY JUST WANT SOMETHING TO GET EXCITED ABOUT.
OH...
!
SINCE THE GOVERNMENT DECIDES WHO WE MARRY...
EVEN A GUY WHO'S AS POPULAR AS NISAKA DOESN'T HAVE AN ADVANTAGE...
IT'S KIND OF EGALITARIAN, IN A WAY...
HEY, NISAKA.

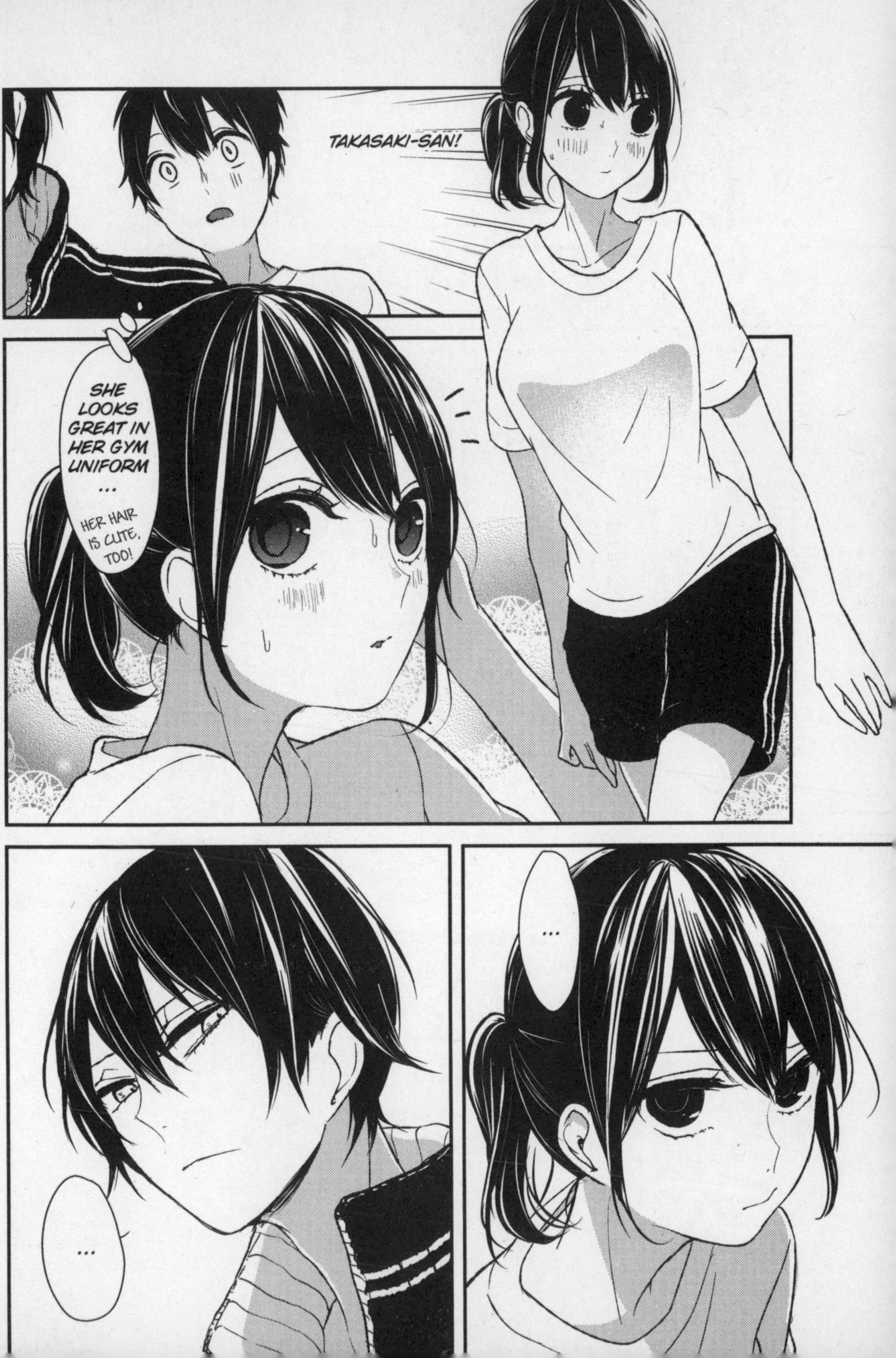
TAKASAKI-SAN!
SHE LOOKS GREAT IN HER GYM UNIFORM ...
HER HAIR IS CUTE, TOO!
...
...

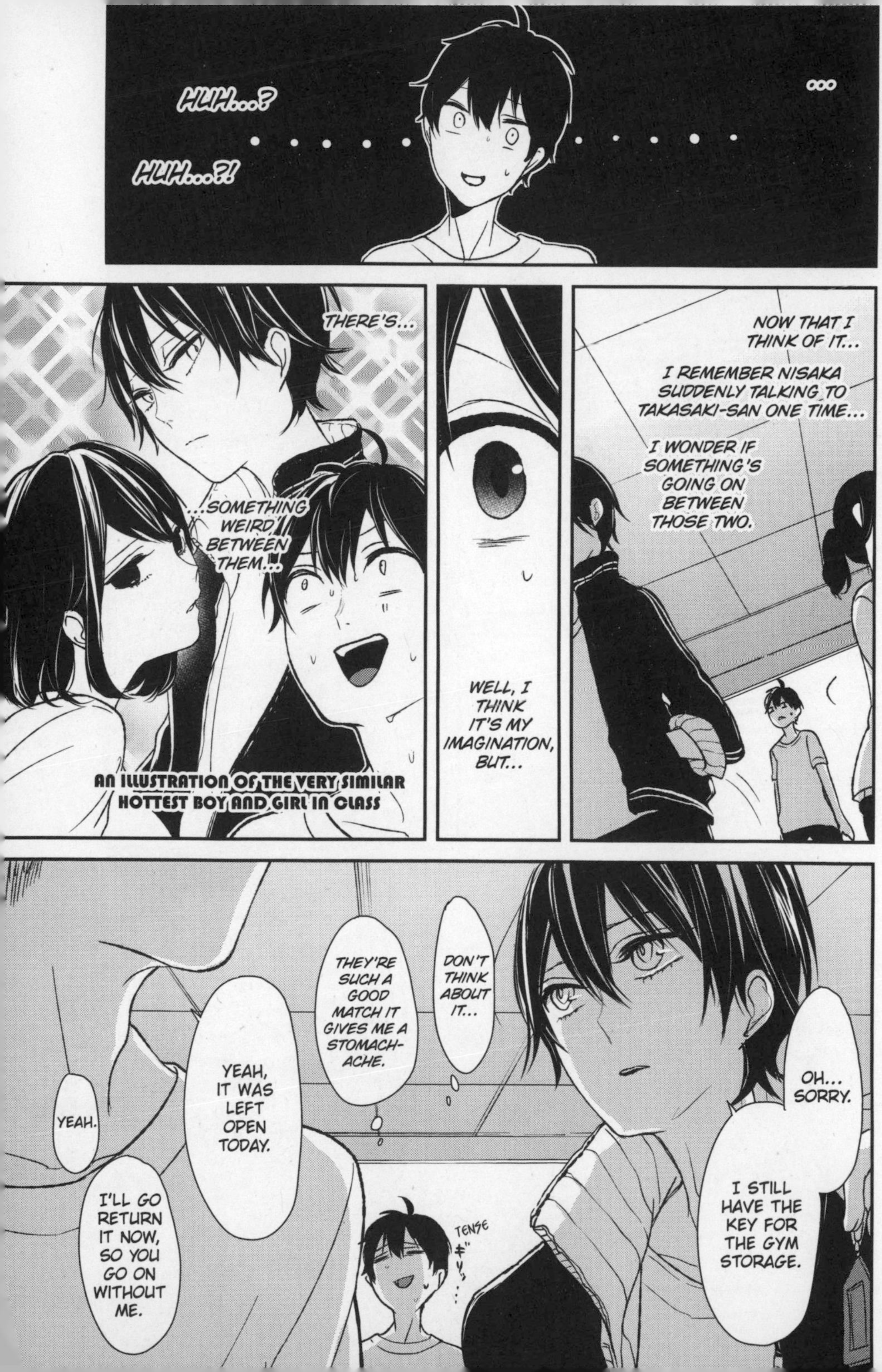
...
HUH...?
HUH...?!
NOW THAT I THINK OF IT...
I REMEMBER NISAKA SUDDENLY TALKING TO TAKASAKI-SAN ONE TIME...
I WONDER IF SOMETHING'S GOING ON BETWEEN THOSE TWO.
WELL, I THINK IT'S MY IMAGINATION, BUT...
THERE'S...
...SOMETHING WEIRD BETWEEN THEM...
AN ILLUSTRATION OF THE VERY SIMILAR HOTTEST BOY AND GIRL IN CLASS
OH... SORRY.
I STILL HAVE THE KEY FOR THE GYM STORAGE.
DON'T THINK ABOUT IT...
THEY'RE SUCH A GOOD MATCH IT GIVES ME A STOMACH-ACHE.
TENSE
YEAH, IT WAS LEFT OPEN TODAY.
I'LL GO RETURN IT NOW, SO YOU GO ON WITHOUT ME.
YEAH.

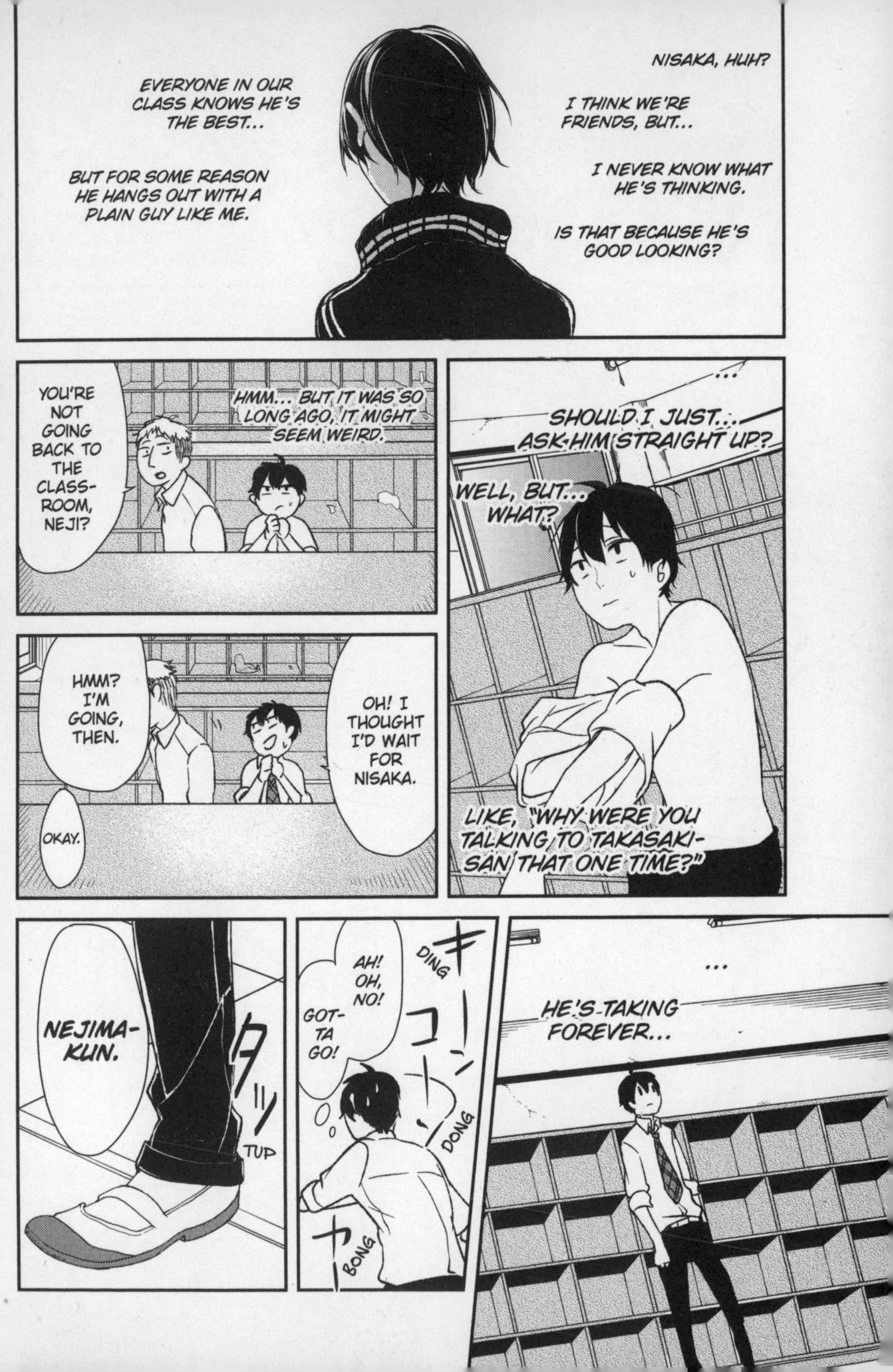
NISAKA, HUH?
I THINK WE'RE FRIENDS, BUT...
I NEVER KNOW WHAT HE'S THINKING.
IS THAT BECAUSE HE'S GOOD LOOKING?
EVERYONE IN OUR CLASS KNOWS HE'S THE BEST...
BUT FOR SOME REASON HE HANGS OUT WITH A PLAIN GUY LIKE ME.
...
SHOULD I JUST... ASK HIM STRAIGHT UP?
WELL, BUT... WHAT?
LIKE, "WHY WERE YOU TALKING TO TAKASAKI-SAN THAT ONE TIME?"
HMM... BUT IT WAS SO LONG AGO, IT MIGHT SEEM WEIRD.
YOU'RE NOT GOING BACK TO THE CLASS-ROOM, NEJI?
OH! I THOUGHT I'D WAIT FOR NISAKA.
HMM? I'M GOING, THEN.
OKAY.
...
HE'S TAKING FOREVER...
DING
DONG
AH! OH, NO!
GOT-TA GO!
BONG
TUP
NEJIMA-KUN.

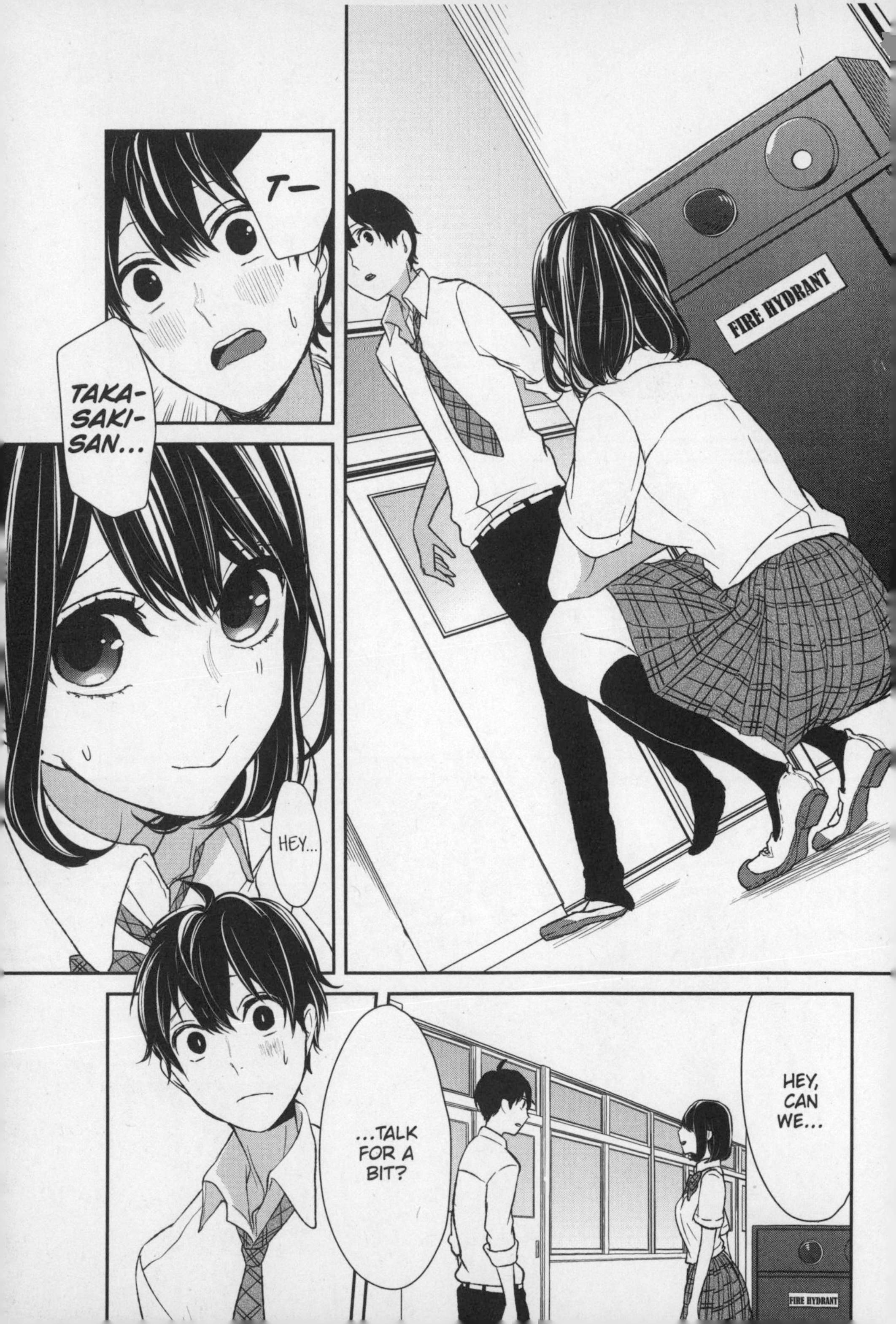
FIRE HYDRANT
T—
TAKA-SAKI-SAN...
HEY...
HEY, CAN WE...
...TALK FOR A BIT?
FIRE HYDRANT

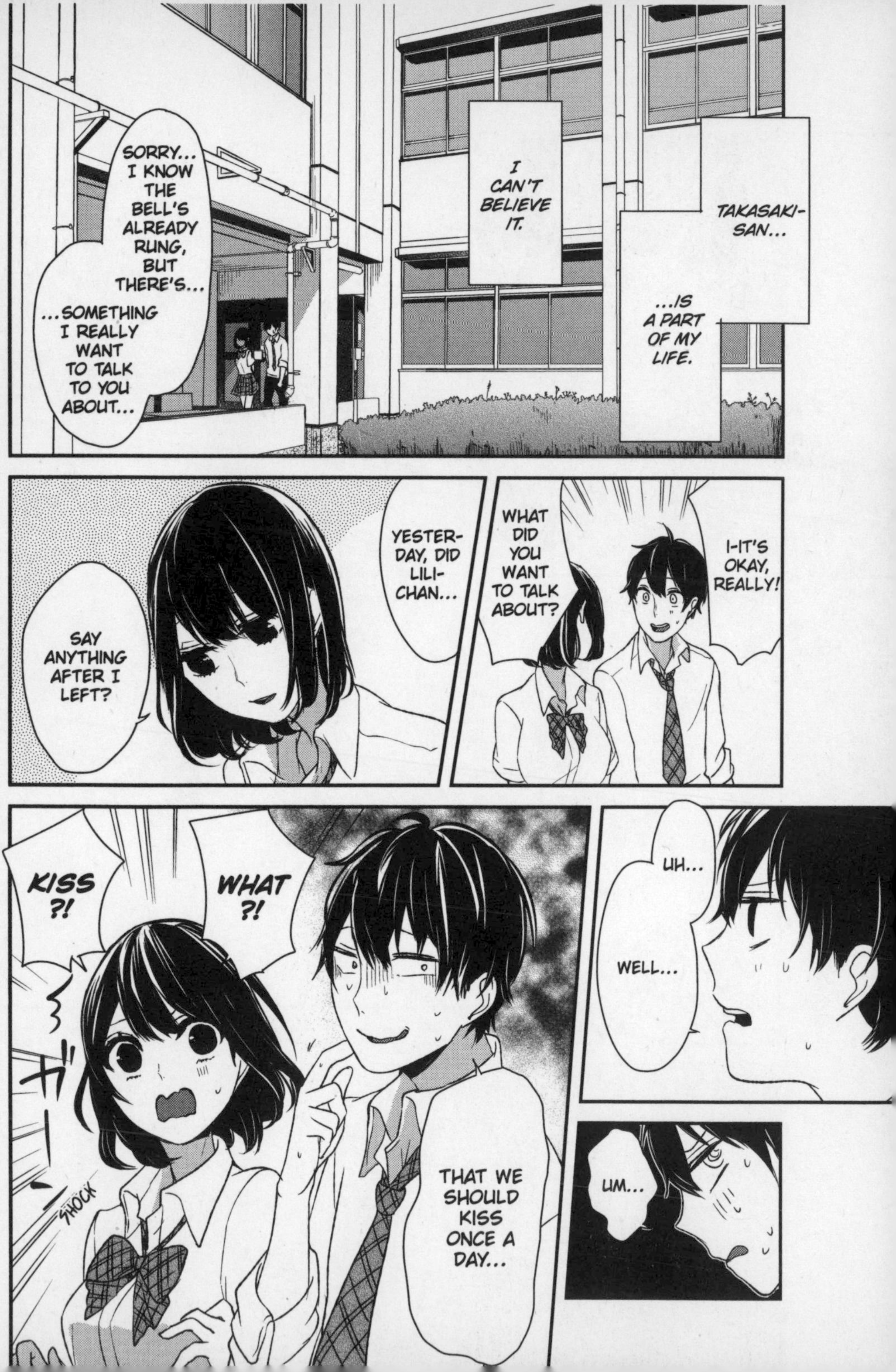
TAKASAKI-SAN...
...IS A PART OF MY LIFE.
I CAN'T BELIEVE IT.
SORRY... I KNOW THE BELL'S ALREADY RUNG, BUT THERE'S...
...SOMETHING I REALLY WANT TO TALK TO YOU ABOUT...
I-IT'S OKAY, REALLY!
WHAT DID YOU WANT TO TALK ABOUT?
YESTER-DAY, DID LILI-CHAN...
SAY ANYTHING AFTER I LEFT?
UH...
WELL...
UM...
THAT WE SHOULD KISS ONCE A DAY...
WHAT ?!
KISS ?!
SHOCK

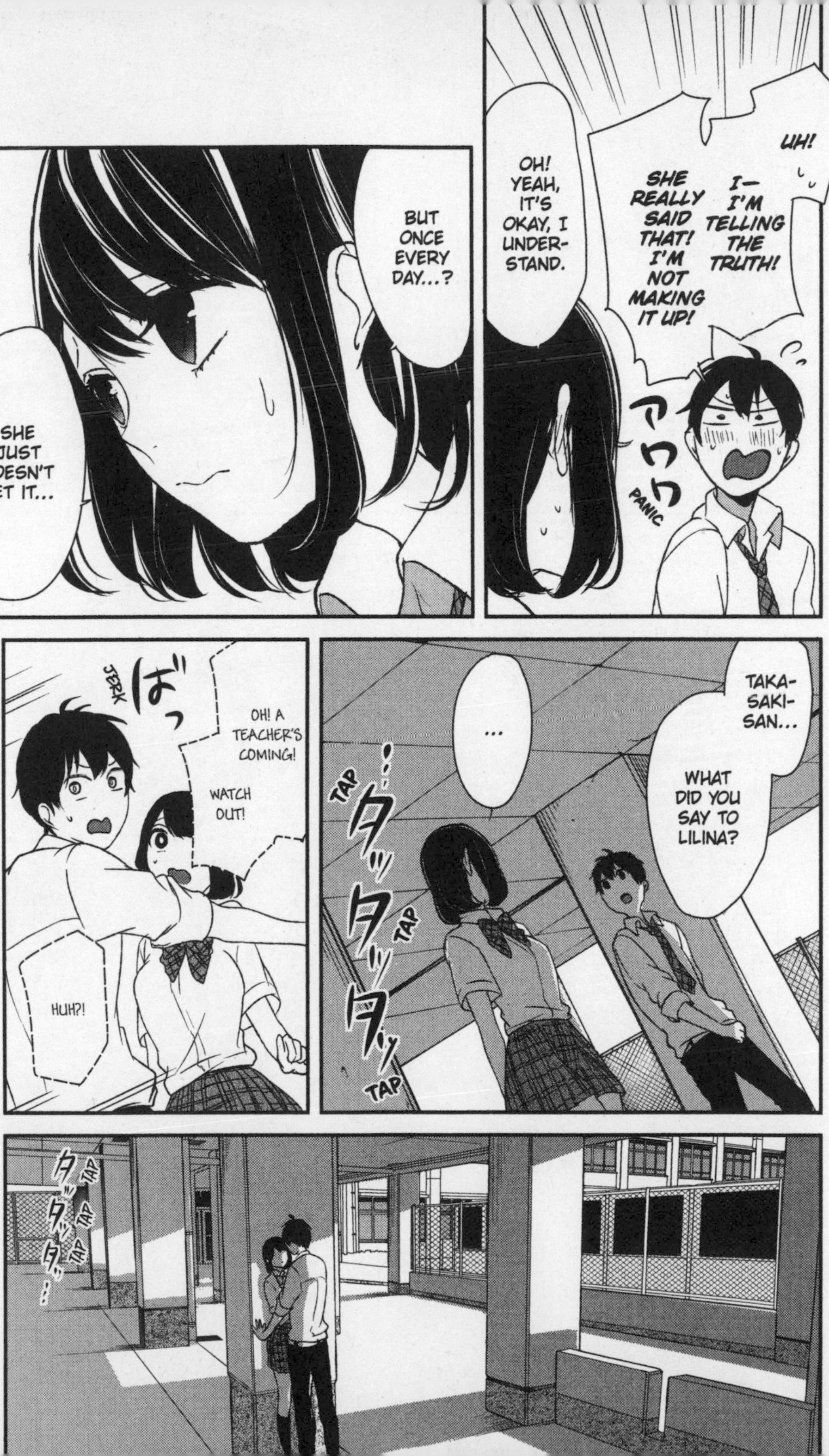
UH!
I— I'M TELLING THE TRUTH!
SHE REALLY SAID THAT! I'M NOT MAKING IT UP!
アワワ
PANIC
OH! YEAH, IT'S OKAY, I UNDERSTAND.
BUT ONCE EVERY DAY...?
SHE JUST DOESN'T GET IT...
TAKASAKI-SAN...
WHAT DID YOU SAY TO LILINA?
...
タッタッタッ
TAP
TAP
TAP
ばっ
JERK
OH! A TEACHER'S COMING!
WATCH OUT!
HUH?!
タッタッタッ...
TAP
TAP
TAP

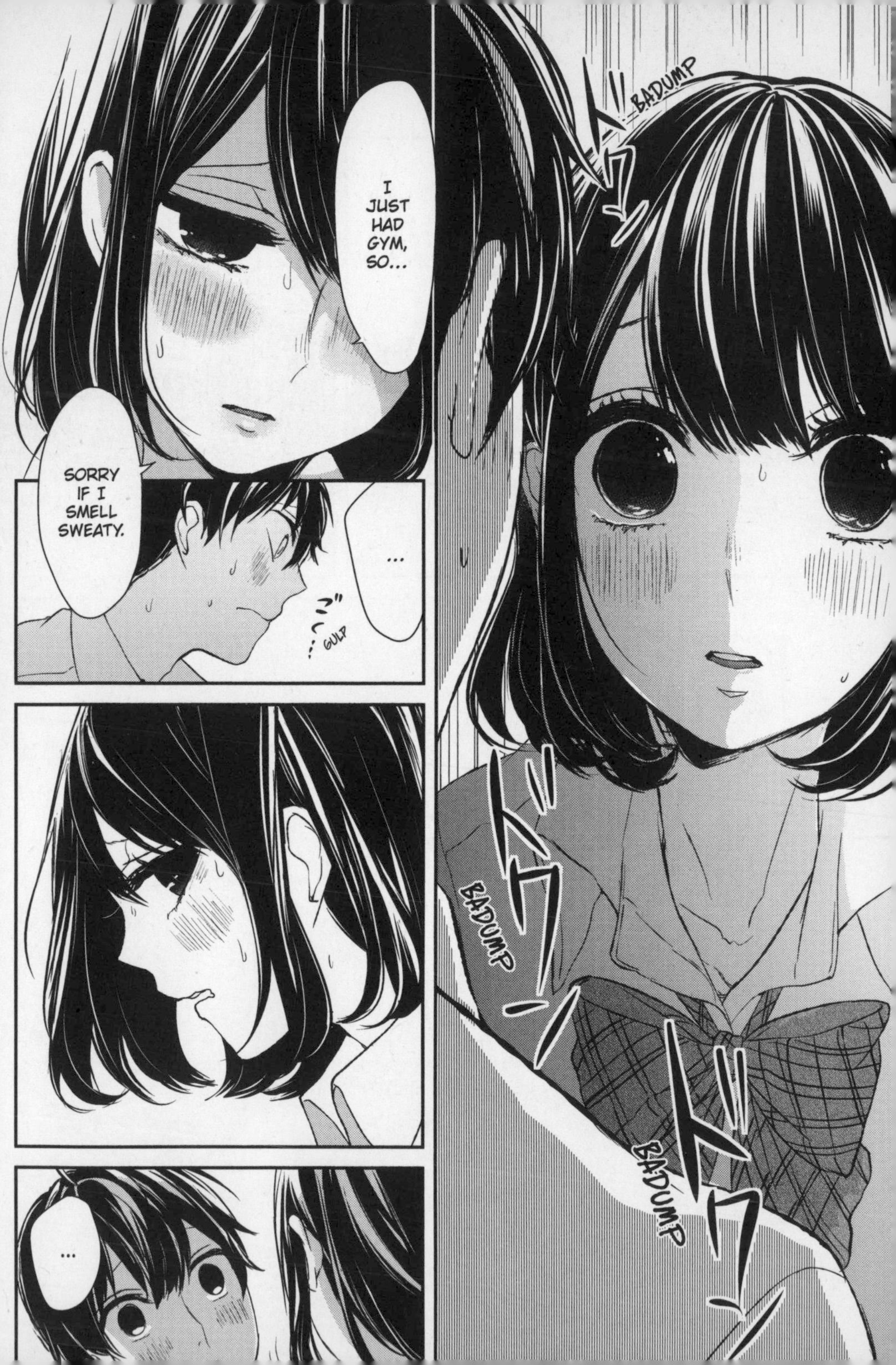
BADUMP
BADUMP
BADUMP
I JUST HAD GYM, SO...
SORRY IF I SMELL SWEATY.
...
GULP
...

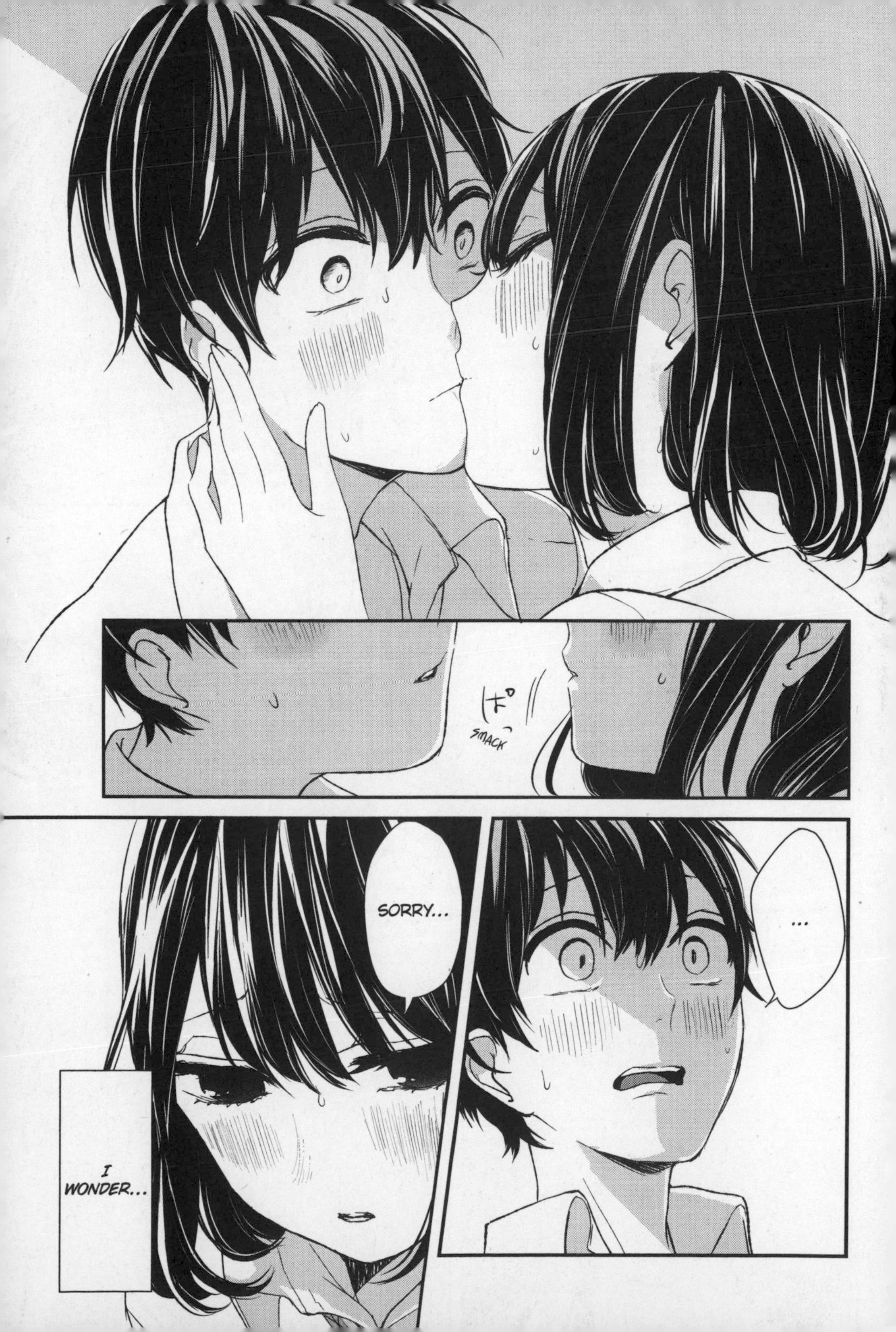
ぽ
SMACK
...
SORRY...
I WONDER...

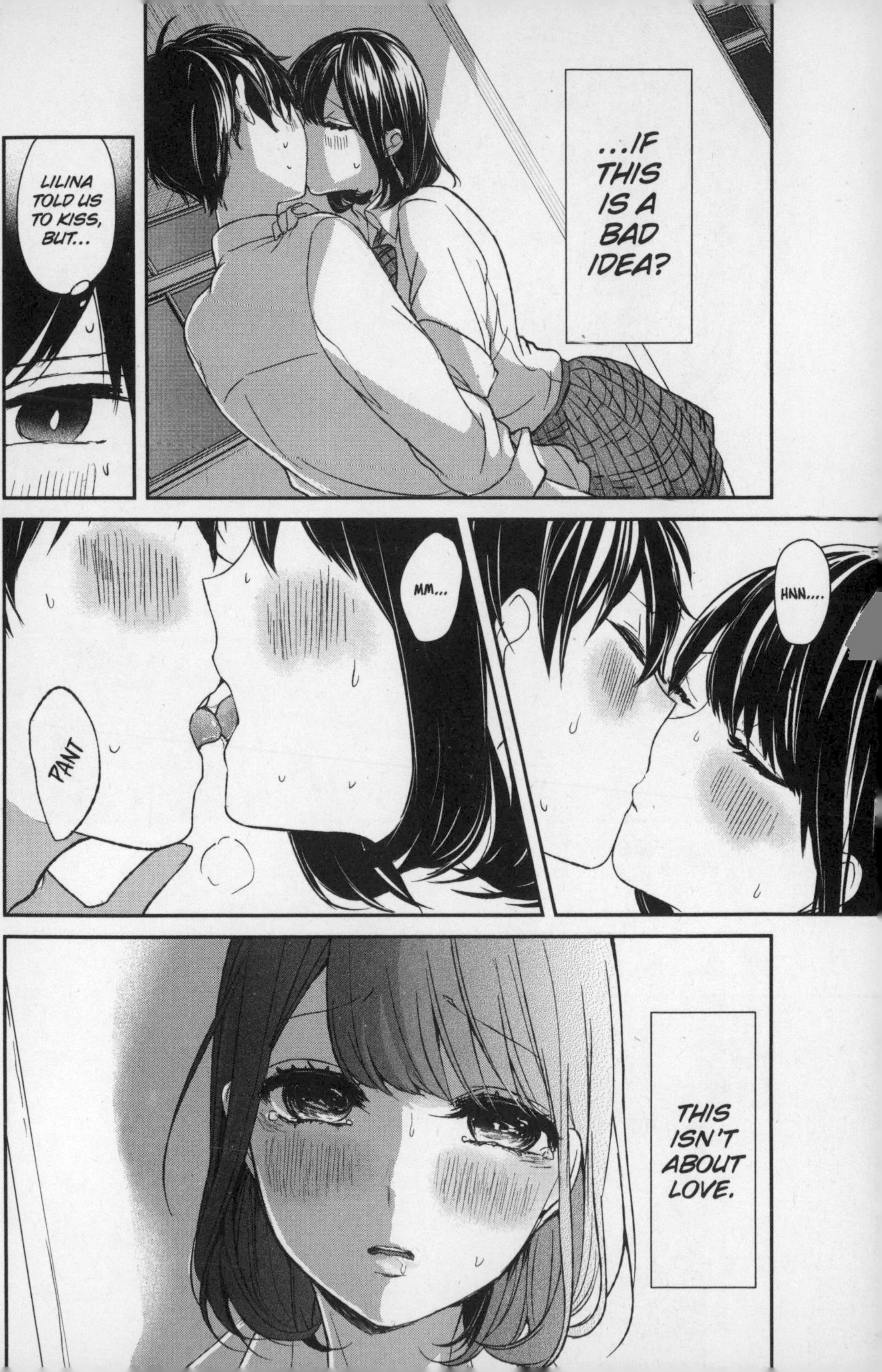
...IF THIS IS A BAD IDEA?
LILINA TOLD US TO KISS, BUT...
HNN....
MM...
PANT
THIS ISN'T ABOUT LOVE.

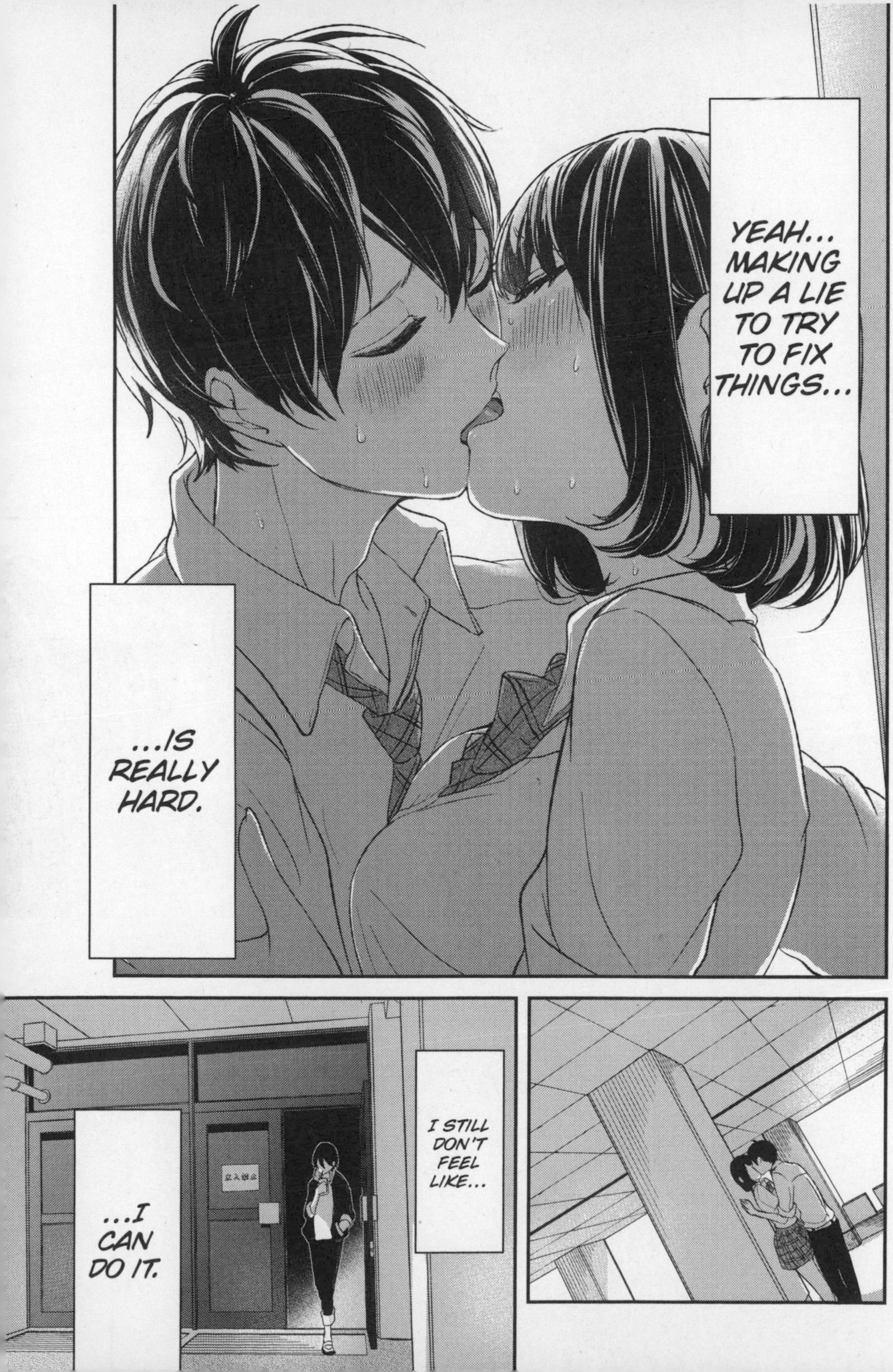
YEAH... MAKING UP A LIE TO TRY TO FIX THINGS...
...IS REALLY HARD.
I STILL DON'T FEEL LIKE...
...I CAN DO IT.

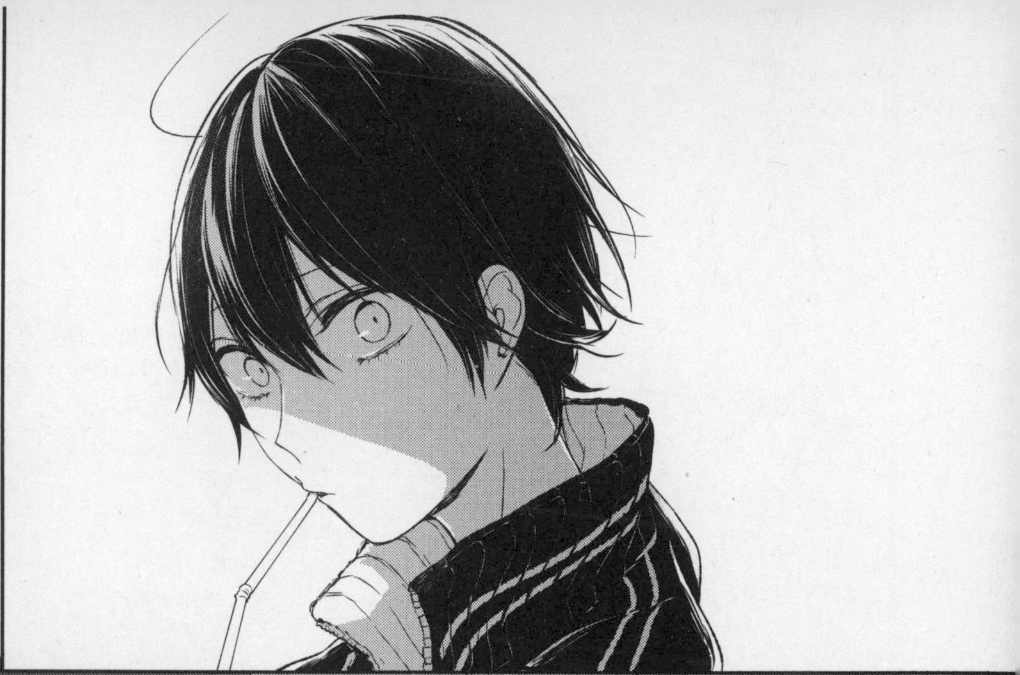
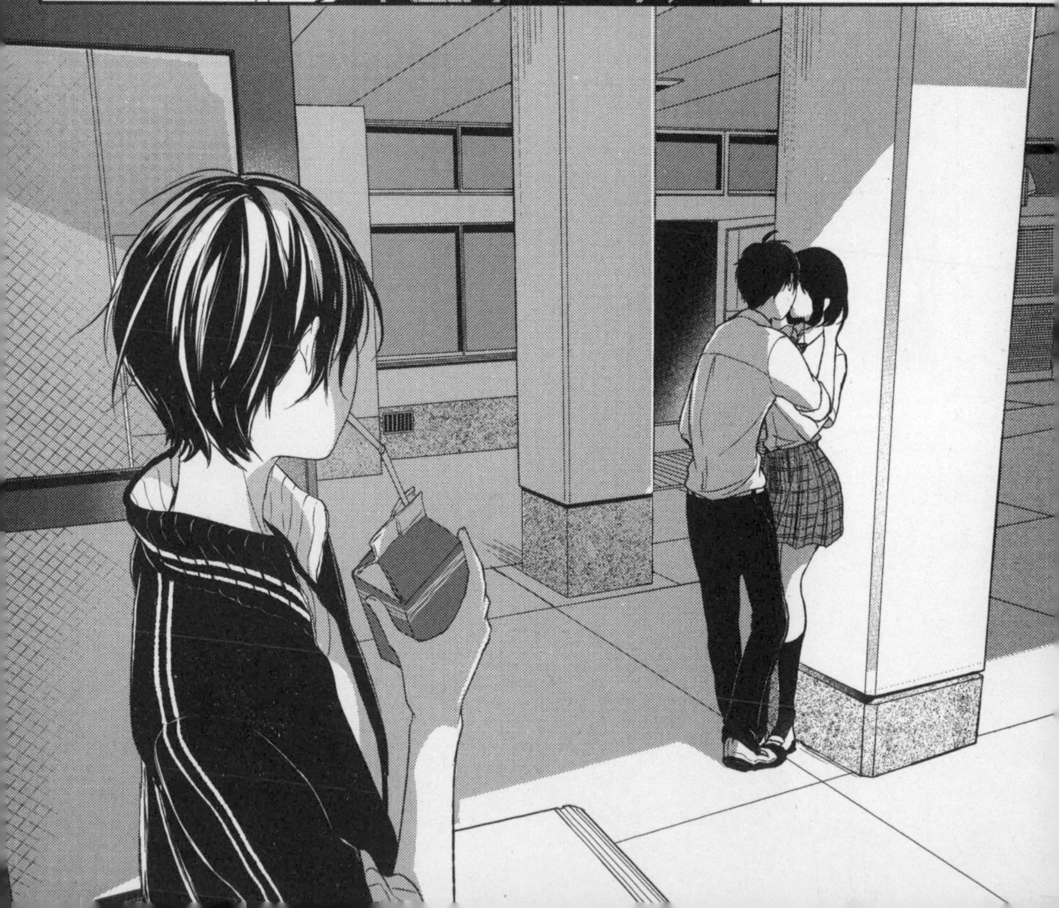

Chapter 4.5: A Friend's Love

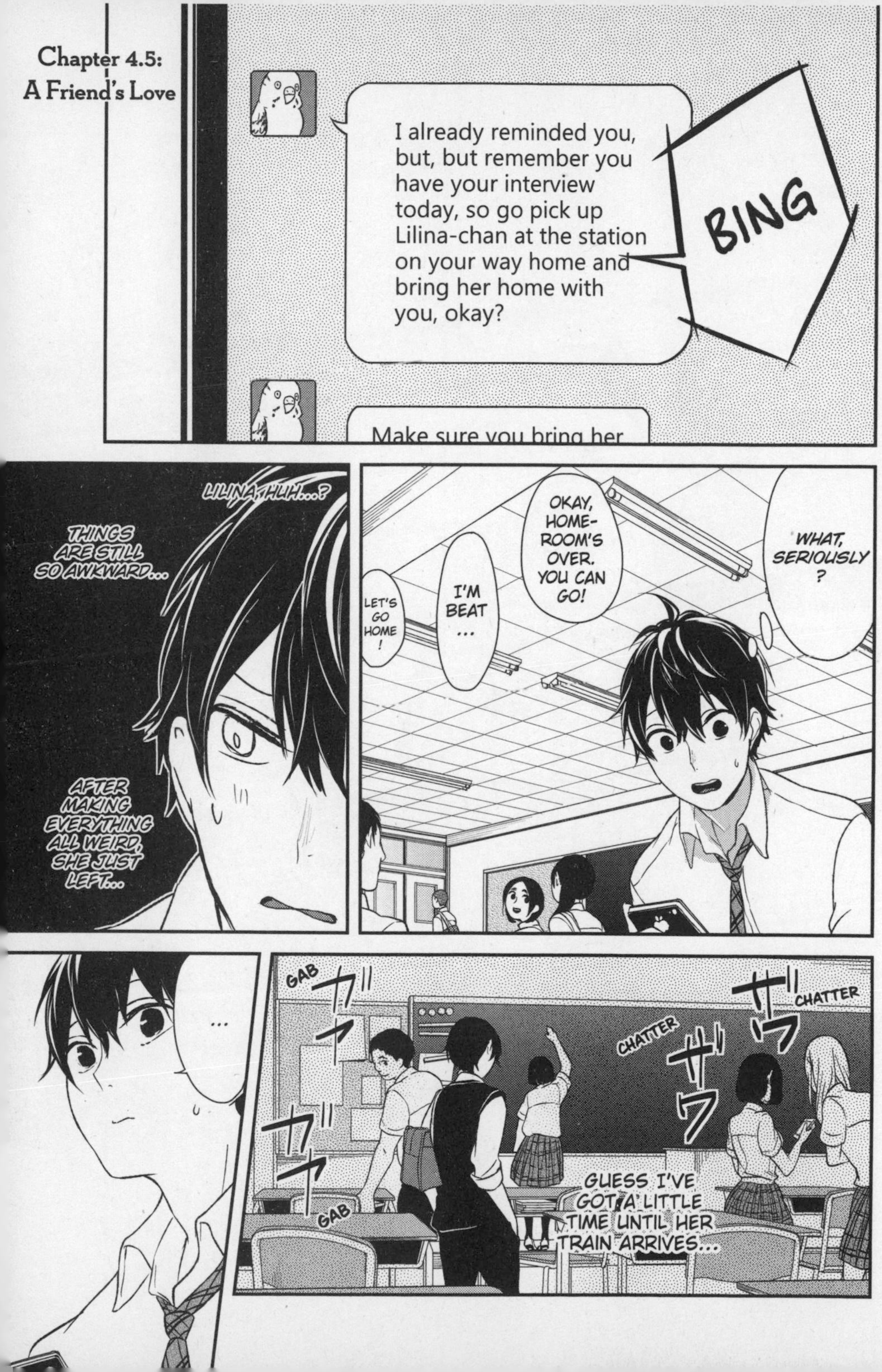
I already reminded you, but, but remember you have your interview today, so go pick up Lilina-chan at the station on your way home and bring her home with you, okay?
BING
Make sure you bring her
WHAT, SERIOUSLY?
OKAY, HOME-ROOM'S OVER. YOU CAN GO!
I'M BEAT...
LET'S GO HOME!
LILINA, HUH...?
THINGS ARE STILL SO AWKWARD...
AFTER MAKING EVERYTHING ALL WEIRD, SHE JUST LEFT...
ザワ
CHATTER
ザワ
CHATTER
ガヤ
GAB
ガヤ
GAB
GUESS I'VE GOT A LITTLE TIME UNTIL HER TRAIN ARRIVES...
...

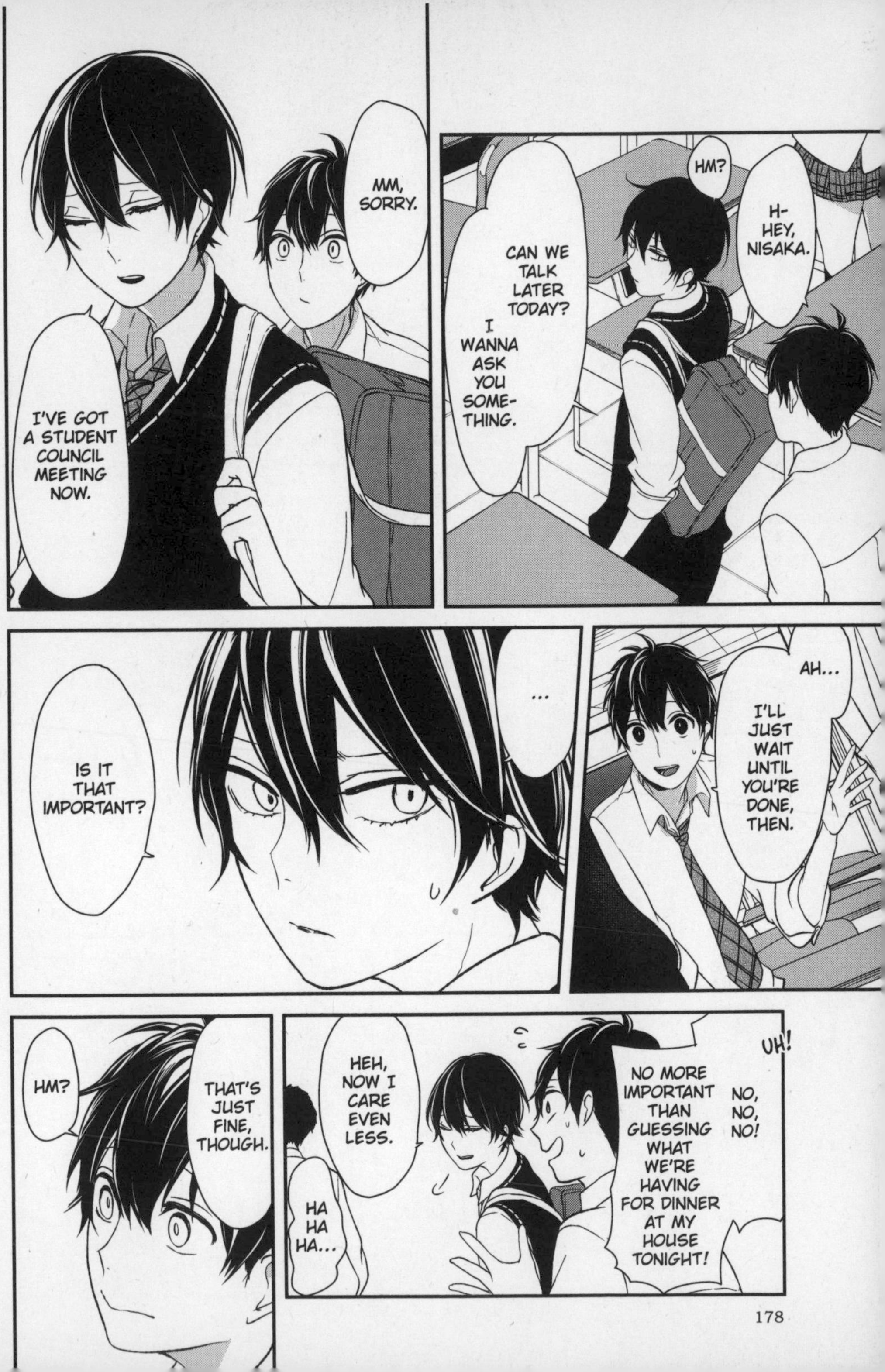
H- HEY, NISAKA.
HM?
CAN WE TALK LATER TODAY? I WANNA ASK YOU SOMETHING.
MM, SORRY.
I'VE GOT A STUDENT COUNCIL MEETING NOW.
AH... I'LL JUST WAIT UNTIL YOU'RE DONE, THEN.
...
IS IT THAT IMPORTANT?
UH!
NO, NO, NO!
NO MORE IMPORTANT THAN GUESSING WHAT WE'RE HAVING FOR DINNER AT MY HOUSE TONIGHT!
HEH, NOW I CARE EVEN LESS.
HA HA HA...
THAT'S JUST FINE, THOUGH.
HM?

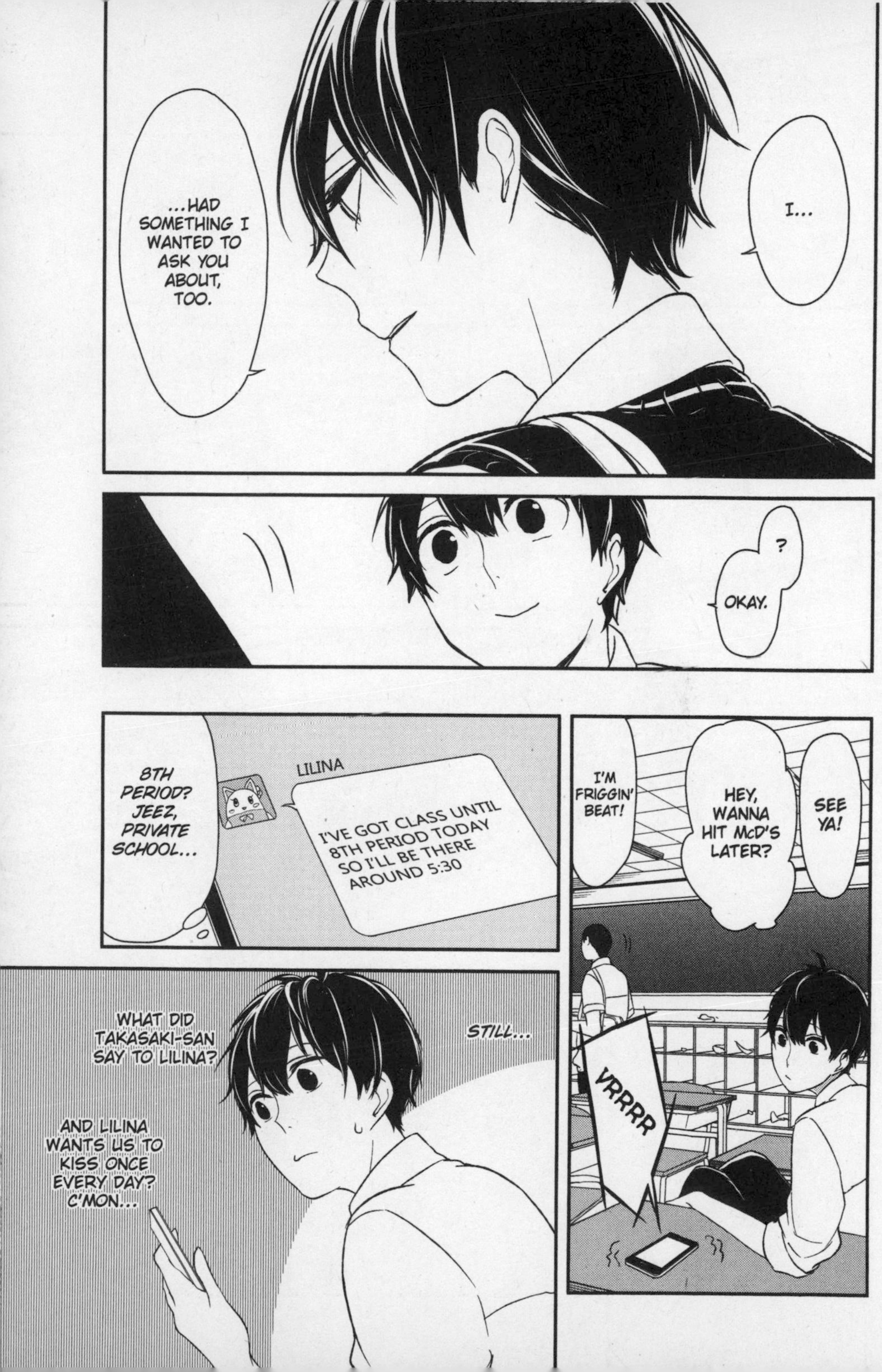
I...
...HAD SOMETHING I WANTED TO ASK YOU ABOUT, TOO.
?
OKAY.
SEE YA!
HEY, WANNA HIT McD'S LATER?
I'M FRIGGIN' BEAT!
VRRRRR
LILINA
I'VE GOT CLASS UNTIL 8TH PERIOD TODAY SO I'LL BE THERE AROUND 5:30
8TH PERIOD? JEEZ, PRIVATE SCHOOL...
STILL...
WHAT DID TAKASAKI-SAN SAY TO LILINA?
AND LILINA WANTS US TO KISS ONCE EVERY DAY? C'MON...

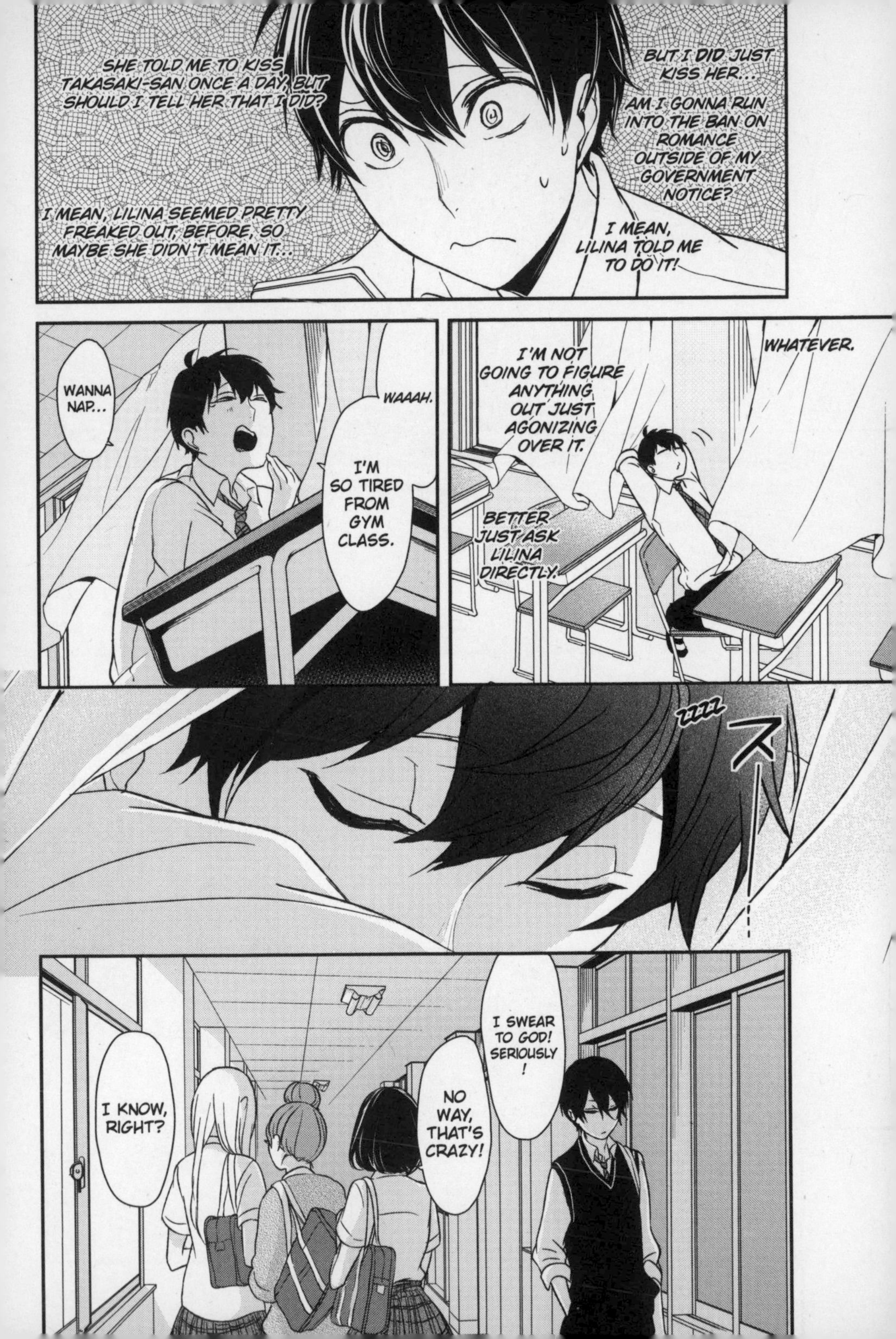
BUT I DID JUST KISS HER...
AM I GONNA RUN INTO THE BAN ON ROMANCE OUTSIDE OF MY GOVERNMENT NOTICE?
SHE TOLD ME TO KISS TAKASAKI-SAN ONCE A DAY, BUT SHOULD I TELL HER THAT I DID?
I MEAN, LILINA TOLD ME TO DO IT!
I MEAN, LILINA SEEMED PRETTY FREAKED OUT, BEFORE, SO MAYBE SHE DIDN'T MEAN IT...
WHATEVER.
I'M NOT GOING TO FIGURE ANYTHING OUT JUST AGONIZING OVER IT.
BETTER JUST ASK LILINA DIRECTLY.
WAAAH.
I'M SO TIRED FROM GYM CLASS.
WANNA NAP...
ZZZZ
ス
I SWEAR TO GOD! SERIOUSLY!
NO WAY, THAT'S CRAZY!
I KNOW, RIGHT?

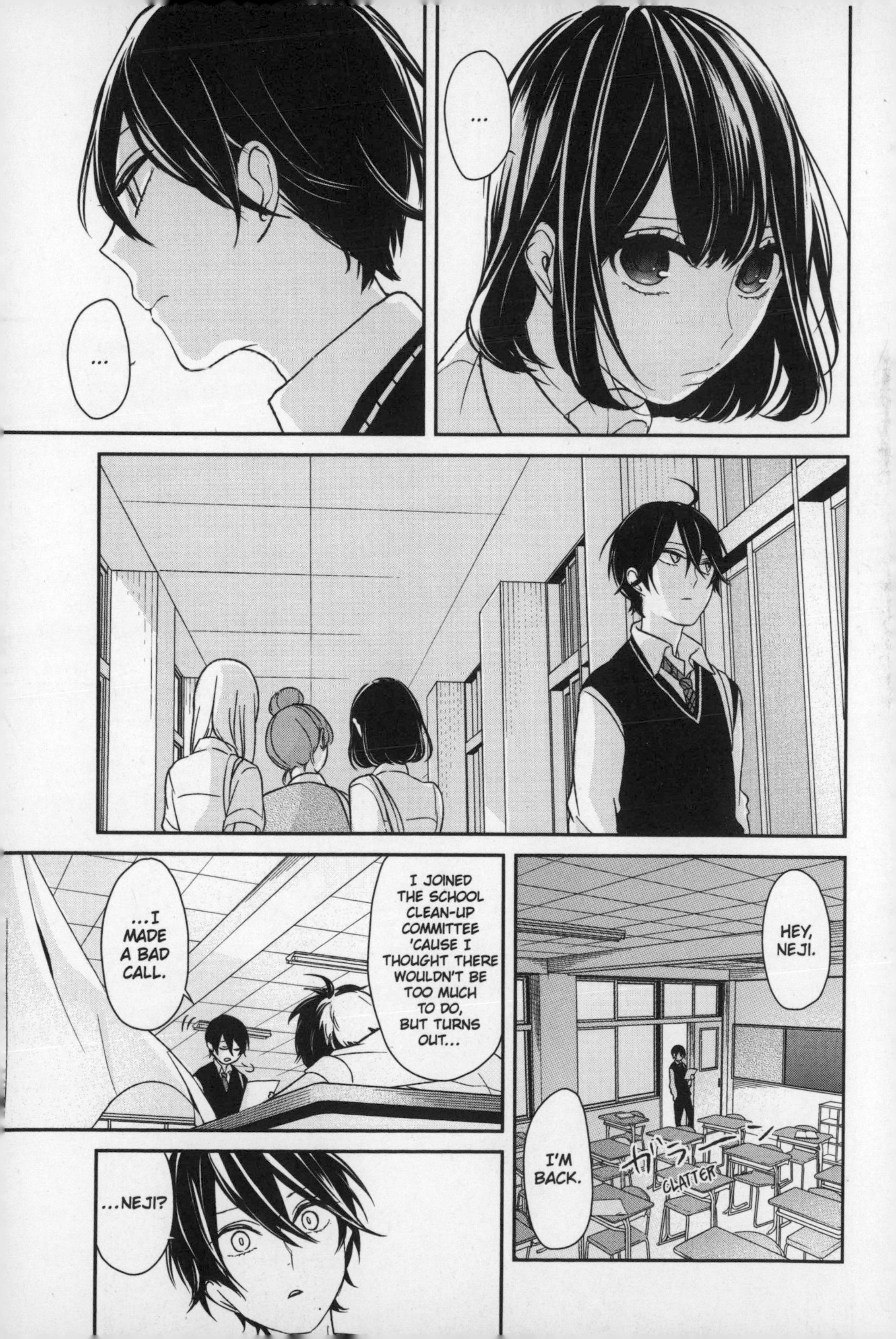
...
...
HEY, NEJI.
I'M BACK.
CLATTER
I JOINED THE SCHOOL CLEAN-UP COMMITTEE 'CAUSE I THOUGHT THERE WOULDN'T BE TOO MUCH TO DO, BUT TURNS OUT...
...I MADE A BAD CALL.
...NEJI?

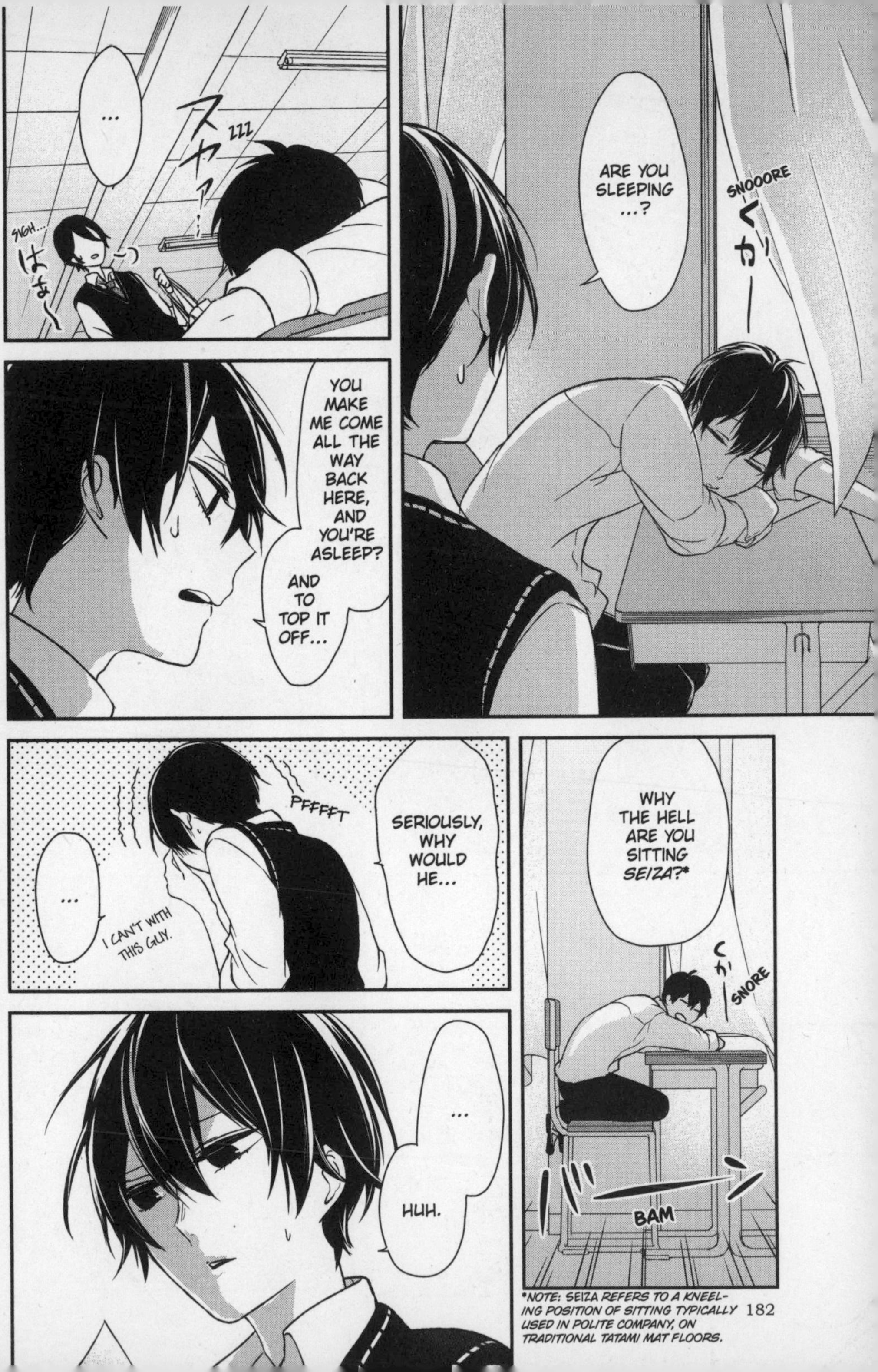

ARE YOU SLEEPING ...?
SNOOORE
...
ZZZ
SIGH...
YOU MAKE ME COME ALL THE WAY BACK HERE, AND YOU'RE ASLEEP?
AND TO TOP IT OFF...
WHY THE HELL ARE YOU SITTING *SEIZA?**
SNORE
BAM
SERIOUSLY, WHY WOULD HE...
PFFFFT
...
I CAN'T WITH THIS GUY.
...
HUH.

NOTE: SEIZA REFERS TO A KNEELING POSITION OF SITTING TYPICALLY USED IN POLITE COMPANY, ON TRADITIONAL TATAMI MAT FLOORS.

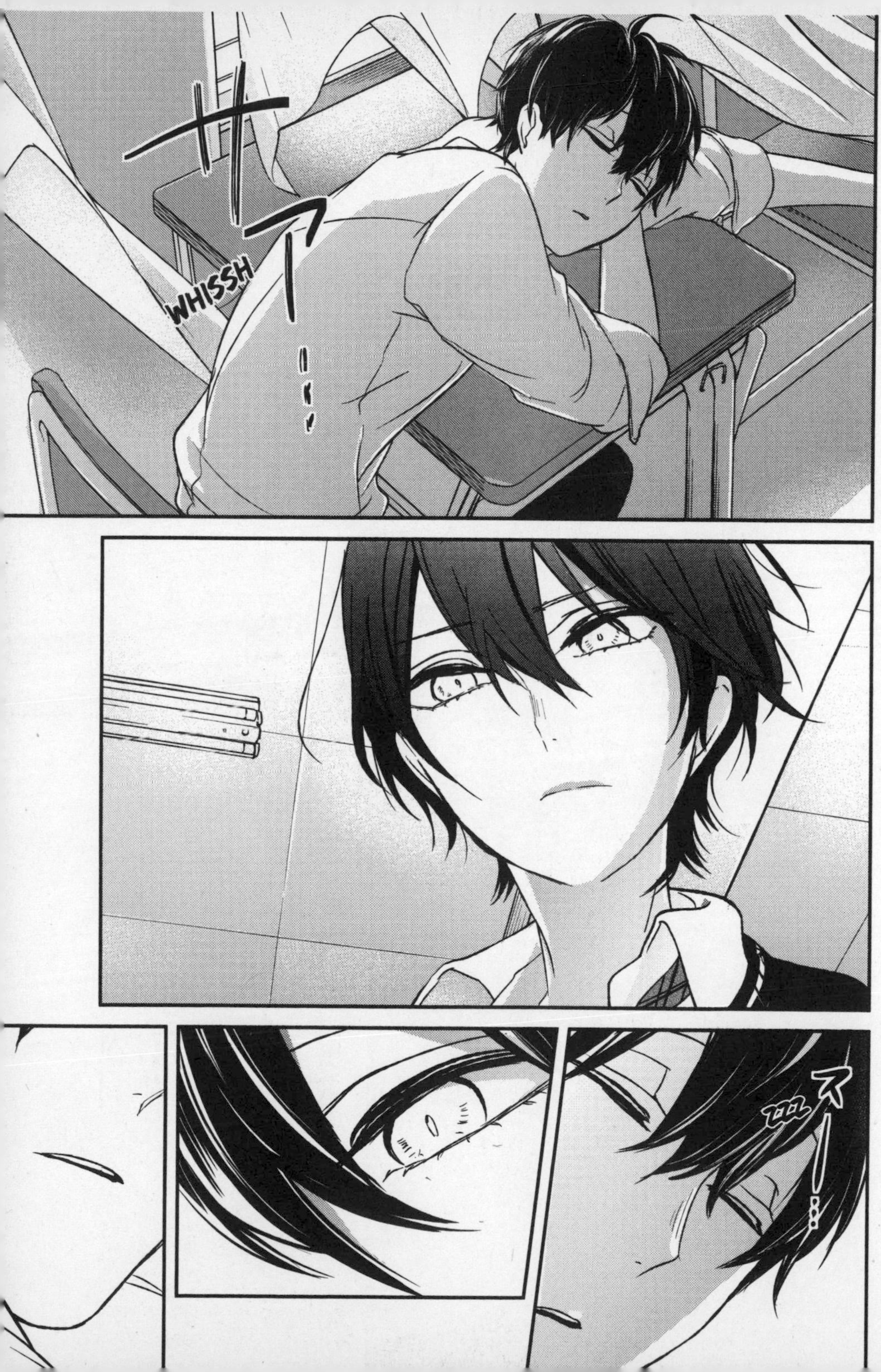
サァー
WHISSH
スー…
ZZZ

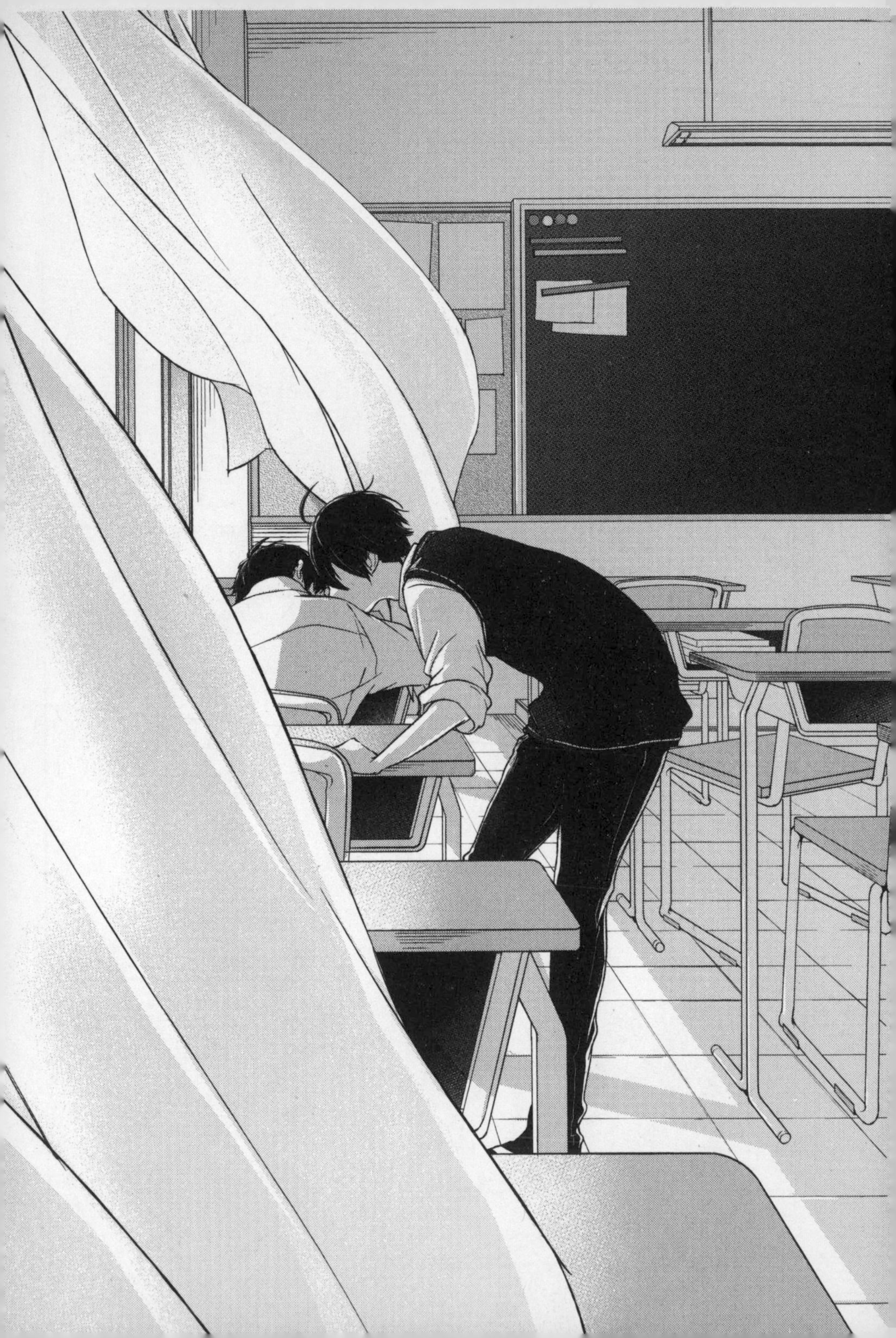

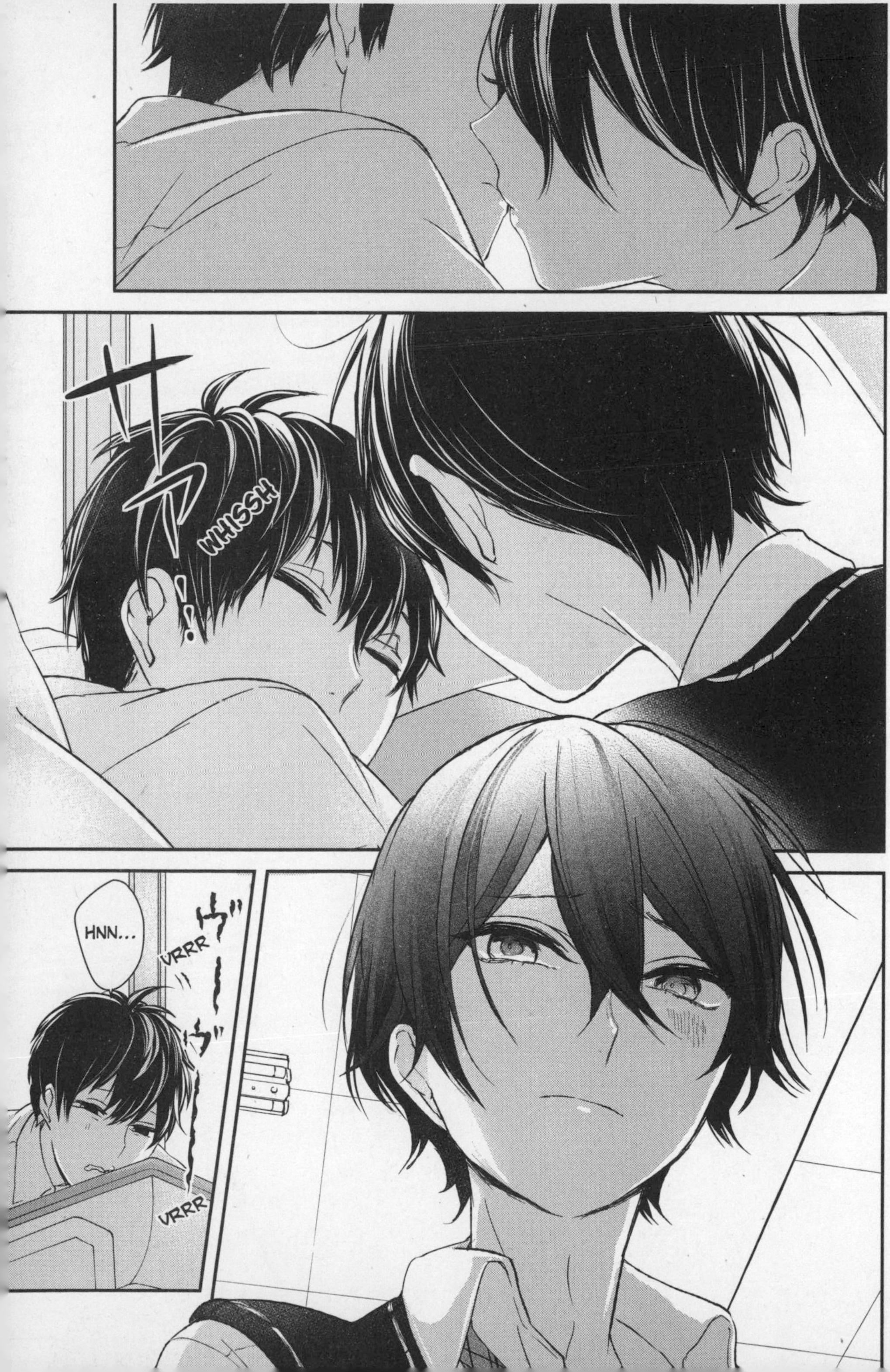
WHISSH
!!
HNN...
VRRR
VRRR

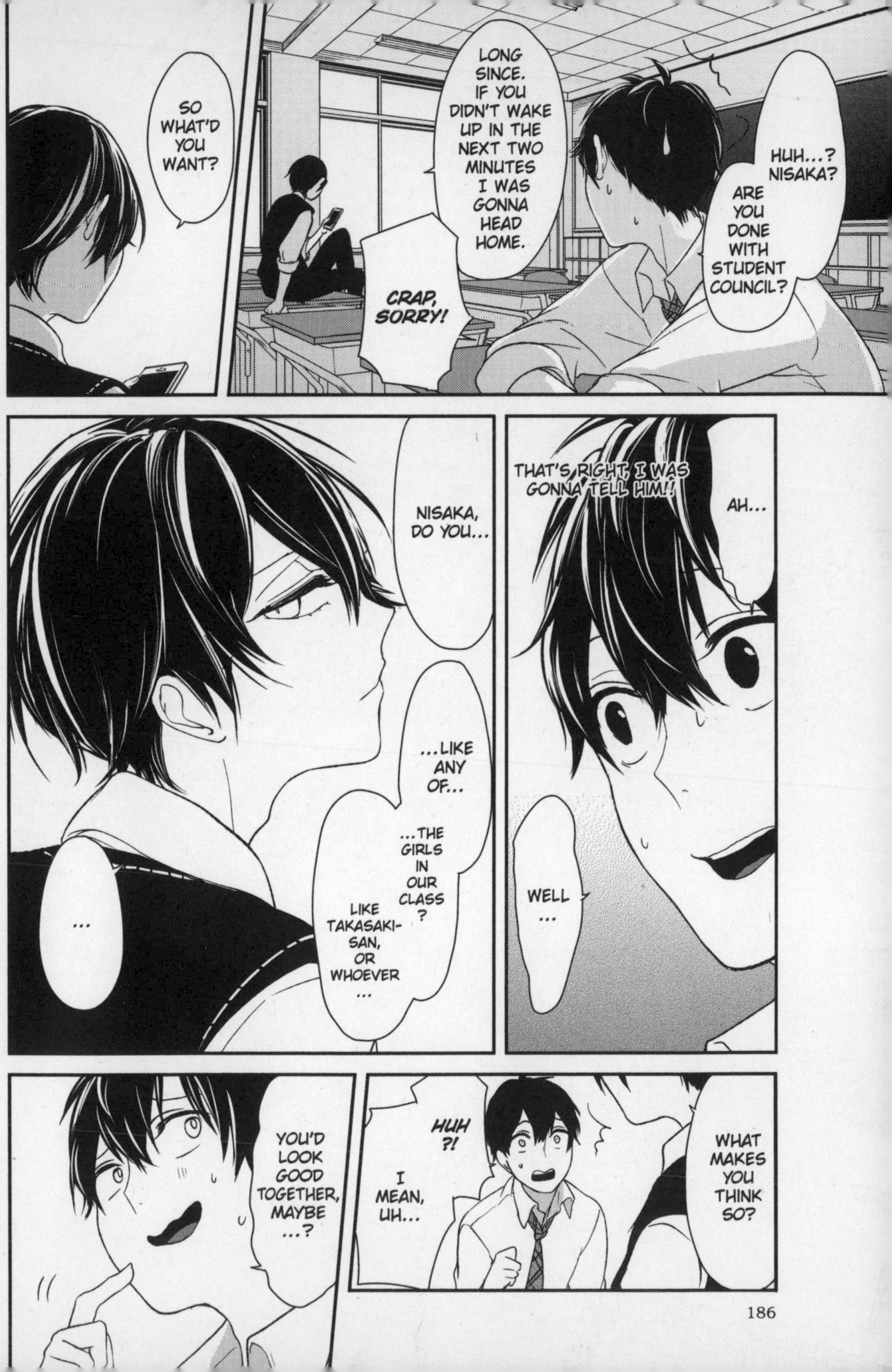
HUH...? NISAKA?
ARE YOU DONE WITH STUDENT COUNCIL?
LONG SINCE. IF YOU DIDN'T WAKE UP IN THE NEXT TWO MINUTES I WAS GONNA HEAD HOME.
CRAP, SORRY!
SO WHAT'D YOU WANT?
AH...
THAT'S RIGHT, I WAS GONNA TELL HIM!!
WELL ...
NISAKA, DO YOU...
...LIKE ANY OF...
...THE GIRLS IN OUR CLASS?
LIKE TAKASAKI-SAN, OR WHOEVER ...
...
WHAT MAKES YOU THINK SO?
HUH?!
I MEAN, UH...
YOU'D LOOK GOOD TOGETHER, MAYBE ...?

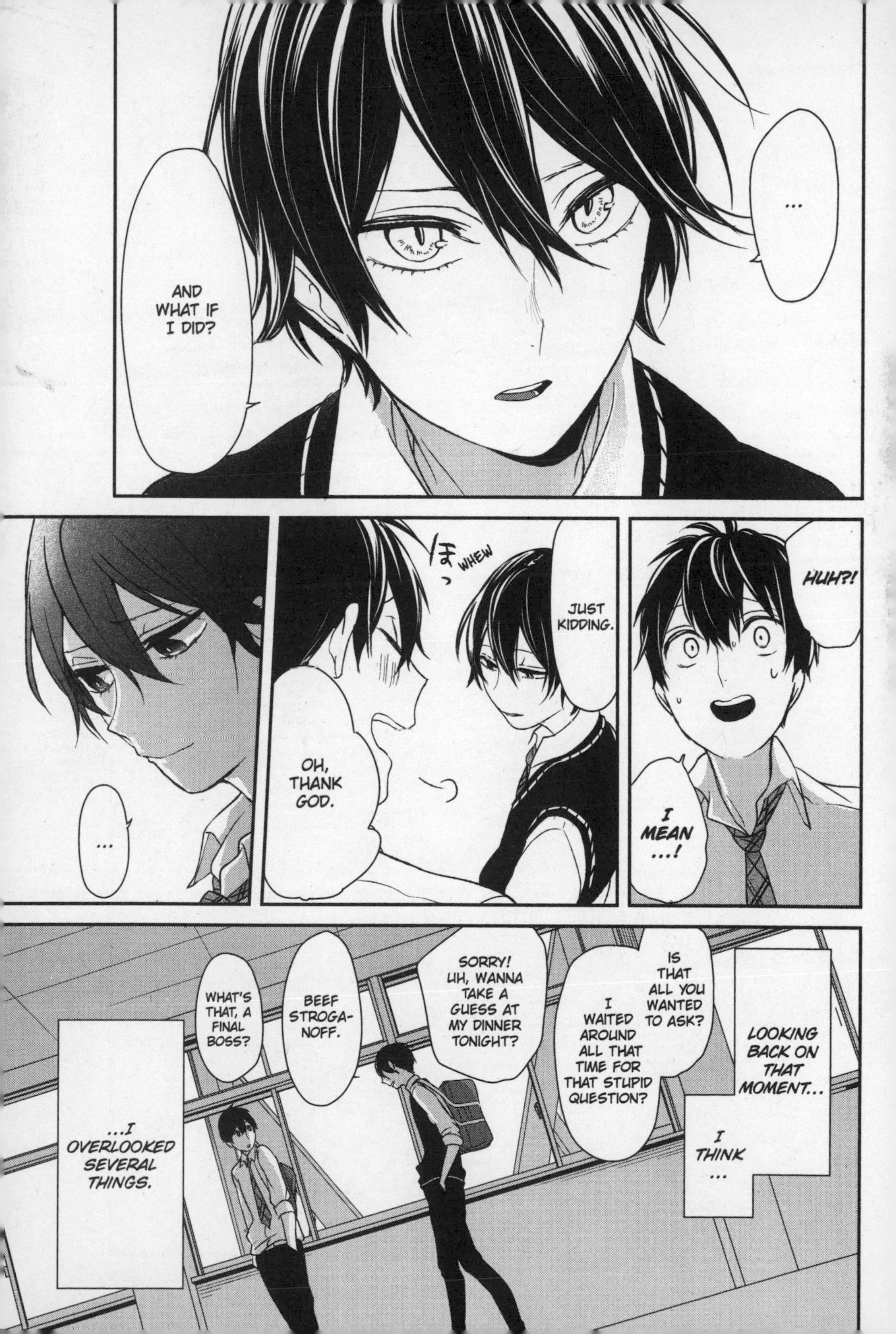
...
AND WHAT IF I DID?
HUH?!
I MEAN ...!
JUST KIDDING.
ほっ WHEW
OH, THANK GOD.
...
LOOKING BACK ON THAT MOMENT...
I THINK ...
IS THAT ALL YOU WANTED TO ASK?
I WAITED AROUND ALL THAT TIME FOR THAT STUPID QUESTION?
SORRY! UH, WANNA TAKE A GUESS AT MY DINNER TONIGHT?
BEEF STROGA-NOFF.
WHAT'S THAT, A FINAL BOSS?
...I OVERLOOKED SEVERAL THINGS.

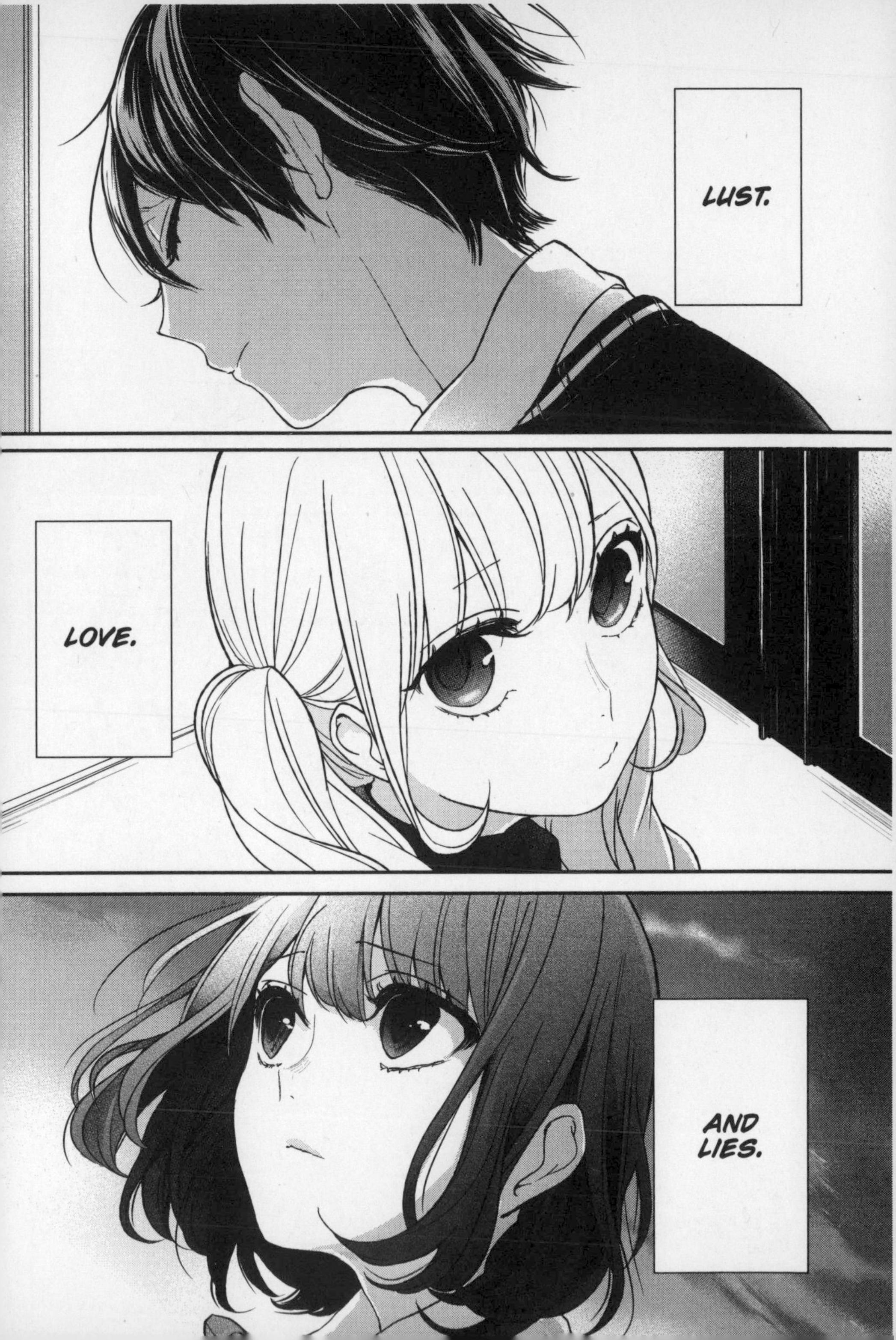
LUST.
LOVE.
AND LIES.

Love & Lies

Next Volume...

I'M ICHIJOU FROM THE MINISTRY OF HEALTH, LABOR, AND WELFARE.
The Ministry of Heath, Labor, and Welfare arrives...
...to conduct their first interview!
GOOD EVENING!
I'M YAJIMA.
SO YOU SEE, THE YUKARI LAW...
...IS ACTUALLY QUITE ROMANTIC, DON'T YOU THINK?

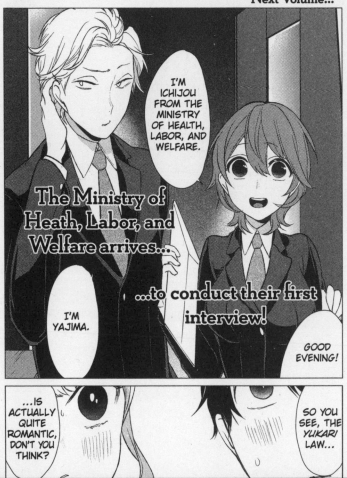

The full scope of the **Yukari Law** becomes clear...but does it really lead to the **ultimate love**, or is it a **trap** laid by science?

Love & Lies

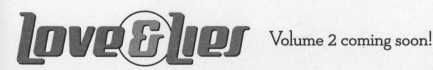

Volume 2 coming soon!

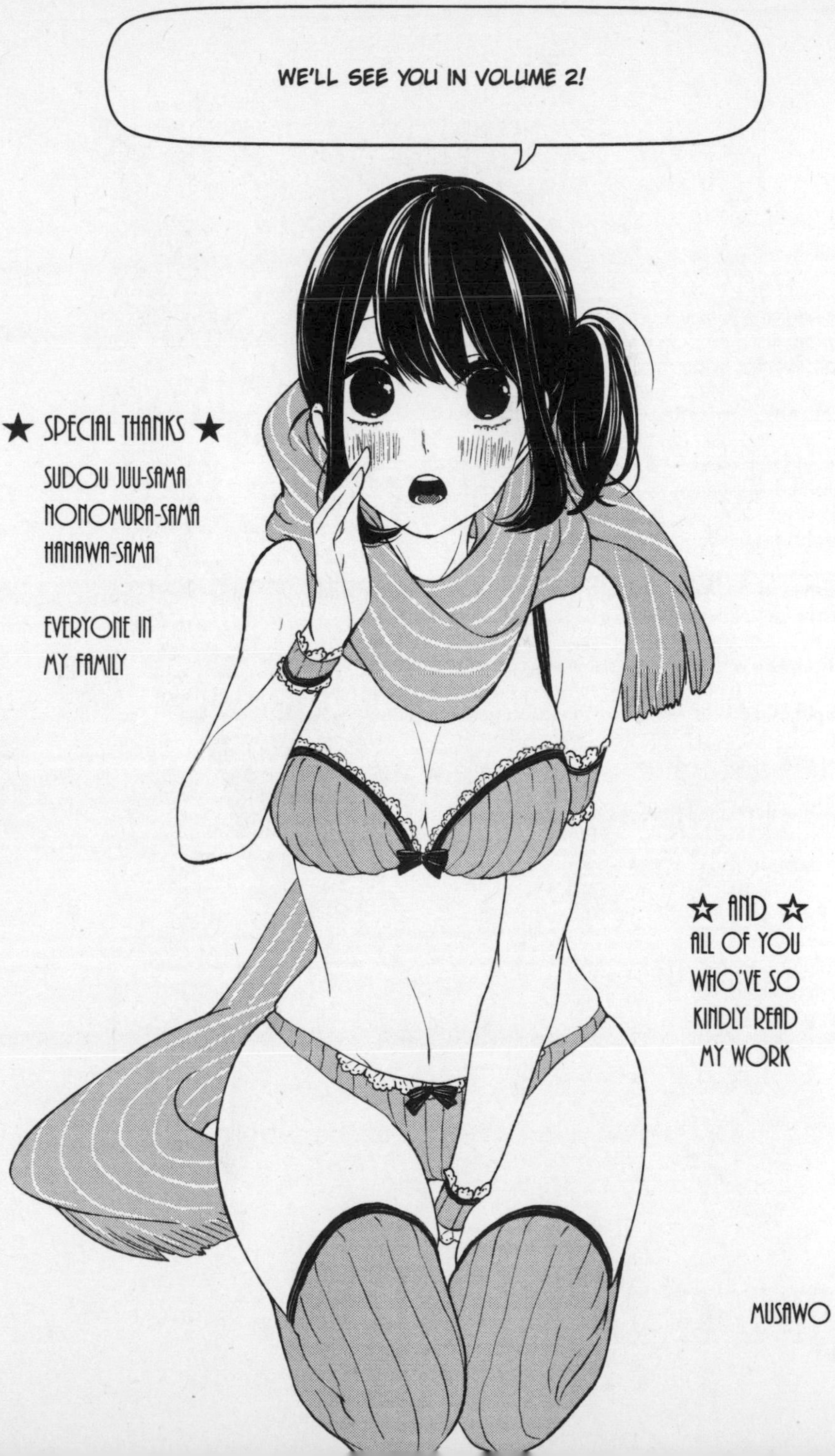
WE'LL SEE YOU IN VOLUME 2!
★ SPECIAL THANKS ★
SUDOU JUU-SAMA
NONOMURA-SAMA
HANAWA-SAMA
EVERYONE IN
MY FAMILY
☆ AND ☆
ALL OF YOU
WHO'VE SO
KINDLY READ
MY WORK
MUSAWO

A Kodansha Comics Trade Paperback Original.

Love and Lies Volume 1 copyright © 2015 Musawo
English translation copyright © 2017 Musawo

All rights reserved.

Published in the United States by Kodansha Comics, an imprint of Kodansha USA Publishing, LLC, New York.

Publication rights for this English edition arranged through Kodansha Ltd., Tokyo.

First published in Japan in 2015 by Kodansha Ltd., Tokyo, as *Koi to Uso* Volume 1.

ISBN 978-1-63236-499-9

Printed in the United States of America.

www.kodanshacomics.com

9 8 7 6 5 4 3 2 1

Translator: Jennifer Ward
Lettering: Daniel CY
Editing: Paul Starr
Kodansha Comics edition cover design by Phil Balsman